Translation, Translanguaging and Machine Translation in Foreign Language Education

David Coulson · Christopher Denman
Editors

Translation, Translanguaging and Machine Translation in Foreign Language Education

palgrave
macmillan

Editors
David Coulson
Language Education & Information
Science
Ritsumeikan University
Kyoto-shi, Japan

Christopher Denman
Postgraduate Studies & Research
Sultan Qaboos University
Muscat, Oman

ISBN 978-3-031-82173-8   ISBN 978-3-031-82174-5   (eBook)
https://doi.org/10.1007/978-3-031-82174-5

This Palgrave Macmillan imprint is published by the registered company Springer Nature Switzerland AG
The registered company address is: Gewerbestrasse 11, 6330 Cham, Switzerland

If disposing of this product, please recycle the paper.

Foreword

The important role of translation in language teaching and learning was summarily dismissed by fashionable Anglophone theorists from the late nineteenth century until the beginning of the twenty-first. Based on flimsy psycholinguistic theory and unfounded pedagogic dogma, the idea was that a language would be best learned and taught without reference to the language(s) of the student(s). This approach, though often posing as liberal and progressive, particularly in its indignant dismissal of the Grammar-Translation Method as authoritarian, was in fact chauvinistic to an extreme, making the language being taught ascendant over all others involved in what must always be, by definition, a bi- or multi-lingual process. No mention was made of translation as an important skill in itself, as a lynchpin of intercultural understanding, or as a formidably useful teaching and testing device. Most parochial of all, there was no recognition of the cultural and intellectual achievement of moving skillfully between two languages.

Recent years have thankfully seen the weakening of such dogma. To a large extent, we may now treat this strange and counter-intuitive monolingual approach to language teaching and learning as a matter of history, at least in the academic literature. Translation is again recognized not only for its pedagogic effectiveness but also for its important social and cultural value; there is now also widespread recognition of the importance of translanguaging in the classroom. This welcome new dispensation is evidenced by the stimulating commentaries on the relation of translation, translanguaging, and language pedagogy in this important new collection.

This is no time for complacency, however. New and equally dangerous ideas now present themselves, all the more pernicious for being often implicit and subconscious. We all now have an easy and regular route to apparently successful translation. We click the "see translation" button on social media platforms. We feed our words into Google Translate or Babelfish or ChatGPT and see immediate results. Faced with the ancient human conundrum of how to communicate with someone with whom we have no language in common, we now have an easy solution. We can simply type into our smartphone, hold up the translation for them to read, or just press a button to make the phone speak on our behalf. And we feel the pleasure of success. Especially when our interlocutor understands us and repeats the process in reverse.

And so we deceive ourselves anew.

It is important that translation and interpreting, whether as communication or as an aid to teaching and learning, remain a human experience. Those who do it well, now as ever, show empathy, understanding, subtlety, cultural knowledge, mental agility, erudition, technical skill, and linguistic knowledge. Those who are less successful at it, as language learners will inevitably be, are nevertheless striving to communicate—even a failed translation brings home to us the complicated relationship between our language and that of another. When we type into Google Translate or speak to an AI program, we do none of these things—we just have an illusion that we are translating and interpreting. The process moreover happens within a black box. We see the results but have no idea what is behind them. Our understanding of the two languages, and the people who speak them, is in no way demonstrated or augmented.

Machine translation has certainly gained ground immensely—it is even now possible to read an automatically translated novel without encountering too many glitches to remind us that we are doing so. It is ubiquitous, an integral part of contemporary international and multi-cultural life. It must of course be taken on board and considered by all involved in language teaching and learning—as it is, critically and thoughtfully, in this volume.

But can machine translation be 'good translation'? As things stand, only for the most mundane and practical texts. What makes a 'good translation' in more complex circumstances, surely, is not an absolute quality but its adjustment to specific circumstances and participants. Translation quality is context dependent—successful for particular people in particular circumstances, a feature of discourse rather than text. This applies most obviously to spoken interpretation, but also to written translations for publication, where, although the participants are not present to the translator, decisions must be made about the extent of glossary and explanation needed. These require knowledge of, and constant adjustment to, the projected reader.

It is true that automatic translation is often used to provide a first draft. Yet, in all but the most banal and functional communications, the good interpreter and translator—people upon whom all our hopes of international understanding and compassion still reside—may be aided, but not replaced, by a machine. In our times of news manipulation and unscrupulous political campaigning, disinterested humans with expertise in the two languages are needed more than ever to guard against abuse and manipulation for malign purposes, a danger which can easily pass undetected if everything is handed over to the nation states and corporations which own and control AI programs.

Amid all the current hype about AI, some speculate that things will change, dismissing reservations as outdated and reactionary. Future AI programs, it is surmised, will constantly adjust to their actual or projected audience in the same way as a human interpreter. Indeed, there are already online video presentations in which, with perfect lip-synching, the speaker appears to talk fluently in a language which they do not actually know, thanks to AI. There are legitimate concerns that human interpreters may be replaced with machines. Nevertheless, *as things stand now*, such speculation remains science fictional—and may always remain so. Human and machine translation are ontological chalk and cheese. In human translation, as in all communication, we want to know what the people involved, both speaker and interpreter, not a prosthetic attachment, are saying. So, while we must of course constantly monitor and remain up-to-date with advances in AI technology, and recruit them as helpers in a limited capacity, we do not need to be cowed by them. While automated translation has a role in banal functional transactions—instructions for assembling a shed, for example—it still lacks the depth and subtlety for more meaningful exchanges—creative, interpersonal, controversial—where the human message is more than mere propositional content. To take examples at an extreme of human communication, AI can write or perform a poem, but the results are uninteresting as human activity. They tell us nothing about the person who is the source, as a real poem or performance does, for the obvious reason that there is no-one there.

Meanwhile, the human issues around translation remain as complex and challenging as ever, in teaching, in learning, and in everyday life. This book is firmly committed to the kind of humanistic and context dependent analysis which is still, and will remain, at the cutting edge of language pedagogy.

Guy Cook
Emeritus Professor of Language
in Education
King's College London
Former Chair of British
Association for Applied
Linguistics (2009–2012)

Contents

Notes on Contributors

David Coulson has a background in foreign language learning, translation and second-language teaching and research. He teaches and supervises postgraduate research in English and Japanese applied linguistics at Ritsumeikan University, Japan. His research interests include various topics in applied linguistics. His publications include research on the topic of translanguaging. He has published in internationally peer-reviewed journals and has had chapters published in several books. He is interested in educational reform and acted as the lead editor on *Educational Reform and International Baccalaureate in the Asia-Pacific* (IGI Global, 2021).

Christopher Denman is a Researcher at the Office of the Deputy Vice-Chancellor for Postgraduate Studies at Sultan Qaboos University, Oman. He has a research affiliation with the university's Humanities Research Centre and was previously an instructor at its Centre for Preparatory Studies. He has ELT experience at the secondary and tertiary levels in Australia, South Korea, and Japan, and has been co-editor of several volumes concerned with various aspects of English language instruction in the Arab world and internationally, including *Individual and contextual factors in the English language classroom* (Springer, 2022).

Khalsa Al Aghbari is an Associate Professor of Linguistics at Sultan Qaboos University's Department of English and Translation where she teaches diverse linguistics and translation courses to undergraduate and postgraduate students. Her research on Omani Arabic phonology, morphology, sociolinguistics, and TEFL appears in prestigious journals including *Morphology*, *Anthropological Linguistics*, *Journal of Omani Studies*, *International Journal of Arabic Linguistics* and *Ampersand*.

Mehmet Akıncı is an Assistant Professor in the Department of Foreign Language Education at İstanbul 29 Mayıs University. He holds a Ph.D. in English Language Education from Boğaziçi University. Dr. Akıncı's research focuses on psycholinguistics, the cognitive effects of bilingualism, working memory, attention control, research methodology, language assessment, and English language instruction, particularly in second language acquisition and pedagogy.

Hamid Allami is an Associate Professor in ELT and Applied Linguistics. His areas of interest include Classroom Discourse Analysis, Sociolinguistics, Interlanguage Pragmatics and Intercultural Communication Pedagogy. Currently, he is a faculty member at the English Language Teaching (ELT) department at Tarbiat Modares University in Tehran, Iran.

Antonie Alm (Ph.D., UCLA) is an Associate Professor in Languages and Cultures at the University of Otago, New Zealand. Her research focuses on L2 motivation, learner autonomy, and informal language learning, particularly using digital technologies. Antonie serves as an associate editor for the *CALL Journal* and the *JALTCALL Journal*.

Srbuhi Aydinyan is pursuing her Ph.D. in the Translation Studies Department at Brusov State University and holds a master's degree in Applied Linguistics from Yerevan State University. Srbuhi contributed

to developing Armenian-English parallel corpora of student translations as a part of a research group. Her research focuses on corpus
linguistics, corpus creation, and natural language processing, particularly
multilingual corpora.

Karine Chiknaverova is a Professor at the English Language Department of MGIMO-Odintsovo, specializing in English language teaching.
She holds a Ph.D. in TESOL and focuses on the theory and methods of
teaching foreign languages at the university level. Her research interests
include English for Specific Purposes, legal translation, and error analysis.
Dr. Chiknaverova has authored over 80 scientific publications.

Mehtap Güven Çoban is Director of Studies in the Department of
English Language Preparatory Program at İstanbul 29 Mayıs University.
She is a doctoral candidate in English Language Education at Boğaziçi
University with an MA in Translation Studies. Her research interests
include translation, cognition, memory, language acquisition, and bilingualism. She aims to bridge theory and practice to improve language
education.

Christine Coombe has a Ph.D. in Foreign/Second Language Education
from The Ohio State University. She is an Associate Professor of GARD
at Higher Colleges of Technology, Dubai. Christine has published over
60 books in language testing and assessment, teacher effectiveness,
research methods, leadership, and management in ELT and TBLT. Dr.
Coombe served as President of the TESOL International Association
(2011–2012).

Liubov Darzhinova is a Research Assistant Professor at the Graduate
School of the Education University of Hong Kong. Her research interests lie in the fields of psycholinguistics and teacher education, with a
focus on written language processing and pre-service teachers' language
assessment literacy. Her research findings are disseminated in over 20
publications in high-impact journals and edited volumes.

Adel Dastgoshadeh is a faculty member at the Islamic Azad University, Sanandaj Branch, Iran. He has published books and papers in esteemed journals, including *Language Testing in Asia* and *Smart Learning Environments*. Dr. Dastgoshadeh has taught BA, MA, and Ph.D. programs. His research interests include teacher education, psycholinguistics, and teaching methodologies.

Zahra El Aouri is an Associate Professor of Applied Linguistics and TEFL at the Department of English Studies, Cadi Ayyad University, Morocco. Dr. El Aouri holds a Doctorate Degree in Education from the Faculty of Education, Morocco. Her main research interests remain within the field of Applied Linguistics and TEFL along with research methodology and statistical analysis of data using SPSS.

Kiyono Fujinaga-Gordon is an Assistant Teaching Professor of Japanese Studies at Carnegie Mellon University. Dr. Fujinaga-Gordon has a Ph.D. in Linguistics from the University at Buffalo and an MA from the University of Tokyo. Her research interests include Miyako language, Japanese linguistics, language documentation, sociolinguistics, historical linguistics, multilingualism, and second language acquisition.

Dennitza Gabrakova is Professor at the Institute of Global Initiatives, Wakayama University. Her research and teaching interests are in the area of environmental humanities and the ecologies of foreign language learning and intercultural communication. She is currently working on translating in these areas within the university administration context.

Hayk B. Hambardzumyan, Ph.D., is a Senior Lecturer at the Department of Translation Studies, Brusov State University, Armenia. As a Lecturer, he has over eight years of experience in translation studies and related fields. His research interests include corpus linguistics, translation technology, and interdisciplinary research in translation studies. He is a member of the research group dedicated to creating Armenian-English parallel corpora.

Kristina A. Harutyunova, Ph.D., is a Senior Lecturer at the Department of Translation Studies, Brusov State University, Armenia. She has more than 25 years of teaching experience. Her research interests include translation studies, applied linguistics with an emphasis on corpus linguistics, corpus creation, and natural language processing. She is a member of the research group working on the creation of Armenian-English parallel corpora.

Yoko Hasegawa is a Professor of Japanese Linguistics in the Department of East Asian Languages and Cultures, UC Berkeley. Since her dissertation on Japanese clause linkage (UC Berkeley, 1992), she has worked on such aspects of Japanese linguistics as phonetics/phonology, syntax/semantics, pragmatics, and translation. Her publications include *Cambridge Handbook of Japanese Linguistics, The Routledge Course in Japanese Translation,* and *Soliloquy in Japanese and English* (John Benjamins).

Belén Hernando-Lloréns is an Assistant Professor in Multilingual Education at the University of Iowa. Dr. Hernando-Lloréns's scholarship addresses ongoing histories of educational exclusion regarding multilingual children of color in the United States and internationally. Her work appears in *Harvard Educational Review, Journal of Curriculum Studies, Globalisation, Societies and Education,* and *Curriculum Inquiry.* She has received the AERA's Early Career Award.

Gayane R. Hovhannisyan Doctor of Philology with over 30 years of international teaching experience, leads the Translation Studies Department at Brusov State University. Professor Hovhannisyan has a rich research and publication background, with scientific interests in cultural and cognitive linguistics, psycholinguistics and translation studies, language acquisition, and verbal communication. Her recent research is devoted to taxonomies and translation in digital humanities.

Yu Huiwen teaches English at Ritsumeikan University in Kyoto, Japan. She holds an MA degree in English education. She has taught TOEIC, TOEFL, and IELTS classes for around a decade and has instructed more than 3,000 English-language students. She is interested in all fields of second-language teaching and is particularly focused on the applications of machine translation in writing.

Masako Inamoto is an Associate Professor of Japanese in the Department of World Languages and Literatures at Skidmore College in Saratoga Springs, New York, where she teaches Japanese language, literature, and films, including anime. She received an M.S. in TESOL from the University at Albany-SUNY, and both her MA and Ph.D. in East Asian Languages and Literatures from Ohio State University.

Kaveh Jalilzadeh works for the School of Foreign Languages and is a faculty member at Istanbul University Cerrahpasa, School of Foreign Languages. He has published articles in esteemed journals such as *Language Testing in Asia, Smart Learning Environment, Asian Pacific Journal of Foreign Language Education, Research in Language Teaching*, and *CALL-EJ*.

Jun Kanazawa is an English Lecturer at Daito Bunka University in Japan, within the Department of Political Science, Faculty of Law. She is also a Ph.D. student at the University of Tokyo, where she previously earned her MA. Her research interests include pragmatics, contrastive studies between Japanese and English, second language acquisition, and statistics.

Sora Kim is a Ph.D. student in the Department of Teaching and Learning at the University of Iowa and currently works as a Graduate Assistant at the Center of Translation and Global Literacy. Her research interests include teaching and learning Korean as a foreign/second language and critical pedagogy in world language education.

Elisabet Titik Murtisari is an Associate Professor in the Master of English Language Education Program at Universitas Kristen Satya Wacana. She holds an undergraduate degree in TESOL and both an MA and a Ph.D. in translation studies (applied linguistics). Her research interests include EFL grammar learning, pragmatics in translation, intercultural perspectives in language learning, and the use of translation in language education.

Eri Nakagawa is Lecturer at the University of Tokyo, where she earned her MA and Ph.D. in Translation Studies. Her research interests include literary translation between English and Japanese, creativity in translation, stylistics, short story studies, and translation in language teaching and learning. She also works as an English-to-Japanese translator.

Mohammad Hussein Norouzi is an Assistant Professor of Applied Linguistics at the Faculty of Foreign Languages and Literatures, University of Tehran. He teaches a variety of courses at BA, MA, and Ph.D. levels and has published in local and international journals. His main areas of research interest include discourse analysis and English language teaching.

Louise Ohashi is an Associate Professor at Gakushuin University (Department of English Language and Cultures) who specializes in second language acquisition. Her research interests include motivation, autonomy, and CALL/MALL. In recent years she has been conducting research into the use of GenAI in language education. She is Chair of EUROCALL's AI SIG and a KAKENHI grant recipient.

Carolina García Pérez —Graduate in English literature and linguistics, an MA degree in legal and financial translation, a Ph.D. in pedagogical translation. Professor of English at Alfonso X el Sabio University (Madrid), Department of Foreign Languages. Her research interests include discourse analysis, educational assessment, bilingualism, terminology, methodology, specialized translation, legal translation, literary translation, academic translation, audiovisual translation, post-editing, and localization.

Fatemeh Ranjbaran Madiseh is Assistant Lecturer in the Department of English for Sciences, Center for Preparatory Studies, Sultan Qaboos University, Oman. She holds a Ph.D. in applied linguistics from the

University of Tehran and is an active researcher and peer reviewer, annually presenting her research at international conferences. Her research interests primarily include ESP, technology-enhanced learning, and innovative teaching pedagogies.

Abbas Ali Rezaee is a Professor of Applied Linguistics at the Faculty of Foreign Languages and Literatures, University of Tehran. He has published extensively in national and international journals. He has taught MA and Ph.D. courses and supervised many Ph.D. and MA theses/dissertations. His main research interests include Language Teaching and Testing, ESP, and CALL.

María del Mar Sánchez Ramos is Full Professor of Translation Studies at the Department of Modern Languages (University of Alcalá, Madrid, Spain). Her main research interests are translation technologies (i.e., machine translation and post-editing), corpus-based translation studies, and discourse analysis.

John Rylander (Ph.D.), a faculty member in the Institute for Liberal Arts and Sciences (ILAS) at Kyoto University, is a founding member of the International Academic Research and Resource Center (i-ARRC), and currently teaches courses in the Division of English Language Education. He researchers, publishes, and presents on second language pragmatics, language assessment, conversation analysis, and eye-tracking methodology.

Bettina Schnell is a graduate in French, Spanish, Italian, and English linguistics, and literature. She holds a Ph.D. in foreign language pedagogy. She is a Professor at Comillas Pontifical University Madrid, in the Department of Translation, Interpreting, and Global Communication. She is the former director of the master's degree in legal and financial translation, and coordinator of the Tradyterm research group. Research interests: L3 acquisition, psycholinguistics, digital humanities, natural language processing, Literary Translation, and Translation Pedagogy.

Haniye Seyri obtained her Ph.D. in Teaching English as a Foreign Language (TEFL) from the University of Tehran. She has taught a number of courses in language teaching at high schools, teacher training centers, and universities. Her main research interests include teacher education, positive psychology in language education, and English for Academic Purposes (EAP). She has published papers in prestigious international journals.

Shadi Shivakhah holds an MA in ELT. Her areas of interest include second-language teacher education and classroom discourse analysis. She has been teaching English for over 20 years.

David Singleton is an Emeritus Fellow at the Centre for Language and Communication Studies, Trinity College Dublin. He specializes in second language acquisition and multilingualism, especially focusing on the role of age in language learning and the L2 lexicon. Professor Singleton has published over 230 scholarly works, supervised more than 100 postgraduate students' dissertations and has also held professorships in Hungary and Poland.

Boris Vazquez-Calvo is an Assistant Professor of EFL and L2 Education in the Department of Language Education at the University of Málaga, Spain. His research interests span language teacher education, language learning and translation, and various aspects of technology-mediated language learning and digital discourse, with a focus on intersections with fan practices.

Carl Vollmer is an Instructor of English, Social Studies, and TOK in the immersion program at Ritsumeikan Uji Junior and Senior High School. He received his MA in English education from the Graduate School of Language Education and Information Science at Ritsumeikan University. His research interests include conversation analysis, task-based learning, and language teaching practices.

Larry Walker (M.Ed., Ph.D.) is Professor of Translation Studies in the Department of European and American Linguistic Cultures, Faculty of

Letters, and Graduate School of Letters at Kyoto Prefectural University. His research examines translation histories of the Japanese novel, ethnographic studies on the Japanese-English translation industry and its translators, and the influence of AI on translation practices.

Lauren Walker is a Literature and Theory of Knowledge teacher in the immersion department of Ritsumeikan Uji Junior and Senior High School. She is pursuing an MA in education at the University of Bath. Her research interests include international school leadership and literature teaching in global contexts.

Yuki Watanabe is a Lecturer in Media, Film, and Communication at the University of Otago. She earned her Ph.D. in second language education from the University of Kansas. Her current areas of research include Asian popular culture and media, indigenous media, intercultural communication, and the use of communication technology in education.

Pamela M. Wesely is a Professor of Multilingual Education and Associate Dean at the University of Iowa. Her research interests focus on innovation in K-12 language education and the attitudes and motivation of stakeholders (students, parents, and teachers). She has authored two books, and her work has appeared in *Foreign Language Annals*, *Journal of Teacher Education*, and *Language Teaching Research*.

List of Figures

List of Tables

1

Introduction: Translation, Translanguaging and Machine Translation in Foreign Language Education

David Coulson and C. J. Denman

1.1 Introduction

"Translation, Translanguaging and Machine Translation in Foreign Language Education" is an edited volume concerned with a wide range of topics about the current and emergent roles of translation and translanguaging in foreign language instruction. These are areas that have been gaining increasing momentum in recent years, with traditional understandings around the uses of translation for foreign language teaching and learning being challenged and, in many cases, disrupted by the rapid development of machine translation (MT) apps such as DeepL and ChatGPT translator. The improving quality and widespread deployment

D. Coulson (✉)
Ritsumeikan University, Kyoto, Japan
e-mail: coulson@fc.ritsumei.ac.jp

C. J. Denman
Sultan Qaboos University, Muscat, Oman
e-mail: denman@squ.edu.om

© The Author(s), under exclusive license to Springer Nature Switzerland AG 2025
D. Coulson and C. Denman (eds.), *Translation, Translanguaging and Machine Translation in Foreign Language Education*,
https://doi.org/10.1007/978-3-031-82174-5_1

of these technologies are causing language instructors in a diverse range of settings to reconsider not only their pedagogic approaches to, and perceptions of, the use of translation in the classroom, but also what form effective instruction should take. This represents a significant paradigm shift in many still current approaches to foreign language instruction in which translation has been viewed with a great deal of scepticism, if not dismissed outright.

From a historical perspective, the significant decline in the relevance of translation in foreign language learning can be seen as a response to traditional grammar-translation approaches in which students were required to learn about the target language rather than developing proficiency in it. As communicative competence began to take centre stage in language classrooms, exemplified by the rise of communicative- and content-oriented approaches (Ellis, 2003; Snow, 1998; Stoller, 2004), the use of translation became increasingly marginalised (Nguyen, 2024).

However, the resultant disempowerment of translation in foreign language learning brought with it a number of unfortunate consequences, with many of these associated with the fact that translation naturally occurs in the minds of bilingual and multilingual individuals and can hence give rise to increased awareness of their languages (Linares, 2022; Shaekhova & Song, 2024). In fact, both empirical evidence and anecdotal evidence demonstrate that foreign language learners continue to employ translation strategies and approaches, despite frequently encountering institutional policies and educational practices explicitly prescribing "English-only" environments (Paterson, 2020). The use of these translation strategies has continued to be a key, if often wilfully ignored, part of foreign language learning as they are recognised by many learners as having the potential to enhance their communicative abilities. Indeed, translation continues to be widely acknowledged in both theory and practice as a natural process for "multicompetent" individuals (Cook, 2008), whether classroom rules permit its use or not. Further, if the pedagogic goal is to facilitate the acquisition of the multilingual repertoire of individuals, denying the use of all the linguistic resources at their disposal has no rational basis, as Cenoz and Gorter (2020) explain in their examination of pedagogical translanguaging.

Even as pedagogical approaches to language instruction continue to evolve, for many years now, little emphasis has been placed on the use of translation (Artar, 2017). However, in recent times, increasing understanding of the natural place of translation in the cognitive processes of foreign language learners has become more widely acknowledged (Murtisari, 2021), with strong opinions being exchanged about the uses and potential abuses of AI translation technologies perhaps heightening the level of both academic awareness and general awareness of the issue. According to Laviosa (2014), the pedagogic use of creative and pedagogically effective tasks has come to be recognised as beneficial to learners' grasp and noticing of structural and lexical contrasts between their languages. As an "ecological practice" (p. 28) that enhances learners' willingness to embrace multilingual skills and recognise their own place in a world of greater cross-cultural interaction, translation activities can be highly effective. Indeed, some of the types of activities which fulfil this role are described in this volume's chapters.

Proponents of incorporating translation in foreign language learning often view it as the "fifth skill" (Ayachia, 2018) complementing reading, writing, listening and speaking. In terms of classroom practice, supporters argue that the use of translation necessarily entails increased interaction in the target language through learner-to-learner questioning and class-wide exploration of word and idiom meanings (Al-Musawi, 2014). It further enables students to develop metalinguistic awareness of structural contrasts between the first and target languages and of the cultural communication norms of both (Fois, 2020; Károly, 2014; Safari, 2020). Work such as that by Pintado Gutiérrez (2018, 2022) stresses the importance of various kinds of tasks to develop translating skills. This includes those not only for formal translation practice, but also for particular skills required for linguistically revealing activities such as subtitling.

Building upon such perspectives, applied linguistics now emphasises the importance of translanguaging strategies in which learners are encouraged to make best use of all their available linguistic resources (González-Davies, 2019). The possibilities offered by creative and engaging translation and translanguaging activities, rather than the orthodoxy of grammar-translation, are rich. Advantages for foreign language instructors include the potential to create opportunities for learners to focus on both language form and meaning, elicit classroom discussion about linguistic and non-linguistic forms, and expose learners to challenging situations requiring the application of problem-solving skills and pragmatic knowledge that move beyond communicating through language alone (Mollaei et al., 2017).

As stated above, the need to seriously consider the effective and beneficial integration of translation technologies into foreign language classrooms is currently reaching a critical point. The improving accuracy of MT tools has the potential to massively transform how foreign languages are taught and learned (Urlaub & Dessein, 2022). Despite evidence of suspicion and mistrust among some in the foreign language teaching community, especially in relation to concerns about the trustworthiness of generative AI and its impact on student academic integrity and creativity (Dehghan, 2024; Murphy et al., 2023), resisting technological and associated pedagogical change runs the risk of ignoring a plethora of potential advantages and the chance to be at the forefront of genuine educational innovation. The time is therefore ripe for a careful examination of the implications of MT for foreign language learning within the framework of translation's wider reemergence in modern classrooms.

It is within the context briefly sketched above that the current volume "Translation, Translanguaging and Machine Translation in Foreign Language Education" offers an up-to-date and detailed view of these areas that encompasses voices from researchers and professional educators around the world. The book takes the current and projected roles of translation and translanguaging in foreign language learning as its foundation, upon which a wide range of topics are explored. Chapters, which encompass theoretical perspectives, research and classroom reports, are presented across three parts.

Part I examines the role that translation can potentially assume in the foreign language classroom. It begins with a study by Wesely, Hernando-Lloréns and Kim under the title "Developing Translation as an Asset-Based Pedagogy in Multilingual Classrooms". The authors present translation as an asset-based approach that incorporates learners' full linguistic repertoires during language learning. They also examine the tenets of translation as an asset-based pedagogy in multilingual classrooms and describe how they introduced the pedagogy to language teachers in the United States through a series of professional development workshops as an example for similar action in other educational contexts.

Murtisari's "Genre-Based Interlingual Focus on Form: Translating for Contextual Grammar Learning and Beyond" next offers an account of an interlingual focus on form method featuring the use of parallel texts and language foci to create pedagogical instruction for EFL learners. After discussing several principles underpinning interlingual focus on form, the chapter provides practical suggestions for sessions and modules illustrating the classroom implementation of the proposed method.

Al Aghbari's "Translation Errors of Third Semester English Specialists at Sultan Qaboos University" presents a study of the translation errors made by English majors in Oman when translating a short text from English into Arabic. Analysis reveals a number of serious semantic and grammatical errors, in addition to learners' limited English vocabulary, which Al Aghbari uses to call for amending courses that English specialists are required to study as part of their majors and for devising teaching materials to enhance their language skills.

Gabrakova is similarly concerned with the effectiveness of pedagogical approaches supporting university learners' translation practices. Her "'Babel Project': Japanese Language Learning through Theatre Translation" reports on the results of an informal, spontaneous Japanese language seminar in which students translated a playscript from Japanese into English. Based on both the author's experiences and participant feedback, Gabrakova argues that the learning space created by the project resulted in the kinds of leadership and self-reflection that are integral for the development of learners' bilingual social identities.

In an English for Specific Purposes (ESP) context, Chiknaverova's "Interlanguage Interference: What Should Tutors Be Aware of When Teaching Vocabulary in the Legal Translation Classroom?" features a contrastive examination of English and Russian legal terms and frequently used lexis that reveals three distinct types of false cognates, in addition to linguistic phenomena also acting as interference triggers. Chiknaverova offers a number of recommendations for teaching strategies and exercises for both English for law purposes and EFL/ESL classrooms more generally.

In the proceeding chapter—"From Foe to Friend: The Role of Fan Translation in Language Education"—Vazquez-Calvo details five proposals for integrating fan translation, in which learners translate L2 media content aligned with their interests, into the curriculum. After offering practical approaches to integrating fan translation into language learning, the author discusses how these approaches can result in more engaging, relevant teaching and research practices.

Next, Schnell and García Pérez's "To Translate or Not to Translate in the Foreign Language Classroom? An Empirical-Experimental Study on Pedagogical Translation in Secondary Language Education" details an empirical-experimental investigation of the effectiveness of pedagogical translation compared to communicative approaches for the teaching of grammar to early-stage English learners in Spain. Following analysis of learners' performance on objective evaluation tasks and error analysis, the authors conclude that pedagogical translation is, in fact, as effective as more traditional communicative teaching approaches.

In "Effects of Translation Practice as Consciousness-Raising on L2 Explicit, L2 Implicit, and Metalinguistic Knowledge", Çoban and Akıncı develop the concern with effective classroom practice by discussing the results of a quasi-experimental study investigating the effects of translation as consciousness-raising on the acquisition of linguistic structures in second language explicit and implicit knowledge and metalinguistic knowledge with English learners in Turkey. Following a six-week period in which experimental group students received grammar instruction supported by translation-based activities, the authors reported that learners exposed to these activities experienced increases in both explicit and metalinguistic knowledge, thus supporting translation's role as a valuable pedagogical tool.

In the final chapter of Part I, El Aouri explores different feedback techniques teachers use to formatively assess university student translation tasks, including how they can close the "feedback loop", thus enabling students to effectively learn from previous work. The author's chapter "Techniques to Assess University Students' Translation Tasks: The Challenge of Closing the Feedback Loop" suggests three feedback techniques to achieve this and concludes with recommendations for pedagogical practice and future translation research.

Chapters in Part II have a focus on translanguaging in foreign language learning. The section begins with Darzhinova and Singleton's scoping review of empirical research on translanguaging—"Mapping Research on Translanguaging in Language Assessment". The review results in a number of significant insights into various dimensions of translanguaging in language assessment, including research foci and geographical and learning contexts and so on, and gives readers several practical suggestions based on these for future research directions.

In "Translanguaging at the Heart of Language Education: A Systematic Review", Rezaee, Seyri and Norouzi adopt a complementary approach to the previous chapter in their systematic review of translanguaging research by focusing on empirically-informed trends in relation to its current status, and teacher and learner perceptions and attitudes. Rezaee et al.'s review reveals generally positive perceptions of translanguaging among these key stakeholders and concludes with pedagogical implications.

Closely concerned with the former chapter's topic, Allami and Shivakhah's "Iranian EFL Teachers' Beliefs on Pedagogical Translanguaging" examines the beliefs about translanguaging as a pedagogical practice of EFL teachers. Analysis of questionnaire and interview data resulted in numerous factors, including teacher familiarity with translanguaging, that influence these beliefs. The authors use these outcomes to argue for the need for developing learning contexts in which learners' dynamic cultural and linguistic repertoires are fully integrated.

"Unveiling the Efficacy of Translanguaging in English Language Teaching: Insights from Turkish Teachers", by Jalilzadeh, Coombe and Dastgoshadeh, provides an account of a phenomenological study of English language teachers' perspectives on translanguaging as an educational strategy in Turkey. Data collected through semi-structured interviews and framed narratives revealed that these instructors had generally positive perceptions of translanguaging, including in terms of its effectiveness across tasks, collaborative work, knowledge enhancement and so on. The authors maintain that these results support the potential of translanguaging as a transformative pedagogy for English language teaching in Turkey and beyond.

Part II concludes with Ranjbaran Madiseh's "Exploring the Affordances and Challenges of Translanguaging: The Context of Oman", which explores teacher translanguaging practices and student challenges and opportunities in English-medium instruction programmes in the sultanate. Following group discussions and interviews with students and teachers, the author describes a number of challenges and opportunities associated with translanguaging and English-medium instruction, which are utilised to argue for the need for further professional development to raise instructors' awareness of the effective use of classroom translanguaging.

Part III is concerned with MT in foreign language learning. Hasegawa, Fujinaga-Gordon, Nakagawa and Kanazawa begin this section with the chapter "College-Level Language Education in the Machine-Translation Era: A Metacognitive Approach", a discussion of the impact of advances in MT engines on Japanese-as-a-foreign-language higher education courses. After considering the importance of changing the curriculum focus from a communication—to a thinking-based design, the authors provide the example of their own ChatGPT experiment thus highlighting how AI can be successfully incorporated into the curriculum.

Next, Ohashi's study, "Machine Translation and Language Learning: Teachers' Perspectives and Practices", investigates teachers' views on the use of MT from personal and pedagogical perspectives. Her results show cautious acceptance of MT's use rather than a wish for a ban. Many participants felt that they require further guidance and training in relation to the pedagogical applications of MT, as this would not only help them with guiding students on its ethical and autonomous uses, but also facilitate their adoption of more effective pedagogical strategies.

Yu and Coulson's "How Can Machine Translation Help Chinese Students in an English Academic Writing Task?" investigates the ways in which MT can have a positive impact on English language learning. The authors find that learners utilising MT can make significant progress not only in words and grammar but also at the paragraph level. Their findings indicate that DeepL can act as source of noticing and result in students retaining newly learned words and phrases. It is due to these outcomes that the chapter concludes by arguing MT can be effectively employed in language learning classrooms.

The chapter by Sánchez Ramos, "Integrating Machine Translation in Language Learning in the Age of Artificial Intelligence: A SWOT Analysis", examines how MT is used by university ESL teachers. Some, but not all, of the instructors in the study employed MT for teaching more effectively. Further, the author's SWOT analysis reveals that, while teachers perceive certain threats posed by MT to their learners and even to themselves in terms of job security, they nonetheless believe that its use can create better teaching and learning chances.

In "Exploring the Use and Perception of Machine Translation in Language Learning: A Study in a Japanese High School Immersion Program", Walker and Vollmer next examine the use of MT with high school learners at different stages of a Japanese high school's study abroad programme. Survey data indicate that the use of MT changes in frequency and type as students move through the programme, thereby suggesting that learners are prone to rely more on their own language abilities as proficiency develops.

"Empowering ESL Translation Studies: Integrating Machine Translation for Enhanced Language Proficiency and Productivity" by Hovhannisyan, Harutyunova, Hambardzumyan and Aydinyan reports on a pilot project in which methods for creating parallel Armenian-English language corpora by translation students were developed and tested with a particular focus on MT. The chapter describes several means for ensuring the efficiency of these methods, before arguing that their integration has the potential to create new opportunities for language learning.

Alm and Watanabe's "Language Teaching in Transition: Educator Perspectives on Integrating Machine Translation Tools in Tertiary Contexts" is an account of a qualitative study into language teachers' perspectives on the integration of MT tools into their teaching. Semi-structured interviews and participant observation of tertiary-level language teachers in New Zealand revealed moderate levels of acceptance of MT tools among participants, while further highlighting concerns about learner dependence upon these. The chapter concludes by detailing teacher insights into how MT can be integrated into the classroom in a responsible and effective manner.

The final chapter, "L2 Translation in US/Japan Classrooms: AI and Peer Feedback in Task-Based Language Teaching", by Walker, Inamoto and Rylander, describes a study into learner beliefs about L2 translation and foreign language learning following translation and exchange of source texts between Japanese and American higher education students through document sharing. Although student interest in using AI in coursework was found to exist, participants were unsure about its most effective use, while peer feedback on translations was seen by learners as more trustworthy.

As this overview reveals, contributors to this volume are drawn from a wide range of educational contexts and subsequently offer diverse perspectives on the use of translation and translanguaging in foreign language learning. However, they all nonetheless share a common interest in increasing understandings of the potential advantages and challenges offered by the integration of translation, translanguaging and MT in the language classroom. Through their efforts, contributors seek to ensure that the approaches to translation use in the language classroom taken by current and future teachers, students, administrators, materials developers, policymakers and all other concerned stakeholders are for the benefit of learners while being employed in empirically- and theoretically-supported ways.

It is imperative that those considering the uses of translation and translanguaging in foreign language learning do not merely echo the passing trends or objections of the times, but consistently bear in mind that, without critical debate built upon systematic examination, no educational reform or paradigm shift can hope to be sustained as a force for improvement. It is with the intention of making a sincere contribution to this debate that this book is offered.

References

Al-Musawi, N. M. (2014). Strategic use of translation in learning English as a Foreign Language (EFL) among Bahrain university students. *Comprehensive Psychology, 3*(4). https://doi.org/10.2466/10.03.IT.3.4

Artar, P. (2017). *The role of translation in foreign-language teaching* [Unpublished doctoral dissertation]. Universitat Rovira I Virgili. http://hdl.handle.net/10803/461885

Ayachia, H. (2018). The revival of translation as a fifth skill in the foreign language classroom: A review of literature. *AWEJ for Translation & Literary Studies, 2*(2), 187–198. https://doi.org/10.2139/ssrn.3187001

Cenoz, J., & Gorter, D. (2020). Pedagogical translanguaging: An introduction. *System, 92*(102269). https://doi.org/10.1016/j.system.2020.102269

Cook, V. (2008). *Second language learning and language teaching* (4th ed.). Hodder Education.

Dehghan, F. (2024). Demystifying the unknown: ChatGPT and foreign language classrooms in the voices of EFL teachers. In Z. Çetin Köroğlu & A. Çakır (Eds.), *Fostering foreign language teaching and learning environments with contemporary technologies* (pp. 70–90). IGI Global. https://doi.org/10.4018/979-8-3693-0353-5.ch004

Ellis, R. (2003). *Task-based language learning and teaching*. Oxford University Press.

Fois, E. (2020). ELT and the role of translation in developing intercultural competence. *Language and Intercultural Communication, 20*(6), 561–571. https://doi.org/10.1080/14708477.2020.1800025

González-Davies, M. (2019). Developing mediation competence through translation. In S. Laviosa & M. González-Davies (Eds.), *The Routledge handbook of translation and education* (pp. 434–450). Routledge.

Károly, A. (2014). Translation in foreign language teaching: A case study from a functional perspective. *Linguistics and Education, 25*, 90–107.

Laviosa, S. (2014). *Translation and language: Pedagogic approaches explored*. Routledge.

Linares, E. (2022). The challenges and promise of classroom translation for multilingual minority students in monolingual settings. *L2 Journal, 14*(2), 51–74. https://doi.org/10.5070/L214251571

Mollaei, F., Taghinezhad, A., & Sadighi, F. (2017). Teachers and learners' perceptions of applying translation as a method, strategy, or technique in an

Iranian EFL setting. *International Journal of Education and Literacy Studies, 5*(2), 67–73. https://doi.org/10.7575/aiac.ijels.v.5n.2p.67

Murphy, R., Wotley, D., & Minn, D. (2023). Integrating ChatGPT into the EFL classroom: Benefits and challenges. *Kiban Kyoiku Center Kiyo Journal, 40*, 97–166.

Murtisari, E. T. (2021). Use of translation strategies in writing: Advanced EFL students. *LLT Journal: A Journal on Language and Language Teaching, 24*(1), 228–239. https://doi.org/10.24071/llt.v24i1.2663

Nguyen, T. T. H. (2024). Translation in language teaching: The need for redefinition of translation. *AsiaCALL Online Journal, 15*(1), 19–33. https://doi.org/10.54855/acoj.241512

Paterson, K. (2020). Disrupting the English-only status quo: Using home language as a vital resource in the classroom. *TESL Ontario CONTACT Magazine, 46*, 5–15. https://contact.teslontario.org/wp-content/uploads/2020/08/Kate-Paterson.pdf

Pintado Gutiérrez, L. (2018). Translation in language teaching, pedagogical translation, and code-switching: Restructuring the boundaries. *The Language Learning Journal, 49*(2). https://doi.org/10.1080/09571736.2018.1534260

Pintado Gutiérrez, L. (2022). Current practices in translation and L2 learning in higher education: Lessons learned. *L2 Journal, 14*(2), 32–50. https://doi.org/10.5070/L214251728

Safari, F. (2020). The relationship between EFL learners' explicit knowledge of Source language and their translation ability. *Journal of Language and Translation, 10*(4), 109–120.

Shaekhova, L., & Song, J. (2024). 'It's normal. That's just my life': Tatar-Russian bilinguals' translanguaging and tranßcripting in multiple linguascapes. *Translation and Translanguaging in Multilingual Contexts, 10*(2), 166–187. https://doi.org/10.1075/ttmc.00132.sha

Snow, M. A. (1998). Trends and issues in content-based instruction. *Annual Review of Applied Linguistics, 18*, 243–267. https://doi.org/10.1017/S0267190500003573

Stoller, F. L. (2004). Content-based instruction: Perspectives on curriculum planning. *Annual Review of Applied Linguistics, 24*, 261–283. https://doi.org/10.1017/S0267190504000108

Urlaub, P., & Dessein, E. (2022). Machine translation and foreign language education. *Frontiers in Artificial Intelligence, 5*(936111). https://doi.org/10.3389/frai.2022.936111

Part I

Translation Practices in the Language Classroom

2

Developing Translation as an Asset-Based Pedagogy in Multilingual Classrooms

Pamela M. Wesely⬤, Belén Hernando-Lloréns⬤, and Sora Kim⬤

2.1 Introduction: Developing Translation as an Asset-Based Pedagogy in Multilingual Classrooms

Translation has been part of the multilingual language classroom for centuries. The use of translation in the teaching of the so-called dead languages, Latin or Ancient Greek, was a mainstream pedagogical practice. However, over the twentieth century, language teaching methods focusing on modern languages moved away from teaching grammar and

P. M. Wesely (✉) · B. Hernando-Lloréns · S. Kim
University of Iowa, Iowa City, IA, USA
e-mail: pamela-wesely@uiowa.edu

B. Hernando-Lloréns
e-mail: belen-hernando@uiowa.edu

S. Kim
e-mail: sora-kim@uiowa.edu

© The Author(s), under exclusive license to Springer Nature Switzerland AG 2025
D. Coulson and C. Denman (eds.), *Translation, Translanguaging and Machine Translation in Foreign Language Education*,
https://doi.org/10.1007/978-3-031-82174-5_2

15

focused more on developing communicative skills and competencies. In that shift, translation was determined by many to be an ineffective teaching method in the multilingual classroom (Colina & Albrecht, 2021; Cook, 2010). Within the context of world language (WL) education (also called foreign language (FL)[1] education), translation has long been viewed negatively and in opposition to a more communicative approach (Kelly & Bruen, 2015; Pym, 2018). Nonetheless, scholars have argued that translation has always been used "under the table" in the WL classroom, as a tool and an aid but without explicitly being articulated in the objectives or outcomes of the classes (Colina & Albrecht, 2021; Cook, 2001).

In recent decades, translation has been reconceptualized as a pedagogical tool in the multilingual classroom. More scholars have started to claim the positive effects of using the students' home/first languages in the learning process, specifically as they can help students "be more aware of their languages, take pride in being bilingual, and interlink L1 and L2 knowledge in their minds" (Colina & Albrecht, 2021, Chapter 1, para. 3; see also Balboni, 2017). Books and guides by scholars including Colina and Albrecht (2021), Cook (2010), and Leonardi (2010) have worked to situate translation as a pedagogical activity in the WL classroom, advocating for the use of Translation in Language Teaching (TILT) as a term to encourage movement away from the historical definition of translation (Cook, 2010; Pintado Gutiérrez, 2021).

Furthermore, as WL classrooms have become more linguistically, culturally, and racially diverse, and our global societies have become more concerned with issues of equity in diverse schools, there has been a call for making WL classrooms more inclusive while finding ways in which teachers can build on the languages and knowledges that students bring to classrooms. Asset-based pedagogies view students' languages and cultures as a strength, in contrast to the pervasive perspective that attributes achievement disparities to deficiencies in the student or the

---

[1] "World language education" is used in this chapter to reference programs and pedagogies in the United States whose primary objective is for students to learn a non-English language and cultures not associated with English-speaking communities. The term "world language" is preferred to "foreign language" in this context, as the term "foreign" can imply otherness, difference, and other negative connotations.

student's culture (López, 2017). Under this perspective, an ideal environment for language learning is created when teachers can build on the languages and knowledges that students bring from their homes and communities (Colina & Albrecht, 2021; González et al., 2005).

In this paper, translation is presented as an asset-based pedagogy that draws on students' full linguistic repertoires in the process of second language learning. After a theoretical and conceptual overview of this argument, the paper will provide a brief description of a professional development (PD) workshop designed to share these concepts and pedagogical ideas with elementary, secondary, and post-secondary WL teachers in the United States.

2.2   Translation as an Asset-Based Pedagogy

2.2.1 Translation in the Sociocultural Paradigm

The concept of translation as an asset-based pedagogy is grounded in sociocultural theories of language learning. Based on the work by Vygotsky (1978), sociocultural theory suggests that one essential aspect of learning languages involves using the new language in interaction with other people. The educational basis for development in this theory is the zone of proximal development (ZPD), the gap between what a learner can do unaided and what they can do jointly with a skilled expert or, for language learners, more capable speaker (Gibbons, 2014). In the ZPD, learners may use tools to help mediate between them and the world, to assist their learning; these mediational tools can vary from discourse patterns to texts to visuals. Many scholars working with this theoretical framing for learning also reference the metaphor of scaffolding, the practical support that assists learners in moving toward new skills, just as scaffolding around a building aids in its construction until it can stand alone (Gibbons, 2014).

Using translation in the language classroom can provide a form of scaffolding and a mediational tool that facilitates rigorous and supportive instructional design. Indeed, translation has been established as a mediational tool since the first draft of the Common European Framework of Reference for Languages (CEFR) (Council of Europe, 2018). The CEFR describes mediation as the fourth mode of communication alongside reception, production, and interaction. The CEFR introduces the concept of mediation as follows:

> In both the receptive and productive modes, the written and/or oral activities of mediation make communication possible between persons who are unable, for whatever reason, to communicate with each other directly. *Translation or interpretation*, a paraphrase, summary or record, provides for a third party a (re)formulation of a source text to which this third party does not have direct access. Mediation language activities, (re)processing an existing text, occupy an important place in the normal linguistic functioning of our societies. (Council of Europe, 2018; CEFR Section 2.1.3; our emphasis)

Mediation language activities are thus not only cross-linguistic according to the CEFR, but also broadly conceptualized as related to communication and learning, as well as social and cultural mediation. This reconceptualization of language mediation beyond its linguistic traits has been key in framing translation as a mediational and asset-based pedagogical tool in the classroom.

2.2.2 Asset-Based Pedagogies and the WL Classroom

Schooling has always been a tool of assimilation and imperialism, where those learners who did not conform to the "cisheteropatriarchical,[2] English-monolingual, ableist, classist, xenophobic and other hegemonic gazes" (Alim et al., 2020, p. 262) were seen as deficient and lacking. Asset-based pedagogies gained currency in the 1990s and 2000s as a way of changing the paradigm in how these learners were viewed (Paris & Alim, 2017). López (2017) states that these pedagogies "view students' culture as a strength, countering the more widespread view that inordinate achievement disparities stem from deficiencies in the child and/

---

[2] The privilege assigned to cisgender, heterosexual men in society.

or child's culture" (p. 193). Asset-based pedagogies focus on critiquing structures of power, developing critical awareness, and interrogating teacher knowledge about students (Alim et al., 2020; Paris & Alim, 2017).

The validation and transformation in asset-based pedagogies center multilingual learners and their cultures. The United States Census Bureau stated that in 2019, 67.8 million individuals (about twice the population of California) spoke a language other than English at home, which is about one in five households or 22% (Dietrich & Hernandez, 2022). Historically, these multilingual learners have been left out of both scholarship on WL education in the United States (Dobbs et al., 2022; Prada et al., 2020) and the preparation of WL teachers (Pascual y Cabo & Prada, 2018). The "native monolingual speaker" has traditionally been the idealized student in the WL classroom (Bui & Tai, 2022, p. 6).

The linguistically diverse WL classroom has thus become a critical space for the development of asset-based pedagogies. In this classroom, the knowledges and linguistic varieties that these multilingual children bring are not only valued but also incorporated as part of a critical, social action curriculum driven by a transformational approach of schools and society (Banks, 2007). Translation has become a powerful pedagogical tool for the exploration of issues of power and linguistic diversity in the WL classroom, and it is an important way to serve the needs of the increasingly multilingual WL classroom. To explore this further, a consideration of bilingualism and translanguaging is necessary.

2.2.3 The New Bilingualism, Translanguaging, and Translation

The traditional understanding of bilingualism often identifies an L1 and an L2 (or in the case of multilingualism, an L1, L2, L3, L4, etc.) for the learner, where the languages are isolated and separate, easily identifiable and named social representations that can be shifted between, but do not overlap or integrate in any way. Translation, under this perspective, has been characterized as a way of bridging two bounded languages and cultures, offering a way of rendering in one language that which was already expressed in another (García et al., 2019). However, newer conceptualizations of multilingualism and translation pedagogy, connected to asset-based thinking about learners, challenge this limited understanding of bilingualism.

More recent perspectives toward what it means to be bilingual have focused attention on the linguistic practices in which multilingual speakers engage within the wide linguistic range (or *repertoire*) they inhabit (García, 2017; Hornberger, 2004). Translanguaging, wherein multilingual learners are seen to have one unitary linguistic system with combined features of different named language categories (Tian, 2020), has become a more inclusive way to describe what multilingual children do with language(s) or, as García (2017) put it, "Translanguaging puts back the emphasis on what people do with language to produce and interpret their social worlds" (p. 257). Rather than approaching the notion of what it means to be bilingual as aligning to the linguistic traits that society assigns to languages and idealized notions of a speaker of a language, translanguaging moves away from a moralizing understanding of what it means to speak a language to tackle a more pragmatic and critical approach of what multilinguals do with language. As Tian (2020) stated, translanguaging offers the opportunity to better address the learning needs of emergent bilinguals, "[incorporating] students' home language practices strategically into classrooms" (p. 217). Bilingualism in this view is an instructional resource in asset-based pedagogies, empowering bilinguals, protecting their language rights, and affirming their identities.

Translanguaging has not always been as prominent in the discourse and scholarship on WL classroom contexts as with bilingual classroom contexts. Just as the idealized student in the WL classroom in the United States has been the monolingual English speaker, mixing languages and calling upon multiple linguistic repertoires in the WL classroom have been viewed as language deficits or errors (Bui & Tai, 2022). However, more critical frameworks in recent years have suggested that monolingual and multilingual students bring language varieties (e.g., Spanglish, Chinglish, African-American Vernacular English or AAVE) into the classroom that provide opportunities for translanguaging. Nijhawan

(2022) presented the idea of "trans-FL" as classroom pedagogy—a teacher-initiated policy with judicious and principled L1 use. This move shifts translanguaging out of the space for multilingual learners for whom translanguaging might be more of a natural phenomenon and into a space where FL/WL learners, who may not have a much less considerable mastery of their L2 and would not be inclined to switch between them, are instead directly encouraged to do so by classroom practices. Situating WL students as capable of translanguaging is not without its issues or concerns (see Bui & Tai, 2022), but it challenges the idea of translanguaging as the domain of students with a high level of proficiency, upends the binary conceptualization of WL learning, and normalizes the continuum of linguistic repertoires that exist in our students as part of the WL classroom.

If we move away from simplistic cross-linguistic approaches to translation, and instead conceptualize translation as a mediational tool of learning, it becomes a rich asset-based pedagogical tool that produces sense-making opportunities and spaces for students to reflect on the practice of not only translation of linguistic utterances, but of all the semiotic and non-semiotic elements involved in communication. As García et al. (2019) articulated, teachers who use translation in a translanguaging framework "extend the meaning-making repertoire of [learners] and make them understand the complexity of their own repertoire and that of their listeners" (p. 87). Translanguaging practices work with the asset-based pedagogy of translation insofar as they support the learners' subjectivities and ways of knowing.

2.2.4 Translation as a Tool for Critical Language Awareness

Another vital component of translation as an asset-based pedagogy extends to its consideration as a tool for critical language awareness. Leeman (2018) defines critical language awareness as an approach to teaching that helps "encourage students to question taken-for-granted assumptions about language and to analyze how such assumptions are tied to inequality and injustice, with the ultimate goal of promoting positive social change" (p. 345). The approach is sustained in the understanding of language beyond a vehicle for communication and as "imbued with social meaning and power relations" (Leeman, 2018, p. 348). The theorization of critical language awareness draws significantly from the work done around critical pedagogies, critical discourse analysis, and new literacy studies, grounded in social theory that examines issues of power, equity, and justice in education (Leeman, 2018).

Translation is immediately implicated in any critical consideration of language. As Baker (2014) articulated:

> the mere act of writing or translating into a minority language then becomes a political statement against the majority language and culture… Translation *out of* the minority language is usually undertaken to raise awareness of the minority language and literature and allow its writers to reach a larger audience. (p. 18; emphasis hers)

In the language classroom, translation serves to shift the approach to language teaching from appropriateness (correct use of a language is based on idealized, moralized notions of what speaking a language entails) to situatedness (the when, where, who, and to whom of language use). Translation becomes a resourceful asset-based pedagogical tool in making students reflect on how multilingual speakers use language within a linguistic repertoire and how different language varieties used within that repertoire have different social prestige. In a way, translation can serve as a reflective space for students to learn about issues of language and power, as well as the situatedness of language use. It can be used to contribute to "undoing standard language ideologies and promote more inclusive educational spaces" (Linares, 2022, p. 69). Making a translation thus is less about aligning a final text in the target language to idealized notions of appropriateness and language use and more about the decisions around the situatedness of language use, stressing the different kinds of language varieties and practices that are valued and/or penalized in different spaces (Phipps & Gonzalez, 2004).

Translation as a pedagogical tool for critical linguistic awareness entails a resignification of translation in the classroom from a focus on the product (as traditionally used in the language classroom) to a focus on the process. This understanding of translation makes the reflexive practice around the task of translation the core practice of the learning process and its evaluation. Translation as a tool for linguistic awareness becomes a feature of how translation can be used as an asset-based pedagogy in the WL classroom because it involves drawing on the knowledges that students bring into the classroom. In the next section, we will explain how we approached and developed these concepts in a PD opportunity with WL teachers in the United States.

2.3   Professional Development Workshop

As Tian (2020) argued, teacher education can provide unique opportunities to help teachers access translanguaging pedagogy in their classrooms. The importance of teaching about translanguaging, modeling translanguaging, and practicing translanguaging has been shown to interrupt and shift teachers' thinking about the ways that multiple languages can interact in the classroom (Tian, 2020). Therefore, to disseminate these principles and concepts of translation as an asset-based pedagogy and to provide opportunities for teachers across our state, our research team developed and enacted an online PD workshop in Spring 2023, entitled *Translation as a Pedagogical Tool for Change: A More Humanizing Understanding of Teaching Languages*. Participants included ten experienced in-service WL teachers from institutions across Iowa. Seven of the teachers taught Spanish, two taught French, and one taught Chinese. Eight teachers taught at the high school level, one at the community college level, and one at both a high school and community college. Due to grant funding, participants who attended all three workshops received a stipend of US$330 and a free licensure renewal credit if they were licensed in Iowa. These teachers were recruited via the state organization of language teachers, which sent out emails and posted on social media about the opportunity.

The instructional team for the three sessions of this workshop was led by the second author, assisted by the first and third authors and other experts in the field mentioned in the descriptions below. The workshop had three five-hour sessions taking place over three Saturdays. This length of fifteen hours was dictated by state requirements for licensure renewal credits. Each session went from 10:00 a.m. to 12:00 midday, with a one-hour break for lunch, before continuing from 1:00 to 4:00 p.m. The workshops were entirely conducted via Zoom.

The workshop mirrors the teacher development work on translation and translanguaging outlined by González-Davies and Ortínez (2021, p. 23), which moved from phases that encouraged reflection ("Where are we now?", "What do we do?", "How do we do it?", and "Why do we do it?") to inquiry seminars that analyzed and modeled new perspectives, to designing and implementing new models. The topics of the three sessions are summarized in Table 2.1.

Table 2.1 Session overview for translation workshop

Session	Morning Topics	Afternoon Topics
Session 1: March 4, 2023	• Foundations 1: Sociocultural Theories of Language Learning; Multimodal Literacies; Plurilingual Repertoire	• Foundations 2: Critical Perspectives on Language Learning • Expert Presentation on Translation as a Pedagogical Tool
Session 2: May 6, 2023	• Review of March 4 Workshop • Presentation of Sample Lesson 1 • Presentation of Sample Lesson 2	• Presentation of Sample Lesson 3 • Presentation of Sample Lesson 4 • Small Group Discussion of Written Lesson Plans • Preview of Final Session and Activities
Session 3: June 17, 2023	• Review of Previous Workshops • Assessment: Evaluating a Lesson • Pre-Planning Participants' Lessons • Designing Participants' Lessons	• Worktime and More Lesson Designing • Lesson Presentations • Review of Workshop

2.3.1 Session One: Foundational Concepts

In Session One, the team focused first on establishing and situating theoretical foundations and content matter. This component of teacher PD is necessary, especially when establishing a new approach or new way of considering the field (Sancar et al., 2021). Additionally, the session focused on how these theories could be related to student learning and how they were situated in practice, which are other key components included in many frameworks of teacher PD (Borko et al., 2010).

The primary four concepts addressed in the session were: (1) *socio-cultural theories of language learning*; (2) *multimodal literacies* (reviewing the modes of communication and the multiple ways to communicate beyond linguistic exchanges); (3) *plurilingual repertoires* (addressing the different forms of, and ways to, conceptualize bilingualism); and (4) *critical perspectives on language learning* (directly addressing the concept of asset-based pedagogies). As each of these areas was addressed, the teacher participants were first asked to reflect on the topic and to report on their thoughts either in the chat or in small-group breakout rooms. Brief quotes, videos, and short passages cited earlier in this chapter and drawn from Colina and Albrecht (2021), Gibbons (2014), Phipps and Gonzalez (2004), and Leeman (2018) were displayed for participants to encourage discussion and review. Finally, participants were guided through discussions and illustrations of how to connect each concept to translation pedagogy.

In the last part of the session, participants were shifted from education studies to translation studies. The teacher participants listened to a presentation by an experienced literary translation expert and translation educator, Dr. Aron Aji, the co-director of the Center for Translation and Global Literacy at the University of Iowa. In this one-hour presentation, Dr. Aji reviewed the central tenets of literary translation, explaining that literary translation concerns not just language but also the text. The response to "What gets translated?" is language, but also literary/aesthetic characteristics, intertextualities, the cultural context of the original, and the literary effect/affect. He reviewed the role and agency of the translator when working between the source text and the target, translated text. He offered one example from his own experience as a translator, describing his thinking and his own decision making. Finally, Dr. Aji reviewed the basic components of translation pedagogy, including the learning objectives, the methodological focus and goals, the instructor's roles, the students' roles, and the classroom as a hermeneutic space and imaginarium. Importantly, Dr. Aji emphasized the point that the aim of translation pedagogy is not to create consummate translations or outstanding translators.

To end the session, participants were encouraged to reflect on their learning in breakout rooms with questions about what they had learned and how they could relate it to their teaching. Participants were also directed to complete a survey where they could give their feedback on the first session and make suggestions for subsequent sessions.

2.3.2 Session Two: Sample Lessons

Examples and models of practice are vital components of high-quality teacher PD. Almost all frameworks for contemporary PD include substantive recommendations for how to help teachers learn from other examples (Borko et al., 2010; Sancar et al., 2021). In this spirit, Session Two was focused almost exclusively on introducing, presenting, and processing sample lessons that used translation pedagogy.

Session Two began with four sample lesson presentations that involved translation positioned as an asset-based pedagogy. The first presentation was given by Dr. Irene Lottini, an Associate Professor of Italian and Director of Italian Studies at the University of Iowa. Her presentation focused on audiovisual translation in language and culture learning. First, she showed a video in the target language and asked students to discuss it. Then, she provided a script in the target language for students to translate, followed by a discussion and revisions of the translation. Finally, she created a final video with subtitles added that represented the translation. This lesson offered participants the opportunity to understand the focus on process involved in critical language awareness, where engagement with the languages was prioritized over the creation of a perfect final product. Dr. Adrienne K. Ho Rose, the Director of Undergraduate Studies and a Lecturer in Comparative Literature, Literary Translation, and the Classics at the University of Iowa, gave the second lesson plan presentation. She invited the participants to look at a short poem in Latin by Catullus and then to consider over thirty different English translations for the same poem. In considering the extant translations, the participants did not engage in the process of translation themselves. Rather, they considered the decisions that others had made and the impact of those decisions on the overall impression made by the poem in English. In this, participants were encouraged to reflect on the translators' own language backgrounds and cultural identities, connecting the process of translation with a focus on the assets that each translator brought to the translation process.

Delivered by Melanie Carbine, a doctoral student in Literacy, Culture, and Language Education at the University of Iowa, the third lesson presentation investigated language varieties via translation, featuring a fast-food commercial where four women spoke in AAVE about a delicious hamburger. The workshop participants reflected on how they would translate the commercial into their non-English language, focusing on specific individual terms used in the advertisement and talking about how different translations of those terms would have different meanings. After small group discussion, she offered a Spanish version of the commercial created by the company for Spanish-speaking audiences and made them reflect on the decisions made by the translators. Language varieties were thus the focus of this presentation, offering an example of how the teacher participants could teach lessons on translation that acknowledged the existence of multiple language varieties and incorporated them into the process of translation. The final presentation was delivered by Sora Kim, a doctoral student in Literacy, Culture, and Language Education. It addressed the topic of machine translation, something that the teacher participants had indicated on their intake surveys as being of great interest to them. The workshop participants looked into how different sentences were translated in different ways by machine translators. They were guided through ways of getting students to reflect on machine translations and to use them as a tool in creating more polished translations. In this activity, participants were also encouraged to question and challenge how machine translators reinforced the prioritization of specific language varieties, adding an aspect of critical language awareness along with the focus on process over product.

After the four lesson plan presentations concluded, the teacher participants were invited to reflect on what they had learned, particularly in light of the concept of translation as an asset-based pedagogy that prioritized process over product. The final activity gave participants the opportunity to look at written lesson plans from Colina and Albrecht (2021). The participants were encouraged to share the plans they had read, to discuss how they might implement similar lessons in their own classrooms, and, more broadly, to share the ideas that they had that day about incorporating translation into their classrooms. Session Two thus ended with the opportunity for participants to actively reflect in discussion and to start thinking about integrating translation pedagogy into their own practice.

2.3.3   Session Three: Creating Lessons

Session Three was organized around the principle that effective PD for teachers is focused on situating the new knowledge in their specific contexts. As Sancar et al. (2021) stated, "The new generation of PD design is responsive to the unique needs of each teacher and structured in response to their individual concerns, strengths, and missions in their real school context" (p. 8). As such, all development of lessons or ideas for the teacher participants in this workshop encouraged them to reflect on their own students. Session Three took place just after the end of most school years in the United States, so the teacher participants were able to reflect on starting their new year in the fall.

This session was focused mainly on curriculum design, utilizing the theory and concepts of translation as an asset-based pedagogy to engage in planning effective instruction. After short, directed reflection on what the teacher participants had learned in the previous sessions, Session Three started with a focus on assessment in translation as a pedagogical tool, moving from product to process. Several participants in Session Two had struggled with conceptualizing how to assess the use of translation in the language classroom if the emphasis was not on the finished product. Therefore, the instructional team attempted to work collaboratively with the teacher participants, identifying their areas of confusion, and tailoring the instruction in Session Three to the learning opportunities that they wanted (Borko et al., 2010).

In emphasizing the difference between the focus on product and the focus on process, the team encouraged the teacher participants to shift their thinking from literal translation to creative or situated translation. Assessment, in this conceptualization, would only be 20% focused on grammatical, lexical, or morphosyntactic conventions in the final product. 80% of the focus would be on meetings or feedback with the teacher, reflexive writing or translators' notes, presenting translations, or meeting with peers and peer evaluation. Teacher participants were then given two sample assessment rubrics from lessons reviewed during Session Two. They were divided into small groups and asked to report on their observations using an online collaboration site, Google's Jamboard. They were asked to answer the questions: "In what ways do you see this assessment tool using process versus product?" and "What are your thoughts and reactions to this way of assessing translation?".

After this discussion and reflection, the session moved into a more active consideration of the teacher participants' own planning and lesson ideas. Participants were asked to create a one-day lesson plan. First, they were given some guiding questions about the setting, objectives, assessments, goals, use of translation, materials, pacing, and sequencing of their lessons. After that 30-minute work session, the teacher participants met in small groups to discuss their ideas. They were then given a simple lesson plan template that they could then use as a guide as they built their lessons, and time to work on their lessons while the instructional team made themselves available for consultation.

The final part of Session Three offered teacher participants time to share their lesson plan ideas with one another and with the instructional team. They were asked to upload their materials to the course management system so that other participants could consult them. Some teacher participants created lessons that expanded on work they had already done with translation in their classrooms. Others adapted extant lessons by adding in elements of translation pedagogy. Still others created brand new lessons involving translation that were unrelated to prior lessons. Their lessons varied in length and scope, and the teachers actively modified the requirements created by the instructional team to fit their priorities and contexts.

2.4   Conclusion: General Reactions and Engagement

As mentioned above, the instructional team worked to be responsive to, and collaborative with, the teachers participating in the workshop. Each session was followed by a brief survey that invited teacher participants' thoughts on what was beneficial and what was challenging to them in each session. After Session Three, participants were asked to reflect on what they had learned and what they still wanted to know. Although an in-depth analysis of the responses is beyond the scope of this paper, it was clear that the participants appreciated two things above all: the connection of translation studies and language education experts, and the chance to collaborate and work on their own translation lessons. They also responded positively to the asset-based framing of translation, and challenging the traditional notion of translation as a problem in the WL classroom.

Establishing translation as an asset-based pedagogy in the WL classroom represents important conceptual developments in how WL learners are viewed, as well as how much criticality is welcomed in the WL classroom. The teachers in the workshop on this topic were receptive to the topics and the reconceptualization of translation in their classrooms. The workshop provided a useful template for future PD related to the establishment of translation as an asset-based pedagogy.

References

Alim, H. S., Paris, D., & Wong, C. P. (2020). Culturally sustaining pedagogy: A critical framework for centering communities. In N. S. Nasir, C. D. Lee,

R. Pea, & M. M. de Royston (Eds.), *Handbook of the cultural foundations of learning* (pp. 261–276). Routledge.

Baker, M. (2014). The changing landscape of translation and interpreting studies. In S. Berman & C. Porter (Eds.), *A companion to translation studies* (pp. 13–27). Wiley.

Balboni, P. E. (2017). Translation in language learning: A 'what for' approach. *Revista EntreLínguas, 3*(2), 276–299. https://doi.org/10.29051/rel.v3.n2.2017.9546

Banks, J. A. (2007). Approaches to multicultural curriculum reform. In J. Banks & C. A. McGee Banks (Eds.), *Multicultural education: Issues and perspectives* (pp. 247–266). Wiley.

Borko, H., Jacobs, J., & Koellner, K. (2010). Contemporary approaches to teacher professional development. In P. Peterson, E. Baker, & B. McGaw (Eds.), *International encyclopedia of education* (3rd ed., pp. 548–556). Elsevier. https://doi.org/10.1016/B978-0-08-044894-7.00654-0

Bui, G., & Tai, K. W. (2022). Revisiting functional adequacy and task-based language teaching in the GBA: Insights from translanguaging. *Asian-Pacific Journal of Second and Foreign Language Education, 7*(1), 40. https://doi.org/10.1186/s40862-022-00160-7

Colina, S., & Albrecht, S. (2021). *Incorporating translation in the World Language classroom.* University of Arizona Center for Educational Resources in Culture, Language and Literacy. https://opentextbooks.library.arizona.edu/scolina/

Cook, G. (2010). *Translation in language teaching.* Oxford University Press.

Cook, V. (2001). Using the first language in the classroom. *The Canadian Modern Language Review, 57*(3), 402–423. https://doi.org/10.3138/cmlr.57.3.402

Council of Europe. (2018). *Common European Framework of Reference for Languages: Companion volume with new descriptors.* Council of Europe Publishing.

Dietrich, S., & Hernandez, E. (2022). *Language use in the United States: 2019.* United States Census Bureau.

Dobbs, C. L., Leider, C. M., & Tigert, J. (2022). A space for culturally and linguistically diverse learners? Using S-STEP to examine world language teacher education. *International Multilingual Research Journal, 16*(3), 237–245. https://doi.org/10.1080/19313152.2022.2082781

García, O. (2017). Translanguaging in schools: Subiendo y bajando, bajando y subiendo as afterword. *Journal of Language, Identity & Education, 16*(4), 256–263. https://doi.org/10.1080/15348458.2017.1329657

García, O., Aponte, G. Y., & Le, K. (2019). Primary bilingual classrooms: Translations and translanguaging. In S. Laviosa & S. González-Davies (Eds.), *The Routledge handbook of translation and education* (pp. 81–94). Routledge.

Gibbons, P. (2014). *Scaffolding language, scaffolding learning*. Heinemann.

González, N., Moll, L. C., & Amanti, C. (2005). *Funds of knowledge: Theorizing practices in households, communities, and classrooms*. Lawrence Erlbaum.

González-Davies, M., & Ortínez, D. S. (2021). Use of translation and plurilingual practices in language learning: A formative intervention model. *Translation and Translanguaging in Multilingual Contexts, 7*(1), 17–40. https://doi.org/10.1075/ttmc.00059.gon

Hornberger, N. H. (2004). The continua of biliteracy and the bilingual educator: Educational linguistics in practice. *International Journal of Bilingual Education and Bilingualism, 7*(2–3), 155–171. https://doi.org/10.1080/13670050408667806

Kelly, N., & Bruen, J. (2015). Translation as a pedagogical tool in the foreign language classroom: A qualitative study of attitudes and behaviours. *Language Teaching Research, 19*(2), 150–168. https://doi.org/10.1177/1362168814541720

Leeman, J. (2018). Critical language awareness and Spanish as a heritage language: Challenging the linguistic subordination of US Latinxs. In K. Potowski (Ed.), *Handbook of Spanish as a minority/heritage language* (pp. 345–358). Routledge.

Leonardi, V. (2010). *The role of pedagogical translation in second language acquisition: From theory to practice*. Peter Lang.

Linares, E. (2022). The challenges and promise of classroom translation for multilingual minority students in monolingual settings. *L2 Journal, 14*(2), 51–74. https://doi.org/10.5070/L214251571

López, F. A. (2017). Altering the trajectory of the self-fulfilling prophecy: Asset-based pedagogy and classroom dynamics. *Journal of Teacher Education, 68*(2), 193–212. https://doi.org/10.1177/0022487116685751

Nijhawan, S. (2022). Translanguaging… or trans-foreign-languaging? A comprehensive Content and Language Integrated Learning (CLIL) teaching model with judicious and principled L1 use. *Translation and Translanguaging in Multilingual Contexts, 8*(2), 143–185. https://doi.org/10.1075/ttmc.00087.nij

Paris, D., & Alim, H. S. (Eds.). (2017). *Culturally sustaining pedagogies: Teaching and learning for justice in a changing world*. Teachers College Press.

Pascual y Cabo, D., & Prada, J. (2018). Redefining Spanish teaching and learning in the United States. *Foreign Language Annals, 51*(3), 533–547. https://doi.org/10.1111/flan.12355

Phipps, A., & Gonzalez, M. (2004). *Modern languages: Learning and teaching in an intercultural field.* Sage.

Pintado Gutiérrez, L. (2021). Translation in language teaching, pedagogical translation, and code-switching: Restructuring the boundaries. *The Language Learning Journal, 49*(2), 219–239. https://doi.org/10.1080/095 71736.2018.1534260

Prada, J., Guerrero-Rodriguez, P., & Pascual y Cabo, D. P. (2020). Heritage language anxiety in two Spanish language classroom environments: A comparative mixed methods study. *Heritage Language Journal, 17*(1), 92–113. https://doi.org/10.46538/hlj.17.1.4

Pym, A. (2018). Where translation studies lost the plot: Relations with language teaching. *Translation and Translanguaging in Multilingual Contexts, 4*(2), 203–222. https://doi.org/10.1075/ttmc.00010.pym

Sancar, R., Atal, D., & Deryakulu, D. (2021). A new framework for teachers' professional development. *Teaching and Teacher Education, 101*, 103305. https://doi.org/10.1016/j.tate.2021.103305

Tian, Z. (2020). Faculty first: Promoting translanguaging in TESOL teacher education. In S. M. C. Lau & S. Van Viegen (Eds.), *Plurilingual pedagogies: Critical and creative endeavors for equitable language in education* (pp. 215–236). Springer Nature.

Vygotsky, L. S. (1978). *Mind in society: The development of higher psychological processes.* Harvard University Press.

3

Genre-Based Interlingual Focus on Form: Translating for Contextual Grammar Learning and Beyond

Elisabet Titik Murtisari[iD]

3.1   Introduction

A natural means to access foreign languages since ancient times, translation has had a perennial association with foreign language teaching and learning. As language learning was traditionally perceived in terms of a language's formal aspects, translation was employed to assist students in learning grammar at the sentence level through the Grammar Translation Method (GTM). Originally designed for the study of archaic languages and intellectual exercises (Dakowska, 2005), traditional GTM relied on decontextualized and inauthentic sentences. It was unable to develop students' active communication skills in the target language, leading to its decline with the advent of the Direct Method. As a result, translation has been sidelined in language instruction, often

E. T. Murtisari (✉)
Universitas Kristen Satya Wacana, Salatiga, Indonesia
e-mail: elisabet.murtisari@uksw.edu

© The Author(s), under exclusive license to Springer Nature
Switzerland AG 2025
D. Coulson and C. Denman (eds.), *Translation, Translanguaging and Machine Translation in Foreign Language Education*,
https://doi.org/10.1007/978-3-031-82174-5_3

linked with uncommunicative teaching practices that deviate from its communicative nature.

Nonetheless, with the growing recognition of the role of the native or first language (L1) in language education, translation is being reevaluated and gradually reintegrated to assist language learning. A mounting body of research affirms that there is no compelling reason against the use of translation in L2 classrooms (e.g., G. Cook, 2010; Machida, 2008). Moreover, translating/mediation skills have also been included as descriptors of language proficiencies in the Common European Framework of Reference (CEFR) Companion Volume (Council of Europe, 2020). Regardless, its long-standing association with GTM has left a mark on how translation is perceived, making it "highly stigmatized" especially in grammar learning (Murtisari et al., 2020). As a result, innovations on its use in grammar learning remain scarce. In contrast, current approaches often remain confined to refined versions of GTM, focusing primarily on focus on forms activities.

Focus on forms, rooted in traditional grammar teaching, has its own merits (Ellis, 2016; Graus & Coppen, 2015) and is still widely practiced in English as a Foreign Language (EFL) contexts. Even though the declarative knowledge gained from focus on forms may not be immediately applicable in communication, it can enhance noticing and be internalized to support further language learning processes (Newby, 2006). Nevertheless, students will benefit by attending to form in communicative tasks (focus on form) to help them develop further form-function mapping. By emphasizing the integration of form and meaning in communicative contexts at the discourse level, focus on form fosters a deeper and more comprehensive understanding of the target language, ultimately enriching the language learning experience. While González-Davies (2014) suggests that focus on form, originally developed in a monolingual context, is not really applicable in multilingual contexts, its utility becomes apparent in an interlingual setting through the practice of translating from L1 to L2 at the discourse level (Lv, 2016; Machida, 2008; Murtisari & Bonar, n.d.). With this in mind, and building on the author's previous work (e.g., Murtisari, 2016; Murtisari & Bonar, n.d.; Murtisari et al., 2020), this paper explores the interlingual focus on form approach in specific genres, demonstrating its application based on pedagogically-informed principles.

3.2 Literature Review

3.2.1 Translation and Language Learning

Facilitating communication across linguistic and cultural barriers, translation has been a crucial tool for multilingual interaction throughout history. However, it has often been undervalued in language teaching due to the impression that it is not communicative. Far beyond a mere change of forms, translation is primarily an act of mediation that involves various interlingual and intercultural aspects. Consequently, it is not a skill that every L2 speaker can effectively perform.

With its need to enhance students' L2 communicative skills, translation training aligns closely with language learning objectives. Additionally, given that effective communication in L2 requires intercultural skills (Liddicoat & Scarino, 2013), translation can promote language learning by fostering these skills. Proper translation training assists students in recognizing intercultural differences by highlighting formal, semantic, pragmatic, and ultimately semiotic incompatibilities, while also teaching them how to negotiate these differences. These abilities surpass the capabilities of machine translation, which falls short in capturing the implicit context for successful intercultural communication. Cross-linguistic and cross-cultural insights acquired through translation may assist learners in navigating L2 use, promoting a more comprehensive and authentic command of the language. Without these skills, there is a potential risk that learners may rely on their own linguistic constructs and cultural assumptions when employing L2 grammar and vocabulary.

Furthermore, with the growing recognition of the role of students' L1 in language learning, the relevance of translation in language education has become even more apparent. As part of an L2 learner's prior knowledge, L1 is a natural means for them to learn an L2 (Titford, 1983). It also enhances students' comprehension and offers a metalinguistic tool to explain complex concepts and unfamiliar forms (V.

Cook, 2001; Edstrom, 2006), making teaching more efficient (Atkinson, 1987). Moreover, allowing L1 use can also increase the confidence of lower-proficiency students (Carson & Kashihara, 2012). Finally, recognizing L1 as a valuable component of students' identities is crucial, considering it holds equal importance to L2, especially in contexts where L2 is dominant. Embracing the multifaceted role of one's first language enhances language learning and fosters a more inclusive and supportive learning environment.

Professional translation training necessitates high L2 proficiency for handling complex texts. However, the teaching of translation can be tailored for L2 learners at varying competence levels and difficulty levels (González-Davies, 2014). The main goal is not flawless translation but rather fostering awareness of formal, semantic, and pragmatic differences between L1 and L2. The objective is to equip learners with skills for negotiating meaning across these incompatibilities, aiming to expand their interlanguage by addressing gaps in L2 proficiency (see Machida, 2011). More challenging translation tasks with parallel texts may benefit students with different levels of L2 proficiency (Murtisari, 2016; Murtisari & Bonar, n.d.). Murtisari and Bonar's study suggests that such flexibility is primarily attributed to the utilization of L1, which serves as scaffolding for students' comprehension of L2 forms, including grammar and vocabulary.

3.2.2   Skopos Theory, Genres, and Parallel Texts

Skopos theory, a prominent functionalist perspective on translation, views translation as a form of communication between individuals facing linguistic and cultural barriers (Nord, 2022). This theory views translation as an act of mediation, requiring a shift in contexts influenced by various cultural factors. Advocates of skopos theory argue that the translation process should be guided by the communicative purpose or skopos, not merely by formal or semantic equivalents. Consequently, translation strategies are employed based on the target text's function, such as serving as an advertisement or a manual, and considering factors such as communication goals, media, and the target audience

(Nord, 2022). Before embarking on a translation, the translator identifies these aspects, outlined in a brief, either explicitly provided by the commissioner or discerned independently by the translator through consideration of the skopos.

Skopos may be applied to any text's rendering and may be used as a basis for teaching translation with a focus on form in various ways. However, employing it with specific genres allows students to learn specific linguistic features by applying them while producing similar texts for pedagogical purposes. Although the complex concept of "genres" (Lee, 2001; Swales, 1990; Tuffs, 1993) is beyond the scope of this chapter, it can generally be perceived as somewhat fluid categories of texts linked to their typical social or communicative purposes. Broadly defined, genres encompass various text types and their sub-types, such as narratives, advertisements, and academic texts. Teaching genres offers an additional benefit by helping learners establish connections between form and function at the discourse level, which is inseparable from contextual grammar learning. Moreover, the ability to recognize and reproduce genres may play a pivotal role in determining a student's success within academic contexts (Davies, 1988, as cited in Tuffs, 1993).

Another aspect of the genre-based interlingual focus on form is the use of parallel texts. These texts, consisting of a source text and its corresponding translation, are commonly used in Translation Studies for comparative analyses of various translational aspects. Parallel texts, which naturally lend themselves to bilingual language learning, are an efficient way of making inputs comprehensible to L2 learners (Butzkamm & Caldwell, 2009). Aiding comprehension at formal and functional levels, such texts can assist learners to turn L2 input into intake and subsequently to produce L2 more appropriately (Butzkamm & Caldwell, 2009). They may also offer learners repeated exposures to diverse linguistic forms in use, promoting the internalization of their usage in communicative contexts.

With such benefits, both quantitative and qualitative studies on the use of parallel texts or corpora for L2 learners have shown positive results on reading, writing, vocabulary, and grammar learning (e.g.,

Dolgunsöz & Kimsesiz, 2021; Lo, 2023). Through the practice of translating a text similar to the parallel text's source text, supported by a translation model and corrective feedback (CF), students can continuously compare their L1 and interlanguage with L2. This direct comparison promotes a more meaningful awareness of gaps, further enhanced by the contextual support of L1.

3.2.3   Grammar Learning: Focus on Form

The emergence of form-focused language learning stemmed from the recognition that meaning-focused language instruction is inadequate for L2 acquisition (Long, 1991). Long (1998) supports Schmidt's (1993) Noticing Hypothesis, emphasizing the importance of form attention for successful L2 learning. Introducing two form-focused approaches, Long advocates for focus on form, which overtly draws attention to linguistic elements during meaning-focused activities (Long, 1991). Through the application of brief, reactive, incidental, interactive, and implicit techniques, focus on form retains L2 learners' focus on their communicative tasks while addressing their linguistic issues (Long, 1991, 1998). Therefore, Long contends it is superior to focus on forms, which involves the explicit instruction of grammatical structures and may overlook students' needs.

However, Ellis (2016) critiques Long's concept of focus on form as too narrow. Ellis suggests that focus on forms can also encompass formal elements within communicative tasks. Expanding on Long's idea, Ellis defines focus on form as "various techniques designed to attract learners' attention to form while they are using the L2 as a tool for communicating" (p. 409). In this way, it may also be explicit, pre-planned, and non-interactive. In contrast, focus on forms involves "various devices (such as 'exercises') designed to direct learners' attention to specific forms that are to be studied and learned as objects" (p. 409). Simply put, focus on form emphasizes attention to L2 formal elements while teaching communicative skills, whereas focus on forms occurs when form becomes the primary focus of instruction (Doughty & Williams, 1998).

With this relatively flexible principle, scholars have suggested different techniques to perform focus on form (e.g., Doughty & Williams, 1998). These techniques include exposing students to repeated use of specific forms (input flood), using language features essential for communicative tasks (task-essential language), and raising awareness through marking forms for identification (consciousness raising). Long (1998) emphasizes the importance of CF, providing negative evidence for language production errors. Diverse strategies can integrate focus on form effectively, dependent on unique learning contexts (Long, 1998). Focus on form may also be supported with a focus on forms technique like production practice after communicative activities, aiding learners in automating linguistic forms (Ellis, 2009). Both approaches are seen as complementary (Ellis, 2015).

Furthermore, as focus on form occurs within a communicative context, Long (1998) suggests its implementation in Task-Based Language Teaching (TBLT). Emphasizing "purposeful and functional language use" through real-life tasks, TBLT has four key principles (Ellis, 2009, pp. 222–223):

1. The primary emphasis should be on meaning, encompassing both semantic and pragmatic aspects.
2. Tasks should create "gaps" requiring active language usage for communication, such as providing information, expressing opinions, or inferring meaning.
3. Learners should rely on their own resources, whether linguistic or non-linguistic, to accomplish the task.
4. The approach is outcome-based, extending beyond L2 use alone.

In contrast to spoken language activities, translation tasks often require students to use dictionaries and thesauruses for accurate rendering. While this is standard in L2 written tasks to enhance vocabulary, students generally rely on their own resources otherwise. Nevertheless, despite being a "real-world activity" and meeting all the criteria, translation is not classified as a task in TBLT literature (G. Cook, 2010, pp. 30–31). Moreover, parallel texts, facilitating access to L2 meaning through L1 and allowing direct comparison of L1 and L2, align with TBLT principles, particularly the clarity of contextual meaning (Nunan, 2004). Consistent with this, Ellis et al. (2012) assert that the intake of new linguistic forms is only achievable when input is easily comprehensible. In this context, the use of translation has the potential to promote the learning of form.

Research on using translation as a focus on form activity is limited. In Machida's (2008) study on Japanese learning in Australia, in-class translation activities were implemented over 12 weeks. Sentence-level translation targeted specific linguistic elements in lessons (seemingly employing focus on forms), while short article translation (300–350 words) integrated into reading exercises covered various genres (focus on form). The focus was on pedagogical benefits, excluding translation as an end. Thus, translating from L2 to L1 served as evidence for L2 comprehension, while L1-L2 comparison raised awareness of how form conveys meaning. The detailed integration of focus on form is not explained, but the class relied on translation practice and teacher feedback. Assessments included tests into both L1 and L2, allowing the use of bilingual dictionaries. The study showed that advanced learners found the subject useful, interesting, and challenging but manageable. Despite vocabulary-related errors in text translation, Machida emphasized the significance of grammatical issues, suggesting more opportunities for focusing on form.

In contrast to Machida's (2008) comprehensive study, Lv's (2016) less in-depth research offers insights into implementing a focus on form through translation. The process involves translating a short text, exposure to an English model translation, consciousness-raising activities, re-translation, and a test through translating a similar Chinese text. Although improvements were observed in the case study's student works, there was a more notable enhancement in lexical elements compared to grammar, which echoes Machida's finding. However, meaningful conclusions were limited due to the study's somewhat constrained nature, focusing on one student's work in a class of 20 Chinese pupils. Regardless, studies like Machida's and Lv's demonstrate that grammar needs more processing for uptake in translation activities, highlighting the need to attend more to form during translating.

Building on Murtisari's (2016) work, subsequent studies by Murtisari et al. (2020) and Murtisari and Bonar (n.d.) investigated Indonesian EFL learners' translation experience for grammar learning. In their third year of English language education, the students in both studies were at intermediate to post-intermediate levels of English. Using genre-based parallel texts, the research highlights the potential of developing translation into engaging focus on form tasks for grammar learning, catering to students with varying language proficiency levels. The findings reveal heightened awareness of grammar's role in meaning making and the benefits of parallel texts for L1-L2 comparison, transparent contextual meaning, L2 modeling, and repeated exposure to forms in authentic contexts during translation for grammar learning. Despite the positive outcomes, the studies lack sufficient details on techniques to enhance translation activities for grammar learning. Addressing this gap, this chapter examines how interlingual focus on form may be effectively implemented to direct students' attention to language features.

3.3 Genre-Based Interlingual Focus on Form

3.3.1 Principles for Interlingual Focus on Form

To illustrate how translation can be integrated into a focus on form instructional approach, it is essential to first establish theoretically-informed principles that ensure its effectiveness. The principles below serve as guidelines for educators in implementing translation and enhancing students' overall experience through integrated and purposeful learning activities.

1. Awareness: This principle aligns with Batstone and Ellis's (2009) principle for effective grammar teaching under the same name, which refers to awareness of the form of language features and form-function mapping. To promote these, strategically aligning the parallel texts is essential to allow students direct comparison between the source and target texts to assist them with noticing. The intentional comparison serves as a valuable tool for raising awareness of the differences and similarities between the languages, aiding students in refining their language usage and gaining a deeper understanding of the subtleties

involved in effective translation. Furthermore, while translating practice (into L1 or L2) and discussing the appropriate translation alone may constitute a focus on form, it is important to create more focus on form opportunities for grammar learning. This may be achieved by employing different focus on form techniques, such as asking students to mark particular language features and discussing their forms and meanings, and providing a model translation after a translation practice task in addition to CF.

Furthermore, in the context of translation, it is essential that students are also aware of the pragmatic aspects relevant to the translation's communicative purpose. Therefore, learners need to attend to skopos-related factors such as the purpose of the translation, media, register, and target audience. Such information will guide students in re-expressing the intended meaning in the target text while attending to the higher order elements of communication, rather than just transferring the semantic meaning of the source text.

Additionally, students also need to understand the concept of translation as a means of communication and what it entails. This understanding involves recognizing that languages are often incompatible in terms of form and meaning (semantic and pragmatic) due to structural and cultural differences, making translation an act of mediation. In fact, there are few "semantic primes" or fundamental concepts that have universal meaning, such as "good", "bad", "think", and "feel" (Goddard, 2012). Unless understanding such incompatibilities, EFL students, who tend to have less knowledge on L1-L2 differences, may be prone to faulty literal rendering.

Increasing depth of awareness should be tailored to the specific teaching context and the needs of learners. For younger learners, it may be sufficient to briefly address how languages have different ways of expressing meaning, emphasizing the need to use more natural forms illustrated by examples. Conversely, tertiary language learners may benefit from a more theoretical explanation on the concept of translation, formal and meaning incompatibilities across languages and cultures, and general strategies to mediate these differences.

2. Scaffolding: In sociocultural theory, scaffolding involves providing support to help learners carry out activities and develop specific skills through structure and collaboration (Walqui, 2006). Since translating effectively is a specific skill that students do not automatically acquire when learning another language, providing support is essential.

Introducing scaffolding in the form of parallel texts at the beginning serves as an example of translating a particular type of text. Offering a comparison between the source text and its translated version, parallel texts serve as tangible examples of how form can be used in L2 and how to mediate meaning between L1 and L2. Scaffolding is also needed to show how a specific genre, including its language features, operates in an L2. This serves as a preparation for subsequent translation tasks, equipping students with the understanding of the language and style of the text they need to translate. For this purpose, potentially challenging L2 words, especially those reflecting meaning shifts in the translation, must also be dealt with to ensure that students understand the differences between the source and target texts.

Additionally, students will also benefit from group work to practice translating before they translate on their own. This approach aligns with the principles of Vygotsky's (1978) zone of proximal development, allowing students to work together at a level beyond their current capabilities. Although students, as per previous research (e.g., Murtisari & Bonar, n.d.), did not perceive group work as very helpful for grammar learning, engaging in group practice may still offer additional support, thereby contributing to task completion and enhancing their overall involvement in the translation process.

3. Authenticity: Authenticity is a crucial aspect in preparing parallel texts, translation tasks, and models to align with communicative functions, reflecting Batstone and Ellis' (2009) principle of real-operating conditions for grammar instruction. In the context of translation practice, it is essential to select genres relevant to students' needs and topics that interest them to ensure engagement. Texts that are employed in pedagogical translation activities should also use natural language, and target texts must accurately reflect the source texts.

This authenticity is vital for authentic comparisons of how meaning is negotiated between L1 and L2 in various communicative contexts. Teachers can gather materials from bilingual references or create them, but it is paramount to edit both source and target texts for naturalness and accuracy. Notably, not all bilingual materials may be suitable for general language learning due to radical shifts that result in adaptations rather than translations.

4. Repeated Practice for Iterative Exposure and Use (Recycling): In addition to increasing the likelihood of forms being noticed, repetition is also a technique of focus on form to develop awareness (Hawkes, 2012). However, I have made this a separate principle in the context of using translation as an interlingual focus on form due to the complexity of the task and various language forms it involves. By reiterating use of linguistic forms in different contexts, utilizing translation as an interlingual focus on form may create "grammaring" experience (Larsen-Freeman, 2015, p. 273). Besides making forms more salient, such repetition may benefit students by providing opportunities for language production (Tannen, 2007) and expand their range of using particular language features through recycling (British Council, n.d.).

To reinforce recycling, the assessment is a test where students individually translate a similar text. In cases of larger classes, this may be completed collaboratively in groups. This approach ensures ongoing practice and application of the learned material.

3.3.2 Implementing the Genre-Based Interlingual Focus on Form

Building on these pedagogically-informed principles, this section explores how interlingual focus on form can be implemented within specific genres for tertiary EFL post-intermediate and intermediate levels. Both L1-L2 and L2-L1 directions may be used for language learning, but in the context of grammar learning, L1-L2 may offer more benefits for the practice of using L2 in communication. While similar procedures have been outlined in previous of the author's studies (Murtisari, 2016; Murtisari & Bonar, n.d.; Murtisari et al., 2020), the sessions detailed here provide additional details to further illustrate the proposed approach. An introductory session on the concept of translation, form and meaning incompatibilities across languages, and common translation strategies is recommended prior to these sessions.

Well-prepared learning modules are necessary for the following steps, which may be implemented in two sessions of 90–100 minutes each. Shorter sessions are possible by reducing the length of the parallel texts and translation tasks.

Session 1.

1. Pre-Task before Translating a Specific Genre (5–10 minutes)

    This initial segment acts as an awareness-raising activity regarding the pragmatic context of the subsequent task. Here, the class engages in a brief discussion on the general characteristics of the genre, including its common communicative purpose. The instructor may initiate by prompting the students to share their prior knowledge about the text type.

2. Receptive Communicative Task (approximately 30 minutes)

    This step primarily serves as scaffolding by giving students an example of how translation works. It starts by students silently reading an L1 text aligned side by side with its translation in L2 (parallel texts) to allow direct comparison between L1 and L2. Each text consists of 250–300 words or less depending on instructional needs. Following this, students engage in a reading-aloud session, taking turns reading the source text and its corresponding translation in chunks. The teacher then checks the students' general comprehension and connects further with the parallel texts based on the aspects of the translation they find interesting. Subsequently, the class discusses specific communicative elements like media, intended audience, communicative objectives, and formal/informal register in the translation.

3. Vocabulary Exercise (approximately 15 minutes)

    After the reading activity, students have a short vocabulary exercise focusing on difficult L2 words and idiomatic expressions by finding their L1 source expressions in the parallel texts. In order to do this, students need to skim through the reading to discover the answers, exposing themselves to the pair of texts again. It is essential that the instructor explains to students if there is any significant difference between the L1 and L2 expressions and why such translation remains effective in the pragmatic context of the translation. For instance, the word "lontong" (an Indonesian rice cake wrapped in banana leaf) may be just translated as "rice cake" in English when the context does not justify the inclusion of the details (e.g., when they are not important in the context or the space is limited).

4. Analysis of Translation Strategies (20–30 minutes)

Aiming to raise students' awareness of L1-L2 differences and pragmatic aspects, this segment focuses on specific translation strategies relevant for the genre by pairing specific parts of the L1 and L2 texts. For example, when translating instructions, certain implicit details may require explicit expression to suit the new readership. In instances like dealing with the passive voice, prevalent in Indonesian, there might be a need to rephrase into an active voice in L2, as a literal transfer may sound unnatural. An essential aspect is the discussion of why a particular strategy is employed and its appropriateness in the translation's communicative context. This dialogue aids students in comprehending language incompatibilities and the broader pragmatic context of intercultural communication, providing insights into mediating meanings in interlingual communication.

Session 2.

5. Language Focus Task (20–30 minutes)

This step primarily serves as a task-essential language segment. In this segment, the class examines specific grammatical features found in the parallel texts. It acts as a follow-up to the previous task and a pre-task to the practice session. Students may mark the corresponding forms in L1 and L2, identifying their functions with the instructor's assistance. For example, in the context of translating tourism texts, the English locative inversion (e.g., *Further north is the majestic State Guest House, formerly home to the Dutch Resident*) is emphasized.

This stylistic form is prevalent in the tourism genre and can enhance the aesthetic quality of the translation in L2. To further enhance their understanding, students engage in a short exercise translating sentences into L2 using the language feature. It is crucial that these sentences maintain relevance to the parallel texts' topic, ensuring the exercise remains contextual.

6. Productive Communicative Task (60–70 minutes)

This practice section is collaborative. Students are asked to translate a similar text in pairs or a group of three using dictionaries. It is crucial that the translation implements the language features previously discussed to create recycling opportunities. This step is followed by students suggesting their group translations. The teacher explores alternative translations and presents a model translation.

To reinforce recycling, the assessment is a test where students individually translate a similar text. In cases of larger classes, this may be completed collaboratively in groups with other assessments given to discriminate individual grades. As mentioned earlier, the feedback should aim for the text's ideal translation, but the assessment standards are set below those intended for professional translators.

3.4   Implications and Conclusion

This paper has advanced the discussion on how translation can be developed to enhance students' learning of form in a holistic manner. With its use of L1, this approach not only diminishes ambiguities but also plays a crucial role in assisting students to develop form-function mapping in grammar learning through reiteration and more chances for focus on form. Treating translation as a skill, the interlingual focus on form inherently encompasses an intercultural perspective that considers culture as inseparable from language and language learning. This aligns with Liddicoat and Scarino's (2013, p. 6) view that "language learning is fundamentally engagement in intercultural communication".

The approach helps bridge the gap in language teaching, where intercultural aspects are frequently overlooked due to the predominant emphasis on L2.

As L1 is a dominant means of thinking among EFL students, expressing ideas in L2 for many learners often amounts to an act of translation, albeit mentally. Therefore, it is crucial for these learners (see Murtisari, 2016, 2021) and bilingual EFL teachers to develop translation skills. This is especially pertinent considering the value of translation in today's increasingly multicultural societies. Despite the widespread use of machine translation, this technology falls short in comprehending implicit pragmatic contexts in the input and is often insufficient for effective intercultural communication. Furthermore, analyzing the purpose and context of communication, negotiating meaning and employing translation strategies for communication, and understanding different genres are valuable skills that extend beyond language learning.

Despite the potential benefits, more research is necessary to further explore how the translation approach may assist students in language learning and how to maximize its benefits. This includes investigating the effectiveness of integrating genre-based translation in various contexts and understanding its impact on students' overall language proficiency and intercultural communicative competence. Additionally, exploring variations in implementation across different proficiency levels and cultural contexts can provide valuable insights for refining and tailoring this approach to diverse learning environments.

References

Atkinson, D. (1987). The mother tongue in the classroom: A neglected resource? *ELT Journal, 41*(4), 241–247. https://doi.org/10.1093/elt/41.4.241

Batstone, R., & Ellis, R. (2009). Principled grammar teaching. *System, 37*(2), 194–204. https://doi.org/10.1016/j.system.2008.09.006

British Council. (n.d.). *Recycling*. https://www.teachingenglish.org.uk/professional-development/teachers/knowing-subject/q-s/recycling

Butzkamm, W., & Caldwell, J. A. (2009). *The bilingual reform: A paradigm shift in foreign language teaching*. Narr Francke Attempto Verlag.

Carson, E., & Kashihara, H. (2012). Using the L1 in the L2 classroom: The students speak. *The Language Teacher, 36*(4), 41–48. https://jalt-publicati ons.org/sites/default/files/pdf-article/36.4_art1.pdf

Cook, G. (2010). *Translation in language teaching: An argument for reassessment*. Oxford University Press.

Cook, V. (2001). Using the first language in the classroom. *Canadian Modern Language Review, 57*(3), 402–423. https://doi.org/10.3138/cmlr.57.3.402

Council of Europe. (2020). *Common European framework of reference for languages: Learning, teaching, assessment—Companion volume*. www.coe.int/ lang-cefr

Dakowska, M. (2005). *Teaching English as a foreign language: A guide for professionals*. Wydawnictwo Naukowe Pwn.

Dolgunsöz, E., & Kimsesiz, F. A. (2021). Parallel texts in EFL reading classroom: Can they enhance EFL vocabulary learning through reading? *I-manager's Journal on English Language Teaching, 11*(4), 1–10. https://doi. org/10.26634/jelt.11.4.17866

Doughty, C., & Williams, J. (1998). Issues and terminology. In C. Doughty & J. Williams (Eds.), *Focus on form in classroom second language acquisition*. Cambridge University Press.

Edstrom, A. (2006). L1 use in the L2 classroom: One teacher's self-evaluation. *The Canadian Modern Language Journal, 63*(2), 275–292. https://doi.org/ 10.3138/cmlr.63.2.275

Ellis, R. (2009). Task-based language teaching: Sorting out the misunderstand-ings. *International Journal of Applied Linguistics, 19*(3), 221–246. https:// doi.org/10.1111/j.1473-4192.2009.00231.x

Ellis, R. (2015). The importance of focus on form in communicative language teaching. *Eurasian Journal of Applied Linguistics, 1*(2), 1–12. https://doi.org/ 10.32601/ejal.460611

Ellis, R. (2016). Focus on form: A critical review. *Language Teaching Research, 20*(3), 405–428. https://doi.org/10.1177/1362168816628627

Ellis, R., Basturkmen, H., & Loewen, S. (2012). Preemptive focus on form in the ESL classroom. *TESOL Quarterly, 35*(3), 407–432. https://doi.org/10. 2307/3588029

Goddard, C. (2012). Semantic primes, semantic molecules, semantic templates: Key concepts in the NSM approach to lexical typology. *Linguistics, 50*(3), 711–743. https://doi.org/10.1515/ling-2012-0022

González-Davies, M. (2014). Towards a plurilingual development paradigm: From spontaneous to informed use of translation in additional language learning. *The Interpreter and Translator Trainer, 8*(1), 8–31. https://doi.org/10.1080/1750399X.2014.908555

Graus, J., & Coppen, P. (2015). Student teacher beliefs on grammar instruction. *Language Teaching Research, 20*(5), 571–599. https://doi.org/10.1177/1362168815603237

Hawkes, M. L. (2012). Using task repetition to direct learner attention and focus on form. *ELT Journal, 66*(3), 327–336. https://doi.org/10.1093/elt/ccr059

Larsen-Freeman, D. (2015). Research into practice: Grammar learning and teaching. *Language Teaching, 48*(2), 263–280. https://doi.org/10.1017/S0261444814000408

Lee, D. Y. W. (2001). Genres, registers, text types, domains and styles: Clarifying the concepts and navigating a path through the BNC jungle. *Language Learning and Technology, 5*(3), 37–72.

Liddicoat, A. J., & Scarino, A. (2013). *Intercultural language teaching and learning*. Wiley-Blackwell.

Lo, S. (2023). Pedagogical translation for vocabulary learning: The parallel-text approach. *Taiwan Journal of TESOL, 20*(2), 97–135. https://doi.org/10.30397/TJTESOL.202310_20(2).0004

Long, M. H. (1991). Focus on form: A design feature in language teaching methodology. In K. DeBot, R. Ginsberg, & C. Kramsch (Eds.), *Foreign language research in cross-cultural perspective* (pp. 39–52). John Benjamins.

Long, M. H. (1998). Focus on form in task-based language teaching. *University of Hawai'i Working Papers in ESL, 16*(2), 35–49. https://core.ac.uk/download/pdf/77238837.pdf

Lv, B. (2016). Double construction in translation and its effect as a learning tool. In Y. S. Fong & M. Brooke (Eds.), *Strengthening connectivity in the ELT: Selected papers from the Fifth CELC Symposium for English Language Teachers* (pp. 61–77). National University of Singapore.

Machida, S. (2008). A step forwards to using translation to teach a foreign/second language. *Electronic Journal of Foreign Language Teaching, 5*(1), 140–155.

Machida, S. (2011). Translation in teaching a foreign (second) language: A methodological perspective. *Journal of Language Teaching and Research, 2*(4), 740–746. https://doi.org/10.4304/jltr.2.4.740-746

Murtisari, E. T. (2016). Translation skill in language learning/teaching: EFL learners' point of view. *Kalbų Studijos: Studies about Languages, 29*, 102–113. https://doi.org/10.5755/j01.sal.0.29.14580

Murtisari, E. T. (2021). Use of translation strategies in writing: Advanced EFL students. *LLT Journal: A Journal on Language and Language Teaching, 24*(1), 228–239. https://doi.org/10.24071/llt.v24i1.2663

Murtisari, E. T., & Bonar, G. J. (n.d.). *Rethinking translation through an interlingual focus on form: Pedagogical implications for grammar learning* [Manuscript submitted for publication].

Murtisari, E. T., Bonar, G. J., & Widiningrum, R. (2020). Learning grammar through learning to translate: A means and an end. *Journal of Asia TEFL, 17*(2), 715–723. https://doi.org/10.18823/asiatefl.2020.17.2.30.715

Newby, D. (2006). Teaching grammar and the question of knowledge. In A. Fenner & D. Newby (Eds.), *Coherence of principles, cohesion of competences: Exploring theories and designing materials for teacher education* (pp. 1–11). European Centre for Modern Languages/Council of Europe Press.

Nord, C. (2022). Action/skopos theory. In F. Zanettin & C. Rundle (Eds.), *The Routledge handbook of translation and methodology* (1st ed., pp. 11–25). Routledge. https://doi.org/10.4324/9781315158945

Nunan, D. (2004). *Task-based language teaching.* Cambridge University Press.

Schmidt, R. W. (1993). Awareness and second language acquisition. *Annual Review of Applied Linguistics, 13*, 206–226.

Swales, J. (1990). *Genre analysis: English in academic and research settings.* Cambridge University Press.

Tannen, D. (2007). *Talking voices: Repetition, dialogue, and imagery in conversational discourse.* Cambridge University Press.

Titford, C. (1983). Translation for advanced learners. *ELT Journal, 37*(1), 52–57.

Tuffs, R. J. (1993). A genre approach to writing in the second language classroom: The use of direct mail letters. *Revue Belge De Philologie Et D'histoire, 71*, 699–718.

Vygotsky, L. S. (1978). *Mind in society: The development of higher psychological processes.* Harvard University Press.

Walqui, A. (2006). Scaffolding instruction for English language learners: A conceptual framework. *International Journal of Bilingual Education and Bilingualism, 9*(2), 159–180. https://doi.org/10.1080/13670050608668639

4

Translation Errors of Third-Semester English Specialists at Sultan Qaboos University

Khalsa Al Aghbari ⓘ

4.1 Introduction

The act of translation encompasses shifts, or transfers, of form, meaning, style and culture communicated by a source or original text, with the ultimate goal of interpreting its message accurately (Hatem & Mason, 1990; Mohammed, 2011). It is believed that a successful translation is one that produces the same effect as the source text (ST) (Mohammed, 2011). The ability to translate a message into another language is an indicator of proficiency in that language.

The field of translation studies has recently witnessed a high level of renewed interest as evidenced by a significant increase in the number of translation programs offered (Gamal, 2010; Moga, 2021). This has led to the proliferation of studies that evaluate the curricula and teaching and

K. Al Aghbari (✉)
Sultan Qaboos University, Muscat, Oman
e-mail: khalsah@squ.edu.om

© The Author(s), under exclusive license to Springer Nature
Switzerland AG 2025
D. Coulson and C. Denman (eds.), *Translation, Translanguaging and Machine Translation in Foreign Language Education,*
https://doi.org/10.1007/978-3-031-82174-5_4

assessment approaches within these programs, with the goal of improving the teaching and practice of the translation profession.

Translation has been investigated from a number of theoretical perspectives, such as formal vs. dynamic (Mroczek, 2022; Nida, 1964), semantic vs. communicative (Mohamed, 2022; Newmark, 1991), semantic vs. functional equivalence (Bell, 1992; Wang, 2018), covert vs. overt (House, 2018) and non-pragmatic vs. pragmatic translation (Lathifah & Mujiyanto, 2021; Wilss, 1993). Regardless of these dichotomies, there has been a consensus among scholars and translators on the traits of a successful translation. For example, accuracy, clarity, precision and stylistic effects are widely discussed as important to preserve the essential meaning of the text in various languages (Mohammed, 2011). Moreover, in spite of the existence of various approaches employed to explore translation, the term 'equivalence' is strongly stressed. However, equivalence is flexible as the varied translations of a ST may be equivalent in meanings, forms or cultural perspectives to that of the target one. It is also important to acknowledge that the closer in form a ST is to its translation, the higher the probability of it resulting in a literal translation which fails to adequately express the intended meaning and culture. For translation to be effective, it needs to focus on the message and meaning of the ST as translation is ultimately an interpretation of messages.

One of the recurrent observations made in the field of translation studies is that "students either translate the original utterances literally, or they avoid totally translating them when they fail to find an equivalent in the target language or when they do not understand the source utterance" (Triki, 2013, p. 49). In translation, the focus should be on the message of the ST, as translation is the act of interpreting the message. Successful translation should reject the bottom-up approach to translation which reduces translation to the act of code switching whereby the structure and grammar of the ST take precedence over meaning and the communicative purpose of the text. This is in line with Nord's (1997) belief that translation problems cannot be addressed at the linguistic text surface level at the expense of foregrounding the pragmatics of the ST.

It is within this framework that the study detailed in this chapter explores the most common translation errors committed by third-semester English specialists using Halliday's Systemic Functional Grammar (SFG) in an attempt to inform translation programs about how best they can design their study plans.

4.2 Literature Review

4.2.1 Studies on Translation Errors Made by Arabs

Errors made by Arab students learning English as a second language have been explored in a variety of studies. For example, Triki (2013) investigated errors made by fourth-year Algerian students specializing in translation following the supposition that "differences between English and Arabic at the pragmatic level can lead to different errors when translating" (p. 40). He attributes his learners' errors in translation to two main causes: lack of pragmatic knowledge and lack of awareness of its importance in the task of translation.

Al-Jarf (2022) identified the problems encountered by advanced undergraduate Saudi student translators when translating word + preposition in long texts from English into Standard Arabic. Her study described translation aspects such as type of error, its frequency and source, while also discussing the strategies employed by students when translating a preposition highlighting collocation errors. Findings revealed that 81% of errors made are intralingual, referring to students' lack of competency in English. Al-Jarf classified students' faulty strategies into "deletion, insertion (addition) or substitution of prepositions in the Arabic translation" (p. 63).

Two further studies were conducted by Al-Jarf (2016a, 2016b) on translating binomials, neologisms, *om-* and *abu-* expressions, and color-based metaphorical expressions. She found that the translation of binomials, color-based metaphorical expressions whose form and meaning are similar in both English and Arabic, is easy, while those which are particular to one of these languages but not the other are more difficult.

Hamdan and Fareh (1999) studied the errors committed by Arab learners of English in translating the linking word '*wa*' in relation to its six meanings: resumptive, sequential, alternative, comitative, adversative and circumstantial. Through a translation task designed specifically to examine the student translators' competency in translating '*wa*' into English, the researchers found that the student translators encountered serious difficulties in translating the comitative, circumstantial and resumptive '*wa*' leading to the disruption of the understanding of the ST.

Qassem (2014) explored problems fourth-year students experience in translating political terms, including expressions, abbreviations and names of government institutions or organizations, contained in three authentic texts from English into Arabic. He described how 64% of the errors committed by students were attributed to their insufficient knowledge of political culture and lack of training in this crucial area of translation. As a result, the author suggested that students use strategies such as omission and avoidance to get around unknown political terms.

Zhiri (2014) explored the errors committed by Moroccan undergraduate students when translating tense and aspect, especially the present perfect and present perfect progressive from English into Arabic. He concludes that "Moroccan students tend to consider the imperfect as an equivalent to the English present simple or present progressive and the perfect as an equivalent to simple past" when rendering English texts containing these tenses into Arabic (p. 293).

Sabtan (2020) discusses the necessity of including a course in machine translation in the study plans of translation programs in the Arab world as he reflected on his experience teaching a machine translation course to translation undergraduate students in Oman. The course assigned students post-edit Arabic and English machine-translated texts which were the output of three free online machine translation systems (e.g., Systran, Babylon and Google Translate). Students were asked to discuss the linguistic problems found in each system in order to select the one with the fewest number of errors. Based on these discussions, Sabtan concludes that there is a pressing need to integrate technology into the curricula of translation departments in the Arab world.

As the above studies indicate, Arab students generally confront a variety of problems in their translation. These range from syntactic and semantic to cultural and communicative errors. The current study attempts to expose the most common translation errors made by bachelor-level English specialists in an attempt to help translation programs adopt the most suitable and effective curriculum.

4.3 Methodology

In this study, 22 third-semester English specialists at an Omani university (see Table 4.1) were instructed to translate an English text composed of 223 words into Arabic. Students were recruited from one translation course at the research site after being informed of the nature of the study, their rights to non-participation and withdrawal, and the confidentiality of their participation.

The text is composed of ten sentences, and the text difficulty level is intermediate, as determined by a translation professor at Sultan Qaboos University (SQU). The students were allowed an hour to complete their translation of the text and for revision. No use of dictionaries was permitted. The text given to participants to translate is a speech about the exploitation of energy sources in Africa by Europeans (Museveni, 2022). Difficult words were glossed for students; all possible meanings were supplied to test their ability to pick the best equivalency based on the context of the translated text. Students had to decide on the best collocations for the glossed words based on the text topic and sentential requirements.

The author next listed the 22 translations of each sentence under its source sentence in an Excel sheet. This totaled 2,230 sentences that were studied and examined for the most common translation errors.

The study employed both qualitative and quantitative approaches to address the types of errors made by students in their translation of the

Table 4.1 Participant backgrounds

Major	English Language and Literature
Age	20–23 years old
Academic Level	Third semester
Language Proficiency	Medium with a 4.5–5 IELTS score

text from English into Arabic. More specifically, the study hinges on Halliday's (1994) concept of SFG. Halliday argues that SFG "is a theory of grammar that is oriented towards the discourse semantics" (p. 15). The errors committed by students were classified into two categories: semantic and discoursal. Semantic errors resulting from limited English proficiency are particularly highlighted to reflect the misunderstanding that frequently characterized students' translation. Mohammed (2011), conversely, attributes translation errors to:

> structural and cultural differences between the two languages, the reliance on the dictionary rather than the meaning in use of lexical items, the differences in the cohesion and coherence systems of Arabic and English, the negligence of the role of context in translation as well as unfamiliarity with text-typologies and genre conventions (p. iv).

The number of translation errors determined to be caused by misunderstanding of the text and by language errors was tallied and is reported below.

4.4   Results and Discussion

Errors at the semantic level were the most frequently encountered in the study. They range from omission of information in the ST, due to either a lack of understanding of the ST, to transposing one word with another word, resulting in a communication breakdown. Below, the text with its ten numbered sentences is presented. The typical translation of each sentence is provided followed by an exploration of the errors committed by participants in its translation.

> [1] For many years we have been told that in order to protect the environment **fossil** fuel investment in Africa for Africans is unacceptable. [2] Now with Europe reinvesting in its own fossil fuel power industry to bring **mothballed** power plants back online, in a truly **perverse** twist, we are told that new Western investment in African fossil fuels is possible— but only for oil and gas resources that will be shipped to Europe. [3] This is the purest hypocrisy. [4] In Africa, we believe what we see, not what

we hear. [5] We see hundreds of millions of our own citizens without access to electricity. [6] We see Western investment in African energy concentrated into wind and solar resources that create **intermittent** electricity which could not provide the consistent energy required to power factories or produce employment. [7] We see Europeans with jobs made possible by diverse means of electricity production, and Africans with neither, forcing tens of thousands to make life-threatening crossings of the Mediterranean Sea to Europe. [8] We will not accept one rule for them and another rule for us. [9] We will not allow African progress to be the victim of Europe's failure to meet its own climate goals. [10] It is morally **bankrupt** for Europeans to expect to take Africa's fossil fuels for their own energy production but refuse African use of those same fuels for theirs.

(1) لقد قيل لنا لسنوات عديدة أنه بغرض حماية البيئة فإن الاستثمار في الوقود الأحفوري لصالح الأفارقة في أفريقيا يعد أمرا مرفوضا

The phrase 'in order to protect the environment' was misplaced by 16 students (73%) who were uncertain about the meaning of the sentence. There were two students (9%) who omitted the phrase altogether. This resulted in the translation missing an important piece of information. The resulting translations are:

- لسنوات عديدة تم إقناعنا بأن استثمار الأفارقة للوقود الأحفوري في أفريقيا غير مسموح إطلاقا
- لقد تم إخبارنا على مر السنوات بأن احتكار صناعة الوقود الأحفوري الطبيعي الأفريقي غير مسموح للأفريقيين .

The second translation is particularly interesting since it translated 'environment' into طبيعي and used it to modify الوقود الأحفوري. There were about 14 (64%) translations which used 'environment' as a modifying phrase to 'fossil fuel investment' resulting in wrong translations and producing a meaning different from the one intended by the ST. Below are a few faulty translations:

- لقد قيل لنا لسنوات عديدة أنه من أجل حماية الإستثمار في الوقود الأحفوري البيئي في أفريقيا أمر غير مقبول للأفارقة.

- لقد قيل لنا منذ العديد من السنوات أن حماية استثمار الوقود الأحفوري البيئي في أفريقيا لا يعد مقبولا للأفارقة.

- لعدة سنوات قيل لنا أنه من غير الممكن حماية التنقيب عن الوقود الأحفوري البيئي في أفريقيا للأفارقة.

- لسنوات عديدة، أخبرنا أن حماية لبيئة استثمار الوقود الأحفوري في أفريقيا للأفارقة عبارة عن شيئ مستحيل.

The first three translations used 'environment' as an adjective to 'fossil fuel'. On the other hand, the verb 'protect' is mistakenly used to refer to protecting the investment in fossil fuels. This evidently produces a different meaning. The final example above approached the translation differently. Although it kept the phrase 'protect the environment' intact, it used it to mean protecting the environment of investment. This meaning is also flawed as it does not reflect the meaning intended by the source sentence.

I assumed that confusion arises due to missing commas in the ST. Furthermore, the student translators failed to linguistically analyze the sentence to break it into meaningful phrases. This could have helped them understand the intended meaning and render the English text into Arabic correctly. As stated above, the English level of the translators is medium, which makes analysis of the structural elements in the source sentence a difficult task. These students were taught explicitly to perform sentence analysis to identify the subject and predicate of the sentence, and to separate other modifying phrases as well. This advanced technique is often performed by professional translators to avoid mistranslating and hence produces the same meaning intended in the source sentence.

The first sentence also has another potentially difficult phrase which is 'for Africans'. Misplacement of this phrase in the translation will yield different meanings or, at the most extreme level, may result in an incorrect structure. Namely, the following Arabic translation places للأفارقة at the end of the sentence which results in ambiguity. *Do Africans themselves invest or does Europe invest for them?* There are two possible intended meanings in the English text for the phrase 'for Africans' which are *Africans investing their own fossil fuels* or *Europeans do that for the benefit of Africans*. In the translation below, the students placed the phrase 'for Africans' sentence, finally producing a meaning different from the ST:

— لعدة سنوات قيل لنا أنه من غير الممكن حماية التنقيب عن الوقود الأحفوري البيئي في أفريقيا <u>للأفارقة</u> —

Therefore, two (9%) student translators used the words من أجل and لصالح to translate the phrase 'for Africans', while 12 (55%) used the preposition للأفارقة/للأفريقيين allowing two interpretations of the English text.

The phrase 'is unacceptable' is translated into various translations including مرفوض, مسموح غير and غير مقبول.. All these equivalents are possible in the context. However, the translation غير مقبول is the most faithful.

The second sentence in the text also has potentially difficult phrasing to translate. Its typical translation is:

(2) والآن مع قيام أوروبا بإعادة الاستثمار في إنتاج الطاقة من وقودها الأحفوري لإعادة محطات الطاقة المتوقفة عن العمل مرة أخرى وفي حبكة عكسية قيل لنا أن الاستثمار الغربي الجديد في الوقود الأحفوري في أفريقيا ممكن ولكن فقط لموارد النفط والغاز التي سيتم شحنها إلى أوروبا

The meaning of this sentence is integrated with the previous one. It explains how Africans were told not to invest in their fossil fuels in order to protect the environment while Europeans freely exploit Africans' fossil fuels to their advantage. Europeans were able, as a result, to bring to life their power plants using the oil and gas of Africa.

Ten students (45%) were confused by the word 'plants' which is equivalent to power stations. Due to the fact that they have not come across this meaning before, these students translated the word into 'trees', producing flawed translations as discussed further below and shown here:

— الان مع الاستثمار الأوروبي لصناعة قوة وقود احفوري وذلك باستعادة قوة النباتات المخزونة —

Examining the faulty translation above reveals a range of serious language errors made by students. To illustrate, the words 'power' and 'industry' are literally translated as قوة and صناعة without paying attention to either their context or their collocations. The phrase 'power station', in which the word 'power' refers to محطات الطاقة, is a collocated phrase that is unlikely to have been encountered by students in their previous reading skills courses. Participants opted for a word-for-word translation producing a translation that is both linguistically flawed and nonsensical. The translation produced is وقود لصناعة قوة, , a sequence of three unrelated nouns. This can also indicate that the student translators failed to read the text as meaningful phrases. They read it word by word and supplied each word with its equivalent. This unconscious reading led to a disjointed rendering of the text.

The sentence is complex because it expresses two ideas: 'Europe rein-vestment in their power plants' and 'new Western investment in African fuels is possible but only for oil and gas resources that will be shipped to Europe'. These two ideas are linked by the phrase *in a truly perverse twist* to show the contradictory stand taken by Europe in its investment of fossil fuels in Africa.

Furthermore, the sentence involves a possessive determiner with a complex noun that has four different words its own fossil fuel power industry. The translation of this four-words compound requires the use of transformation skills whereby the possessive structure is restructured to allow a well translated Arabic equivalent. As students lack the necessary ability for this strategy, about 10 (45%) student translators render the phrase to لطاقة مصانع الوقود الاحفوري الخاصة بها, incurring a serious language error and importing a foreign equivalent الخاصة بها which experienced translators reject altogether. Below, I list two representative faulty translations for this sentence:

- والان مع استخدام أوروبا لطاقة مصانع الوقود الاحفوري الخاصة بها فانها تقوم بإعادة استخدام طاقة الكواكب بطريقة فاسدة حيث تم اشعارنا عند وجود محتمل لمصدر جديد للوقود الاحفوري في افريقيا ولكنها فقط لمصادر الزيت والغاز التي سيتم شحنها الى أوروبا
- وتعيد أوروبا النظر الان في قوة صناعات الوقود الأحفوري الخاصة بها وتعيد قوة النباتات المتجمدة إلى العمل مرة أخرى وحقيقة الأمر المعاكس أنه قيل لنا أن استثمار الغرب الحديث في الوقود الاحفوري الافريقي ممكن ولكن فقط من اجل موارد الغاز والنفط التي سترسل الى أوروبا

The second translation listed above is particularly interesting as it shows both literal understanding and misunderstanding of the English text. The translator wrongly translated 'mothballed power plants' into قوة النباتات المتجمدة, resulting in discontinuity with the meaning expressed by the sentences before it, and ignoring the main topic of the text. More-over, the student translator made language errors demonstrated by the use of من أجل،، a prepositional phrase that has nothing to do with the intended meaning of the ST which states that the investment is limited, and not for shipped oil and gas.

The produced translations also reveal inefficiency in the knowledge of Arabic indicated by placing the translation of the phrase 'in a truly perverse twist' in the wrong position in the Arabic translation, disregarding the need to make the sentence both readable and understandable. It also shows that the student's ultimate goal of translation is only to supply Arabic equivalents to every single English word in the ST.

(3) وهذا هو النفاق بعينه.

Sentence 3 is short but it contains the word *hypocrisy* which can be challenging if the student has not encountered it before. This word, if linked well with the previous phrase 'in a truly perverse twist', can be readily understood. In the collected translations, around 9 (41%) student translators produced wrong equivalents to 'purest hypocrisy' as listed below:

- الاستغلال الخالص
- استغلالا ممنهجا
- أمر شنيع
- انقى المصادر النفطية
- انقى نظرية
- الفرضية الصافية
- الاحتيال الانقى
- افقر مصدر متجدد
- انقى واطهر هيبوقراطية

The majority of participants translated 'hypocrisy' as either الاستغلال or. الاحتيال Although both words are equally negative and may serve as instantiations of النفاق, they do not serve the intended meaning in the ST.

Another striking mistake in the translations is collocating النفاق with أنقى, reflecting literal translation of the word 'purest'. The Arabic word انقى never goes with 'hypocrisy' as it has positive connotations. In the translations above, there are two unacceptable renderings of the English text. These are انقى المصادر النفطية and افقر مصدر متجدد. These support the assumption made earlier that the student translators lack proficiency in English despite their exposure to the language for three semesters. Two student translators (9%) translated 'hypocrisy' as فرضية (hypothesis), showing inattentive reading of the word and associating it phonetically with another word that has similar sounds. It is also observed that three student translators (14%) left the word untranslated while one copied it as is in the Arabic text.

The fourth sentence in the text, discussed below, is easy to understand and may have two translations:

(4أ) في أفريقيا نحن نصدق ما تراه العين وليس ما تسمعه الأذن.

(4ب) ونؤمن نحن في أفريقيا بما نراه وليس بما نسمعه.

As this sentence is accessible grammatically and semantically, all 22 (100%) student translators produced its correct equivalent. However, 10 (45%) participants produced grammatically faulty Arabic sentences which leave out the object pronoun هاء that should be attached to the verbs *see* and *hear*, نراه and نسمعه, respectively. Below, a representative faulty translation is shown:

-    في أفريقيا نحن نؤمن بما نرى وليس بما نسمع

The fifth sentence was:

(5) ونحن نر مئات الملايين من مواطنينا ممن لا يملكون الكهرباء

The student translators seemed to have an overall understanding of the meaning of the sentence. In fact, some even used poetic language, demonstrating their high-level use of Arabic. Below, I show various translations which stylistically differ from each other:

-    وحين تقع أعيينا على البلاد فإنها تقع على مئات الملايين من المواطنين بلا إمكانية للوصول إلى مصدر كهرباء

-    ونرى مئات الملايين من المواطنين دون كهرباء

-    ونرى مئات الملايين من مواطنينا لا يتم إمدادهم بالكهرباء

In terms of understanding, all student translators produced the correct translation to this sentence. The first translation above is creative as it employs a complex structure steering away from the literal meanings of the verb *see*, utilizing a poetic equivalent أعيننا تقع, while the majority opted to literally translate *see* as نرى. The second part of the sentence, 'without access to electricity', receives various translations ranging from لا يتم إمدادهم to بدون المقدرة للحصول and إمكانية للوصول بلا. I observe that the second translation uses literal equivalents to the word *access*, while لا يتم إمدادهم shows a deep reading into the English text; *it accuses the Europeans of depriving locals of electricity*. These variations of the Arabic translations show different competencies in Arabic. As for language errors, 11 (50%) students made some.

Moving to sentence 6 below:

(6) ونرى الاستثمار الغربي للطاقة الأفريقية يتركز في مصدري الرياح والشمس اللتان تنتجان كهرباء متقطعة لا يمكنها أن توفر الطاقة المتواصلة المطلوبة لتشغيل المصانع أو انتاج فرص العمل.

The sentence in the ST is a long, compound one that involves some difficult lexical items. Moreover, the translation requires additional knowledge of Arabic syntax which does not only have the singular and plural form of a noun but it also requires a 'dual' suffix to express the number 'two'. Surveying the translations produced, it was observed that 100% of the translations are characterized by correct understanding of the English text. However, the student translators opt for different translations that vary stylistically and grammatically. Around one-third of respondents (32%) have language errors, including mistakes with prepositions, conjunctions, equivalents and spelling errors as illustrated below:

-    ونرى أيضا أن الاستثمار الغربي في الطاقة الأفريقية يرتكز على مصادر الرياح والطاقة الشمسية والتي تنتج كهرباء متقطع حيث لا يمكنها وفير الطاقة اللازمة المطلوبها لتزويد المصانع بالطاقة أو لتوفير الوظائف

For example, the word المطلوبها has a spelling mistake. Moreover, the word متقطع is also spelt wrongly, missing التاء المربوطة. Below, another faulty translation is shown:

- وفي المقابل فإننا نرى أيضا الاستثمار الغربي لطاقة أفريقيا والتي تتركز في تحويل مصادر طاقة الشمس والريح إلى تيار متناوب من الكهرباء والذي بدوره يساهم في منع وصول الطاقة الغير منقطعة المطلوبة لتشغيل المصانع أو لانتاج العمالة

In this translation, the equivalent to intermittent is not متناوب but متقطع. This mistake reflects the need to teach collocations explicitly in translation courses.

Exploring other flawed translations, I observe that the lack of sufficient vocabulary also led one student to maintain two words from the English text and transliterate them into the Arabic translation. The student translator produced the following translation:

- ونحن نشاهد   الويستريم في أفريقيا كطاقة معتمدة على الرياح ومصادر   السولار التي تولد كهرباء غير منقطعة

The equivalent to *western* and *solar* was not known and apparently could not be guessed by the student. Furthermore, the student used the wrong collocation for *produce employment*, rendering the collocated phrase literally into الإنتاج التوظيفي. However, the equivalent should be توفير الوظائف..

(7) ونرى الأوربيين يحظون بوظائف في قطاع إنتاج الكهرباء المتنوع بينما يحرم الأفارقة من ذلك، ويجبر عشرات الآلاف منهم إلى النزوح إلى أوروبا في عبور للبحر المتوسط يهدد حياتهم

Sentence 7 continues from the previous one by providing readers with evidence of how Europeans treat themselves differently from the way Africans are treated. There are 5 (23%) wrong translations. I show two examples:

- إننا نرى كذلك أن الأوروبيين صنعوا المستحيل عندما تعلق الامر بانتاج الكهرباء على عكس الافارقة الذين يواجهون عشرات الالاف من تهديدات الحياة لعبور البحر المتوسط إلى أوروبا
- ولقد لاحظنا أن الأوروبيين ممكن يملكون وظائف قد هددوا الحياة عبر البحر الأبيض المتوسط إلى أوروبا الافريقيونفقد أجبروا عشرات من الاف الناس للعمل من خلال استخدام مختلف وسائل انتاج الكهربا التي لا يمتلكها

Looking closely at the produced translations reveals that a few students resorted to fronting the final part of the sentence, which produced a different meaning from the one intended by the ST.

I will move to discuss the translations of sentence 8:

(8) وإننا لن نقبل بأن يملي الأوروبيون قوانينهم علينا

In the translation of this construction, 15 (68%) student translators wrongly used قاعدة to translate *rule* which here means قانون. Moreover, participants could have read deeper to see that the author is referring to the double standard used by the Europeans when dealing with the energy resources of the Africans.

The translation of the final two sentences in the text also produced some interesting results. Sentence 9 is:

(9) كما لن نسمح للتقدم الأفريقي أن يكون ضحية لفشل أوروبا في تحقيق أهدافها المناخية

This sentence is both syntactically and semantically simple with a subject *we* and a fairly medium-length predicate: *will not allow African progress to be the victim of Europe's failure to meet its own climate goals.* Difficult vocabulary for participants may include the words 'progress', 'victim' and 'climate'. However, these words are quite common, and the majority of third-semester students had already encountered them in previous reading courses. In terms of accuracy, around 14 students (64%) produced flawed translations. One striking error was committed in translating the word 'progress'. Students used equivalents such as المشروع and التنمية, النجاح, الوسائل, العمليات. The precise translation of the word can either be التقدم or التطور, where both show how the development of Africans falls victim to the exploitation and failure of selfish Europeans. It was also observed that nine students (41%) avoided translating the word 'climate'. This shows that these students did not know the meaning of the word and could not guess it from the context. Moreover, one student wrongly rendered 'victim' into ملكا, meaning 'a possession', as in the following:

- حيث أننا لن نسمح لمصادر أفريقيا أن تصبح ملكا للاوروبيين ليحققوا الأهداف التي يرجونها

It should also be noted that a number of translations (32%) involve language mistakes including grammatical and spelling errors.

The translation of sentence 10 is:

(10) وإنه من الإفلاس الأخلاقي لأوروبا أن تنتزع وقود أفريقيا الأحفوري لانتاج كهربائهم في حين تمنع الأفارقة من استخدام هذا الوقود والذي هم في الأساس من يملكونه

The meaning of 'bankrupt' was given to the students in the gloss. Two students (9%) produced wrong translations for this sentence. It was also observed that there were many grammatical and spelling errors. As this English sentence is quite lengthy, 11 students (50%) produced translations whose length is unnecessarily long. This strategy is employed when the meaning of the sentence is not fully clear to the student translators who decide to reiterate words.

There are two very long Arabic translations produced for this sentence. I include one as an example:

- وإن هذا الفعل الشنيع يعد إفلاسا من الناحية الإخلاقية للاوروبيون حيث أنهم يتوقعون أننا سنسمح لهم بنهب الوقود الاحفوري الخاص بافريقيا واستخدامه لانتاج طاقتهم الخاصة مع الحرص على رفض استخدام الافارقة لحقهم في نفس الوقود الاحفوري.

Table 4.2 below summarizes the types and percentage of translation errors made by students. It shows that the majority of errors fall into two classifications: semantic and linguistic errors. The first type can be due to students' lack of proficiency in English. The second type relates to a lack of knowledge about Arabic writing. For example, the Arabic produced as a translation of the ST exhibits language errors, such as incorrect prepositions, missing and incorrectly used punctuation, faulty conjunctions and flawed collocations.

4.5   Conclusion: Pedagogical Implications

The aim of the study was to identify the types of errors made by third-semester English specialists after taking six language skills courses, including intensive reading, in their first two semesters at a public

Table 4.2 Type and percentage of errors

Sentence #	% of Errors of misunderstanding	% of Language errors
1	74	65
2	46	45
3	41	24
4	0	45
5	0	50
6	0	32
7	23	68
8	68	41
9	64	32
10	9	50

university in Oman using Halliday's SFG. Results should be interpreted, however, with several limitations in mind, foremost among these being the fact that only 22 students in one class were involved in the research, and only their semantic and language errors were examined. Despite these limitations, knowledge of these error types highlights the weaknesses participants have in their English competency. Clarification of this limited knowledge will help enable educators and English instructors to design amended courses and devise teaching materials that enhance learners' language skills which will, in turn, improve students' translation abilities. As discussed above, some of the errors committed need to be explicitly highlighted so that students can become fully aware of them.

The study also revealed insufficient vocabulary in the language repertoire of these students which caused them to avoid translating a number of words or led them to mistranslate them. Many of the words in the text should have been relatively easy for learners at this level, and students were likely to have read them in the texts they took in their reading courses. The study has also revealed poor reading and comprehension skills as manifested through the students' inability to see the interconnected flow of ideas as they progress in their reading of the text. More intensive reading courses are needed to allow students to be guided through the text with an instructor.

Finally, the study has also drawn attention to numerous language errors made by participants on grammatical and semantic levels. These errors, which were made in the students' native language, indicate inefficient writing skills in Arabic. It has almost become axiomatic that the best translators are those who translate into their mother tongue. However, results reported in this chapter suggest that even students who are native speakers of Arabic are unable to produce flawless Arabic translations. The implications of this, therefore, reach well beyond the English language classroom and have potential ramifications for education provision across courses in Oman and beyond.

References

Al-Jarf, R. (2016a). Issues in translating English technical terms to Arabic by Google Translate. In J. Itmazi (Ed.), *3rd International Conference on Information and Communication Technologies for Education and Training (TICET 2016)* (pp. 17–31). Lulu.

Al-Jarf, R. (2016b). Translation of English and Arabic binomials by advanced and novice student translators. In L. Ilynska & M. Platonova (Eds.), *Meaning in translation: Illusion of precision* (pp. 281–298). Cambridge Scholars.

Al-Jarf, R. (2022). Undergraduate student-translators' difficulties in translating English word + preposition collocations to Arabic. *International Journal of Linguistics Studies, 2*(2), 60–72. https://orcid.org/0000-0002-6255-1305

Bell, D. (1992). Racial realism. *Connecticut Law Review, 24*, 363–379.

Gamal, M. (2010). Examining translation experience. *American Journal of Translation Studies, 2*(1), 1–33.

Halliday, M. (1994). *An introduction to functional grammar* (2nd ed.). Edward Arnold.

Hamdan, J., & Fareh, S. (1999). The translation of Arabic *Wa* into English: Some problems and implications. *Dirasat, 26*, 1–22.

Hatem, B., & Mason, I. (1990). *Discourse and the translator*. Longman.

House, J. (2018). Translation studies and pragmatics. In C. Ilie & N. R. Norrick (Eds.), *Pragmatics and its interfaces* (pp. 143–162). John Benjamins.

Lathifah, S. U., & Mujiyanto, J. (2021). Formal shifts use on achieving pragmatic equivalence in English-Indonesian translation of KungFu Panda. *English Education Journal, 11*(4), 465–472.

Moga, L. G. (2021). Literary translation and rewriting: Challenges and perspectives. *Scientific Bulletin of the Politehnica University of Timişoara: Transactions on Modern Languages, 20*(1), 65–75. https://www.sc.upt.ro/att achments/article/499/02_04_Moga.pdf

Mohamed, E. J. (2022). Translation methods: A comparison study between semantic and communicative translation. *International Journal of Linguistics, Literature and Translation, 5*(4), 86–94.

Mohammed, T. (2011). *A taxonomy of problems in Arabic-English translation: A systemic functional linguistics approach* [Unpublished doctoral dissertation]. University of the Western Cape. https://core.ac.uk/download/pdf/589 15199.pdf

Mroczek, P. (2022). *Linguistic differences between formal and dynamic equivalence in selected Polish and English translations of The Epistle to Colossians* [Unpublished bachelor's thesis]. Jagiellonian University in Krakow. https://ruj.uj.edu.pl/entities/publication/2d7d83e3-e2f8-43f3-9eb7-0269d4fa4a32

Museveni, Y. (2022, November 9). Europe's failure to meet its climate goals should not be Africa's problem. *Monitor.* https://www.monitor.co.ug/uga nda/oped/commentary/europe-s-failure-to-meet-its-climate-goals-should-not-be-africa-s-problem-4014320

Newmark, P. (1991). *About translation* (vol. 74). Multilingual Matters.

Nida, E. A. (1964). *Toward a science of translating: With special reference to principles and procedures involved in Bible translating.* Brill.

Nord, C. (1997). A functional typology of translations. *Benjamins Translation Library, 26*, 43–66.

Qassem, M. (2014). The Arab translation students' hindrances in translating political culture from English into Arabic. *Arab World English Journal, 5*(4), 240–253.

Sabtan, Y. (2020). Teaching Arabic machine translation to EFL student translators: A case study of Omani translation undergraduates. *International Journal of English Linguistics, 10*(2), 184–197. https://doi.org/10.5539/ijel.v10n2p184

Triki, M. (2013). A pragmatic approach to the study of English/Arabic translation errors. *Journal Academica, 3*(1), 39–51.

Wang, Z. (2018). Introduction of functionalism and functional translation theory. In *6th International Conference on Social Science, Education and Humanities Research (SSEHR 2017)* (pp. 623–627). Atlantis Press.

Wilss, W. (1993). Basic concepts of MT. *Meta, 38*(3), 403–413. https://doi.org/10.7202/004608ar

Zhiri, Y. (2014). The translation of tense and aspect from English into Arabic by Moroccan undergraduates: Difficulties and solutions. *Arab World English Journal, 5*(4), 288–296.

5

"Babel Project": Japanese Language Learning Through Theater Translation

Dennitza Gabrakova

5.1   Introduction

The "Babel project" was a translation activity undertaken with advanced-level students in a New Zealand university. Institutional financial difficulties in offering courses in foreign languages and cultures impacted the provision of Japanese, which was otherwise a strong course since the 1990s with high levels of enrolment. Being unable to offer foreign language classes for a small number of students meant designing rigid syllabi based on tests, or merging courses and identifying topics of interest that can be shared among learners of various languages. "Translation" and "intercultural communication" were set at the core of advanced language work at the postgraduate level. This provided fertile ground for a collaborative-based approach towards developing Japanese language

D. Gabrakova (✉)
Wakayama University, Wakayama, Japan
e-mail: dennitza@wakayama-u.ac.jp

D. Coulson and C. Denman (eds.), *Translation, Translanguaging and Machine Translation in Foreign Language Education*,
https://doi.org/10.1007/978-3-031-82174-5_5

proficiency. It was at this juncture that the Babel project seminar materialized.

The Babel project involved six advanced-level students who had attended a postgraduate-level course, either as part of their postgraduate studies or who were supplementing credits for their undergraduate degree. The project organically developed as an extension of the author's individual support for the students in the spirit of prioritizing cultural enrichment over educational pragmaticism. This chapter reports on the process leading to producing a complete collaborative translation of a Japanese language play, in which the six students were in charge of the lines of one of the drama's six characters. The students used my university office as a meeting place during which they would read out and translate the lines in my company. These meetings were supplemented by online work among the students on a Google Docs document with the play translation.

5.2   The Babel Project

5.2.1 Creative Labor

The project was implemented at Victoria University of Wellington, New Zealand, to accommodate the interests and aspirations of several students whose level and future goals exceeded the undergraduate curriculum. Adopting collaborative translation of a play from March 2021 to October 2021, with exchange among the author and the students continuing until today, was not perceived as an extracurricular activity, but rather as a space to overcome the insufficient availability of Japanese language coursework among students with ambitious goals for a bilingual future.

The six students were a small group with diverse goals, but with a common interest in mastering the Japanese language. With limited time, as a teacher, I had to make a choice of either addressing their individual concerns within limited consultation slots or adopting an inclusive method involving all of them into a specific language-based task. I chose the second, aiming at the performative creation of an interactive community of Japanese language learners, anchored on the task of translating a piece of authentic drama.

The choice of the literary work was based on prior deliberation with one of the students about assigning it to them as a master's course project. Due to personal reasons, this student chose not to pursue the project. However, in discussion with me, we decided not to waste the plan and instead offered it to a group of peers. These students needed extra credits to fulfil their academic plans and/or displayed eagerness to improve their reading skills, while their interests surpassed the undergraduate curriculum. The task was to team-translate a play by a contemporary Japanese author, Yoko Tawada, emphasizing translation as its very theme. The play has six characters: the dog, the cat, the bear, the rabbit, the squirrel, and the fox. The lines of each were assigned to one student for translation. The Japanese script of the play was the course material for us to base our study and discussions on over a period of seven months, which is roughly two semesters in a New Zealand university.

Using drama for teaching the Japanese language has been advocated by Hewgill et al. (2004) and Fukushima and Fujimoto (2009) as a way to instil an authentic conversation style through acting out scripts in L2 learners. However, our task was translating as a mode of performing, unlike previous practice. Clarification of grammar structures in the dialogic style of Tawada's drama constituted the basis of our activity. The inherently collective nature of the task of rendering this drama into English (the native language of the learners), was essentially distinctive from usual translation activities in group discussions in L2, or translation lessons. Each translation of the lines of one character by one individual student was part of the overall pedagogical assignment, and germane to the theme of the original text. From this setting emerged a situation in which students saw their own group efforts mirrored in the interactions of the animals in the play. In addition, the Biblical motif of a "Babel project", incorporated into Tawada's play, emphasized translation as a prerequisite for achieving a common understanding between discordant worldviews.

The choice of material for translation was based on my long-standing interest in the writings of Yoko Tawada, particularly her efforts to write literary works in her non-native German. The length of the work required longer-term engagement by students than usual. Moreover, for most of the students it was an extracurricular project which accounted for the irregular pace and composition of the seminar sessions. Some of the students were enrolled in other courses, preparing for study and work in Japan, or transitioning to full-time positions after graduation. Since the lines of each of the six characters are separately presented, it was possible to carry out the translation work in a fragmented manner (i.e., brief sessions) so that all the students did not have to attend the seminar at the same time.

The participants varied between one and four in each session. They also independently organized sub-sessions to go over specific parts of the play. This sense of taking charge of their work is also germane to the theme of sustainability in the play. The only occasion, and a symbolic peak in our work, when all six students gathered was to participate and read excerpts of their translation at an online keynote lecture on civil society, moderated by me, for an international graduate student seminar.

Two of the participants continued working on the script, polishing it for submission for publication. This process took nearly two years for the final version of the script to be produced. Additionally, reflective comments by the participants were solicited and are presented in this chapter, which can be interpreted as an extension of the project. In this sense, the translation of Tawada's play was alive, evolving and ongoing, in parallel to the students' engagement with the Japanese language in various capacities from hobby to serious efforts for careers in translation.

5.2.2 The Ecosystem

The outcome of the translation of the play exists as a full script, a record of the six students' collaborative effort, yet at the same time it was an evolving process, a blueprint of a language seminar. In retrospect, this invited us all to further reflect on the pedagogy and potential reach of such a translation project. For me, the retrospective nature of this teaching philosophy provides a precious sense of educational fulfilment. My further reading of studies by other scholars on translation in language teaching (McCreary, 2022; Pintado Gutiérrez, 2018), and also on the labor of performance and creativity (Marinetti & Rose, 2013; Noda, 2014), in retrospect shaped my appreciation of the possibilities of this project, encouraging me to pursue the "life-giving" (Kondo, 2018) potential of the space of performativity. I have also found enormous intellectual comfort in Laviosa's (2014) approach to incorporating translation within language teaching, and especially her embrace of an "ecological approach" (p. 57) to the study of L2. Laviosa stresses the "sense of initiative, autonomy and motivation" that this pedagogy fosters in students in response to the teacher's "high expectations" from the "real challenges" of "authentic forms of assessment" (p. 57).

In the case of the *Animals' Babel* translation, the ecological approach proposed by Van Lier (2010) and honed into a translation-informed language teaching methodology by Laviosa (2014), had two important implications. There was the institutional ecology of the language teaching unit, functioning under financial pressure with high demands for increasing undergraduate language learner numbers, with increased efficiency in delivering well-honed content with a reduced number of teaching staff. When the ambitions of both students and teaching staff surpass the limits of these pedagogic formats, ideally courses above the undergraduate level can be offered. However, such courses were not sustainable within a single foreign language major.

The second ecological aspect of this project was in the choice of the content, namely an explicitly ecologically oriented play with implied references to the Fukushima triple disaster of 2011 (an earthquake followed by a tsunami and nuclear meltdown), accompanied by a critique of efficiency and economic pursuit at the expense of quality of living. The Babel project inside the play is an invitation to six animals to build a sustainable "Babel" structure, after a natural disaster has wiped humanity off the planet. Therefore, the self-reflexivity of the Babel project as a teaching project within a crisis in the humanities and foreign language teaching was quite clear.

Given this insight into language as a whole ecology, Van Lier (2002, 2004) advises teachers to create a learning environment that offers students physical and social opportunities for participating in a variety of open-ended, unpredictable activities aimed at creating a multitude of meanings individually or in groups (Laviosa, 2014, p. 67).

Even though the research on translation in language teaching mentioned above does not have a focus on the adoption of a drama text, the ethos of the ecological perspective is in line with my work with this translation seminar. I am particularly drawn by the reference to the destabilization of the teacher/learner traditional dichotomy and the "open-endedness" of the task, which definitely corresponds to the production of a translation of Tawada's play; as one student translated, "Dog: *Yes, onions should be half translucent. Projects are the same; they lose their appeal if they're totally transparent*".

Interestingly, the so-called role-play, conventionally employed in language learning, takes on a new and authentic meaning when the participants in the seminar are requested to become in charge of a specific theatrical role. As Laviosa (2014) states, "While role-play situations seem to suit risk-taking and extroverted personalities, translation seems to favor reflection and introverted personality traits, since it involves lower levels of interaction" (p. 28). Here, the introvert/extrovert dichotomy is also playfully challenged. This claim is supported by the use of drama in foreign language teaching (Campbell & Tigan, 2022; Hewgill et al., 2004), whereas translation adds reflexivity. In Laviosa's summary, we find evidence of the learners' perception of translation in foreign language learning appreciated in terms of "the intellectual challenge it poses, the linguistic confidence it instils, the improvement of L2 use it brings about, the awareness about cultural differences it raises and the feeling of achievement it gives" (p. 37). Importantly, the *Animals' Babel* project complements an effort to enhance educational experience beyond the numerical value of test scores, and the conformism it engenders, or, as Laviosa puts it:

> …the quality of the linguistic experience is seen as crucially different from educational standards. The latter are measured by exam results and centre on products of learning, while the former places value on the learners' engagement in the educational experience as a whole and on the development of abilities that go beyond the teaching objectives, e.g. patience,

cooperation with fellow students, giving and asking for help, or dealing with the unexpected (p. 46).

In Laviosa's (2014) path-breaking approach, we find her personal dedication to the work of influential language and translation teachers and scholars—Kramsch (1993) and Tymoczko (2007). Laviosa's approach is instructive in that it praises these two specific pedagogical role models and attempts a combination of their approaches in a single "holistic" pedagogy. A lecture by Rod Ellis (2021) inspired me to invest more time and energy into the "teaching" aspect of foreign language teaching.

Here, in our *Animals' Babel* project, we had the students performatively engage with their own expanded selves as multilingual subjects. This constitutes the creation of a social identity, which is equally empowering, and attuned to historical and cultural, and even economic, inequalities.

In the seminar sessions, we sat around the table in my office, reading, drinking tea, and engaging in what Laviosa (2014), based on Kramsch (1993), refers to as "metatalk". We talked about our own experiences, practical as well as intellectual, of translating, from the details for scheduling a session to the intricacies of a grammar structure in the lines of a character. As a lecturer, on numerous occasions I have usurped the "metatalk" by offering my interpretations on current affairs, education, and environmental issues.

To counterbalance the silence or the absence of members of the group, I would use banter as a form of informal brainstorming to encourage the students to create connections between the content of the play and their respective areas of interest. Always stressing the economic burden on internationalized Japan, enabling the welcoming of foreign students and English language teachers, in indirect connection to the Fukushima disaster in 2011, I was also attempting to heighten students' "geopolitical responsibility" (Tymoczko, as cited in Laviosa, 2014, p. 92), for instance vis-à-vis the sensitive issue of nuclear energy in Japan.

In sum, Laviosa's (2014) ideal for a space of foreign language teaching combines insights from Kramsch (1993) and Tymoczko (2007) with the keyword "self-reflexivity" as one common denominator. The choice of text, catalysing the formation of a "cooperative learning environment" is informed by the lecturer's ethic credo (poetry in these two cases), and a multi-media piece—in the case of Laviosa's English and Italian language classrooms. In my case study, quite coincidentally, Tawada is herself a "multilingual subject" in writing and performance, and therefore the self-reflexivity attains a certain thickness, which may not have been achievable otherwise. Finally, at the end of the play, to the surprise of the hard-working student-translators, the main theme crystallizes around the merging of leadership with translation, indirectly conveying my message to the students and my encouragement to them as leaders within a new, decentred, to-be-built Japanese language seminar format. Here, the seminar achieved Laviosa's (2014) vision of transformation in the classroom leading to the "grow[th of] …a self-reflective, interculturally competent and responsible meaning maker[s]" (p. 105).

5.2.3 The Classroom as a Backstage

The students gathered in my office and sat around a table with print-outs of Tawada's text, their mobile phones and writing instruments to take notes in the margins of the play. They read their respective animal's lines in turn in Japanese and proposed an English translation for the purpose of checking meaning. I provided explanations on tricky syntax and vocabulary with ramifications to social and cultural contexts. Students filled in for their absent colleagues, reading lines of the animal characters as needed. We roughly covered one page in single one-to-two-hour session with ample time for chatting, ranging from concerns on balancing work with study to sharing episodes related to students' experiences with certain Japanese expressions. Given my scholarly interest in Tawada's writing, I also provided abundant literary analysis for each section that had been read in those sessions. Since four of the participating students had at different times been enrolled in my Japanese literature class, they were receptive to my interpretations of Tawada's play.

The sessions with the students resembled a rehearsal for an imagined performance in the future. In retrospect, this experience elicited my unwavering admiration for cultural anthropologists with close ties to theater, such as Dorinne Kondo. In her book *Worldmaking*, which is noted for its creativity, Kondo (2018) describes "the willful suspension of disbelief" (p. 27) as one of the reasons for her attraction to theater. We knew we were jokingly pretending to be actors, but pretence and acting merged. In our case, I adopted humour (both in the choice of text and in the translation methodology as a learning and performance method), projecting our bilingual selves onto unique animal characters. It was delightful to exaggerate all points of similarity between the six animals' attitudes and those of the respective students for the purpose of emulating the role of actors to impersonate fictional characters, even in a playful, provisional manner. What was perhaps the most essential make-believe was the fact that the space of our labor was indistinguishable from a backstage, even one without a frontstage.

One of the students created an online word document (a virtual backstage), where the learners could access and write the translation of their lines based on the notes and memory from our sessions. In order to create empathy with the content, I repeatedly encouraged students to read with more expression, which was also supported with laughter. The overlapping members of different sessions would go over the same content, which was useful for retention. Each session was a unique encounter in a unique configuration with a unique mood, and "despite the impossibility of capturing performance" (Kondo, 2018, p. 11), the students in charge of the online document recorded all our discussions conscientiously into coherent sentences that reflected the theatrical atmosphere.

In this way, the backstage was our site of creative labor in a number of ways. We were creating an innovative old-fashioned format (with the encouragement of digital aids and learning technology, the immediacy and messiness of this format has its converse freshness), attuned to the university ecosystem of financial precarity (both in terms of budget for the humanities, and financial support for students) and fast-paced advancing conformism and contract-based attitudes, insisting on measurable reimbursement for study and teaching time, and short-term gratification (Troiani & Dutson, 2021).

Intriguingly, in a profound sense of "reparative mirroring"—a term Kondo (2018) develops in *Worldmaking* to recognize the life-giving power of recognizing oneself onstage—existed on the content-level of the script due to the fact that each of the six animal characters had gathered in response to a certain "recruitment for a Babel project", for which, ironically, they were not paid, but need to pay a fee for working instead.

Hereafter, the six characters' utterances are shown by the students' own translation. In the humorous and apparently disorganized exchanges among the six characters, a recurring theme of social satire is precisely the reference to the unhealthy/hypocritical side of contemporary corporatized labor: Fox says: "Maybe it's healthier to have insomnia than to work in a company". Cat says: "I suppose I wouldn't have left my company if it hadn't been for my boss". Dog says: "I specialize in teaching a few of those languages that are of little economic value. Of course, I only teach students who don't pay tuition… but perhaps I should say 'taught', as I was recently fired". Rabbit says: "I play piccolo in an orchestra, bass in a jazz band, drums in a rock band and wash dishes at home", to which Bear retorts: "Aren't those just hobbies?".

As detailed further below, the translation by the seminar participants of the interaction between Squirrel and Bear reflects this vision of the ideal craft/labor endeavour against the economic imperatives of contemporary society.

SQUIRREL: I do not recall when, but I went to visit the workshop of a walnut artisan as research for a news report. The master of the workshop said that for 10 years one must be devoted to their training and forget all about time, money, and themselves. Using a single chisel, they would carve a palace into the walnut. Decorations were added to chandeliers and harpsichords. Floral patterned plates were set along the dining table. They were all so small that you needed a microscope to see them. Not once did the master praise their apprentice. Though it seemed that this was never an issue, as the both of them were completely transfixed in their walnut work. They forgot entirely about themselves.

BEAR: With things as they are, maybe the ideal job is one where you take as long as possible and turn very little profit. That's my vision of an inhuman future.

Although the work with the Japanese translation was indirectly useful for students' study goals of broadly improving their conversational Japanese and reading skills, the sessions were specifically credit-bearing for none of the members. Kondo (2018) reminds us that "creativity is work, practice, method", and "art is [also] work: sometimes joyous and exciting, sometimes tedious, always requiring craft, prodigious effort, and especially in theater, collaboration" (p. 6). As Fukushima and Fujimoto (2009) warn, "For students as well as the instructor, this was a time- and energy-consuming, bothersome but [low-productivity] project" (p. 87), particularly disliked by high test-scoring students.

The "collaborative" aspect of the project came across in the students' reflections, emphasizing the "experience", the "team", the "camaraderie", and the immersively absorbing "fun" nature of "understanding". This dovetails with Kondo's (2018) view that, in theatrical performance, actors (and students) cannot necessarily grasp the implications of their involvement but can pursue reparative goals (e.g., overcoming low self-esteem, frustration with work/life balance). This type of engagement is also not "necessarily antithetical to 'rigor' but may not yield to easy classification, or abstraction" (Kondo, 2018, p. 312).

5.2.4 Leadership

Despite the open-endedness and messiness of our translation project, there was a sense of direction and a dream of completion, which was due to the firm anchoring in an existing piece of prose. Needless to say, the "final version" of the translation shared on New Year's Eve 2023 by two of the students, who worked on style fixes until the "end", could be simultaneously a destination and an interim point leading to new encounters and teamwork. As a lecturer without a corresponding character in the play, my role was in safeguarding the openness of the backstage, ensuring positivity and mutual respect, and, above all, pleasure and gratitude for the "red thread of fate" (a Japanese idiom referring to deep interpersonal connection in Tawada's play) that gathered us in this project.

While encouraging and admiring gestures of leadership among the participants, such as organizing alternative sessions, reaching out to fellow students, or simply socializing, I was also coming to terms with my own style of leadership as a teacher. Could it be that I was not teaching Japanese language, nor literary appreciation, but a form of leadership expected of the "bilingual self"? I think that the latter was the case. Concerning this, through my support for my students, I find some "reparative mirroring" in Laviosa's (2014) idea to give a research lecture to her students, and Kondo's (2018) reference to the role of the dramaturg; "Translation between cultures and among disciplines is a key dramaturgical function. Simply put, dramaturgs are charged with 'making meaning.' … [Dramaturgical critique is] a step toward the reparative" (p. 41). Connected to this concept, my role was attempting, through comments on the text and social context, to raise appreciation for Tawada's play, and whenever possible to the value of our joint effort to create and maintain this space of translation at the margins of a Japanese language major. It was a little embarrassing for me to have my pedagogic role mirrored in that role of a dramaturg: "A conventional dramaturg is diplomatic, an idealized mother, who 'solves problems, smoothes out the psychosis of production and upon request, must always be able to provide the right answer'" (Lepecki & Brizell, as cited in Kondo, 2018, p. 41).

Kondo points to a more assertive position of dramaturgical critique as interventional and reparative, which had an intense edge in my case, given that I was the one to set up the project, and thus a stage director of sorts. The submerged dramaturgy, in my case, resembles a leadership style, which in Barbuto's (2006) classification is referred to as "Servant Leadership". Barbuto delineates a model of teaching leadership "dramaturgically", which, in the case of "Servant Leadership", "requires the instructors to act caring, open-minded, and unstructured (student-driven)" (p. 7). Since traditional class planning is incompatible with this type of leadership, the open-endedness of the Babel project both as the motif in Tawada's play and as allegory for the translation seminar corresponds to this teaching style. Dog reminds readers: "'Free' means work without pay; that's sometimes called 'slavery'", but I am comfortable to accept such criticism humorously in my capacity as a "zookeeper".

More importantly, the play itself, in a tour de force of self-reflexivity, proposes the "translator" as the best acceptable leader. I hope this is one rhetorical message to be interwoven into this "menagerie" (a description by a participant) of bilingual subjects. Their translation below captures this point:

SQUIRREL: Rather than a boss, what if we were to choose a translator? And what kind of translator would we want? A translator who will not do it for their own benefit, assembles everyone's opinion, creates a tune from that dissonance, attaches the footnotes, and looks for the connecting red thread that gives name to a common wish.

DOG: Neither president, representative, conductor, nor a project director, but a--

RABBIT: Translator!

EVERYONE: Agreed!

5.3 Participants' Comments

The reflections of the six participants in this translation seminar were elicited through email more than a year after the sessions ended. I aimed to assess the lasting impact of my approach on students' self-motivated Japanese learning and team spirit. Students' comments are presented below:

- DOG: It wasn't until I joined this translation project that I really stopped and thought about what I was doing as a Japanese language student. Dog, whose lines I would later translate, declares "...language is all we've got to pass on. Why else would I have become a language teacher?" Dog knew that beyond grammar patterns, grades, and job prospects, language is kind of what *this* is all about. Civilization. Experience. Being. Japanese was to me a part of that, a desire to communicate, but it's easy to lose sight of that sometimes. Translating a work of this length challenged me to use my Japanese language skills and to engage critically with the text, but to me, it was more the experience. I had to think about Dog's world, in Dog's eyes, in Dog's words. As a team translation, I think we were as much a menagerie as the animals in Tawada's fictional world. I hope having had a diversity of translators, the characters' personalities, idiosyncrasies, and world-views might be more naturally replicated. I had fun, I forgot theory, and used Japanese fluently. Not in the high Japanese proficiency sense, but in a kind of lost-in-a-Japanese-infused experience sense.

- BEAR: This project provided me with an opportunity to pause, acclimate and orient myself to a challenging text within a broader learning environment where opportunities to pause are infrequent… Tackling the task of translation invited multiple re-reading sessions. We regularly revisited various parts of the text, often reading for different characters in an attempt to enrich each other's translations. This allowed us to draw a kind of map within our minds, creating connections between our lines and the broader text. This level of attention prompted questions that I would, were I acting as a "reader", not normally ask. For example, I would often ask myself if the meaning in English was drifting away from the original, or if I was carrying over the correct voice for a character in their way of speech. This level of scrutiny allowed me to examine the Japanese more closely. Eventually my understanding started to become more intuitive. It was a very introspective and rewarding experience that taught me the value of "understanding" as a mechanism and how a translator can reach that destination.

- RABBIT: I really enjoyed the Babel Project! I liked the group translation work, it was fun to collaborate in a team with others and cross-check our translations. It was a great exercise in understanding the nuances of translation. I thought that the idea of being tasked with translating an individual character's lines was quite enjoyable. It allowed for the creative freedom to translate a single part of a story but also forced each of us to think about how the others were translating their characters and how they fit into the continuity of the piece as a whole. This prompted a lot of valuable discussions about usage and translation of key words, the style of speech each character uses and how dialogue in a scene flows when each line hasn't always been translated in the context it was originally written in. These discussions helped me to understand and appreciate the intricacies that go on in a translation project and the amount of work it takes to coordinate with others to translate a cohesive piece of text. I loved the experience and I'm proud of what we created as a team. And even though I am loath to doing presentations, I enjoyed performing the play to others.

- CAT: At the beginning of this project, gathered in our ZooKeeper's office, I recall struggling to even read a single line in the play, let alone comprehend the nuances of the language and the general abstractness of the play. I had my phone on my lap so I could frantically search up readings and definitions of kanji ('Chinese characters') to gain some semblance of following the meaning of each line. However, I've appreciated the space this translation project created for self-improvement, developing friendships, a sense of pride and fulfilment. The abstract nature of the author's style, coupled with my initial Japanese language limitations, could cause me to feel quite frustrated sometimes... But as more time was spent with the play, especially among the camaraderie provided by my fellow friends and translators, the contents of the play began to make more sense, as well as taking on a sense of familiarity. Thus, my enjoyment derived from reading and translating the play deepened. In moments when the play got the better of me and/or my fellow translators, we were able to return to the catalyst for this journey, our ZooKeeper, Dennitza. Furthermore, the character pairings she orchestrated infused a unique identity into the translation process. I now associate certain character lines so vividly with their translator counterparts, which has added a lot of depth and joy to the project.

- FOX: I have very fond memories of working on the translation of 'Animals' Babel' alongside 5 of my friends. Meeting up in Dennitza-sensei's office was always something I looked forward to, being able to chat and drink tea together while translating the amazing work of Yoko Tawada... I'm very thankful to everyone who was a part of the project that made it such a fun, valuable, and memorable experience. My time spent working on the 'Animals' Babel' project was undoubtedly a highlight of my undergraduate days.

- SQUIRREL: It was such a privilege to be involved in the translation for 'Animal Babel'! It was my first time translating a play so it was very interesting to get behind a project that involved several characters and personalities! We all had our set characters and different ways of translating which made it difficult at times but when we came together and discussed, it always ended up falling into one piece. A special shout out to "Cat" and "Bear" who spent many hours working on the final piece and flow of the play! Thank you to Dennitza for this opportunity!

5.4   Conclusion

The reflection comments by the six students demonstrate the experiential and enriching value of this translation project, which became highly articulated in retrospect. The challenges and frustrations of working together "for free", the "psychosis" of the theatrical production (in Kondo's (2018) words), give way in the students' memories to a sense of pride and fulfilment derived from the whole process of collaborative translation. As the students described it, the separate lines of each character in Tawada's play, which had been translated in an isolated manner, came to life after they were sequentially assembled together in the seminar, and this led to an outburst of "joy" from the combined effort among all the students. The pleasure was derived from the mediating role of the characters of the play, which gave room to the students to explore their extended bilingual alter egos. The reflexivity and reflectivity fostered by the project were deeply enabled through the pedagogical combination of both the drama and the translation process. However, above all, as students' comments suggest, it was the shared space of this seminar format that produced this reflexivity and reflectivity through a slowdown from the demands of the usual university curriculum. In this way, the project demonstrated that the aspiration for foreign language proficiency, nurtured within a collaborative environment built around performance and translation, is conducive to the goal of creating an attitude of lifelong learning, and a sense of leadership dedicated to identifying and serving a community, one of the crucial, underappreciated tasks of translation.

Acknowledgements The student translation detailed in this chapter was published in full with illustrations by leading contemporary artist Kenji Yanobe as an Ebook from Wai-te-ata Press, Victoria University of Wellington, in November 2024, with the support from New Zealand-Japan Cultural Exchange Programme.

References

Barbuto, J. (2006). Dramaturgical teaching in the leadership classroom: Taking experiential learning to the next level. *Journal of Leadership Education, 5*(2), 4–13.

Campbell, M., & Tigan, A. (2022). Translanguaging and product-oriented drama: An integrated pedagogical approach for language learning and literacy development. *International Journal of Bilingual Education and Bilingualism, 25*(10), 3745–3757. https://doi.org/10.1080/13670050.2022.2104115

Ellis, R. (2021, June 23). *Options in the design of task-based language teaching curriculum: An educational perspective*. LALS Public Lecture, Victoria University of Wellington, New Zealand.

Fukushima Y., & Fujimoto, J. (2009). *Learning and teaching Japanese language through drama* [Paper presentation]. 16th Princeton Japanese Pedagogy Forum, Princeton University, USA. https://pjpf.princeton.edu/sites/g/files/toruqf1151/files/pdf/12%20Fukushima.pdf

Hewgill, D., Noro, H., & Poulton, C. (2004). Exploring drama and theater in teaching Japanese: Hirata Oriza's play Tokyo notes, in an advanced Japanese conversation course. *Sekai No Nihongo Kyoiku, 14*, 227–252.

Kondo, D. (2018). *Worldmaking: Race, performance, and the work of creativity*. Duke University Press.

Kramsch, C. (1993). *Context and culture in language teaching*. Oxford University Press.

Laviosa, S. (2014). *Translation and language: Pedagogic approaches explored*. Routledge.

Marinetti, C., & Rose, M. (2013). Process, practice and landscapes of reception: An ethnographic study of theater translation. *Translation Studies, 6*(2), 166–182.

McCreary, M. (2022). Rancière's *The Ignorant School Master*: Poetic virtue and the method of equality. *Educational Theory, 71*(6), 677–807.

Noda, M. (2014). 'Theatre forms the core around which dialogue develops'— Interview with Oriza Hirata. *Critical Stages/Scènes Critiques, 10*. https://www.critical-stages.org/10/theatre-forms-the-core-around-which-dialogue-develops-interview-with-oriza-hirata/

Pintado Gutiérrez, L. (2018). Translation in language teaching, pedagogical translation, and code-switching: Restructuring the boundaries. *The Language Learning Journal, 49*(2), 219–239.

Tawada, Y. (2014). *Kentōshi*. Kodansha.

Troiani, I., & Dutson, C. (2021). The neoliberal university as a space to learn/think/work in higher education. *Architecture and Culture, 9*(1), 5–23. https://doi.org/10.1080/20507828.2021.1898836

Tymoczko, M. (2007). *Enlarging translation. Empowering translators*. St. Jerome.

Van Lier, L. (2002). An ecological-semiotic perspective on language and linguistics. In C. Kramsch (Ed.), *Language acquisition and language socialization: Ecological perspectives* (pp. 140–164). Continuum.

Van Lier, L. (2004). *The ecology and semiotics of language learning*. Kluwer Academic Publishers.

Van Lier, L. (2010). The ecological approach to classroom teaching and learning: Practice to theory, theory to practice. *Procedia—Social and Behavioral Sciences, 3*, 2–6. https://doi.org/10.1016/j.sbspro.2010.07.005

6

Interlanguage Interference: What Should Tutors be Aware of When Teaching Vocabulary in the Legal Translation Classroom?

Karine Chiknaverova◉

6.1   Introduction

In applied linguistics, extensive research has been conducted on interference (e.g., Baker & Saldanha, 2009; Franko Aixelá, 2009; Hopkinson, 2007). A considerable number of studies to date have examined linguistic interference and its typical generalized manifestations in legal contexts (De Sutter et al., 2013; Muratova, 2016; Stepanova, 2019; Stepanova et al., 2018). To some extent, there are several directions of research that contribute to an understanding of its nature. They include the findings of Calvo and Ortega (2009) and Duběda (2021), which are related to the problem of literality and equivalence in legal translation. Other useful

K. Chiknaverova (✉)
The Branch of the Federal state autonomous institution of higher education "Moscow State Institute of International Relations (University) of the Ministry of Foreign Affairs of the Russian Federation in the town of Odintsovo, Odintsovo, Russia
e-mail: k.chiknaverova@odin.mgimo.ru

© The Author(s), under exclusive license to Springer Nature Switzerland AG 2025
D. Coulson and C. Denman (eds.), *Translation, Translanguaging and Machine Translation in Foreign Language Education*,
https://doi.org/10.1007/978-3-031-82174-5_6

93

insights are revealed in detailed accounts of legal translation and the challenges it poses for learners (Alcaraz & Hughes, 2014; Kajzer-Wietrzny, 2018; Simonnæs, 2013).

Studies of comparative and contrastive nature involving not only linguistic aspects per se but also those of a legal nature are further helpful in comprehending various instances of interference (Biel, 2014; Čavoški, 2017; Dănişor, 2015). Such studies also involve the data of various parallel legal corpora and rely on corpus linguistics methods that open up new dimensions in the corresponding research (Biel, 2010). An additional aspect involved in the complex analysis of the issue of interference is error analysis. Error analysis approaches enable researchers to reveal factors of interference that underlie their learners' errors (Baggio, 2022; Orlando, 2017).

The handful of studies that do investigate interference at the lexical and/or semantic levels in legal contexts focus specifically on legal terminology (Imre, 2015; Stepanova, 2013). These, however, fail to take into account the entire spectrum of vocabulary used in legal texts of various genres, while also not addressing the linguo-didactic aspects of the problem. It is with the aim of filling this gap in the existing literature that the research reported in this chapter seeks to address the following research question: What are the types of lexico-sematic interference in the English-to-Russian legal translation classroom? To achieve this, we explore vocabulary used in a particular legal translation university course, categorize and classify it to identify possible interference mechanisms that can be triggered in the course of translation from English to Russian by Russian-speaking students.

6.2   Literature Review

In one of the primary investigations of interference in linguistic contexts, Weinreich (1979) reported that "cases of deviation from the norms of any of the languages that occur in the speech of bilinguals" result from "knowing more than one language, i.e. due to language contact" (p. 22). In translation studies, interference is seen as the "projection of specific features of the source text onto the target text, resulting in violations of the norms, conventions, and discourse of the target text" (Alekseeva, 2004, p. 170). When teaching translation, it is therefore important to consider the approaches of applied linguists to this matter. For example, in the Dictionary of Foreign Language Teaching Terms (Azimov & Shchukin, 2009), interference is defined as "the interaction of language systems, the influence of the native language system on the target language during the process of mastering it" which "manifests itself in deviations from the norm and the system of the target language under the influence of the native language" (p. 87).

Interference is classified as "interlanguage" and "intralanguage". Intralanguage interference, according to Azimov and Shchukin (2009), is "characteristic of those who have already acquired sufficient experience in language learning and it manifests itself in the way that previously formed and more solid skills interact with new ones, leading to errors" (p. 87). Interlanguage interference arises due to disparities between the native language and the target language systems, impacting meaning and usage at various levels (Azimov & Shchukin, 2009).

Interlanguage interference can be categorized into different types based on the specific aspect of the translated text it impacts. These categories include lexical composition, grammatical structure, subject-content, linguo-textual, and cultural aspects (Gerasimova, 2007). Alimov (2005) identified the following types of interlanguage interference: phonetic (phonological and sound-reproductive); orthographic; grammatical (morphological, syntactic, and punctuation); lexical; semantic; and stylistic.

Lexical interference is understood as "the intrusion of the vocabulary of one language system into another" (Alimov, 2005, p. 17). Several discreet research directions are associated with lexical interference: the borrowing of lexical units, the structure of foreign lexical units, the meanings of lexical units, and their connection with units of the intended expression (Semchinskiy, 1974). In this regard, borrowing, calquing, and semantic interference, as well as changes in the meaning of a word under the influence of another language, are identified as types of lexical interference (Zhluktenko, 1974).

Semantic interference most often manifests itself in the use of lexical units, which have been referred to as "false friends of the translator" that "completely or partially differ in meaning from their phonetic and graphical counterparts in the target language" (Latyshev, 2005, p. 184). Following the semantic meaning of a native language word, the meaning of foreign words can be expanded or narrowed. This kind of vocabulary is divided into three types that are referred to as diaparonyms: synonymous, which may coincide in certain contexts without leading to an error; contact, whose semantic relations do not imply lexical equivalence but rather imply intuitively recognizable similarity; and distant, in that they lack semantic similarity but having formal correlative (formal similarity) (Kuznetsova, 2016).

The vocabulary that is affected by interlanguage interference belongs to a broader group of words similar in their external form—lexical internationalisms, or interonyms. They are defined as words or expressions that are used by several world languages with the same meaning and in a phonetically similar form (Kuznetsova, 2016). Within this group of words, different degrees of semantic closeness are distinguished; the more similarities there are in semantic fields, the more grounds there are to consider a particular unit as a full equivalent.

Thus, different authors interpret the concepts of lexical and semantic cross-linguistic interference differently. In one case, semantic interference is a type of lexical interference, while in another case, it is an independent phenomenon. In a very generalized way, lexical interference is mainly referred to when there is a similarity in the form, while semantic interference is based on a similarity in the meaning. Since in most cases these types of interference overlap, in this chapter the term "lexico-semantic interference" is used. Therefore, the mixing of formally similar but semantically different words, and cases where there is mixing of formally similar and semantically equivalent counterparts, are examined. Such phenomena are referred to as lexico-semantic interference, with three varieties considered in the context of legal language: synonymous, contact, and distant.

6.3   Methodology

In the investigation reported here, the directions of potential lexico-semantic interference were examined within an English-to-Russian legal translation course through the use of methods of analysis and synthesis, classification, description, and a continuous sampling technique. For the purpose of this research, texts specifically selected and, in some instances, adapted for the International Legal English Certificate course (Krois-Lindner, 2006), with a particular focus on commercial law, were used. The reason for only focusing on commercial law was predetermined by the majors of students on the course. The authors of the corresponding textbook used explain its focus on commercial law by stating that the specific aspects of it covered by the book are widely recognized as those in high demand internationally. The teaching materials are directed toward learners of upper-intermediate and advanced levels of English. The topics covered mainly include the following: company law, contract law, intellectual property, real property law, employment law, and the sale of goods, with a particular emphasis on company law and contracts.

   In the first stage of the research, using the method of continuous sampling, diaparonyms, internationalisms, and full equivalents were selected from the materials of the legal translation course (Krois-Lindner, 2006). Internationalisms were chosen for further analysis due to the possibility of categorizing them as false internationalisms. For example, 'penalty' or 'instrument' have Russian counterparts, but in legal English they are false internationalisms. All identified cases included random graphical and/or phonetic similarity, instances of borrowing from common sources, and from the English language into Russian. The identified vocabulary included both industry-specific and cross-industry terms, as well as commonly used economic, business, financial, and general English vocabulary that appeared in the texts at least twice. Upon removing loanwords that had direct equivalents, the proximity and distance of the identified diaparonyms were analyzed based solely on their dictionary correspondences. For this purpose, a selection of English-Russian and Russian-English dictionaries was used, both specialized and general-purpose. Information about these sources is provided following the References.

The materials selected for our research include the legal concepts of the UK and US legal systems. The choice of the concepts was predetermined by the widest coverage possible in different jurisdictions. The types of authentic text material are those commonly used by practicing lawyers. For the purposes of the research, non-written texts in addition to introductory texts created by the author for teaching purposes were excluded as these were not authentic. Both the texts were presented in full and broken down into their typical components in order to focus on the language functions typically used in each of these parts of a text.

The genre of a legal text is one of the important factors when analyzing cases of lexico-semantic interference as it predetermines the lexis used: the thematic varieties, mainly dictated by a specific branch of law, frequency of other vocabulary and collocations, and their stylistic and lexico-grammatical characteristics.

6.4   Results

Initially, the documents, or excerpts from them, extracted from the teaching content were classified as follows: various types of law (directives, statutes, by-laws (ordinances), regulations, bills, laws, codes); local government and parliamentary documents; documents compiled by lawyers for their clients and/or colleagues (answers, briefs, letters of advice, legal opinions, law reviews and law updates summaries, checklists), as well as those written by companies and individuals (affidavits, complaints, promissory notes); court documents (court rulings, injunctions, motions, notices, pleadings, writs, legal decisions); corporate documents (articles of incorporation/memorandums of association, by-laws, general partnership agreements, board resolutions, LLM/partnership bills, minutes of a meeting, contracts, informative memos (internal memos), competency statements of companies; and advertisements of seminars.

The groups of vocabulary typical for these types of legal texts were further addressed. A continuous sampling technique was used to analyze the vocabulary. The analysis revealed the following frequent groups of vocabulary:

- Cross-sectoral, sector-specific, and general legal terms;
- Financial, economic, and business terms;
- Other vocabulary (general English) frequently used in these texts.

Cross-sectoral vocabulary are those used in different branches of law and, generally, have differences in meaning when used in different branches. For example, *appellant, petition, directive, convention, mediation, reparation*. Sector-specific vocabulary are words mainly used in one branch of law retaining the usual meaning. An example is *copyright*.

In addition to cross-sector and sector-specific vocabulary, there are many general legal terms or semi-terms used across various branches of law retaining the same meaning, such as *valid, effect (in effect), confidential, confiscate, arbiter/arbitrator, delegate/delegate* (v. & n.), *proceeding(s)/procedure, discriminatory/discriminating, corporate, legal, case, penalty, instrument, default* (v. & n.). Terms such as *margin, financial/monetary, rent, firm, principal* (amount), *option* come from the sphere of finance, business, and economics and are widely used in commercial law.

A large proportion of the vocabulary is general English words which mainly retain the same meaning as they have in plain English contexts, although their frequency in the texts under study is very high. They include *alternative(s), argument(s), competence, prospect(s), accumulate, limit* (n. & v.), *practice(s), activit(ies), exclusive(ly), secret, corresponding, equivalent, private, pause* (meaning "suspend"), *intention, fitness* (meaning "suitability"), *assist, start, show, recommend, inform, intimate, objective, (in) opposition to*.

Moreover, there are also word combinations typically used in certain syntactic functions and that are largely stylistically predetermined by the genres of legal texts. These include *subject to, result from, as is* (in the present condition), *to reserve a right*, etc.

Within the contexts mentioned above, all three types of diaparonyms—synonymous, contact, and distant—were identified. The number of synonymous diaparonyms is overwhelming; the contact ones, however, are rare. In fact, it is sometimes difficult to distinguish these from the synonymous ones. The distant type is also not common. Further, several subtypes of diaparonyms were identified in the given contexts.

Synonymous diaparonyms include those that have at least one overlapping seme. Usually there are no more than three overlapping meanings. Contact diaparonyms are those that have close meanings so one can draw certain parallels between the accordances in the source and target languages, mainly based on metonymy or metaphor. They can also have one overlapping meaning but are replaced by other words in the target language due to certain stylistic restrictions. Distant diaparonyms have no overlapping meanings. However, if the etymology and how the meaning of the word has developed are explored, certain analogies can be traced. Another characteristic of the diaparonyms is that different derivatives with the same root form either different types of diaparonyms, or only one/two of them act as diaparonyms while the others do not have any similar accordances in the target language. Below the description and special features of each are provided.

Synonymous Diaparonyms
Examples include:

- One or more meanings coincide(s): **General** meaning—**общее** собрание; **General** director—**генеральный** директор (out of seven dictionary definitions one coincides; *it should be noted that different dictionaries can have different approaches to describing a word's meanings; hence, this paper relies on the dictionaries given in the references);
- The same category as the previous one. However, the non-overlapping meanings are never invoked in the given contexts: Arguments of the parties—споры/**аргументы** сторон (the meaning of 'disagreement' is not invoked);
- Can be treated as internationalisms but often other words are preferred in the target language due to the stylistic restrictions: (The liability is limited) and the **limit** is always clear—ответственность ограничена и это ограничение/**лимит** всегда прозрачно (прозрачен)—in this case the choice of the word 'ограничение' is stylistically predetermined

Contact Diaparonyms
Examples include:

- **Charter** [Чартер] of the company—**Устав** компании; The **aggregate** [агрегат] amount/value—**Совокупная** стоимость/ценность; **Execution** [экзекуция] of an agreement—**выполнение** договора; To fulfill the conditions **precedent** [прецедент] to the satisfaction of the lender—Выполнять **предварительные** условия; **Article** [артикль] #5 of the federal law—Статья 5 данного федерального закона
- The subtypes mainly include variations of metaphorical (very rare) and metonymic relationships (more common) and instances when one can imply intuitively easily determined similarity (the most common)
- For example:

Aggregate (adj.): formed by combining into a single whole or total < aggregate income >

Агрегат [Agregat]—a collection of elements forming a system or its part

The correspondence in Russian is a noun. However, the overlapping seme denotes 'combining several elements into a whole'

Distant Diaparonyms
The examples include:

- *The Party shall perform its* **obligations [obligatsii]** *hereunder (сторона обязуется исполнить свои* **обязательства** по договору); **Tort**—торт; **Associate** lawyer—ассоциация; **bar** association—бар; **instrument**—инструмент; **case** law—кейс; **parol** evidence—пароль; **passage** of title exchange of ownership in a property—пассаж; **penal** law—пенал; **sex** discrimination—секс; to the order of—ордер; **Uniform** Commercial Code (UCC) (US)—униформа*
- For example:

tort—торт

tort: *a civil wrong, other than breach of contract, for which a remedy may be obtained, usu. in the form of damages; a breach of a duty that the law imposes on persons who stand in a particular relation to one another*

торт: a confectionery product, usually in the form of a stack of sweet cakes (layers) made of sponge, shortcrust, or puff pastry, soaked or covered with cream, syrup, jam, etc

As mentioned above, different derivatives with the same root can act as diaparonyms. There are also instances when only some derivatives can be classified as false cognates or interonyms. For example:

1) *Legal **practice*** (n.)—*Юридическая **практика** [praktika]* (n.)
*Legal **practitioner*** (n., doer)—*Юрист, Практикующий юрист, юрист-**практик** [praktik]* (n., doer)
*To **practice** law* (v.)—*Заниматься юридической **практикой**, **практиковать** [praktikovat']* (v.)

2) ***Competence** of the registration authorities* (n.)—*Компетенция [kompetentsia]* (n.) *регистрационных органов*
*They are **competent** bodies* (adj.)—*Они являются **компетентными*** (adj.) / *уполномоченными органами*

3) ***Pension** fund* (n.)—*пенсионный* (adj.) *фонд*
*To **fund** a project* (v.)—*финансировать проект* (no accordances in the target language)

4) ***Arguments** of the parties* (n.)—*аргументы* (n.) *сторон*
*To **argue** the case*—*оспорить дело, иск* (no accordances in the target language)

As stated above, the semantic meaning of the identified pairs was determined by consulting their dictionary definitions, and within the context of legal language. The meanings identified within the domain of special-purpose language significantly differ from the dictionary definitions of the words, although there have also been cases where the same meanings and corresponding translations are found within the context of general-purpose language and the professional language. Below, findings are presented in detail.

1. In general language, they are synonymous diaparonyms, but in the given legal context, they do not have matching meanings and hence act as distant ones.
2. The corresponding word in the target language conveys generally the same meaning but cannot be used in the target text in legal contexts due to stylistic or structural constraints, or word compatibility of the TL. In general texts, at least one meaning is denoted with a word of the same graphical or pronunciation pattern.
3a. In a broad context, they are synonymous diaparonyms; in the given legal contexts, they act as interonyms.
3b. Meanings and forms of several (but not all) derivatives match in both plain and legal contexts.

3c. Correspondences of some derivatives are absent in one of the languages, or they acquire different meanings and cannot be either considered as interonyms or diaparonyms in both general and legal contexts.

3d. Two or more derivatives are diaparonyms but of different types in legal and general contexts.

4. The lexical units are distant diaparonyms both in plain and legal language.

The next step included specifying the linguistic phenomena typical for the vocabulary identified that can cause a negative intralanguage interference on the lexico-semantic level. To identify these phenomena, the errors of Russian-speaking learners of legal translation, collected during three years of teaching legal translation to second-year university students of law faculties, were analyzed (see Chiknaverova, 2018).

Upon analyzing the errors, the researcher identified the following instances: polysemy, homonymy, paronymy, and synonymy within the range of words that were selected as those potentially causing interlanguage lexico-semantic interference.

Polysemy of the selected terms mainly included instances of cross-sectoral terms and terms/non-terms having different meanings in legal and/or non-legal contexts. Some of these can also act as homonyms. This can be traced through the use of such words as*: clerk, delegate, consolidation, cartel, associate, beneficiary, certificate, bar, balance, capitalization.*

Example: A cross-sectoral term, **_respondent:_**

1. *The party against whom an appeal is taken; in some appellate courts, the parties are designated as petitioner and respondent. Often the designations depend on whether the appeal is taken by writ of certiorari or by direct appeal.*
2. *The party against whom a motion or petition is filed.*
3. *At common law, the defendant in an equity proceeding.*
4. *Civil law. One who answers for another or acts as another's security.*

Most of the terms mentioned above as cross-sectoral can also acquire different meanings in legal and non-legal contexts (e.g., *bill, associate, bar, balance, clerk*).

Example: ***Bill*** (n.) (general English):

1. *An itemized list or a statement of particulars (such as a list of materials or members of a ship's crew).*
2. *Written document or note.*
3. *An itemized account of the separate cost of goods sold, services performed, or work done.*
4. *An amount expended or owed.*
5. *A statement of charges for food or drink.*
6. *Written or printed advertisement posted or otherwise distributed to announce an event of interest to the public.*
7. *A programmed presentation.*
8. *A piece of paper money.*
9. *An individual or commercial note.*

Bill (n.) (legal English):

1. *A formal written complaint, such as a court paper requesting some specific action for reasons alleged.*
2. *An equitable pleading by which a claimant brings a claim in a court of equity.*
3. *The premises, which state the plaintiff's case.*
4. *The confederating part, in which the defendants are charged with combination.*
5. *The charging part, in which the plaintiff may try to overcome defenses that the defendants may allege.*
6. *The jurisdictional clause, showing that the court has jurisdiction.*
7. *The interrogating part, inserted to try to compel a full and complete answer.*
8. *The prayer for relief.*
9. *The prayer for process to compel the defendants to appear and answer.*

Instances when there are different meanings of a term in different English-speaking countries were also considered. For example, the term 'bankruptcy' applies to individuals and partnerships (United Kingdom) and also to legal entities (USA). In American law, the term 'insolvency' has another meaning: "A court decision that allows a company's assets to be sold to pay creditors" (Black's Law Dictionary).

There are also cases when identical phenomena are described by different words in different English-speaking countries. Examples: 'to lift corporate veil' / 'to pierce corporate veil', 'articles of association' / 'bylaws', 'memorandum of association' / 'articles of incorporation', 'extraordinary meeting' / 'special meeting' (Krois-Lindner, 2006).

Such pairs as *"principal"* and *"principle"* are the most common examples of paronymy in the texts:

princi**pal** (adj.): chief; primary; most important;

princi**pal** (n.): one who authorizes another to act on his or her behalf as an agent;

Principle (n.): a basic rule, law, or doctrine.

Often, there are cases where two or more forms of the same part of speech can be derived from one root. These words can be wrongly perceived as interchangeable.

Examples: delegate and delegator.

Delegate:

1. *One who represents or acts for another person or a group.*
2. *Parliamentary law. A voting member of a convention, whether entitled to vote as an elected or appointed delegate, as an upgraded alternate, or ex officio.*

Delegator:
One who delegates (a responsibility, etc.) to another.

Words, mainly terms, that cause interlanguage interference have synonyms which in most cases have no graphic or phonological similarities with the ones in the target language and, if there are any, they have no semantic correlations. Moreover, in the overwhelming majority of cases, the target language correspondence tends to have fewer synonyms or no synonyms at all. Below are examples of such synonyms; the ones that are treated as diaparonyms are bolded.

Examples:

Claimant **appellant** *petitioner.*
   Option *choice* **alternative**
   Arbitration mediation *conciliation*
   Responsibility duty **obligation**
   Agreement covenant **contract**
   Adjourn **pause** *suspend*
   Valid *enforceable in effect*
   Solely **exclusively** *only.*

For instance, in the case of synonyms 'claimant/appellant/petitioner' in the source language, in the target language the term 'appellant' (апеллянт [appell'ant]) will have a synonym 'истец по апелляции' [istets po apell'atsii] which has no similarity to the word of the source language. It should also be noted that the word 'petitioner' may give rise to the analogy of 'петиция' [petitsia] but there are no accordances to the doer of the action in the target language. In the case of 'option/choice/ alternatives', which are treated as synonyms in the source language, there are two diaparonyms out of the three synonyms, but they are not synonyms in the target language. The correspondence of 'option' in the target language 'опцион' [optsion] is *the right (but not the obligation) to buy or sell a given quantity of securities, commodities, or other assets at a fixed price within a specified time*, whereas 'альтернатива' [alternative] (the correspondence of 'alternative') is an 'option'. However, among the synonyms *'arbitration/mediation/conciliation'*, the diaparonyms *arbitration* and *mediation* (in the target language—'арбитраж' [arbitrazh] and 'медиация' [mediatsia]) can be treated as synonyms in the target language as well.

6.5   Recommendations

The texts chosen for analysis were initially designed for a legal English course. In order to adjust the course for translation purposes specifically targeting issues of interference in lexico-semantic interlanguage, the classroom activities are best divided into pre-translation, translation, and post-translation. Below, exercises that can be designed to address the specific features of the legal vocabulary specified above are provided.

6.5.1 Pre-Translation Exercises

Pre-translation vocabulary exercises are, generally, designed to build a foundation for learners, enabling them to approach the translation process with a comprehensive understanding of the words they will encounter.

The initial set of exercises aims to build students' metalanguage and linguistic analysis skills. It includes providing definitions and examples of cognates, false cognates (and their three types), homonyms, polysemous words, synonyms, hypernyms, hyponyms, meronyms, and collocations. Tutors are expected to ensure that the learners can identify all parts of speech and provide a basic morphological analysis of the words as well as parts of the sentence, and are able to conduct a basic syntactic analysis of a sentence. It also involves being able to compile a glossary of false cognates, and cognates that a particular legal text contains. The next step involves raising awareness and checking understanding of the key linguistic terms. Exercises on this level embrace:

- Matching words in one language with their corresponding false friends in another language.
- Sorting given vocabulary into cognates and false cognates.
- Classifying false friends into three groups: synonymous, contact, and distant.
- Identifying relationships between words, considering hypernyms, hyponyms, and meronyms.

- Focusing on word roots, prefixes, and suffixes to understand complex words.

This stage can be enriched by mnemonic and annotating exercises. They include:

- Encouraging learners to create mnemonic devices or memory aids for false cognates.
- Annotating the source text by marking challenging or unfamiliar false cognates. Discussing these annotations as a class to build a shared understanding.
- Developing core lexical skills by exploring dictionary definitions. The most efficient activities include:

  - Comparing the meanings of words in plain and legal contexts in one language and then in both languages; finding the differences and similarities.
  - Identifying general legal, cross-sectoral, sector-specific terms and Anglo-American correspondences in legal English-English dictionaries.
  - Formulating term definitions, comparing them with dictionary definitions, and further practice of definition-making skills.

The work with synonyms should be incorporated as a separate block, focusing on:

- Cognate synonym exercise: Providing a set of synonyms for false cognates (in the source language) and asking learners to match each term/word with its corresponding synonym.
- Synonym exploration: Providing a set of cognates and three types of false cognates and asking learners to find synonyms to them in both languages.

The most challenging part of translating is choosing equivalents in the target language in specific contexts, which in turn presupposes the basic skills of identifying meaning in context. In this respect, potentially beneficial exercises include:

- Contextual analysis: Selecting source text paragraphs/sentences with specific types of false cognates, prompting learners to identify lexical chunks and underline words indicating the context.
- Word context prediction: Providing sentences with gaps, including false friends, and asking learners to predict missing words based on context, with clarifying referents.
- Collocation practice: Supplying a list of false cognates and prompting learners to provide all possible collocations in both languages.
- Culture-specific vocabulary exploration: Identifying words that may have specific cultural connotations among the previously identified false cognates; discussing the cultural nuances associated with these words and exploring possible translation challenges.

6.5.2 Translation Exercises

For translation exercises, it is important to start by providing a list of word pairs, some being false friends, and asking learners to match them with their correct counterparts in the target language in addition to translating lexical chunks containing cognates or false cognates in a given context. In the next stage, the work shifts to sentence translation and then to paragraph and whole text translation in different contexts and with the different frequency of the target vocabulary focusing more on continuity and coherence in translation and the flow of ideas. The activities include:

- Translation relay: Organizing a translation relay, where teams work to translate sentences or paragraphs, adding an element of competition and urgency to vocabulary practice.
- Back-and-forth translation: This requires learners to translate a sentence from the source language to the target language and then back, enhancing bidirectional language skills and understanding of vocabulary.

6.5.3 Post-Translation Exercises

Exercises here aim to consolidate the understanding and application of false friends and cognates, allowing learners to reflect on their translation choices and refine their skills. Suggested activities include:

- Error correction with intentionally inserted errors in translation either by the tutor or groupmates.
- Translation case studies, discussing translations with specific vocabulary challenges and different approaches.
- Feedback reflection, providing feedback on translations with reflection on alternatives; a translation reflection paper, a reflective essay on the translation process emphasizing cognate usage.
- Review and revision, focusing on clarity, accuracy, and style improvement.

6.6   Conclusion

Before stating the conclusion of the current research, certain limitations need to be acknowledged. First, the material selected for analysis included only commercial law documents; as such, the findings are restricted to this area of law. Additionally, the negative interlanguage interference included only one language pair—English and Russian. Embracing more languages and different groups would provide more comprehensive results.

Despite these limitations, the research identified three possible zones of negative interlanguage interference that manifest themselves when translating legal documents of commercial law from English to Russian. The majority of cases fall within these three groups: synonymous, contact, and distant diaparonyms. In addition, the results indicate that, in legal English and plain English contexts, the distribution of different types of diaparonyms can be significantly different, and the overlapping and non-overlapping semes can vary dramatically. In addition, different derivatives of the core pair of diaparonyms can act differently, mainly showing the same type of lexico-semantic interference, a different type or not having any graphical or phonological similarities.

Apart from the mechanisms that result in interference at the interlanguage level, the same vocabulary can cause additional difficulties that manifest themselves at the level of intralanguage interference. Even in the case of the nearest diaparonyms, both the paradigmatic and syntagmatic relationships are different for the source and target language, which can be seen through the synonymous relations, polysemy, homonymy, and collocations.

The concluding part of the article provided three sets of recommended exercises divided into pre-translation, translation, and post-translation ones, which can be applied to specifically target the negative lexico-semantic interlanguage interference. These practical exercises can be employed in not only legal translation and other English-for-specific-purposes classrooms around the world, but also can be readily adapted for use in English as a Second/Foreign Language learning contexts.

References

Alcaraz, E., & Hughes, B. (2014). *Legal translation explained*. Routledge.

Alekseeva, I. S. (2004). *Introduction to translation studies*. Akademiya.

Alimov, V. V. (2005). *Interference in translation (based on professionally oriented intercultural communication and translation in the field of professional communication)*. Editorial URSS.

Azimov, E. H. G., & Shchukin, A. N. (2009). *New dictionary of methodology terms*. IKAR.

Baggio, G. (2022). *The challenges of legal translation: An error analysis of trainees' translations* [Unpublished master's thesis]. Università degli Studi di Padova. https://thesis.unipd.it/retrieve/8a6eac95-d7e7-4e87-a83d-90ddd2763f0f/Baggio_GiuliaMaria.pdf

Baker, M., & Saldanha, G. (Eds.). (2009). *Routledge encyclopedia of translation studies*. Routledge.

Biel, Ł. (2010). Corpus-based studies of legal language for translation purposes: Methodological and practical potential. In C. Heine & J. Engberg (Eds.), *Reconceptualizing LSP: Online proceedings of the XVII European LSP symposium 2009* (pp. 1–15). Aarhus. https://asb.dk/fileadmin/www.asb.dk/isek/biel.pdf

Biel, Ł. (2014). *Lost in the Eurofog: The textual fit of translated law.* Peter Lang.

Calvo, E., & Ortega, J. M. (2009). A functional approach to legal translation teaching: Combating literality. In L. Sočanac, C. Goddard, & L. Kremer (Eds.), *Curriculum, multilingualism and the law* (pp. 349–372). Globus.

Chiknaverova, K. G. (2018). Analysis of errors at the introductory level of teaching legal translation at university. *Vestnik Kostromskogo Gosudarstvennogo Universiteta. Seriya: Pedagogika. Psihologiya, Sociokinetika, 3,* 181–187.

Čavoški, A. (2017). Interaction of law and language in the EU: Challenges of translating in multilingual environment. *The Journal of Specialised Translation, 27,* 58–74.

Dănișor, D. D. (2015). Legal translation within the European Union: Current stakes and challenges. In I. Boldea (Ed.), *Discourse as a form of multiculturalism in literature and communication* (pp. 138–144). Arhipelag XXI Press.

De Sutter, G., Cappelle, B., & Loock, R. (2013). Competing motivations in Dutch/French legal translation: A quantitative corpus-based study of the interaction between interference and normalisation. Paper presented at *ICLC 7-UCCTS 3: 7th International Contrastive Linguistics Conference and 3rd Edition of Using Corpora in Contrastive and Translation Studies,* Ghent, Belgium.

Duběda, T. (2021). Direction-asymmetric equivalence in legal translation. *Comparative Legilinguistics, 47*(1), 57–72.

Franko Aixelá, J. (2009). An overview of interference in scientific and technical translation. *The Journal of Specialised Translation, 11,* 75–87.

Gerasimova, N. I. (2007). Interlingual interference in translation: The didactic aspect of the problem. *Vestnik Rostovskogo Gosudarstvennogo Ekonomicheskogo Universiteta (RINKh), 1*(23), 178–183.

Hopkinson, C. (2007). Factors in linguistic interference: A case study in translation. *SKASE: Journal of Translation and Interpretation, 2*(1), 13–23. http://www.skase.sk/Volumes/JTI02/pdf_doc/2.pdf

Imre, A. (2015). Translation problems of legal terms. In E. Buja & S. Mada (Eds.), *Structure, use and meaning in intercultural settings* (pp. 97–108). Editura Universității Transilvania.

Kajzer-Wietrzny, M. (2018, September 12–14). Translationese, interpretese and foreignese: What do they have in common? Paper presented at *Using Corpora in Contrastive and Translation Studies Conference,* Université Catholique de Louvain, Louvain-la-Neuve, Belgium.

Krois-Lindner, A. (2006). *International legal English certificate*. Cambridge University Press.

Kuznetsova, I. N. (2016). Translator's false friends, or diaparonymy as a phenomenon of interlingual lexical interference. *Ritorika-Lingvistika, 12*, 290–302.

Latyshev, L. K. (2005). *Translation technology: Textbook for students of linguistic universities and faculties*. Akademiya.

Muratova, E. N. (2016). Training in the translation of legal texts in a foreign language: Overcoming interlingual interference. *Current Issues in Combating Crimes and Other Violations of Law, 16*(2), 229–231.

Orlando, D. (2017). Calling translation to the bar: A comparative analysis of the translation errors made by translators and lawyers. *Translation and Translanguaging in Multilingual Contexts, 3*(1), 81–96. https://doi.org/10.1075/ttmc.3.1.06orl

Semchinskiy, S. V. (1974). *Semantic interference of languages*. Vysshaya Shkola.

Simonnæs, I. (2013). Challenges in legal translation—Revisited. *Linguistica, 53*(2), 91–102. https://doi.org/10.4312/linguistica.53.2.91-102

Stepanova, O. K. (2013). Linguistic and semantic aspects of translating English legal terminology. Naukovyi Visnyk Mizhnarodnoho Humanitarnoho Universytetu. *Filolohiia, 6*, 103–109.

Stepanova, V. V. (2019). Interference challenge to translation quality in multilingual translation. *XLinguae: European Scientific Language Journal, 12*(4), 3–17.

Stepanova, V. V., Meshkova, I., & Sheremetieva, O. (2018). Interference in legal translation: Addressing challenges. *XLinguae: European Scientific Language Journal, 11*, 294–301. https://doi.org/10.18355/XL.2018.11.01.24

Weinreich, U. (1979). *Language contacts. Status and research problems*. Vishcha Shkola.

Zhluktenko, Y. A. (1974). *Lingvisticheskie aspekty dvuyazychiya* [Linguistic aspects of bilingualism]. Vishcha Shkola.

Dictionaries

Garner, B. A. (2014). *Black's law dictionary*. Thomson Reuters.

Mamulyan, A. S., & Kashkin, S. Y. U. (1993). *English-Russian law dictionary*. https://envoc.ru/edictionary/anglo-russkij-polnyj-yuridicheskij-slovar (Accessed March 3, 2021).

Merriam-Webster Dictionary. (n.d.). https://www.merriam-webster.com/dictio
    nary/file (Accessed March 3, 2021).
Novyy Bol'shoy Anglo-Russkiy Slovar [New Large English-Russian Dictionary].
    https://dic.academic.ru/contents.nsf/eng_rus_apresyan (Accessed March 3,
    2020).

7

From Foe to Friend: The Role of Fan Translation in Language Education

Boris Vazquez-Calvo ⓘ

7.1 Introduction

The significance of fan translation in language education has been magnified in today's digital landscape, with teaching methodologies undergoing continuous evolution to meet modern demands. This evolution is evident in the rise of technology-driven pedagogical strategies enhancing task-based language learning in and out of traditional classrooms, as demonstrated by the integration of mobile technologies (Jarvis, 2015) and the exploration of the feasibility of fully online Task-Based Language Teaching (TBLT) innovations (Baralt & Morcillo Gómez, 2017). Concurrently, there is a growing emphasis on utilizing contemporary popular culture in language education. Easy access to textbooks, extensive reading texts and authentic materials, which are a staple in language classrooms (Gilmore, 2007), has been revolutionized by digital

B. Vazquez-Calvo (✉)
University of Málaga, Málaga, Spain
e-mail: bvazquezcalvo@uma.es

© The Author(s), under exclusive license to Springer Nature Switzerland AG 2025
D. Coulson and C. Denman (eds.), *Translation, Translanguaging and Machine Translation in Foreign Language Education*,
https://doi.org/10.1007/978-3-031-82174-5_7

technologies, making a variety of cultural products readily available and redefining their role in language pedagogy (Werner & Tegge, 2020).

Beyond educational resources, these cultural products give rise to animated fan communities. United by shared interests, individuals in communities of fans (or "fandoms") facilitate dynamic exchanges that typically gain public visibility through online platforms. Celebrating Taylor Swift's latest hit with a tweet as a dedicated "Swiftie," cosplaying as one's favorite anime or manga character and posting a selfie, or writing and publishing fanfiction that explores alternate universes inspired by Harry Potter—these activities exemplify the breadth of fan engagement, showcasing the creative ways fans express their admiration and participate in their favorite fandoms. Among these fan activities, fan translation stands out as a particularly unique form of engagement, intensive in language use and offering rich opportunities for linguistic and cultural exchange.

Fan translation involves fans translating cultural products for other fans within their fandoms (Vazquez-Calvo et al., 2019). For example, this practice allows fans to access content, such as Korean dramas, in their native languages faster than commercial releases, often preserving the original text's integrity or sometimes being the sole access point if official translations are never released. These fan-contributed translations, emblematic of a strong community and shared identity (Sauro, 2017, 2021), are primarily shared online, broadening global reach. However, this phenomenon goes beyond sharing content; it highlights a grassroots strategy in disseminating language and culture.

As globalization intensifies the demand for cross-lingual communication, the significance of incorporating translation into future language education becomes paramount. This approach is supported by the Common European Framework of Reference for Languages (CEFR), which recognizes mediation as a mode of communication for an integral understanding of communicative competence (Council of Europe, 2020). To harness the potential role of translation in modern language education, in this chapter the case of fan translation, its dynamics, role, challenges, and potential rapport with relevant language learning and teaching practices is explored, drawing on past research and the pedagogical framework of *bridging activities*. Bridging activities refer to a pedagogical approach to connect formal language teaching and informal uses of language found in digital spaces (Thorne & Reinhardt, 2013). This approach posits that fan translation amalgamates language skills, cultural awareness, and digital literacies, presenting a modern alternative to a traditional understanding of translation, which was typically focused on literal equivalence and linguistic decoding.

The chapter begins by exploring the integration of translation in language education, with a specific focus on fan translation and its implications, before detailing a proposed framework for incorporating fan translation-inspired activities into L2 classrooms.

7.2   Translation in Language Education

Translation's role in language education has shifted from traditional grammar-focused exercises to a holistic tool bridging linguistic and cultural divides, reflecting pedagogical and societal changes. The overview offered here traces its evolution from its foundations to today's fan translation, merging fan-infused enthusiasm with language-learning opportunities.

7.2.1   Traditional Role of Translation in Language Education

In the study of language and communication, the notion of translation is multi-dimensional. At its core, it can be seen as both a cognitive activity (*translating*) and the tangible outcome of that activity (the *translation* or translated text). Whether interlinguistically (between two distinct languages) or intralinguistically (between varieties or modes within the same language), translation as the act of linguistic and textual replacement requires deep interpretation and context-aware adaptation. Its aim extends beyond linguistic precision; it seeks to capture the intent, tone, and cultural subtleties of the original message while meeting the requirements of the target text, making it a context-dependent, function-oriented intercultural and, most often, interlinguistic process (House, 2009; Nord, 1997).

Translation's role in language education has evolved alongside changing perceptions of language and L2 pedagogy. Previously, the Grammar-Translation method in L2 pedagogy aimed to enhance technical language skills for philological study but lacked effectiveness in casual communication or fluency development. This method's shortcomings, such as its emphasis on memorization and neglect of communicative and oral skills, became apparent in the late 20th century's global context (Richards & Rodgers, 2014). In response to Grammar-Translation, subsequent teaching approaches, like the Oral Approach and the Audiolingual Method, emphasized immersive L2 use and verbal practice, often sidelining anything remotely close to translation or L1 use. Richards and Rodgers (2014) highlight that, in these methods, the L2 dominates classroom interactions while the L1 is relegated or frowned upon.

The translation debate extends beyond its mere application in language learning. Cook (2010) argues that L1 hinders L2 acquisition, leading to teaching methods that separate L2 learning from L1 experience. Conversely, Widdowson (2014) notes that learners naturally use translation to connect new L2 structures with existing L1 knowledge. Traditional methods, such as the Audiolingual Method, imply that "translation or use of the native language is discouraged" (Richards & Rodgers, 2014, p. 70). However, translation plays an inherent role in learners' cognitive processes, highlighting a mismatch between (emergent) bilingual/multilingual learners' needs and prevalent monolingual teaching practices. Widdowson (2014, p. 229) critiques the neglect of L1-L2 mediation and translation, stating that "teachers create adverse conditions for learning, so that many, if not most, of the difficulties that learners have to cope with are pedagogically induced."

7.2.2 Shift in Perception of Translation and Emergence of Fan Translation

In the 21st century, translation in language teaching transformed from a mechanical task to a more dynamic activity interweaving language, culture, and thought. Translation evolved to encompass cultural contexts and idiomatic nuances, leading to its promotion as a fifth skill in communicative competence, alongside listening, speaking, reading, and writing (Colina & Lafford, 2017; Naimushin, 2002). Consequently, educators acknowledged translation's dual role as a teaching strategy and communicative task.

As previously noted, the 2020 companion volume of the CEFR (Council of Europe, 2020) incorporated mediation, emphasizing skills like summarizing, paraphrasing, note-taking, and translating. Such skills are pivotal in enhancing comprehension and promoting intercultural understanding. This inclusion emphasizes translation's expansive role in contemporary language education, moving beyond mere word-to-word conversion to a more pluricultural dimension, equipping learners to decipher meanings, correlate information across contexts, and navigate intricate linguistic and cultural landscapes.

Besides institutionally backed discourses and proposals revaluing translation within the conceptualization of communicative competence, several other factors, including the surge in global media and internet usage, have been instrumental in repositioning translation in language education. With global media's widespread availability, fan communities have grown rapidly, and, with them, the increasing practice of fan translation. Wongseree et al. (2019) remark how many fans take the initiative to translate and share online content themselves rather than waiting for official translations. This phenomenon highlights translation as a diverse cultural and linguistic activity, illustrating the proactive and engaged practices of common internet users within the framework of participatory culture. Participatory culture, as described by Beer and Burrows (2010), refers to a culture in which private individuals (the public) do not act only as consumers, but also as contributors or producers (e.g., so-called prosumers). This context emphasizes the collaborative and interactive nature of fan translation, where fans not only consume media but also contribute to its production, dissemination, and localization according to their own standards.

7.3   Fan Translation in Language Education

Fan translation dovetails with contemporary pedagogical values, emphasizing communicative, context-aware, and culturally immersive language education. It transcends traditional rote learning, offering engaging, authentic interactions and cultural insights, key in evolving language teaching practices. The following section frames fan translation, its connection with language learning in informal contexts and its potential to motivate learning.

7.3.1 Definition and Examples of Fan Translation

In the current media-rich landscape, fan translation has flourished, driven by globalization and fans' desire to share content across language boundaries. To understand the intricacies of fan translation, categorizing its diverse forms is crucial. Table 7.1 outlines five common types of fan translation, using criteria such as modality, content type, and the target audience of the fan-translated material.

Essentially, fan translation unfolds as a heterogeneous field, reflecting the diverse practices fans employ to make popular culture and media content universally accessible and celebrated. With that, fan translators and consumers of fan translation stand in a privileged position to learn language and culture. This privileged position arises from their active engagement with both the source and target languages, as well as the cultural contexts, enabling a deeper and more nuanced understanding of both.

Table 7.1 Types of fan translation

Type	Modality	Translated texts	Audience	Description
Fansubbing	Audiovisual	Films, TV shows, and anime	Viewers unfamiliar with the source language	Adding subtitles to audio-visual content, emphasizing cultural nuances and idiomatic expressions
Fandubbing	Audiovisual	Films, anime, and TV series	Viewers who prefer dubbed content	Replacing original audio with voiceovers in another language, requiring voice modulation and emotional understanding
Scanlation	Print and digital	Manga and comics	Readers of graphic novels and manga outside origin countries	Scanning and translating manga or comics, contributing to their global popularity
Fan translation of fanfics	Digital	Fan-created fiction	Fans of a media franchise or literary universe	Translating fan-authored narratives that extend or reimagine established storylines
Romhacking (fan translation of video games)	Digital and interactive	Video games	Gamers seeking non-localized titles	Translating a video game's original script, at times demanding a blend of software programming skills, such as modifications to game code, and linguistic skills

7.3.2 Intersection of Fan Translation and Language Learning

The integration of fan translation and language learning highlights the growing relevance of informal, digital learning environments. A skilled fan translator exemplifies key traits of an effective language learner, engaging in informal, incidental, and self-directed learning. Vazquez-Calvo's (2018) case study of Selo, a dedicated game translator, reveals how these activities facilitate rich linguistic exchanges in online forums. Selo's participation ranged from player to beta-tester and reviewer, demonstrating digital, linguistic, and sociocultural competencies. His experience, enriched by community feedback, illustrates how fan translation merges fandom and authentic language learning, extending beyond conventional classrooms.

Like Selo's experience, fan translation draws learners into rich situations for cultural and linguistic use and learning. Studies of Catalan fan translators (e.g., Vazquez-Calvo, 2021; Vazquez-Calvo & Thorne, 2022) showcase these complexities, particularly in translating puns and wordplays. The riddle "What letter hurts you if it gets too close? B" proved to be very challenging for these fan translators due to the homophone play between "bee" (the insect) and "B" (the letter). Their clever solution integrated Mediterranean culture, utilizing a Roman numeral pun and a homograph reference to "wine" in Catalan: "Quin número emborratxava els romans? El VI.", a play on "six" or VI in Roman numbers and "wine" or "vi" in Catalan as the answer to the question, "Which number made the Romans drunk?".

This meticulous fan translation work, particularly in preserving humor, demonstrates deep engagement and investment, transforming translation into a meaningful experience. These examples highlight fan translation's potential in language learning, indicating strong intrinsic motivation and emotional connections within digital spaces (Sauro & Zourou, 2019), which pave the way for exploring the psychological aspects of fan-driven learning.

7.3.3 The Role of Fan Translation in Motivating Language Learning

Affect and motivation in language learning are crucial, and fan translation, along with other fan activities, may enhance these aspects. Traditional motivation theories categorize motivation into intrinsic and extrinsic types (Gardner, 1985), while Crookes and Schmidt (1991) proposed a more nuanced, fluid continuum of motivation, identifying dimensions of interest, relevance, expectancy, and satisfaction. Selo's example, as a gamer and fan translator translating video games from English to Spanish (Vazquez-Calvo, 2018), concretely demonstrates these motivational dimensions in action, highlighting the impact of personal interest and community participation in language learning.

1. *Interest*. Central to intrinsic motivation, this concerns a learner's authentic desire to engage with content. Selo's fascination was not just about translating words. He embarked on a nostalgic quest, revisiting beloved video games from his teenage years. In translating them, he not only grasped game narratives more deeply but also aimed to share that understanding with a broader Spanish-speaking audience, thus broadening access to content.

2. *Relevance*. Selo's translation work aligns with his personal goals and caters to niche communities, enhancing the relevance of his learning. He navigates both linguistic and technical challenges, such as embedding unique Spanish characters in English-coded games. Sharing his translations online, he fosters a learning community and encourages peer feedback, embodying the collaborative and communicative potential of fan practices with a link with TBLT (Sauro, 2014).

3. *Expectancy*. This involves a learner's perceived potential for success. In fan communities, continuous feedback can shape these perceptions. Each interaction on the forums marked Selo's evolving competence. Praise and critiques both refined his self-view, transforming him into a more confident and competent translator over time.

4. *Satisfaction*. Selo finds joy and fulfillment in his fan translation work, blending intrinsic pleasure with external recognition. His efforts, evident in the popularity and high download rates of his games, have earned him respect within the fan gaming community. Despite external accolades, his reward is the personal satisfaction derived from bridging linguistic gaps for his community. Following the presentation of his case in Vazquez-Calvo (2018), Selo described how fan translation significantly boosted his confidence in using English.

Regardless of the approach to motivation, the fundamental principle remains consistent: fan practices, by connecting with learners' affinity identities (Ito et al., 2019), appear to fuel motivation for learning while tapping into the dynamic, community-centric nature of fandoms, and enhancing language learning through real language use. The challenge now is to optimize this potential. Below, various practical examples are explored as to how fan translation can be effectively employed in language education.

7.4   Methodology

Construing fan translation as a task and a bridging activity, this section provides insight into its integration into language teaching, thereby enhancing learners' linguistic and cultural skills. It further outlines strategies for engaging with fan communities.

7.4.1   Fan Translation as a Task and a Bridging Activity

Drawing on TBLT (Van den Branden et al., 2009), fan translation intertwines academic learning and practical application, aligning individual tasks with real-world objectives and necessary linguistic skills. This approach harmonizes set goals with essential language use, illustrating the synergy between educational objectives and authentic language practice.

Fan translation may serve as a conduit between formal classroom learning and global fan practices, creating authentic learning experiences. Among others, Sauro (2014) reports on her own TBLT proposals based on fan practices through real-world tasks for advanced, literature-focused learners, encouraging the exploration of literary language and text analysis via blogging about video game characters. Building on this, classroom activities can incorporate fan translation and related practices, such as conducting surveys on subtitling preferences and engaging in practical fansubbing projects.

Concerning the example of TBLT and subtitling preferences, students navigate through stages such as identifying the target population, designing a detailed survey on fan and subtitling practices, collecting and processing data, and compiling a comprehensive report. These stages provide numerous linguistic learning opportunities. For instance, crafting a variety of question types, including yes/no, wh-, and multiple-choice questions, enhances grammatical proficiency. Sample questions could include: *What are your favorite shows? Where do you typically watch them? Are they in your native language or another? Do you use subtitles, and, if so, how often and in which language? Do you find subtitles helpful for language learning?* This project exemplifies the integration of fan translation-related practices, such as using and reading subtitles while watching media, into TBLT, underscoring the potential for fan translation to play a central role in educational tasks.

This type of pedagogic proposal organically integrates fan translation into TBLT as a bridging activity, a pedagogic framework introduced by Thorne and Reinhardt (2013) and supported by studies by Reinhardt and Ryu (2014) and York (2023), among others. This approach blends classroom instruction with L2 engagement in real-world communities, positioning fan translation activities (such as engaging with, analyzing, or creating fan-made subtitles) at the intersection of formal learning and authentic communication in the target language. The structure of the bridging activities framework is threefold:

1. **Observe and collect**. Here, students delve into communities that align with their personal interests, actively observing and collecting media items earmarked for subsequent classroom analysis.
2. **Guided analysis**. Under instructor mentorship, students undertake a detailed examination of the selected media, exploring textual intricacies, cultural nuances of the L2 community, and even multimedia elements, whether they be emojis, videos, or memes.
3. **Creation and participation**. Armed with a foundational understanding of the community's sociocultural dynamics, students next become active community participants. They may craft original content or reimagine existing artifacts. Importantly, the feedback and responses from the community to these contributions circle back to the initial stage, fostering a cyclical, iterative learning process.

The following section presents examples of the bridging activities framework, adapted to each of the five modalities of fan translation identified in Table 7.1.

7.4.2 Bridging Fan Translation for Language Learning and Teaching

When students engage in fan translation, they delve deeper than merely understanding surface content; they explore cultural, contextual, and linguistic complexities. In Lakarnchua's (2017) survey of Thai fansubbers learning Korean, one respondent stated that:

> making subs is a form of language practice in itself. There are both vocabulary words that I know and do not know. Any vocabulary words that I do not know, I go find the meaning of. Seeing the word in passing and seeing it frequently, I'll remember it. (p. 41)

This highlights that fan translation is not only language-intensive but also helps in identifying and addressing knowledge gaps. As a result, it encourages learners to overcome these gaps and leads to repeated exposure, which is vital for vocabulary learning and retention (Rodgers & Webb, 2011).

However, integrating fan translation in the classroom necessitates careful design and scaffolding, considering the content type, translation task structure, student roles (in collaborative tasks), and the overarching objectives of assignments. The proposal to adapt the bridging activities framework aims to facilitate fan translation across various instructional contexts, assuming students are at an upper-intermediate to advanced proficiency level.

Proposal 1 Fansubbing primarily caters to international viewers unfamiliar with the source language, aiming to bridge the linguistic gap. Consequently, content can encompass foreign films, series, or anime clips, offering opportunities to tackle cultural and linguistic diversity (Table 7.2).

Table 7.2 Bridging fansubbing

Stage	What students can do
Observe and collect	– Choose a 5-minute clip from a film, series, or song without existing subtitles in the target language – Alternatively, teachers can use a student video created for past projects
Guided analysis	– Analyze the dialogue, idiomatic expressions, and cultural references in the clip – Discuss the challenges of translating humor, sarcasm, or local dialects
Creation and participation	– Add subtitles to the clip, ensuring synchronization. Free software is available such as Aegisub or even YouTube. Refine translations based on peer feedback. If including aspects of diversity, ensure students know the difference between subtitles for the general public and those for the hearing impaired. For example, subtitles for the hearing impaired often include additional information such as sound effects, speaker identification, and color coding. By doing so, fansubbing provides opportunities for both interlinguistic and intralinguistic mediation, potentially emphasizing aspects of accessibility, inclusivity, and diversity

Students work collaboratively, dividing into roles such as primary translator (who conducts a first translation draft), time-coder (who ensures synchronization), and reviewer (who checks for inconsistencies in L2-L1 transfer). The task teaches linguistic adaptation and understanding of cultural nuances, aiming to produce a subtitled clip that feels both authentic and accessible to new audiences.

Proposal 2 Fandubbing affords a work of oral speech, delving beyond written text to capture real talk and characters' personalities. Content can originate from various genres, ranging from animated films to live-action series or songs, each presenting unique challenges (Table 7.3).

In this more individualized task, students reflect on and analyze the decision-making process that fandubbers employ. An intriguing case study for comparing Japanese/Korean to Spanish/Catalan songs might

Table 7.3 Bridging fandubbing

Stage	What students can do
Observe and collect	– Select one or more songs that have been fandubbed in the local language available on YouTube. Conduct an initial comparison based on the number of viewers, likes, and other aspects of audience engagement
Guided analysis	– Analyze the personalities, emotions, and motivations of singers and fandubbers. Consider voice modulation and intonation for some lines
	– Compare the L2 original video clip with the L1 fandubbed version in terms of matching the storyline or emotion conveyed in the song. Identify the fandubbing translation strategies employed by the fandubber
Creation and participation	– Post a complimentary comment on both the original and fandubbed songs, highlighting what students appreciated most about them, based on the prior analysis

be the fandubs created by @miree_music. The fandubber @miree_music fandubs K-pop and J-pop songs into Spanish and Catalan, and her work, particularly the skillfully crafted, multimodal orchestration of her videos, gestures, and translated language in the Spanish fandubbed version of BTS's "Fake Love," has been extensively analyzed (Zhang & Vazquez-Calvo, 2022). This analysis helps students understand the function and importance of coherent multimodal texts as a unified semiotic whole.

Proposal 3 Scanlation revolves around manga or comics, content often full of cultural connotations, visual cues, and constrained text spaces (Table 7.4).

Students can collaborate as translators, image editors (adapting visual layouts), or cultural consultants, ensuring cultural nuances are preserved. This involves maintaining narrative integrity while being linguistically concise, and developing image editing skills, especially for comic-based genres like manga where onomatopoeia and non-verbal symbols are key. The task also requires sophisticated organizational skills for optimized teamwork.

Table 7.4 Bridging scanlation

Stage	What students can do
Observe and collect	– Select a few pages from a manga or comic in the original language and check if there are translated versions in the local and/or target languages; for instance, the Japanese-English–Spanish triad
Guided analysis	– Analyze official translations to determine the extent of localization in the L2 versions – Examine how imagery correlates with dialogue, considering the spatial limitations of speech bubbles and the narrative's core – Investigate scanlation processes through relevant websites[1] or discussions, such as the Reddit thread "How to scanlate??",[2] to understand the intricacies involved
Creation and participation	– Utilize online editing software to translate comics so that the text fits within the speech bubbles while preserving the integrity of the story – Engage in peer reviews to identify areas for improvement

Beyond traditional manga scanlation, other materials, such as works by Spanish comic author Ibáñez, can be used for Spanish-L2 learners. Translating comics like *Mortadelo y Filemón*, which are rich in cultural humor and parodic gags reflecting a stereotypical and self-deprecating image of Spanish culture, challenges students to handle cultural references through techniques that include domestication, neutralization, or localization, thus extending their advanced language skills in an engaging context.

Proposal 4 Fanfiction involves fan-created narratives, often interwoven with established storylines and intricate fan theories (Table 7.5).

Students take on roles of translators, editors, and outreach coordinators, interacting with authors or fan communities. The task involves language translation and navigating fandom dynamics and etiquette.

---

[1] See, for instance: https://manga.fandom.com/wiki/Scanlation.

[2] https://www.reddit.com/r/Scanlation/comments/egseeq/how_to_scanlate/?rdt=65228.

Table 7.5 Bridging fanfic translation

Stage	What students can do
Observe and collect	– Choose an L2 fanfic community and platform such as Fanfiction.net to study common themes, genres, and discussions –Select an untranslated fanfic from a known media series and subgenre, such as a *dramiones* or *drarries* from the Harry Potter world[3] – Make contact with original authors for informal interviews or chats about their fanfic activity and permission to translate
Guided analysis	– Explore the fanfic's themes, character portrayals, and narrative arcs – Analyze the author's voice and style and discuss potential cultural adaptations into the L1
Creation and participation	– Set up a translator profile on a social media or other chosen platform, either multimodal or text-based – Translate the fanfic, preserving the original tone and style. Post it in fan communities for feedback and prepare students to handle various types of criticism and comments

Fanfic translators, like Cristy, who translates English fanfics into Spanish and identifies closely with the Harry Potter series, often exhibit a strong sense of identity engagement (Vazquez-Calvo et al., 2020). In her online persona, Cristy adopts a Harry Potter character's identity, dressing in a yellow Hogwarts uniform to represent Hufflepuff house, known for traits like loyalty and inclusiveness. This reflects the community-oriented nature of fan translation and fanfiction circles (Vazquez-Calvo et al., 2020). Fan translation enables the integration of L2 learning with affinity identities. For further exploration, authors like Barkhuizen and Strauss (2020) offer detailed lesson plans and activities that focus on identity in language education, incorporating affinity identities such as those of a gamer or a fanfic enthusiast.

---

[3] In fanfiction, a literary universe can generate multiple subgenres. In Harry Potter fanfics, *dramiones* are stories depicting a romance between Draco Malfoy and Hermione Granger, while *drarries* feature a romance between Draco Malfoy and Harry Potter.

Proposal 5 Fan translation of video games is a deep dive into the digital gaming universe, extending beyond narrative to include interactive mechanics and user interfaces (Table 7.6).

In this activity, students take on roles of translators and game testers, focusing not just on translation but also on cultural adaptation and design thinking to maintain gameplay integrity and language accessibility. Video game translation combines narrative text with real-life conversational language, challenging fan translators to manage screen space and character limits through skillful paraphrasing. This refers to the available text space within the game, which can be limited by the game's design. An example is the Catalan translation of English video games led by a community of Catalan-speaking gamers and fan translators aspiring to valorize Catalan as a language for video game consumption and production (Vazquez-Calvo, 2021). To fit the game's text space, these Catalan translators had to shorten their translation, illustrating the need for a deep understanding of both the source and target languages and

Table 7.6 Bridging fan translation of video games

Stage	What students can do
Observe and collect	– Select a narrative-rich, non-localized video game and play a section. As an alternative to playing a video game, which may be costly or challenging in some contexts, educators could opt for utilizing silent or commented gameplay videos available online as materials for translation and analysis. Game developers often open calls for participation for fan translators to help in localizing games
Guided analysis	– Analyze game mechanics, user interface, and storyline
	– Reflect on the difficulty of translating such aspects with the constraints inherent to video games, such as a limited number of characters per line
Creation and participation	– Translate elements of the game, such as dialogue or item descriptions
	– Implement feedback mechanisms through playtesting or peer reviews
	– Respect the character limitation set by the characteristics of the game or by the teacher

the ability to critically appraise the meaning of the original text and effectively paraphrase and utilize advanced grammatical structures in the target language. This showcases fan translation as a powerful component of language learning, bridging learners' L1 knowledge with the L2.

Though each proposal for each modality is rooted in the overarching principles of the bridging activities framework, they offer distinct experiences and task cycles, with each presenting unique linguistic challenges, collaborative dynamics, and potentially significant learning outcomes. Not directly covered in the bridging activities framework are evaluation and assessment. Options for these include the integration of peer feedback loops, revision stages throughout the execution of tasks, maintenance of digital portfolios, and a commitment to ongoing individual, group, and teacher-guided reflection. Additionally, active participation in online communities would require navigating real-world feedback and responding appropriately, providing real-life interaction and learning. By incorporating these layers of reflective practice and structured evaluation, students are afforded the opportunity not only to think critically about their work but also to ensure a high level of autonomous and self-guided learning, suitable for the target student demographic of the proposals in this chapter.

7.5   Conclusion

Active participation in fan translation as a real-life task for language learning resonates with Widdowson's (2014) conceptualization of translation, intertwining culture, context, and communicative nuances. Such an approach leads to a more inclusive and culturally attuned language education paradigm. Fan translation transforms learners from passive recipients to active participants in digital environments, enhancing digital literacies and critical skills, and thus extends its benefits to developing soft skills like online collaboration and intercultural understanding (Dooly & Thorne, 2018).

Educators play a crucial role in guiding this exploration. They leverage frameworks such as the bridging activities paradigm (Thorne & Reinhardt, 2013; York, 2023) and task-based approaches (Sauro, 2014) to ensure structured and enriching learning experiences. However, integrating fan translation poses challenges, such as exposure to non-standard linguistic forms and ethical dilemmas, including potential copyright issues (Vazquez-Calvo, 2021). York (2023) emphasizes wise community selection in response to these concerns, while Sauro (2017, 2021) recommends the integration of informal fan practices in formal education with caution about the over-domestication of practices that have a deeply rooted social meaning outside the classroom. These aspects highlight the need for educators skilled in the contextual, linguistic, and methodological knowledge of fandom and fan practices, ensuring effective language learning through fan translation.

Despite these challenges, and further echoing Sauro (2021), fan practices, including fan translation, offer vast opportunities for linguistic, intercultural, and skill development. This chapter has attempted to promote an initial exploration of the potential of fan translation in language education, treating it as a valuable area for pedagogical exploitation and further research interest. By bridging linguistic barriers and cultural horizons, fan translation not only helps reconfigure L2 pedagogy for the digital age but also ushers in a new era of participatory and meaningful language learning where students' passions potentially become a gateway to other languages and cultures.

References

Baralt, M., & Morcillo Gómez, J. (2017). Task-based language teaching online: A guide for teachers. *Language Learning & Technology, 21*(3), 28–43. http://llt.msu.edu/issues/october2017/baraltmorcillogomez.pdf

Barkhuizen, G., & Strauss, P. (2020). *Communicating identities*. Routledge.

Beer, D., & Burrows, R. (2010). Consumption, prosumption and participatory web cultures: An introduction. *Journal of Consumer Culture, 10*(1), 3–12. https://doi.org/10.1177/1469540509354009

Colina, S., & Lafford, B. A. (2017). Translation in Spanish language teaching: The integration of a 'fifth skill' in the second language curriculum. *Journal of Spanish Language Teaching, 4*(2), 110–123. https://doi.org/10.1080/23247797.2017.1407127

Cook, G. (2010). *Translation in language teaching*. Oxford University Press.

Council of Europe. (2020). *Common European Framework of Reference for Languages: Learning, teaching, assessment—Companion volume*. www.coe.int/lang-cefr

Crookes, G., & Schmidt, R. W. (1991). Motivation: Reopening the research agenda. *Language Learning, 41*(4), 469–512. https://doi.org/10.1111/j.1467-1770.1991.tb00690.x

Dooly, M., & Thorne, S. L. (2018). *Knowledge for network-based education, cognition and teaching: Key competencies for the 21st century. KONECT white paper*. KONECT. https://doi.org/10.6084/m9.figshare.7366982

Gardner, R. C. (1985). *Social psychology and second language learning: The role of attitudes and motivation*. Edward Arnold.

Gilmore, A. (2007). Authentic materials and authenticity in foreign language learning. *Language Teaching, 40*(2), 97–118. https://doi.org/10.1017/S0261444807004144

House, J. (2009). *Translation*. Oxford University Press.

Ito, M., Martin, C., Pfister, R. C., Rafalow, M. H., Salen, K., & Wortman, A. (2019). *Affinity online: How connection and shared interest fuel learning*. New York University Press.

Jarvis, H. (2015). From PPP and CALL/MALL to a praxis of task-based teaching and mobile assisted language use. *Teaching English as a Second or Foreign Language Electronic Journal, 19*(1), 1–9. https://www.tesl-ej.org/pdf/ej73/a1.pdf

Lakarnchua, O. (2017). Examining the potential of fansubbing as a language learning activity. *Innovation in Language Learning and Teaching, 11*(1), 32–44. https://doi.org/10.1080/17501229.2015.1016030

Naimushin, B. (2002). Translation in foreign language teaching: The fifth skill. *Modern English Teacher, 11*(4), 46–49.

Nord, C. (1997). *Translating as a purposeful activity*. Routledge.

Reinhardt, J., & Ryu, J. (2014). Using social network-mediated bridging activities to develop socio-pragmatic awareness in elementary Korean. *International Journal of Computer Assisted Language Learning and Teaching, 3*(3), 18–33. https://doi.org/10.4018/ijcallt.2013070102

Richards, J. C., & Rodgers, T. S. (2014). *Approaches and methods in language teaching*. Cambridge University Press.

Rodgers, M. P. H., & Webb, S. (2011). Narrow viewing: The vocabulary in related television programs. *TESOL Quarterly, 45*(4), 689–717. https://doi.org/10.5054/tq.2011.268062

Sauro, S. (2014). Lessons from the fandom. In M. González-Lloret & L. Ortega (Eds.), *Technology-mediated TBLT: Researching technology and tasks* (pp. 239–262). John Benjamins. https://doi.org/10.1075/tblt.6.09sau

Sauro, S. (2017). Online fan practices and CALL. *CALICO Journal, 34*(2), 131–146. https://doi.org/10.1558/cj.33077

Sauro, S. (2021). Online fanfiction for language teaching and learning. *Alsic, 24*(2), https://doi.org/10.4000/alsic.5763

Sauro, S., & Zourou, K. (2019). What are the digital wilds? *Language Learning & Technology, 23*(1), 1–7. https://doi.org/10125/44666

Thorne, S. L., & Reinhardt, J. (2013). 'Bridging activities', New media literacies, and advanced foreign language proficiency. *CALICO Journal, 25*(3), 558–572. https://doi.org/10.1558/cj.v25i3.558-572

Van den Branden, K., Bygate, M., & Norris, J. (2009). Task-based language teaching: Introducing the reader. In K. Van den Branden, M. Bygate, & J. Norris (Eds.), *Task-based language teaching: A reader* (pp. 1–19). John Benjamins.

Vazquez-Calvo, B. (2018). The online ecology of literacy and language practices of a gamer. *Educational Technology & Society, 21*(3), 199–212. http://www.jstor.org/stable/26458518

Vazquez-Calvo, B. (2021). Guerrilla fan translation, language learning, and metalinguistic discussion in a Catalan-speaking community of gamers. *ReCALL, 33*(3), 296–313. https://doi.org/10.1017/S095834402000021X

Vazquez-Calvo, B., García-Roca, A., & López-Báez, C. (2020). Domesticar la 'selva digital': El fanfiction a examen a través de la mirada de una fanfictioner. *Edmetic, 9*(1), 21–51. https://doi.org/10.21071/edmetic.v9i1.12239

Vazquez-Calvo, B., & Thorne, S. L. (2022). Catalan identity and language attitudes through fan translation of video games in the digital wilds. *Journal of Language, Identity & Education, 1–18.* https://doi.org/10.1080/15348458.2022.2137168

Vazquez-Calvo, B., Zhang, L. T., Pascual, M., & Cassany, D. (2019). Fan translation of games, anime, and fanfiction. *Language Learning and Technology, 23*(1), 49–71. https://doi.org/10125/44672

Werner, V., & Tegge, F. (Eds.). (2020). *Pop culture in language education.* Routledge. https://doi.org/10.4324/9780367808334

Widdowson, H. G. (2014). The role of translation in language learning and teaching. In J. House (Ed.), *Translation: A multidisciplinary approach* (pp. 222–240). Palgrave Macmillan.

Wongseree, T., O'Hagan, M., & Sasamoto, R. (2019). Contemporary global media circulation based on fan translation: A particular case of Thai fansubbing. *Discourse, Context and Media, 32.* https://doi.org/10.1016/j.dcm.2019.100330

York, J. (2023). Engaging with the world: Applying connected learning in a university language learning context. *Foreign Language Annals, 56* (2), 334–361. https://doi.org/10.1111/flan.12691

Zhang, L.-T., & Vazquez-Calvo, B. (2022). '¿Triste estás? I don't know nan molla': Multilingual pop song fandubs by @miree_music. *ITL—International Journal of Applied Linguistics, 173*(2), 197–227. https://doi.org/10.1075/itl.21007.zha

8

To Translate or Not to Translate in the Foreign Language Classroom? An Empirical-Experimental Study on Pedagogical Translation in Secondary Language Education

Bettina Schnell⊙ and Carolina García Pérez⊙

8.1 Introduction

Common inquiries within the foreign language (FL) classroom frequently involve questions such as *"What is the English word for this?"* or *"What does this mean in my language?"* These questions articulated by learners to satisfy their communicative needs essentially boil down to *"How do I translate this?"*, and unmistakably underscore that foreign language learning (FLL) and translation are inextricably intertwined, as the native language profoundly influences the way learners construct all subsequent languages they learn. As posited by Widdowson (2003) and Cook (2007), the learning process, regardless of its nature, entails actively

B. Schnell (✉)
Universidad Pontificia Comillas, Madrid, Spain
e-mail: bschnell@comillas.edu

C. G. Pérez
Universidad Alfonso X El Sabio, Madrid, Spain
e-mail: carogape@uax.es

© The Author(s), under exclusive license to Springer Nature Switzerland AG 2025
D. Coulson and C. Denman (eds.), *Translation, Translanguaging and Machine Translation in Foreign Language Education*,
https://doi.org/10.1007/978-3-031-82174-5_8

linking the unfamiliar to the already familiar in order to better comprehend. In this regard, translation may be beneficial by directing learners'
attention to the similarities and differences between languages. Yet, the
utilization of translation in the FL classroom has evolved from the
grammar-translation method being the teaching approach par excellence
toward it being widely disregarded based on the assumption that it might
divert learners' attention from their primary goal of "learning another
language and conforming to its quite different norms and standards"
(Widdowson, 2014, p. 236).

However, in recent decades, growing advocacy has emerged for the
vindication of pedagogical translation (PT) accompanied by a substantial body of research that delves into the role of translation in FLL
and instruction (Carreres & Noriega Sánchez, 2013; Cook, 2007, 2010;
Widdowson, 2014). Notably, Pintado Gutiérrez (2018) highlights that
there is still a dearth of research addressing translation as a pedagogical tool. Consequently, the present study aspires to contribute to the
ongoing debate about the reassessment of PT in FLL and teaching, and
to provide empirical evidence regarding the use of translation as a pedagogical instrument in the context of the English as a foreign language
(EFL) secondary education classroom. Therefore, the primary research
concern was to evaluate the effectiveness of PT as a learning tool through
a comparative analysis of the outcomes attained by participants in both
PT and communicative approach (CA) learning sessions.

8.2   Theoretical Framework: Pedagogical Translation and Error Analysis

When inquiring into the nexus of PT and FLL, it is crucial to clarify
and delineate the notion of PT, ensuring a clear-cut distinction between
the conventional grammar-translation method and translation pedagogy
(TP). The former, historically employed in the instruction of Latin and
Greek and widely criticized for being detrimental to the development
of communicative language skills (Newson, 1998), solely focuses on the
acquisition of the target language (TL) rules and their subsequent application in translation between source and TLs. In contrast, TP pertains to

the education of professional translators centering on aspects related to cognitive processing, as well as considerations regarding teaching materials, activities, and agents in teaching and learning, and their impact on pedagogical practices, in professional translator training (Colina & Angelelli, 2015).

Furthermore, in the context of PT, it is essential to establish a distinction from professional translation. As emphasized by Klaudy (2003) and Vermes (2010), these concepts differ across three dimensions: addressee, object, and function. Professional translation is characterized by an addressee who is the TL reader lacking knowledge of the source language (SL). The ultimate objective in professional translation is the target text (TT), serving as the TL representation of the source text (ST), with the aim of effectively conveying the content of the ST. In this context, the function of professional translation is to overcome the language barrier confronted by the TL reader.

Contrastingly, in line with Klaudy (2003) and Vermes' (2010) considerations, the purpose of PT within FLL is to enhance the learners' proficiency in the FL. The object of PT is to provide information about language learners' level of language proficiency, while the addressee is the teacher or examiner.

Moreover, a third differentiation emerges between PT in professional translator training and PT in FLL. Following Schäffner (1998), PT in FLL directs its attention to different linguistic structures with the objective of enhancing the learners' proficiency in the FL. In contrast, PT in professional translator training focuses on TT production and is geared toward the development of translation competence.

Drawing on the conceptualizations proposed by Schäffner (1998), De Arriba García (1998), Klaudy (2003), Vermes (2010), and Widdowson (2014), PT is conceived as a pedagogical instrument raising language awareness, assisting learners in recognizing the interconnectedness of their non-native (L2) and native (L1) languages, rather than viewing them as entirely distinct linguistic systems, and empowering learners to use their L2 skills by leveraging previous knowledge about their L1. Moreover, the concept of PT, as understood here, aligns with what De

Arriba García (1998) refers to as 'explicative' or 'explanatory' translation, an instructional method employed by teachers to clarify grammar content or to assess students' comprehension of provided explanations.

In the scope of this study, error analysis (EA) assumes particular relevance in analyzing participants' performance in evaluation tasks, since the errors, characterized as systematic deviations from the TL rules, offer valuable insights into the learning process, challenges associated with learning a FL, and the development of learners' linguistic competence. Drawing upon the theoretical framework of EA, as established by Richards (1974), Corder (1967, 1971, 1975), Alexopoulou's (2006) error taxonomy, which itself builds on Richards, and Faerch and Kasper (1983), is useful for identifying the prevalence of intralingual and interlingual error types based on whether participants were exposed to PT or CA. Table 8.1 shows Alexopoulou's (2006, p. 29) error taxonomy.

Table 8.1 Alexopoulou's (2006) error taxonomy

Interlingual errors	Interference (IF)
	→ L1 interference
	→ L3 interference
	→ Literal Translation
	→ Avoidance
Intralingual errors	System-simplification
	→ Simplification (SPL)
	→ Neutralization (NTR)
	→ Incomplete Application of Rules (IAR)
	→ Avoidance
	Generalization
	→ Overgeneralization (OG)
	→ Analogy (AN)
	→ Cross-association (CrA)
	→ Hypercorrection (HC)
	→ Ignorance of Rule Restrictions (IRR)

8.3   Methodology

8.3.1   Rationale, Objective, and Research Questions

The rationale of the study, characterized by its exploratory nature, was to investigate the effectiveness of PT for English learners at early proficiency levels when compared to the standard communicative approach (CA) employed in the Spanish secondary education context. For this purpose, two grammar topics—namely the usage of present perfect/simple past tenses and the gradation of adjectives—were specifically selected. The selection of these grammar topics is grounded in the consideration that the acquisition of both linguistic aspects is integral to the prescriptive first- and second-year English syllabus in Spanish secondary education, given the significance of grammatical competence for early-stage learners. Moreover, these grammar topics are amenable to pedagogic intervention, accommodating both the CA and the translation-based approach.

Beyond the previously mentioned reasons, there are additional factors associated with disparities in the linguistic systems of Spanish and English. Specifically, concerning comparative and superlative formation, morphological distinctions arise. Spanish utilizes a singular morphological process for both the comparative and superlative irrespective of the number of syllables (i.e., 'más alto/peligroso que', 'la más veloz/inteligente'), while English employs distinct morphological processes depending on the number of syllables (i.e., one-syllable or two-syllable adjective ending in -y, -ow, -er, o -le, 'taller than'/'the easiest'; or polysyllabic ones, such as 'the most intelligent/talkative person'). This discrepancy can give rise to instances of L1 interference and overgeneralization.

The selection of the present perfect is driven by the fact that the primary difficulty for Spanish learners lies in its conceptual dimension, since grammatical distinctiveness can be found between temporal features specific to the present perfect and the simple past in spoken Spanish. De Biase (2006) asserts that Spanish speakers in general, and particularly those originating from the north of Spain, the Canary Islands, and Latin America, where the use of the *pretérito perfecto simple* (i.e., the simple past perfect) prevails, present coupling problems and possess a more limited repertoire of morphologically marked options to convey the conceptual nuances associated with the present perfect. Consequently, they resort to periphrasis or alternative linguistic resources to convey these distinctions (i.e., '*Acaba de llegar*' for 'She has just arrived').

Hence, the overall objective was to explore the acquisition of these two specific grammatical aspects in the English language by employing distinct pedagogical approaches. Through a comparison of the participants' results in the evaluation tasks conducted throughout the teaching units, the study sought to determine whether one of the two methodologies demonstrated superior effectiveness in terms of assimilation of these linguistic aspects, or whether both methodologies yielded comparable outcomes. Consequently, the research questions posed in the study were the following:

- RQ1: Is PT equally effective as CA, or does one method exhibit superior effectiveness?
- RQ2: Is there a variation in the effectiveness of PT compared to CA based on the specific grammatical aspect being learned?
- RQ3: How do PT and the CA impact the occurrence of interlingual and intralingual errors?

8.3.2 Research Setting and Participants

The present empirical-experimental investigation was conducted between 2016 and 2019 in the first and second years of the Spanish secondary education system. The study involved the collaboration of three secondary schools located in the Spanish autonomous regions of Madrid and Asturias, with a sample population consisting of 211 pupils aged 12 years. The selection of schools was guided by convenience criteria, driven by the limited response received from secondary schools to the request for collaboration. The subdued response rate was largely due to the scope of the investigation, along with the complexity of the teaching units and the substantial time commitment required for implementation and data collection. Notably, the pedagogical intervention required between seven and nine 50-minute sessions, depending on the grammar topic, resulting in an approximate duration of three-to-four weeks of class time for each grammar topic. Hence, participation in the study had a significant impact on the scheduling of the course content, demanding a steadfast and sustained commitment from school principals and teachers during both the pre-instructional and instructional phases.

The participants exhibited a proficiency level ranging from A2 to B1 according to the Common European Framework of Reference for Languages (CEFR). The decision to involve early-stage learners stems from the positioning of these levels between the beginner and intermediate language learning stages. During this learning stage, learners actively develop their interlanguage and acquaint themselves with the grammar basics of the second language (L2). Following Selinker's (1972) theoretical framework, translation becomes particularly relevant at this stage of interlanguage development, as learners engage in the comparison of the linguistic systems of their L1 and their L2. In a similar vein, Arbuckle (1990) advocates for translation into the L2 in FLL as it prompts learners to apply grammar rules appropriately. Consequently, this phase of language learning proves suitable for an exploration of PT as a methodology in FLL.

8.3.3 Implementation and Data Collection

Before commencing the study, ethical approval was obtained by the Ethics Committee at the Universidad Pontificia Comillas. Permissions were sought and granted both by parents and school principals of the participating institutions. Additionally, participating pupils were briefed by their school teachers about the research objectives and the voluntary nature of their participation, and were given the explicit assurance that their performance in the learning and evaluation activities would not impact their final grades in the English course.

Upon securing consent from the school principals, an orientation session was held with the heads of the English departments and the designated teachers responsible for implementing the teaching units. During this session, teaching materials were provided, accompanied by precise instructions regarding the timing of the activities and the assurance of the anonymity of all participants' personal data. Participants were allocated to experimental groups involved in PT learning activities, or to control groups undertaking learning activities rooted in the CA.

The assignment of participants into experimental and control groups was non-random, with school principals exercising the prerogative to make decisions based on internal organizational criteria. The teaching units for both studies, focusing on adjective gradation (Study 1), and present perfect/simple past tense (Study 2), were administered within the same experimental and control groups. Evaluation samples were collected at various stages of the learning process (see Table 8.2) through objective evaluation tasks graded according to the Spanish grade marking system ranging from 0 to 10. The teachers in charge collected the data, employing an alphanumeric code to ensure anonymity, while grading was carried out by the researchers overseeing the study.

Table 8.2 Leonardi's (2010, p. 88) Pedagogical Translation Framework basic structure

Pretranslation Activities:	Translation Activities:	Post-Translation Activities:
Brainstorming	Speaking and Listening	Written or oral translation commentary
Vocabulary Preview	Reading Activities	Written or oral summary of the ST
Anticipation guides	Writing	Written composition about ST-related topics
	Literal translation	
	Summary translation	
	Parallel texts	
	Re-translation	
	Grammar explanation	
	Vocabulary builder and facilitator	
	Cultural mediation and intercultural competence development	

8.3.4 Design of the Teaching Units

The methodological foundation of the pedagogical intervention based on PT builds on Leonardi's (2010) Pedagogical Translation Framework (PTF). As Table 8.2 illustrates, Leonardi's PTF encompasses three types of activities: pre-translation activities, translation activities, and post-translation activities.

As shown in Table 8.3, distinct teaching units, adhering to a consistent overall structure, were devised for each grammar topic. The conceptualization of the teaching units linked to PT draws from Leonardi's (2010) PTF, while those grounded in CA are rooted in the perspective of language as a tool for communication, as articulated by Colina (2002), La Rocca (2007), and Sánchez Cuadrado (2015).

The teaching units for both grammar structures, employing PT and CA, adopted a comparable framework of three types of learning activities, and, diverging from the classic pre-post-evaluation model, a sequence of shared evaluation activities, encompassing initial, intermediate, and final evaluation tasks, was integrated.

Table 8.3 Design of the teaching units

Activities	Approach	
	Communicative approach (CA)	Pedagogical translation (PT)
Learning activity 1	1. Warming-up activities	1. Pre-translation activities
Evaluation activity 1	2. Initial evaluation	2. Initial evaluation
Learning activity 2	3. Reinforcement activities	3. Translation activities
Evaluation activity 2	4. Intermediate evaluation 1	4. Intermediate evaluation 1
Learning activity 3	5. Extension activities	5. Post-Translation activities
Evaluation activity 3	6. Intermediate evaluation 2	6. Intermediate evaluation 2
Evaluation activity 4	7. Final evaluation	7. Final evaluation

8.3.5 Data Analysis

To provide empirical support for the application of PT and to explore its effectiveness compared with the CA, four teaching units were developed—two based on PT and two based on the CA. As stated above, the teaching units targeted two specific aspects of the English language: adjective gradation (Study 1) and the use of the present perfect/simple past tense (Study 2). Evaluation samples were gathered through objective evaluation tasks (gap-filling tests) and graded from 0 to 10. Participants' grades were calculated based on correct answers relative to total gaps, and the average grade for each participant was determined across all evaluation tasks.

Thus, statistical analysis relied on participants' mean scores obtained throughout the learning process, given the design of teaching units which consisted of initial, intermediate, and final evaluations. Statistical analysis incorporated the independent variables of applied methodology (the PT experimental group vs. the CA control group) and grammar topic (adjective gradation and present perfect/simple past verb tenses). The dependent variable was the participants' achievement across the evaluations measured by mean scores. SPSS was used to conduct descriptive statistical analysis, with a focus on mean scores obtained in evaluation tasks and inter-group comparisons using independent samples t-tests and one-way ANOVA tests. Levene's tests were performed to assess whether the assumption of homogeneity of variances was met for the ANOVAs. Acceptable probability levels for these parametric tests were set at $p \leq 0.05$.

8.4 Results and Discussion

To address RQ1 regarding the effectiveness of PT and CA, regardless of the grammar topic taught, the entire sample (i.e., all participants from Study 1 and Study 2) was divided into two groups: an experimental group in which two teaching units based on PT were applied, and a control group exposed to two teaching units employing the CA (see Table 8.4).

Table 8.4 Descriptive statistics of the sample population

				Std.	Std.
	Group	N	Mean	deviation	error
Participants' mean score	Control group	241	5.48	2.34	0.15
	Experimental group	145	6.13	1.75	0.15

Note N represents the total number of responses obtained by participants in both Study 1 and Study 2

As Table 8.4 shows, the mean scores obtained in the evaluation tasks by the experimental group exposed to PT were slightly higher ($M = 6.13$) compared to those obtained in the control group ($M = 5.48$). An independent samples t-test was conducted to determine if these differences in means were statistically significant at the $p \leq 0.05$ level. As seen in Table 8.5, Levene's Test indicated that equality of variances could not be assumed. However, the mean difference of -0.65 between the two groups was found to be statistically significant ($p = 0.00$) which supports the assumption that the application of teaching units based on PT yields slightly higher results than the application of the teaching units based on CA.

Given the statistically significant difference in favor of the experimental group (PT), and to address the second research question (RQ2) concerning significant differences in mean scores related to the specific grammar topic, the sample was subsequently divided into four groups, as shown in Table 8.6. This was based on the examined grammar topic and participants' affiliation with either the experimental or the control group.

Considering the implemented methodology, it can be observed that the mean scores in the experimental groups 1 and 2 ($M = 6.43$ and 5.70, respectively) again slightly surpass those in control groups 1 and 2 ($M = 5.86$ and 5.06). Regarding the grammar topic, both experimental and control groups exhibit marginally superior results in adjective gradation compared to the present perfect/simple past tense. To ascertain the statistical significance of these differences, a one-way ANOVA was conducted with the grouping variables of experimental groups 1 and 2 and control

Table 8.5 Independent samples t-test for the control and experimental groups

		Levene's test		T-test				95% confidence interval of the difference	
		F	Sig.	t	df	Sig. 2-tailed	Mean difference	Std. error mean difference	Lower	Upper
Participants' Mean Score	Equality of variances	12.66	0.000*	−2.91	384.00	0.00	−0.65	0.22	−1.09	−0.21
	Difference of variances			−3.12	365.96	0.00	−0.65	0.21	−1.06	−0.24

Table 8.6 Descriptive statistics of the sample population

Participants' mean score	N	Mean	Std. deviation	Std. error deviation	95% confidence interval for the mean		Min	Max
					Lower	Upper		
Control group 1 (Study 1, adj. gradation)	126	5.86	2.49	0.22	5.418	6.296	0.275	9.400
Experimental group 1 (Study 1, adj. gradation)	85	6.43	1.69	0.18	6.069	6.798	2.625	9.300
Control group 2 (Study 2, PP/simple past)	115	5.06	2.09	0.20	4.671	5.443	0.000	8.788
Experimental group 2 (Study 2, PP/simple past)	60	5.70	1.76	0.23	5.242	6.150	1.025	9.375
Total	386	5.72	2.16	0.11	5.505	5.936	0.000	9.400

groups 1 and 2. Table 8.7 indicates that the differences in the mean scores of the participants were statistically significant.

The ANOVA results revealed a statistically significant difference in the means among the designated groups ($p = 0.000$) (Table 8.7). However, upon conducting the Tukey HSD as shown in Table 8.8, statistically significant differences were observed solely between control group 2 (present perfect/simple past) and experimental group 1 (adjective gradation) ($p = 0.000$), as well as control group 1 (adjective gradation) and control group 2 (present perfect/simple past) ($p = 0.018$), as illustrated in Tables 8.8 and 8.9.

Concerning whether statistically significant differences exist between the results obtained by participants with either methodology regarding the grammar structures, post-hoc analysis (Table 8.9) reveals that there are neither statistically significant differences between control group Study 1 (adjective gradation) and experimental group Study 1 (adjective

Table 8.7 One-way ANOVA test

Participants' mean score

	Sum of squares	df	Root mean square	F	Sig.
Between groups	96.23	3	32.07	7.23	0.000*
Within groups	1694.80	382	4.44		
Total	1791.03	385			

Table 8.8 Tukey HSD

Participants' mean score

			$\propto\ = 0.05$	
	Group	N	1	2
Tukey HSD	Control group 2 (Study 2, PP/simple past)	115	5.057	
	Experimental group 2 (Study 2, PP/simple past)	60	5.696	5.696
	Control group 1 (Study 1, adj. gradation)	126	5.857	5.857
	Experimental group 1 (Study 1, adj. gradation)	85		6.434
	Sig.		0.057	0.093

Note Means for groups in homogeneous subsets are displayed

Table 8.9 Post-hoc analysis

Multiple comparisons

	Dependent variable: participants' mean score		Mean difference (I – J)	Std. error deviation	Sig.	95% confidence interval	
						Lower	Upper
Tukey HSD	Control group 1 (Study 1, adj. gradation)	Experimental group 1	−0.577	0.296	0.209	−1.339	0.186
		Control group 2	0.800	0.272	0.018*	0.099	1.501
		Experimental group 2	0.161	0.330	0.962	−0.692	1.013
	Experimental group 1 (Study 1, adj. gradation)	Control group 1	0.577	0.296	0.209	−0.186	1.339
		Control group 2	1.377	0.301	0.000*	0.599	2.154
		Experimental group 2	0.737	0.355	0.163	−0.179	1.654
	Control group 2 (Study 2, PP/simple past)	Control group 1	−0.800	0.272	0.018*	−1.501	−0.099
		Experimental group 1	−1.377	0.301	0.000*	−2.154	−0.599
		Experimental group 2	−0.639	0.335	0.228	−1.505	0.226
	Experimental group 2 (Study 2, PP/simple past)	Control group 1	−0.161	0.330	0.962	−1.013	0.692
		Experimental group 1	−0.737	0.355	0.163	−1.654	0.179
		Control group 2	0.639	0.335	0.228	−0.226	1.505

Note * mean difference significant at the $p \leq 0.05$ level

gradation) ($p = 0.209$), nor between control group Study 2 (PP/simple past) and experimental group Study 2 (PP/simple past) ($p = 0.228$).

In summary, no statistically significant differences were identified in the mean scores obtained by participants in the control and experimental groups when differentiating between the grammar topics. In essence, both PT and the CA demonstrated equal effectiveness in the acquisition of adjective gradation and present perfect/simple past tense.

To address RQ3 concerning the impact of PT and CA on the frequency of intralingual and interlingual errors among participants, Alexopoulou's (2006) error taxonomy was employed, resulting in the subsequent categorization of error types related to adjective gradation and present perfect/simple past tense (see Table 8.10).

To conduct the EA, a subsample was created from each school's control and experimental groups based on the median value of the participants' mean scores. This approach was chosen to avoid potential bias that could arise from selecting high or low performers which tend to produce a very low or very high number of errors. For Study 1 (adjective gradation), the subsample included 14 participants (7 from the control group and 7 from the experimental group). Study 2 (PP/simple past) comprised 18 participants (9 from the control group and 9 from the experimental group). In both studies, error profiles were generated for each participant in the subsample, and the total number of errors was calculated for each error type for the control group and the experimental group.

In regard to adjective gradation (Study 1), the findings indicated that the experimental group exhibited a slightly higher overall frequency of simplification (SPL_1), overgeneralization (OG_1), hypercorrection (HC_1), and ignorance of rule restriction (IRR_1) errors resulting from omission or avoidance of error detection compared to the control group.

In the case of cross-association errors (CrA) and IRR_1 errors related to ignorance of rule restrictions, the error frequency of the experimental group is slightly lower than that of the control group. While these findings suggest a positive effect of PT on the correct association of comparatives and superlatives and the assimilation of rule restrictions, it is important to note again that the numerical differences between the results of the experimental group and the control group in the studied subsample are small (Fig. 8.1).

Table 8.10 Error patterns

Type of error		Definition	Example
Study 1 Adj. gradation	Interference (IF₁)	Redundancy of comparative and superlative structures	*more taller than; *the most faster
	Simplification (SPL₁)	Omission of particles (than/the)	Her trainer says she is *best player
	Overgeneralization (OG₁)	Deviant structures in synthetic comparatives and superlatives	He is *more rich than Arthur
	Hypercorrection (HC₁)	Deviant structure in analytic comparatives and superlatives	My bed is *incomfortabler than the sofa
	Cross-association (CrA)	• Confusion over superiority comparatives and superlatives • Deviant structure in comparisons of equality • Deviant structure in inferiority comparatives	I'd like to have *the faster car *Joe is as intelligent than his teacher *less higher than
	Ignorance of Rule Restrictions (IRR₁)	• Unawareness of grammatical rules for irregular adjectives • Avoidance of error detection and correction	*gooder than; *the most clever
Study 2 PP/simple past	Interference (IF₂)	• Inadequacy between simple past and time adverbs (so far, just, yet, still, already) • Incorrect choice of simple past for unfinished actions and time periods	*I didn't see that film yet *John never understood the present perfect (he's still alive)

(continued)

Table 8.10 (continued)

Type of error	Definition	Example
Overgeneralization (OG$_2$)	• Wrong position of auxiliary verbs and time adverbs in present perfect tense structures	*I **never have tasted** champagne
Hypercorrection (HC$_2$)	Deviant structure in irregular verbs for simple past and present perfect tenses	*Our cat **brang** home a mouse
	Deviant structure in simple past interrogative and negative sentences	***Did you were** at home last night?
Ignorance of Rule Restrictions (IRR$_2$)	• Incorrect choice of present perfect for finished actions and time periods	*What **have you done** at the weekend?
	• Incorrect choice of simple past for past actions still in force	How often ***did you travel** till now?
Simplification (SPL$_2$)	Failure to use past participles or auxiliary verbs in present perfect sentences	He never ***seen** the ocean
Overgeneralization (OG$_3$)	Deviant structure in present perfect with main verbs in simple present or base form	***Have you eat** Thai food before?
Incomplete Application of the Rules (AIR)	Deviant structure in 0 with main verbs in simple past	***Have you ever rode** an elephant?
Neutralization (NTR)	Number disagreement in present perfect auxiliary verbs	*Nobody **have ever succeeded**

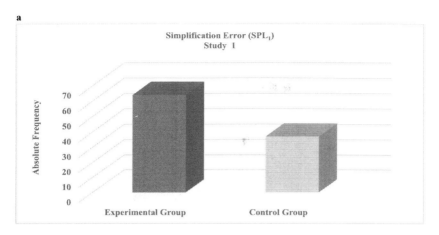

Fig. 8.1   Absolute error frequency: adjective gradation (Study 1)

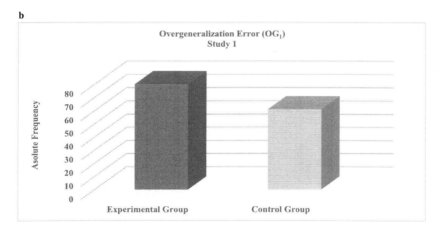

Fig. 8.1   (continued)

Moreover, the error profiles of the selected participants of the experimental group and the control group largely coincide, thereby emphasizing that both methodologies yield very similar results within the subsample (Fig. 8.2).

c

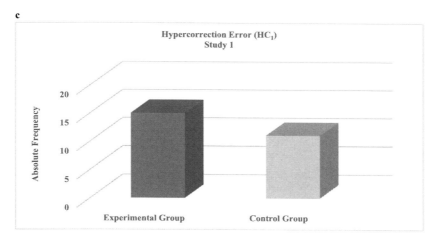

Fig. 8.1 (continued)

d

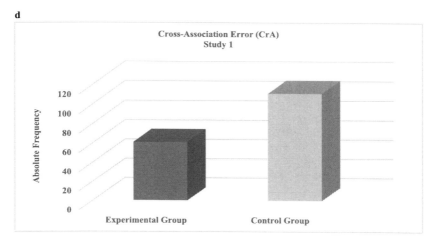

Fig. 8.1 (continued)

In the EA conducted in Study 2 (PP/simple past), the experimental group exhibited a reduced occurrence of interference errors (IF), corroborating the assertion of González Davies and Celaya Villanueva (1992) that PT can contribute to mitigating IF. In terms of intralingual errors,

e

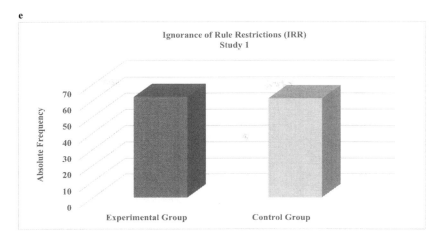

Fig. 8.1   (continued)

the total frequency of errors in overgeneralization (OG_2), hypercorrection (HC_2), incomplete application of rules (IAR), neutralization (NTR), and ignorance of rule restrictions (IRR_2), the results slightly

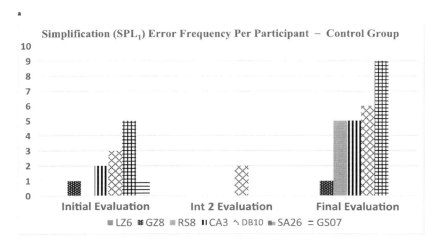

Fig. 8.2   Participants' error profiles: adjective gradation (Study 1)

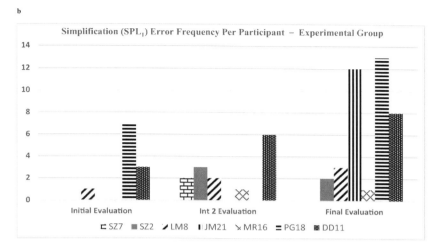

Fig. 8.2 (continued)

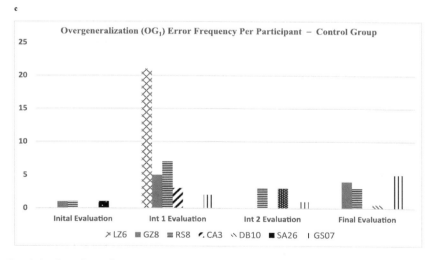

Fig. 8.2 (continued)

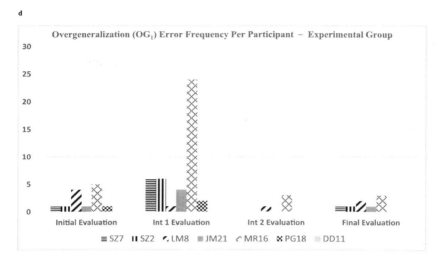

Fig. 8.2   (continued)

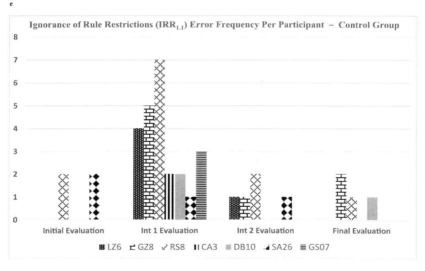

Fig. 8.2   (continued)

f

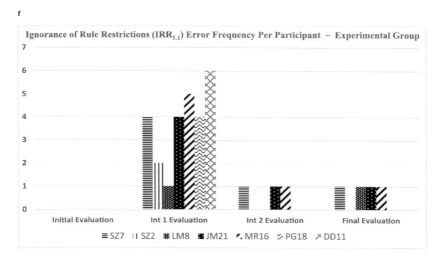

Fig. 8.2 (continued)

favor the control group (Fig. 8.3). However, it is essential to note that this difference again is marginal.

a

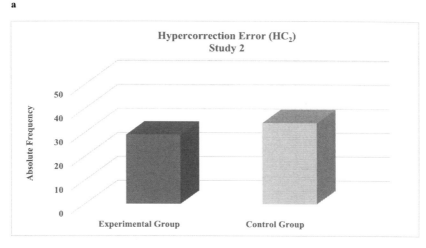

Fig. 8.3 Absolute error frequency: present perfect/simple past tense (Study 2)

b

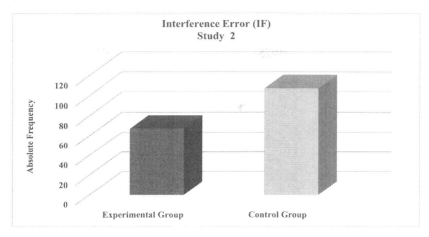

Fig. 8.3 (continued)

c

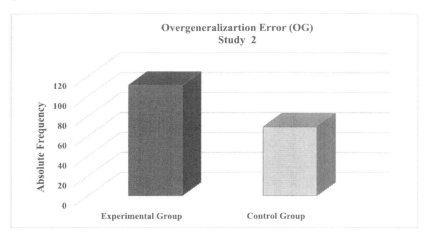

Fig. 8.3 (continued)

d

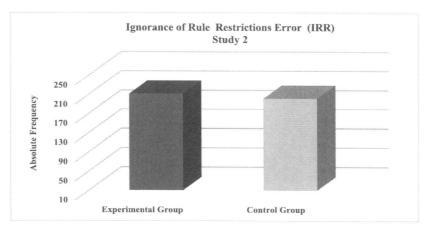

Fig. 8.3 (continued)

e

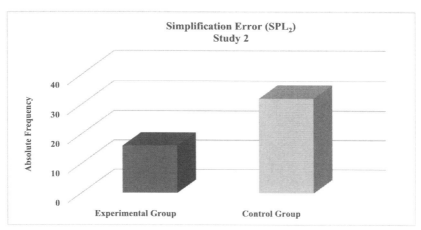

Fig. 8.3 (continued)

The error profiles in Study 2 indicated a convergence in the minimum and maximum error ranges per participant within both the experimental and control groups. Moreover, the error profiles of participants once again demonstrated a notable degree of homogeneity, as illustrated by the examples provided in Fig. 8.4.

After analyzing the overall error frequencies and error profiles of the participants within the subsample, the final synthesis of the EA indicates that PT outperforms CA in Study 1 regarding certain types of errors (SPL_1, OG_1, HC_1, and IRR_1), and in Study 2 regarding the occurrence of interference errors (IF). However, the magnitude of these differences is modest. Consequently, they suggest the equal effectiveness of both approaches, which aligns closely with the findings of the statistical analysis, revealing equal effectiveness of PT and CA in acquiring adjective gradation and present perfect/simple past tense.

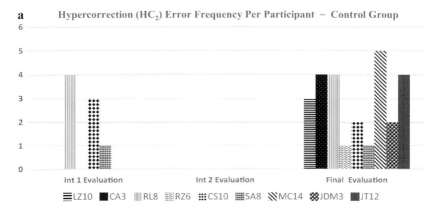

a   Hypercorrection (HC_2) Error Frequency Per Participant − Control Group

Fig. 8.4 Participants' error profiles: present perfect/simple past tense (Study 2)

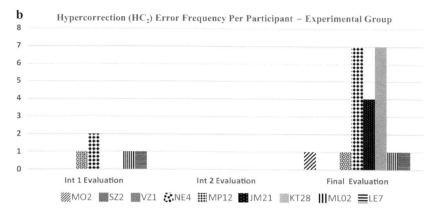

Fig. 8.4 (continued)

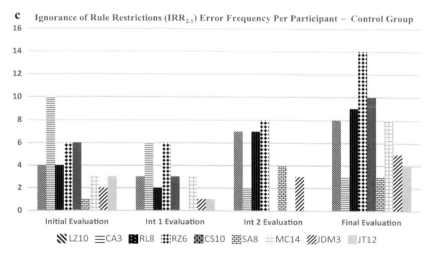

Fig. 8.4 (continued)

8.5   Conclusion

The current study aimed to contribute to the reevaluation of PT in FLL and teaching and sought to provide empirical insights into the application of translation as a pedagogical instrument within the context of

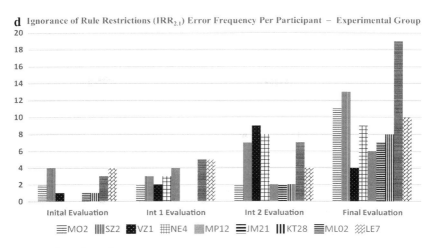

d Ignorance of Rule Restrictions (IRR$_{2.1}$) Error Frequency Per Participant – Experimental Group

Fig. 8.4 (continued)

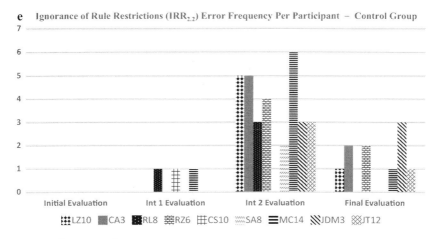

e Ignorance of Rule Restrictions (IRR$_{2.2}$) Error Frequency Per Participant – Control Group

Fig. 8.4 (continued)

the EFL secondary education classroom in Spain. To attain this objective, teaching units were developed for PT and CA ensuring uniformity in terms of learning activities and evaluation tasks. These units targeted two distinct grammar structures—adjective gradation and the present

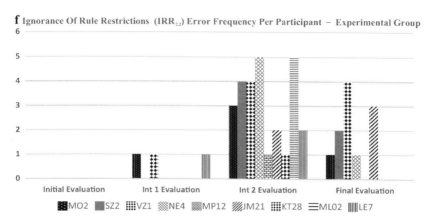

f Ignorance Of Rule Restrictions (IRR$_{2.2}$) Error Frequency Per Participant – Experimental Group

Fig. 8.4 (continued)

perfect/simple past tense—as integral components of the EFL syllabus in Spanish secondary education.

Quantitative analysis of the entire sample disclosed a slight superiority in the results obtained through the application of teaching units based on PT in comparison to those grounded in CA. However, it is crucial to note that this difference lacks statistical significance when considering the mean scores obtained by participants in the control and experimental groups, particularly in relation to the examined grammar structures.

The assessment of errors, employing Alexopoulou's (2006) error taxonomy, further supported these findings. The overall error frequencies, error range, and error profiles exhibited strikingly similar outcomes between the application of PT and CA for the subsample and the linguistic aspects in question.

In summary, both the statistical analysis of mean scores and the subsequent EA converge in highlighting the comparable effectiveness of PT and CA. Thus, our study suggests that PT is equally effective as CA in facilitating the acquisition of both the present perfect/simple past tense and the gradation of adjectives among the examined sample of Spanish early-stage learners of English.

In light of these findings and the acknowledgment that learners naturally leverage their linguistic experience by engaging in translation "as a general pragmatic process", so that eventually "learning and translating become essentially the same thing" (Widdowson, 2014, p. 237), the importance of translation in the FL classroom becomes evident. In conclusion, the following quote from Malmkjær (1998) may serve as a fitting closure to our study:

> All of this is not intended as an argument that all foreign language teaching be carried out through translation. It is intended only as an argument that translation might profitably be used as one among several methods of actually teaching language. (p. 9)

References

Alexopoulou, A. (2006). Los criterios descriptivo y etiológico en la clasificación de los errores del hablante no nativo: Una nueva perspectiva. *Porta Linguarum: Revista Internacional de Didáctica de las Lenguas Extranjeras, 5*, 17–35. https://doi.org/10.30827/digibug.30431

Arbuckle, F. (1990). Translation into the second language in language teaching and for professional purposes. In G. Anderman & M. Rogers (Eds.), *Translation in teaching and teaching translation* (pp. 23–32). University of Surrey.

Carreres, A., & Noriega Sánchez, M. (2013). Traducción pedagógica y pedagogía de la traducción: un diálogo necesario. In B. Blecua, B. S. Borrell, B. Crous, & F. Sierra (Eds.), *Plurilingüismo y enseñanza de ELE en contextos multiculturales: XXIII Congreso Internacional ASELE* (pp. 253–261). Asociación para la Enseñanza del Español como Lengua Extranjera (ASELE).

Colina, S. (2002). Second language acquisition, language teaching and translation studies. *The Translator, 8*(1), 1–24. https://doi.org/10.1080/13556509.2002.10799114

Colina, S., & Angelelli, C. V. (2015). Translation and interpreting pedagogy. In C. V. Angelelli & B. J. Bear (Eds.), *Researching translation and interpreting* (pp. 108–117). Routledge.

Cook, G. (2007). A thing of the future: Translation in language learning. *International Journal of Applied Linguistics, 17*(3), 396–401. https://doi.org/10.1111/j.1473-4192.2007.00160.x

Cook, G. (2010). Translation in language teaching: An argument for reassessment. *ELT Journal, 65*(2), 192–193. https://doi.org/10.1093/elt/ccr007

Corder, S. P. (1967). The significance of learners' errors. *International Review of Applied Linguistics in Language Teaching, 5*(1–4), 161–170. https://doi.org/10.1515/iral.1967.5.1-4.161

Corder, S. P. (1971). Idiosyncratic dialects and error analysis. *International Review of Applied Linguistics in Language Teaching, 9*(2), 147–160. https://doi.org/10.1515/iral.1971.9.2.147

Corder, S. P. (1975). Error analysis, interlanguage and second language acquisition. *Language Teaching & Linguistics: Abstracts, 8*(4), 201–218. https://doi.org/10.1017/s0261444800002822

De Arriba García, C. (1998). Uso de la traducción en clase de lenguas extranjeras: La traducción pedagógica. In P. Orero Clavero (Ed.), *Actes III Congrés Internacional sobre Traducció* (pp. 519–529). Universidad Autónoma de Barcelona. https://dialnet.unirioja.es/servlet/articulo?codigo=7894236

De Biase, A. (2006). *Problemas conceptuales en el aprendizaje de segundas lenguas: La adquisición del 'present perfect simple' para los hablantes de español: Un caso paradigmático* (Unpublished doctoral dissertation). Universidad Autónoma de Madrid. http://hdl.handle.net/10486/2619

Faerch, C., & Kasper, G. (1983). Plans and strategies in foreign language communication. In C. Faerch & G. Kasper (Eds.), *Strategies in interlanguage communication* (pp. 20–60). Longman.

González Davies, M., & Celaya Villanueva, M. L. (1992). *New teachers in a new education system: A guidebook for the reforma.* Promociones Publicaciones Universitarias.

Klaudy, K. (2003). *Languages in translation.* Scholastica.

La Rocca, M. (2007). *El taller de traducción como metodología didáctica experimental en un marco epistemológico socioconstructivista y humanista* (Unpublished doctoral dissertation). Universidad de Vic. http://dspace.uvic.cat/xmlui/bitstream/handle/10854/1724/treinv_a2004_larocca_marcela_taller.pdf?sequence=

Leonardi, V. (2010). *The role of pedagogical translation in second language acquisition.* Peter Lang.

Malmkjær, K. (Ed.). (1998). *Translation and language teaching: Language teaching and translation.* Jerome Publishing.

Newson, D. (1998). Translation and foreign language learning. In K. Malmkjær (Ed.), *Translation and language teaching: Language teaching and translation* (pp. 63–68). St. Jerome Publishing.

Pintado Gutiérrez, L. (2018). Translation in language teaching, pedagogical translation, and code-switching: Restructuring the boundaries. *The Language Learning Journal, 49*(2), 219–239. https://doi.org/10.1080/095 71736.2018.1534260

Richards, J. C. (1974). *Error analysis: Perspectives on second language acquisition.* Longman.

Sánchez Cuadrado, A. (2015). *Aprendizaje formal de ELE mediante actividades cooperativas de traducción pedagógica con atención a la forma* (Unpublished doctoral dissertation). Universidad de Granada. https://digibug.ugr.es/han dle/10481/41765

Schäffner, C. (1998). Qualification for professional translators: Translation in language teaching versus teaching translation. In K. Malmkjær (Ed.), *Translation and language teaching: Language teaching and translation* (pp. 117– 133). St Jerome Publishing.

Selinker, L. (1972). Interlanguage. *International Review of Applied Linguistics in Language Teaching (IRAL), 10*(1–4), 209–232.

Widdowson, H. G. (2003). *Defining issues in English language teaching.* Oxford University Press.

Widdowson, H. G. (2014). The role of translation in language learning and teaching. In J. House (Ed.), *Translation: A multidisciplinary approach* (pp. 222–240). Palgrave Macmillan. https://doi.org/10.1057/978113702 5487_12

Vermes, A. (2010). Translation in foreign language teaching: A brief overview of pros and cons. *Eger Journal of English Studies, 10*, 83–93. https://ojs.uni-eszterhazy.hu/index.php/ejes/article/view/571/

9

Effects of Translation Practice as Consciousness-Raising on L2 Explicit, L2 Implicit, and Metalinguistic Knowledge

Mehtap Güven Çoban⬚ and Mehmet Akıncı⬚

9.1 Introduction

During the rise of Communicative Language Teaching (CLT) in the 1970s and the early 1980s, second language (L2) teaching methodologies displayed a hesitant approach toward the inclusion of translation as part of L2 instruction. This cautious stance predominantly resulted from the inadequacies of the grammar-translation method (GTM) in achieving desired language learning outcomes. While the use of translation for reading and writing skills was given a prominent role, the importance of spoken skill development was neglected. These practical limitations of GTM, with its overemphasis on grammatical rules, as well as its under-emphasis on providing opportunities to improve communicative skills,

M. Güven Çoban (✉) · M. Akıncı
İstanbul 29 Mayıs University, Istanbul, Turkey
e-mail: mcoban@29mayis.edu.tr

M. Akıncı
e-mail: makinci@29mayis.edu.tr

© The Author(s), under exclusive license to Springer Nature Switzerland AG 2025
D. Coulson and C. Denman (eds.), *Translation, Translanguaging and Machine Translation in Foreign Language Education*,
https://doi.org/10.1007/978-3-031-82174-5_9

171

encouraged educationalists, practitioners, and methodologists to seek a new framework for teaching an L2.

The shift in pedagogic focus gave priority to spoken skills through the use of conversational tasks, including by adopting an inductive approach to grammar teaching and offering phonetic training. This orientation further emphasized listening skills over reading skills. However, it was also stated that the use of a mother tongue (L1) should be substantially avoided, leading to a gradual transition to a monolingual L2 teaching environment. This was the inevitable corollary of the monolingualism principle, positing that translation activities make little contribution to L2 learning, which is due to limited L2 input and encouragement to think in one language before translating into another (Newson, 1998).

A good deal of translation studies and foreign language education research seeks ways of drawing on the merits of translation in language teaching both as a part of language instruction and translator training. The ultimate goal of these studies is, of course, enhanced language acquisition. To this end, Pym et al. (2013) conducted ten case studies in various countries including Finland, China, Spain, Germany, and the UK to investigate the effects of translation on English learning success. The results showed that, based on the 2012 EF Proficiency Index, the use of translation in L2 instruction does not present any drawbacks to language learning. The authors conclude that translation should, therefore, be viewed as both a channel for communication and a new pedagogical method, aiming to prioritize communication while offering learners diverse linguistic and pragmatic contexts for translation practice.

As an additional benefit, the use of translation in language instruction can facilitate learner access to innovative classroom resources, including online machine translation and associated technologies. Moreover, research from scholars such as González-Davies (2017) has highlighted the potential for translation to promote plurilingualism. As such, translation has been suggested as an efficient translanguaging scaffolding strategy for improving language learning and multilingual communicative competence.

Despite these potential benefits, only a limited number of studies have a focus on incorporating translation into FLT curricula (e.g., De Florio-Hansen, 2013; Weydt, 2009; Whyatt, 2009). Of these, Whyatt (2009) and Weydt (2009) both concluded that translation offers a promising foundation for improving L2 proficiency, especially if it is reconceptualized as a tool for overcoming reading comprehension barriers and as a means of gaining higher levels of language control in L2 learners' minds. Developing this stance, De Florio-Hansen (2013) suggests embracing translation in L2 classes to facilitate learners' strategic competence in target language use.

The area of teaching skills-based approaches and/or grammar and lexical items is one that has also only witnessed a limited amount of investigative attention. Studies here include O'Malley and Chamot (1990), who consider translation as a potentially beneficial cognitive strategy for reading, while Koletnik Korošec (2013) reports that translation can play a valuable role in language teaching for advanced level learners.

As the above indicates, the frequently debated "proper" position of translation in FLT has continued to evolve as teaching methods have themselves developed and changed. This is explicitly evidenced by recent discussions about the reintroduction of translation into foreign language instruction (Kerr, 2014; Machida & Schaubroeck, 2011; Pintado Gutiérrez, 2019; Vermes, 2010), which have brought the issue back into the center of FLT once again, this time within the framework of bilingualism/multilingualism.

With reference to this debate, Vermes (2010) reports that translation can potentially serve as a facilitative tool in L2 teaching as it contributes to the development of interlanguage competence. On the other hand, Machida and Schaubroeck (2011) emphasize translation as a holistic approach through which learners can be encouraged to develop increased awareness both of form and meaning leading to improvement in reading and writing skills. The authors further claim that this provides conditions in which learners can strengthen their noticing of linguistic structures. Kerr (2014) also supports the importance of the use of L1 and translation tasks to enhance the bilingual atmosphere in L2 teaching settings.

Similarly, Pintado Gutiérrez (2019) argues for an enlargement of the role of translation in L2 instruction.

These developments indicate new perspectives in extending the merits of language learning and teaching. Additionally, they promise to maintain a more inclusive standpoint for making full use of the bilingual nature of L2 instruction (Cook, 2010; Howatt & Widdowson, 2004). Additionally, it is apparent from the literature that, among researchers and educators, there is a renewed interest in the use of the L1 in FLT settings, especially with regard to teaching grammar structures (Widdowson, 2014). In particular, as of the beginning of the twenty-first century, translation has been re-evaluated with respect to its potential as a consciousness-raising activity (Scheffler, 2013), which can support meaning-focused language use for communicating in an L2 (R. Ellis, 2002).

These perspectives inspired us to undertake this research. Against the background and framework described above, the study aimed to analyze and clarify the effects of the use of translation as a consciousness-raising activity. This was performed through the close examination of the development of linguistic knowledge of Turkish English language learners.

9.2   Literature Review

As outlined above, the general attitude toward translation in the educational philosophy of the twentieth century resulted in it being isolated from FLT approaches and methodologies. The reason for this mainly emerged from the acceptance of monolingualism and communication-oriented perspectives in language teaching. These perspectives can be viewed, in many ways, as a reaction to an earlier era during which teachers and materials writers made wide use of the GTM to teach language, which involved the sole use of translation to learn decontextualized sentences. The outcomes of this method were not considered efficient in terms of fostering communicative language skills.

In communication-oriented teaching approaches, the use and incorporation of L1s into FLT curricula were traditionally considered detrimental since they were believed to lead to interference and negative transfer, thus impeding the rate of progress in L2 learning. In the GTM, teaching grammar was mostly based on the translation of sentences, while communicative aspects were largely neglected. Many linguists, such as Richards (2004) and Stern (1992), do, of course, maintain that grammatical competence is an important component of communicative competence. As a result, despite the widespread demise of the GTM, effective instructional methods for grammar continue to be discussed, especially as they perform a key role in the development of reading and writing skills. In response to these discussions, Thornbury (2001) suggested the teaching of grammar in context, while R. Ellis (2006) argued that instruction should encourage learners to pay explicit attention to certain linguistic forms for metalinguistic comprehension and/or processing in order to internalize grammatical structures. Despite these calls, grammar instruction continues to be undervalued within communication-based curricula.

Although the use of L1 has been excluded from FLT settings for a long time, at present translanguaging is a rising trend in bilingual education. García and Lin (2016) emphasized the potential pedagogical advantages of translanguaging. They emphasize the various advantages it offers: first, it can promote a deeper grasp of the linguistic content; second, it may be efficient in augmenting the learners' participation and engagement in lessons; third, the use of L2s can help the native language to develop as well. Indeed, translanguaging has been applied in classroom environments as an effective tool in empowering L2 instruction (Fang et al., 2022).

Alongside these developments, there has been a great deal of research inviting a reexamination of the role of translation in FLT (e.g., Cook, 2010; Dagilienė, 2012; Ebbert-Hübner & Maas, 2018; Pintado Gutiérrez, 2018). The literature reveals that translation is frequently used for testing and measurement purposes, specifically with a focus on accuracy (Tsagari & Floros, 2013). The post-CLT (post-method) has also opened up a way to create a meaningful place for grammar instruction. Post-CLT refers to an environment where both the strengths and weaknesses of CLT are scrutinized and a more macrostrategic framework is offered (Kumaravadivelu, 2006). There has been a wide acceptance of the pedagogic focus on encouraging students to implicitly learn new languages through contextualized grammar "focus-on-form" syllabi (Long, 1991). In this context, an intense debate has been initiated concerning whether grammar instruction should be carried out explicitly or implicitly (R. Ellis, 1993). The position of grammar instruction within FLT curricula is still under discussion.

A large number of studies have been conducted to investigate the effectiveness of L1 use (DeKeyser, 2005). While some of them find using L1 ineffective, others indicate that including translation as a part of explicit grammar teaching contributes to metalinguistic awareness and knowledge (Koletnik Korošec, 2013). In the post-method era, translation and FLT might be claimed not to stand so far from each other. This position may be supported by the findings of studies in the field of bilingualism stressing that all the linguistic systems in the human brain depend on a shared conceptual system (Grosjean, 2010).

In line with these perspectives, studies on bilingualism reveal that bilinguals tend to code-mix and code-switch for communicative purposes. In the field of translation studies, Nord (2005) claims that, in her functional textual approach, conducting a contrastive analysis of both source text and target texts can facilitate student development of an elaborate and solid awareness of linguistic structures of both languages.

Considering the limited number of studies suggesting the use of translation as a pedagogical instrument within FLT curricula, the present research aims to provide a new perspective to address this gap. The existing negative attitude toward the use of translation predominantly stems from the periods in which the GTM was used to teach language by solely emphasizing and encouraging the use of mechanical translation of decontextualized sentences. It came to be widely accepted, however, that this method of language learning did not result in the fostering of communicative language skills. Recent literature concerning the potential of utilizing translation in FLT settings highlights a number of areas in which translation can make an important contribution to language learning, including in terms of the development of communicative competence.

For example, Kim (2010) describes how the GTM helps learners develop awareness concerning how important accuracy is for achieving high-level skills in written output. Additionally, Dagilienė (2012) claims that translation creates and fosters language awareness as learners make an effort to identify differences in linguistic properties by utilizing and negotiating both the source and target language. The author goes on to state that activities based on the use of translation could be adopted as effective pedagogical tasks and instruments when, and if, they are incorporated into the language learning curriculum as a part of in-class activities designed to improve learners' four main skills (i.e., reading, listening, writing, and speaking) in addition to grammatical competence and lexical knowledge.

Pintado Gutiérrez (2018) points out that integrating translation into FL pedagogy could provide significant benefits as a form of scaffolding to facilitate the early stages of L2 learning, as a complex multi-skill task. Hartmann and Helot (2019) underline the importance of translation as a kind of pedagogical affordance in bilingual education by increasing metalinguistic awareness in foreign language learning. The translingual nature of translation provides multiple tools such as text, context, and intertextuality, while learners focus their attention on various linguistic structures. This cognitive engagement with the text can potentially foster metalinguistic awareness, and interdisciplinary and holistic pedagogic frameworks can pave the way for an innovative reconceptualization of translation in FL pedagogy.

Indeed, Hartmann and Helot (2019) report that translation can act as a significant technique to promote noticing during the learning of grammatical structures in English language learning. Widdowson (2014) suggests all language users are "translators," referring to their ability, to varying degrees, to interpret the given text, and context to extract pragmatic meanings. According to the author, it is natural for learners to seek ways to interpret knowledge to infer meaning and extract the message from the text and discourse. This capability is considered a skill to be mastered through practice resulting in an enriched multilingual repertoire. Leonardi (2010) introduced the term "pedagogical translation" into foreign language learning and teaching contexts. Since its introduction, the concept has come to the fore as a way of improving learners' metalinguistic and intralinguistic knowledge (Li, 2018) by utilizing the didactic aspect of translation to facilitate learning processes.

Based on extensive analysis of the research literature, Ebbert-Hübner and Maas (2018) conclude that translation has the potential to bring about improvement in learners' grammatical knowledge, especially in the area of tenses, prepositions, and cognates, even if the evidence is inconclusive about its effect on accuracy in spontaneous language production. As a result, they propose translation as a useful pedagogical tool that could be given a prominent place in FLT curricula. In addition to its linguistic affordances, Adil (2020) suggests that the use of translation, particularly in the earlier stages of language learning, increases learner motivation which can help compensate for their limited linguistic competence.

Overall, as the above overview indicates, although the use of translation in applied linguistics has been marginalized for a very long time, a paradigm shift has started toward the adoption of a more comprehensive perspective in today's bilingual/multilingual world. Despite this, there remains relatively little research investigating what translation might potentially offer in terms of providing cognitive, pedagogical, and functional support for language learning processes. The present study aims to help fill this gap by investigating the effects of translation practice on promoting consciousness-raising and the development of linguistic structures in L2 explicit, implicit, and metalinguistic knowledge.

9.3   Methodology

9.3.1   Research Design

The overarching goal of the present study is to elucidate whether translation practice, as a means of consciousness-raising, positively impacts the acquisition of linguistic structures. To this end, it aims to investigate the following research questions: (i) Does translation practice improve learners' L2 implicit and/or explicit knowledge? (ii) Does translation practice contribute to improvement in learners' metalinguistic knowledge?

In the pre-test post-test design, data were collected through the use of tests designed to measure implicit and explicit knowledge. Metalinguistic knowledge tests were also administered at the beginning and the end of the study period.

9.3.2 Participants

Participants in this study were 74 Turkish learners of English at the B1 level of the Common European Framework Reference for Languages (CEFR). These participants were selected from a pool of 600 high school graduates enrolled in the English Language Preparatory Program at İstanbul 29 Mayıs University. The university primarily conducts instruction in Turkish, with some courses offered in English. To proceed to their faculty studies across approximately 17 different departments, students are required to obtain a passing score on the institutional proficiency test, which is equivalent to a score of 78 in TOEFL iBT. A convenience sampling method was employed in this study due to the researchers' affiliation with the research site university.

Prior to data collection, official permission was obtained to conduct the study from the relevant university authorities. Participants signed an informed consent form which outlined the research aims, steps taken to ensure respondent confidentiality, the voluntary nature of participation, and their right to withdraw at any stage. The researchers were not teaching on the participants' academic program during the study period.

Students from four B1-level classes agreed to participate in the research. Two of these classes, comprising 41 students, constituted the experimental group, while the other two classes, with 33 students, were assigned to the control group. As stated above, although both groups were aware that they were part of a study and of its general aims, they were not explicitly informed about the expected outcomes of the translation-based practice. This was to help avoid the Hawthorne effect.

The experimental group received translation-based practice activities targeting relatively difficult grammar structures, including tenses, past-present-future aspects, gerunds and infinitives, modal verbs, passive voice, conditionals, and reported speech. These activities consisted of tasks such as the translation of sentences from Turkish to English or vice versa, choosing the best translation for a given sentence, completing the translation of a sentence, and finding the best Turkish or English equivalent for a particular structure. Instruction was provided across six weeks, with six hours of study each week. In contrast, the control group spent the same amount of time engaged in regular L2 grammar practice activities on the same syntactic structures. These activities included fill-in-the-blank and rewriting exercises, and multiple-choice questions. These were all conducted in English.

9.3.3   Materials and Instruments

The translation-based study materials encompassed a range of tasks. The tasks included multiple-choice questions that require selecting the correct translation of a given sentence from Turkish to English or vice versa, open-ended exercises that ask for the translation of individual sentences, dialogues, or paragraphs, and fill-in-the-blank exercises that involve completing partially translated sentences.

To measure the outcomes before and after the intervention, three of R. Ellis's (2009) tests were administered to both the experimental and control groups in a counterbalanced order: a timed grammaticality judgment test for implicit knowledge; an untimed one for explicit knowledge; and a metalinguistic knowledge test for metalinguistic knowledge. The timed grammaticality judgment test, delivered via computer, consists of 34 sentences (equally divided between grammatical and ungrammatical) where participants indicate the grammaticality of each sentence within a fixed time limit, with each item worth one point. The untimed grammaticality judgment test follows the same format but features different sentences and no time limit. The metalinguistic knowledge test includes 15 ungrammatical sentences with the target grammar points underlined. Participants had to correct the mistake (one point) and explain the error (one point). The Cronbach alpha reliability coefficients for these tests have been reported in R. Ellis (2005) as $a = 0.81$, 0.83, and 0.90, respectively.

9.3.4 Data Analysis

Dependent variable data were interpreted as interval in nature. Descriptive analysis was initially performed to obtain means, standard deviations, and minimum and maximum scores, while skewness and kurtosis values were calculated to determine if the data were normally distributed. Independent samples t-tests were performed to examine if the experimental and control groups differed from each other on the language tests in a statistically significant way at the start of the study. To assess the effect of intervention, two-way mixed ANOVAs were conducted, while calculations were performed to ensure they met assumptions of normality, homogeneity of variance, and sphericity. The significance level for the t-tests and ANOVAs was set at $p \leq 0.05$.

9.4 Results

Table 9.1 presents descriptive statistics separately for participants in the experimental (i.e., taking translation-oriented exercises) and control (i.e., regular exercises) groups. Overall, despite marginal variations, participants in both groups showed comparable performances at both Time 1 as the pre-test and Time 2 as the post-test.

Table 9.1 Descriptive statistics for both groups at Time 1 and Time 2

Tasks	Time	Group	N	Min	Max	Mean	SD	Skewness	Kurtosis
Implicit	1	Experimental	41	15	31	22.83	3.96	0.28	−0.53
		Control	33	17	33	24.03	4.16	0.27	−0.61
	2	Experimental	41	16	32	23.54	4.09	−0.02	−0.36
		Control	33	16	31	24.24	3.70	−0.26	−0.12
Explicit	1	Experimental	41	18	33	26.24	4.08	−0.11	−0.81
		Control	33	17	34	26.70	4.09	−0.40	−0.47
	2	Experimental	41	20	33	27.76	3.34	−0.71	−0.34
		Control	33	15	33	26.27	4.06	−0.69	0.71
Metalinguistic	1	Experimental	41	2	26	12.22	6.24	0.23	−0.65
		Control	33	4	27	12.52	5.23	0.50	0.19
	2	Experimental	41	3	30	14.41	6.70	0.42	−0.36
		Control	33	5	23	14.18	5.18	−0.05	−0.99

Although there are slight differences between both groups on the measures at Time 1, independent-samples t-tests indicated that there were no statistically significant differences between the groups in their performances across the tasks (implicit: $t(72) = -1.27$, $p > 0.05$; explicit: $t(72) = -0.47$, $p > 0.05$; metalinguistic: $t(72) = -0.22$, $p > 0.05$).

Table 9.2 indicates the correlation matrix for the measures of all participants at both Time 1 and Time 2. All language tasks were correlated with each other. The highest magnitude of correlations was observed between the implicit and explicit tasks at both Time 1 and Time 2.

Concerning the exploration of the interaction between group and time for the enhancement of implicit, explicit, and metalinguistic knowledge, three separate ANOVA analyses were performed. A two-way mixed ANOVA was conducted to investigate the impact of the group and time on implicit knowledge with the group as a between-participants factor, and time as a repeated factor. Regarding preliminary assumption testing, normality, univariate outliers, and homogeneity of variance–covariance matrices were checked and no violations were found. The findings revealed neither interaction between group and time nor the main effects of group or time at the $p \leq 0.05$ level.

To explore the effect of group and time on explicit knowledge, a two-way mixed ANOVA was conducted. Although no main effects of group or time were found, the results indicated an interaction between group and time ($F(1, 72) = 10.07$, $p < 0.01$, Wilks' Lambda $= 0.88$; $\eta^2 =$

Table 9.2 Correlation matrix for the language measures administered at Time 1 and Time 2

	1	2	3	5	6
1. Implicit_T1	1				
2. Explicit_T1	0.727*	1			
3. Metalinguistic_T1	0.559*	0.660*	1		
4. Implicit_T2	0.702*	0.727*	0.543*	1	
5. Explicit_T2	0.563*	0.751*	0.557*	0.611*	1
6. Metalinguistic_T2	0.455*	0.566*	0.779*	0.506*	0.510*

Note T1 (measured in Time 1 as pre-test); T2 (measured in Time 2 as post-test)
*$p < 0.001$

0.123 observed power = 0.88). As can be seen in the graphical represen-
tation in Fig. 9.1, although the mean of the control group was higher at
Time 1, the experimental group showed relatively better performance at
Time 2.

The effect of group and time on metalinguistic knowledge was investigated by conducting a two-way mixed ANOVA. The findings revealed
no interaction between group and time, and no main effect of group.
However, the main effect of time was observed ($F(1, 72) = 17,470$,
$p < 0.001$, Wilks' Lambda = 0.81; $\eta^2 = 0.195$, observed power =
0.97). A pair-wise comparison indicated an enhancement of metalinguistic knowledge of the participants between Time 1 ($M = 12, 37$,
$SE = 0, 68$) and Time 2 ($M = 14, 30$, $SE = 0, 71$).

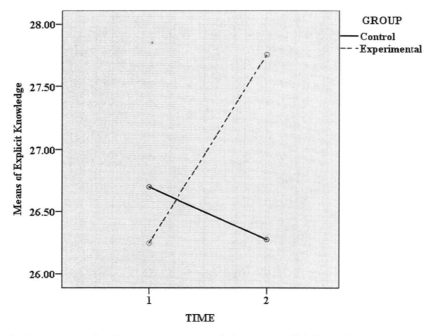

Fig. 9.1 Interaction between group and time on explicit knowledge

9.5   Discussion

The role of translation in FLT and learning has long been disregarded. In the period after the decline in dominance of the GTM, the pedagogic focus shifted to a monolingual approach to develop learners' communicative skills. This mainly resulted from the common assumption that a monolingual approach to FLT is essential to provide learners with contexts in which their primary focus is on target language structures. Considering this assumption, translation or any form of L1 use has been regarded as an interference in the learning process (Widdowson, 2014). In line with this view, from a historical perspective, the paradigm in FLT shifted toward monolingual dominance with the emergence of CLT. In this respect, translation has been seen as a hindrance to language teaching (Cook, 2010).

Following post-CLT (post-method), the importance of referring to learners' L1 in foreign language education has been widely acknowledged. More recently, in light of these developments, grammar teaching approaches have been scrutinized. Fotos and Ellis (1991) investigated the advantages and drawbacks of explicit instruction as consciousness-raising and reported the positive effects of explicit instruction. Similarly, the results of the present study indicate that participants showed better performance in the explicit knowledge test after receiving translation-based practice which enabled them to focus on the linguistic structures through having developed an increased awareness. N. C. Ellis (2005) proposes that implicit learning follows the explicit instruction of linguistic structures. In other words, learners' conscious grasp of grammatical features and forms provides facilitation of the learning processes, which is essential for the acquisition of L2 development. In line with the rationale explained here, the present study also indicates a high correlation between explicit and implicit knowledge.

Similarly, DeKeyser (1998) stated that explicit knowledge advances to implicit knowledge through sufficient amounts of communicative practice. Additionally, as a distinctive part of acquisition processes, noticing plays a prominent role in converting explicit knowledge into implicit knowledge (Schmidt, 1990). Long (1991) and DeKeyser (1998) argue that proceduralization of explicit knowledge can effectively be achieved via the focus-on-forms approach.

Relying upon the results of the present study, enhancement in metalinguistic knowledge witnessed in participants suggests that translation-based activities can be regarded as an essential component in FL curricula to sustain the proceduralization process in learning by encouraging learners to raise their consciousness of grammatical features while employing two languages simultaneously. Findings also reveal that the use of translation in grammar instruction contributes to metalinguistic knowledge by placing explicit attention on forms of the language. The high level of correlation between explicit and implicit knowledge observed here may be attributed to the effect of noticing in converting explicit knowledge into implicit knowledge as part of proceduralization.

These results show a significant enhancement in metalinguistic knowledge among learners after experiencing explicit grammar instruction supported by translation-based activities. As such, it can be inferred that explicit knowledge entails conscious analysis of how linguistic structures and forms function. Being able to explain and understand grammatical rules necessitates a good command of metalinguistic knowledge. Based on this inference, it can be assumed that they are interrelated. Considering the results of the present quasi-experimental investigation, it can also be argued that translation should be revisited and reconceptualized as a pedagogical tool to aid the cognitive processes of L2 acquisition.

9.6   Conclusion and Pedagogical Implications

In conjunction with the rise of bilingualism/multilingualism, a new wave is being observed in the field of applied linguistics. Boundaries are being reconsidered and the question of the usefulness of learners' L1s and the role of translation in L2 acquisition is yet again being raised. The present study has shown that translation practice positively influences the development of explicit knowledge and enhances metalinguistic knowledge. The act of translating involves learners in a deep and detailed analysis of both their L1 and L2. Such cognitive engagement likely provides conscious understanding, especially on relatively complex grammatical structures.

Before drawing final conclusions, however, it is necessary to acknowledge limitations in the current research. For example, the relatively limited sample size means findings may lack external validity, while the focus on only six weeks of class is too short to understand the potential impact of translation-based activities across an entire academic course or program. In this regard, longitudinal research designs may yield more nuanced results. Finally, the opinions of learners, or any other key stakeholders such as teachers and administrators, were not elicited, with test results not giving any real idea about their actual experiences of intervention methods.

However, building on the view that linguistic structures are learned incrementally in a gradual manner through the proceduralization of explicit knowledge (DeKeyser, 1998), results here support the argument that translation may find a place in foreign language programs as a new dimension to facilitate learning, and especially the learning of grammatical features. To this end, a variety of tasks could be designed, ranging from translation of discrete sentences and contextualized short texts to intertextual translation targeting the usage function of specific linguistic items. Overall, translation as a pedagogical tool could potentially enrich both the content and provision of foreign language curricula.

References

Adil, M. (2020). Exploring the role of translation in communicative language teaching or the communicative approach. *SAGE Open, 10*(2). https://doi.org/10.1177/2158244020924403

Cook, G. (2010). *Translation in language teaching*. Oxford University Press.

Dagilienė, I. (2012). Translation as a learning method in English language teaching. *Studies About Languages, 21*, 124–129. https://doi.org/10.5755/j01.sal.0.21.1469

De Florio-Hansen, I. (2013). Translation competence in foreign language learning. Can language methodology benefit from translation studies? *Journal of Linguistics and Language Teaching, 4*(2), 39–68.

DeKeyser, R. M. (1998). Beyond focus on form: Cognitive perspectives on learning and practicing second language grammar. In C. Doughty & J. Williams (Eds.), *Focus on form in classroom second language acquisition* (pp. 42–63). Cambridge University Press.

DeKeyser, R. M. (2005). What makes second-language grammar difficult? A review of issues. *Language Learning, 55*(1), 1–25. https://doi.org/10.1111/j.0023-8333.2005.00294.x

Ebbert-Hübner, C., & Maas, C. (2018). Can translation improve EFL students' grammatical accuracy? *International Journal of English Language and Translation Studies, 5*(4), 191–202.

Ellis, N. C. (2005). At the interface: How explicit knowledge affects implicit language learning. *Studies in Second Language Acquisition, 27*(2), 305–352. https://doi.org/10.1017/S027226310505014X

Ellis, R. (1993). The structural syllabus and second language acquisition. *TESOL Quarterly, 27*(1), 91–113. https://doi.org/10.2307/3586953

Ellis, R. (2002). Grammar teaching: Practice or consciousness-raising? In J. C. Richards & W. A. Renandya (Eds.), *Methodology in language teaching: An anthology of current practice* (pp. 167–174). Cambridge University Press.

Ellis, R. (2005). Measuring implicit and explicit knowledge of a second language: A psychometric study. *Studies in Second Language Acquisition, 27*(2), 141–172.

Ellis, R. (2006). Current issues in the teaching of grammar: An SLA perspective. *TESOL Quarterly, 40*(1), 83–107.

Ellis, R. (2009). Implicit and explicit learning, knowledge and instruction. In R. Ellis, S. Loewen, C. Elder, R. Erlam, J. Philp, & H. Reinder (Eds.), *Implicit and explicit knowledge in second language learning, testing and teaching* (pp. 3–25). Multilingual Matters.

Fang, F., Zhang, L. J., & Sah, P. K. (2022). Translanguaging in language teaching and learning: Current practices and future directions. *RELC Journal, 53*(2), 305–312. https://doi.org/10.1177/00336882221114478

Fotos, S., & Ellis, R. (1991). Communicating about grammar: A task-based approach. *TESOL Quarterly, 25*(4), 605–628. https://doi.org/10.2307/3587079

García, O., & Lin, A. M. Y. (2016). Translanguaging in bilingual education. In O. García & A. M. Y. Lin (Eds.), *Bilingual and multilingual education* (pp. 1–14). Springer.

González-Davies, M. (2017). The use of translation in an Integrated Plurilingual Approach to language learning: Teacher strategies and best practices.

Journal of Spanish Language Teaching, 4(2), 124–135. https://doi.org/10. 1080/23247797.2017.1407168

Grosjean, F. (2010). *Bilingual: Life and reality.* Harvard University Press.

Hartmann, E., & Helot, C. (2019). Pedagogical affordances of translation in bilingual education. In S. Laviosa & M. Gonzalez-Davies (Eds.), *The Routledge handbook of translation and education* (pp. 95–108). Routledge.

Howatt, A. P. R., & Widdowson, H. G. (2004). *A history of English language teaching* (2nd ed.). Oxford University Press.

Kerr, P. (2014). *Translation and own-language activities.* Cambridge University Press.

Kim, E. (2010). Using translation exercises in the communicative EFL writing classroom. *ELT Journal, 65*(2), 154–160. https://doi.org/10.1093/elt/ccq039

Koletnik Korošec, M. (2013). Teaching grammar through translation. In D. Tsigari & G. Floros (Eds.), *Translation in language teaching and assessment* (pp. 23–40). Cambridge Scholars.

Kumaravadivelu, B. (2006). *Understanding language teaching: From method to postmethod.* Lawrence Erlbaum Associates.

Leonardi, V. (2010). *The role of pedagogical translation in second language acquisition.* Peter Lang.

Li, X. (2018). Language enhancement for translation undergraduates: An evaluation of students' reactions to and effectiveness of a comparable and parallel text analysis course. *Journal of Multilingual and Multicultural Development, 39*(6), 475–490. https://doi.org/10.1080/01434632.2018.1439948

Long, M. (1991). Focus on form: A design feature in language teaching methodology. In K. De Bot, R. Ginsberg, & C. Kramsch (Eds.), *Foreign language research in cross-cultural perspectives* (pp. 39–52). John Benjamins. https://doi.org/10.1075/sibil.2.07lon

Machida, M., & Schaubroeck, J. (2011). The role of self-efficacy beliefs in leader development. *Journal of Leadership & Organizational Studies, 18*(4), 459–468. https://doi.org/10.1177/1548051811404419

Newson, D. (1998). Translation and foreign language learning. In K. Malmkjær (Ed.), *Translation and language teaching: Language teaching and translation* (pp. 63–68). St. Jerome Publishing.

Nord, C. (2005). *Text analysis in translation: Theory, methodology, and didactic application of a model for translation-oriented text analysis* (2nd ed.). Rodopi.

O'Malley, J. M., & Chamot, A. U. (1990). *Learning strategies in second language acquisition.* Cambridge University Press.

Pintado Gutiérrez, L. (2018). Translation in language teaching, pedagogical translation, and code-switching: Restructuring the boundaries. *The Language Learning Journal, 49*(2), 219–239. https://doi.org/10.1080/095 71736.2018.1534260

Pintado Gutiérrez, L. (2019). Mapping translation in foreign language teaching: Demystifying the construct. In M. Koletnik & N. Froeliger (Eds.), *Translating and language teaching: Continuing the dialogue* (pp. 23–38). Cambridge Scholars.

Pym, A., Malmkjaer, K., & Gutiérrez-Colon Plana, M. (2013). *Translation and language learning: The role of translation in the teaching of languages in the European Union.* Publications Office of the European Union. https://doi. org/10.2782/13783

Richards, J. (2004). *Approaches and methods in language teaching.* Cambridge University Press.

Scheffler, P. (2013). Learners' perceptions of grammar-translation as consciousness raising. *Language Awareness, 22*(3), 255–269. https://doi.org/10.1080/ 09658416.2012.703673

Schmidt, R. W. (1990). The role of consciousness in second language learning. *Applied Linguistics, 11*(2), 129–158. https://doi.org/10.1093/app lin/11.2.129

Stern, H. H. (1992). *Issues and options in language teaching* (P. Allen & B. Harley, Eds.). Oxford University Press.

Thornbury, S. (2001). *Uncovering grammar.* McMillan Heinemann.

Tsagari, D., & Floros, G. (2013). *Translation in language teaching and assessment.* Cambridge Scholars Press.

Vermes, A. (2010). Translation in foreign language teaching: A brief overview of pros and cons. *Eger Journal of English Studies, 10,* 83–93.

Weydt, H. (2009). Reading books with translations: Getting over the reading barrier. In A. Witte, T. Harden, & A. Ramos de Oliveira Harden (Eds.), *Translation in second language learning and teaching* (pp. 291–308). Peter Lang.

Whyatt, B. (2009). Translating as a way of improving language control in the mind of an L2 learner: Assets, requirements and challenges of translation tasks. In A. Witte, T. Harden, & A. Ramos de Oliveira Harden (Eds.), *Translation in second language learning and teaching* (pp. 181–202). Peter Lang.

Widdowson, H. G. (2014). The role of translation in language learning and teaching. In J. House (Ed.), *Translation: A multidisciplinary approach* (pp. 220–240). Palgrave Macmillan. https://doi.org/10.1057/978113702 5487_12

10

Techniques to Assess University Students' Translation Tasks: The Challenge of Closing the Feedback Loop

Zahra El Aouri[iD]

10.1 Introduction

In higher education, much emphasis is placed on the importance of assessing students' performance because assessment is critical to the teaching/learning process and determines whether or not curriculum objectives have been met. As teachers, we need to assess the effectiveness of our teaching by measuring to what extent our students are learning the course material and meeting course objectives. To do so, we need to ask ourselves some vital questions, such as: Are we teaching what we planned to teach? Are our students learning what they are supposed to be learning? Is there a better way to teach the course material in order to promote better learning?

The concept of assessment is most of the time confused, if not used interchangeably, with other terms such as evaluation and testing.

Z. El Aouri (✉)
Cadi Ayyad University, Marrakesh, Morocco
e-mail: z.elaouri@uca.ac.ma

© The Author(s), under exclusive license to Springer Nature
Switzerland AG 2025
D. Coulson and C. Denman (eds.), *Translation, Translanguaging and Machine Translation in Foreign Language Education*,
https://doi.org/10.1007/978-3-031-82174-5_10

These terms may intersect with assessment as, according to Mundrake (2000, p. 45), "assessment, testing, and evaluation are terms used to describe the outcomes of the educational process". Furthermore, Brown (2004) defines assessment as "any act of interpreting information about student performance, collected through any of a multitude of a means or practices" (p. 304).

In fact, the role of student assessment is to reinforce teachers' critical reflection on their teaching practices. According to Brookfield (2017), this critical reflection on teaching, which results from assessment, is crucial for teachers to develop themselves as educators and enhance their students' learning experiences. Thus, through critical reflective teaching, instructors develop a sense of commitment toward their teaching practice, colleagues, and students. As Brookfield claims, "Critically reflective teachers are well placed to communicate to colleagues and students the rationale behind their practice. They work from a position of informed commitment and convey a confidence-inducing sense of purpose" (2017, p. 81). This indicates that student assessment not only enables teachers to reflect upon and evaluate the effectiveness of their teaching, but also helps them develop the rationale for their pedagogical practices.

Therefore, in the present chapter, the focus is on the techniques used in translation assessment, with a special focus on formative assessment and the concept of feedback in translation teaching. The chapter is divided into five sections. The first presents the two types of assessment—summative and formative—although it is more concerned with the latter. In the second section, the concept of feedback in formative assessment of translation is highlighted, while the third section deals with the techniques used to deliver feedback in translation teaching. The challenge of closing the feedback loop in the translation classroom is the focus of the fourth section, with the fifth being devoted to recommendations for pedagogical practice and academic research in translation.

10.2   Types of Assessment

In the existing body of literature, different forms of assessment are described, although two types are particularly common, especially in language teaching: summative assessment and formative assessment. The focus in this chapter is on formative assessment, due to the fact that it is more closely linked to the concept of feedback than summative assessment.

Summative assessment, which is principally concerned with learning outcomes, occurs at the end of a course of study and has the main purpose of producing a measure to sum up students' learning, usually in the form of grades. This type is an assessment *for* learning. Formative assessment, on the other hand, is an assessment *of* learning, and it occurs during the teaching/learning process and aims to estimate students' achievement and progress in light of the set objectives of the course. Formative assessment is an ongoing process in which teachers gather evidence from various feedback sources such as teacher-student communication, classroom observations, general classroom discussions, peer feedback, self-assessment, and group-work oriented feedback. Then, teachers use it in their instruction either to modify their teaching practices in ways that meet students' needs, or to evaluate students' progress toward achieving course objectives (Black & Wiliam, 1998; Boston, 2002). Through formative assessment, teachers lead learners to "understand their strengths and weaknesses and to reflect on how they need to improve over the course of their remaining studies" (Maki, 2002, p. 11).

The main purpose of formative assessment is to provide immediate feedback on students' achievement, especially individual students' progress in terms of what they did or did not learn, as well as in terms of what they can or cannot do. Hence, formative assessment elicits information about "what, how much, and how well students are learning" (Angelo & Cross, 1993, p. 5). Another purpose of formative assessment concerns instructional effectiveness; that is, through formative assessment and the interaction that takes place between teachers and students, teachers can assess whether their instruction is effective or not. Based on this assessment of instructional effectiveness, teachers can either modify their instruction methods or re-teach the points that they feel are not effectively presented. The main differences between formative and summative assessments are summarized in Table 10.1.

Both summative and formative assessments are helpful in improving student learning. However, research evidence indicates that the latter is usually more effective because teachers can use it to keep students on track and make adjustments to advance the learning process (Wiliam, 2010). This is why Andrade and Heritage (2018, p. 5) state, "Grades and scores stop the action in a classroom: Feedback keeps it moving forward". This implies that formative assessment is more important than summative assessment when it comes to the enhancement of student learning. Black and Wiliam (2009, p. 9) confirm the effectiveness of formative assessment when stating:

> Practice in a classroom is formative to the extent that evidence about student achievement is elicited, interpreted, and used by teachers, learners, or their peers, to make decisions about the next steps in instruction that are likely to be better, or better founded, than the decisions they would have taken in the absence of the evidence that was elicited.

Table 10.1 Overview of formative and summative assessments

Formative assessment	Summative assessment
– is immediately implemented while learning is taking place	– is implemented by the end of a learning period
– focuses on the learning process	– focuses on the end-product of learning
– is an integral part of the teaching/learning process	– is implemented separately from the teaching/learning process
– is a fluid and ongoing process guided by students' needs and teachers' feedback	– is a rigid and static measurement of students' achievement
– involves interaction and collaboration between teachers and students to assess learning progress and check the learning objectives through exchanged feedback	– involves teachers directing and dictating what students must do to complete a certain examination
– has feedback used by teachers and students to make adjustments for continuous improvement of teaching and learning	– has results used by teachers to make pass or fail decisions

A number of researchers support the myriad of merits of formative assessment (see Black & Wiliam, 1998; Hatfield & Gorman, 2000; Steadman, 1998) as teachers use its results to evaluate students' work by highlighting their points of strength and weakness in relation to course objectives. Moreover, formative assessment can be used to increase communication and collaboration between teachers and learners, which leads to changes in instructional practices and meeting students' learning needs. Another potential merit of formative assessment is that it aims to enhance students' learning and growth by providing feedback to facilitate their progress toward achieving learning objectives. Thus, formative assessment targets the quality of learning (Andrade & Cizek, 2010; Shute, 2008).

In addition, formative assessment engages students actively in the learning process, which develops their self-regulation habits (Andrade, 2010) because they try to monitor their learning progress and identify gaps they need to bridge with the help of the feedback received. This makes formative assessment motivating because, when students receive detailed feedback on their work highlighting both well-done parts and those requiring improvement, they become more motivated and interested in the task (Cimpian et al., 2007).

In brief, formative assessment lays emphasis on the critical role of feedback, described as essential for successful teaching and learning (Hattie, 2012). It serves as a vital link between teaching and learning processes, enabling both instructors and students to assess progress and make necessary adjustments (Andrade & Heritage, 2018). Effective feedback not only helps teachers in evaluating their instructional effectiveness, but also supports students in improving their learning performance by identifying strengths and areas of weakness that still need development (Stiggins, 2002). This ongoing interaction fosters motivation and enhances academic achievement, underscoring the importance of formative assessment (Black & Wiliam, 1998).

10.3 Feedback in Formative Assessment of Translation Tasks

Given the potential value of formative assessment in the classroom as discussed above, for instructors of translation to develop students' translation competence, they have to put emphasis on this form of assessment, especially in terms of feedback, as it is the driving force of developing this competence. Fowler (2007) accentuates this point by stating that "the competence development in translators mainly derives from formative assessment" (p. 254).

On the whole, feedback generated through formative assessment can serve both translation teachers and their students in many ways. It can increase student performance when implemented effectively in the flow of learning. It can also increase students' achievement and motivation to take their learning forward. This formative assessment is used by teachers to identify students' capabilities and the areas they excel at, in addition to identifying what learners still need to work on to improve their performance. Furthermore, teachers may use the results of feedback to identify students who are in need of support. Teachers can use formative feedback to reflect on students' progress and modify their teaching practices or instructional methods accordingly (Boston, 2002; Ellis, 2009; Hattie, 2012). In brief, feedback in formative assessment can come from different sources, including teachers, students themselves, and their peers. Teachers receive feedback about their teaching and their students' learning from the things they notice while learning is taking place. In the same way, students receive feedback from their teachers, their peers, and their own self-assessment during the learning process.

10.4 Feedback Techniques in Assessing Translation

Feedback has been described as "the most powerful single moderator that enhances achievement" (Hattie, 1992, p. 9). As a result, it is often an integral part of translation instruction, with successful teachers using a variety of feedback techniques to formatively assess students' translation tasks in the classroom, including teacher feedback, self-assessment, and peer assessment feedback.

10.4.1 Teacher Feedback

Teachers may provide feedback while their students are engaged in translation activities. This teacher feedback can be one-on-one, especially while students are performing a task, or can be collective feedback when the whole class is engaged in negotiating alternatives in translating the source text and trying to make decisions about the final target text. Teachers use a variety of ways to provide their feedback, such as observing individual students' accuracy and commenting on their translations, inquiring about the ideas students have come up with individually, including adjustments made after conferring with classmates about their versions, and engaging in discussions with learners about their translations, thereby creating a triadic (e.g., teacher-student-student) interaction.

Feedback from teachers serves students in different ways. It provides them with hints or cues that draw their attention and help them focus on the translation task. It can also work as a prompt for students to use certain techniques, such as exploring contextual elements of the source text, highlighting key terms, selecting appropriate translation methods, and using dictionaries and glossaries to successfully complete the translation task. Furthermore, teacher feedback can be a motivational source for students to invest more effort in developing their translation skills.

Nevertheless, teacher feedback remains ineffective unless students engage with it (e.g., Handley et al., 2011; Yu et al., 2019; Zheng & Yu, 2018), which makes promoting this engagement a fruitful pedagogical method in teaching translation (Bruton, 2007; Sheen & Ellis, 2011; Washbourne, 2014). Feedback from teachers can enhance students' translation abilities (Sheen & Ellis, 2011), enrich and develop their vocabulary bank (Bruton, 2007), and boost their active learning (Washbourne, 2014).

10.4.2 Self-Assessment Feedback

According to Andrade and Heritage (2018, p. 87), "Teachers are not the sole source of judgment of student learning in the classroom" as there are other sources such as peer- and self-assessment through which students can, under the right conditions, analyze their learning and find ways to improve. Thus, another feedback technique that can be used in addition to teacher feedback is self-assessment, which involves students reflecting on, and evaluating, the quality of their work, assessing how well they meet specific goals or criteria, recognizing strengths and weaknesses in their performance, and making revisions and improvements based on their evaluations (Andrade & Du, 2007).

The purpose of using this technique in a translation course is to help students develop their own judgment of their performance on translation tasks because, as Bourke (2016) claims, "Developing learners' ability to self-assess will contribute to an understanding of themselves and their learning in a fundamental way, often not possible through other assessment practices" (p. 108). Furthermore, through self-assessment, students assess both how they translate and their translation as an end-product. That is, self-assessment is geared toward assessing the process and the product of learning how to translate. In this way, students develop a sense of control over their learning both as process and product, which supports them in developing autonomy in their learning. In this respect, Black et al. (2003) state that students "develop an overview of [their] work so that it becomes possible for them to manage and control it" (p. 49).

Self-assessment helps students develop self-regulation skills in their learning. Further, it also assists teachers in providing specific suggestions about the translation task to promote student competence in translation. As Harris (1997) states, self-assessment "encourages the student to become part of the whole process of language learning, and to be aware of individual progress" (p. 15). Through self-assessment, students learn for themselves how to move up to the next step in their learning, and how to internalize the process, because learning cannot be done for them by their teachers. In this regard, James and Gipps (1998) claim that "the teacher is expected to teach, but only students can do the learning which takes place in their minds" (p. 287).

10.4.3   Peer Assessment Feedback

Alongside self-assessment, peer assessment is a collaborative technique of providing feedback in the translation classroom. This technique can even be a scaffolding basis for self-assessment. As Black et al. (2003) state, "Peer-assessment turns out to be an important complement and may even be a prior requirement for self-assessment" (p. 50). Through this technique, students evaluate each other's translations and can provide a certain degree of feedback by either raising points of weakness in their peers' translations, or by offering a better alternative to certain parts of their peers' versions. This technique is a very active form of feedback because it allows students to interact with each other and pay more attention to the process of learning how to translate. Therefore, peer assessment enables students to "share with one another the experiences that they have undertaken" (Brown & Knight, 1994, p. 52).

Perkins (2003) developed a protocol of peer assessment called the *Ladder of Feedback*, which consists of four steps as shown in Fig. 10.1.

Perkins states that each step on the Ladder of Feedback is equally important. In the first step, the student delivering the feedback asks questions to clarify any unclear points noticed in their peers' versions and understand the output better, while also encouraging further student-student interaction. These clarification questions are intended to seek more information about the provisionally complete task of translation, but not to praise or criticize. It helps students make sound evaluations of their own work and that of their peers, thus providing effective feedback to each other.

In the second step, the student providing the feedback specifies the parts they value about the work. This helps develop their peer's awareness of the strong points of their translated text and offers encouragement and motivation to move forward in their learning. In the third step, the deliverer of feedback expresses any concerns about their peer's rendition

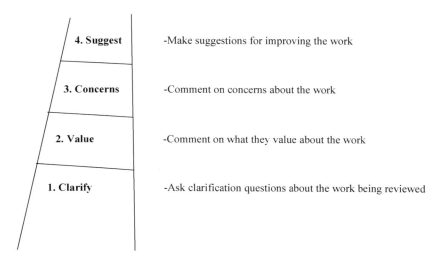

Fig. 10.1 The Ladder of Feedback adapted from Perkins (2003)

of the source text. In this step, students who deliver feedback should be careful with the language they use to express their concerns. They have to choose language for delivering constructive feedback that will improve their peer's work rather than damaging their self-confidence.

In the fourth step, the student who provides feedback offers suggestions on how to improve the work. Again, using language carefully to express these suggestions is of utmost importance because students need to feel that their peers are fellow collaborators in enhancing the quality of their translations, rather than being made to feel that they are being ordered what to do.

Therefore, the Ladder of Feedback can be used as a protocol for providing communicative feedback about an unclear point, or behavior, during the learning process. As Perkins (2003) states:

> Communicative feedback clarifies the idea or behavior under consideration, so that everyone is talking about the same thing. It communicates positive features so that they can be preserved and built on. It communicates concerns and suggestions toward improvement. (p. 46)

In my translation class, I employ the Ladder of Feedback protocol. This involves asking my students to translate a text and to share their versions with their peers. Then, I ask students to raise questions about their peers' work and provide positive comments as well as suggestions for improvements. Next, as described above, the student whose work is being assessed reflects and acts upon the feedback received. This approach allows peer assessment to be an opportunity for high achievers to provide help for less able students, thus ensuring effectiveness for the whole class.

10.4.4 The Challenge of Closing the Feedback Loop in the Translation Classroom

The feedback loop refers to the process of checking students' understanding of what teachers present as content and receiving responses from students. The feedback loop aims to move learning forward. It is initiated by overtly communicating the objective of the task to students. Following this, students engage in the task before presenting their work and exchanging feedback, perhaps in a bidirectional (teacher-student or student-student) or triadic way.

Of course, when feedback is exchanged, students are given time to revise their work and enact the feedback. By the end of this process comes the time to close the feedback loop through students' responses and reflections on the extent to which the task has been successfully accomplished. The feedback loop process is driven by both teachers and students via interaction and collaboration. When feedback loops are effective, everyone benefits. That is, students who receive feedback try to identify strong points in their work and areas where they need to improve.

Students who initiate feedback may develop their self-confidence and come to appreciate the extent of the growth in their learning. Those who observe and listen to feedback benefit from their peers' work and may even view examples of excellent achievement as models to follow. Further, teachers who initiate or simply guide the feedback on offer gain insights about the effectiveness of their instruction and, as a result, either consolidate their teaching practice or modify their teaching methods. Effective feedback loops help students to actively engage in learning, build a strong communication bridge with their teachers and peers, develop metacognitive skills as they learn how to learn, and nurture student agency as they become active owners of their learning and develop self-regulated habits.

In any teaching/learning process, there is always a feedback loop that teachers are challenged to close through effective feedback enabling students to learn from their previous work and develop their skills. This feedback loop is an iterative and continual process involving both teachers and students, with the feedback cycle continuing with each new task. For any feedback loop to be efficiently closed, it should start with instructor feedback and finish with the students' appropriate responses (Barker & Pinard, 2014; Washbourne, 2014).

In order to close the feedback loop, instructors should seek recurrent responses from students to the enacted feedback. For example, teachers may ask their students to respond to the feedback issued by trying either to correct their translation, to retranslate and resubmit their work, or to prepare an oral response for the given feedback. In this way, instructors can overcome the challenge of closing the feedback loop since students' translation skills are enhanced resulting in increased translation competence. When feedback is recurrent, it is more effective (Barker & Pinard, 2014) because it allows students to reflect on their learning process and consequently improve their performance.

Closing a particular feedback loop is important for tackling specific parts of a translation task. However, allowing the cycle to continue, thus creating a continuous cyclical feedback loop to facilitate improvement beyond the given task, is crucial as it allows students to transfer old feedback to other translation tasks. This, as a result, deepens their learning because classroom feedback is "a key practice for both teachers and students to support deeper learning and the development of learning competencies" (Andrade & Heritage, 2018, p. 2). As a result, any feedback cannot meet its goal of formative assessment unless it is actively employed by students to develop their learning skills (Sadler, 2010; Selvaraj & Azman, 2020; Tsagari, 2019).

10.4.5 Recommendations for Pedagogical Practice and Academic Research in Translation

Teaching translation to university students is not an easy task for teachers, and this is especially true when seeking to use different techniques to provide feedback. Further, it is vital to check student understanding of what the instructor planned to teach. To illustrate this point, I will provide a scenario from my own practice in the translation class. To begin, I give a source text to students to translate either from English to Arabic or vice versa. While students are engaging in the task, I assist and facilitate by providing prompts to individual students, pairs, or small groups. When students finish their translation, one volunteers to read their translation, and the whole class listens actively in order to respond later. I try to provide different types of feedback to the student by first asking their peers to comment on the translation, and let the student interact with them. Then, I ask the student to self-assess their work before I provide my own constructive feedback as a last step in the feedback process.

Regardless of the feedback technique used, the challenge of closing feedback loops in learning remains very important because it provides evidence for the instructor of the extent to which the objectives of the teaching unit have been met. In light of the discussion presented in this chapter, the following pedagogical recommendations are offered:

1. Any translation task executed by students should be immediately followed by effective and constructive feedback that students use to move their learning forward and be productive.
2. Students should appropriately implement the received feedback and clearly express their responses.
3. Teachers should urge their students to take an active position in the feedback loop and avoid responding passively to feedback. They should enable them to take in feedback and respond to it in an interactive environment to improve their learning.
4. Teachers should encourage students to support one another by being learning resources for each other and provide peer feedback

because cooperative and collaborative learning has concrete benefits in boosting student performance.

5. Teachers should focus on activating students' agency by encouraging them to become owners of their learning.
6. Teachers should involve all students in opening and closing the feedback loop so that the feedback provided proves effective in boosting students' performance.

In addition to these pedagogical suggestions, these are some further recommendations for academic research in translation:

1. More research is still needed in the area of assessment of student translations, especially in the Moroccan context.
2. As researchers, we need to investigate the effectiveness of summative and formative assessments in diverse translation contexts, especially through the use of comparative research designs.
3. It is also necessary to explore the different feedback techniques teachers use in the translation classroom and find out how these techniques impact students' translation competence.
4. As instructors of translation, we can collaborate and exchange our experiences of teaching translation and face the challenge of closing the feedback loop in translation tasks. This collaboration and exchange of teaching experiences can be done through organizing/attending workshops, round tables, and conferences that have a concern with this specific area.

10.5 Conclusion

Assessment plays a pivotal role in any educational context, which makes it essential for teachers to equip themselves with sufficient knowledge of its different types in order to develop their teaching practices, support their students' learning and respond to their needs, and, finally, meet the requirements of the curriculum. Therefore, assessment remains the most important way to measure student learning and performance in the translation classroom. This means that it should be at the heart of the teaching/learning process through the use of feedback, which acts best as a well-timed interaction between teachers and students concerning an idea or output occurring in the learning process.

Formative feedback should be both constructive and effective in order to boost students' learning and promote their active engagement in the translation classroom. To achieve this, feedback should be generated from different sources, including teacher feedback, peer assessment feedback, and self-assessment feedback.

The implementation of any feedback technique in the translation classroom should engage students and make them responsible for their own learning and, hence, help them become autonomous learners. In fact, involving students in assessing their own learning through self-assessment or peer assessment turns the whole class into an interactive environment, thereby providing an opportunity for teachers to discover more about their students. That is, through student involvement in the feedback process, teachers receive feedback on their own teaching practices via students' questions, comments, opinions, and so on, which makes feedback reciprocal and effective.

Creating feedback loops remains one of the most important methods for ensuring effective student involvement in feedback. However, feedback loops are at the same time challenging as they cannot be effective and fruitful unless they are successfully closed. Teachers must face such challenges, however, by closing these loops, thereby consolidating the impact of feedback on students' learning and validating the entire process. The closure of feedback loops, in fact, guarantees that insights—whether gained through teacher-, peer- or self-assessment—are acted upon and improvements are implemented. This continuous cycle of feedback and response fosters a culture of classroom collaboration, which is essential for nurturing a supportive learning environment where students' agency is celebrated and their voices are both heard and valued.

References

Andrade, H. L. (2010). Students as the definitive source of formative assessment: Academic self-assessment and the self-regulation of learning. In H. L. Andrade & G. J. Cizek (Eds.), *Handbook of formative assessment* (pp. 90–105). Routledge.

Andrade, H. L., & Cizek, G. J. (2010). *Handbook of formative assessment*. Routledge.

Andrade, H. L., & Du, Y. (2007). Student responses to criteria-referenced self-assessment. *Assessment & Evaluation in Higher Education, 32*(2), 159–181. https://doi.org/10.1080/02602930600801928

Andrade, H. L., & Heritage, M. (2018). *Using formative assessment to enhance learning achievement, and academic self-regulation.* Routledge.

Angelo, T. A., & Cross, P. K. (1993). *Classroom assessment techniques: A handbook for college teachers.* Jossey-Bass.

Barker, M., & Pinard, M. (2014). Closing the feedback loop? Iterative feedback between tutor and student in coursework assessments. *Assessment & Evaluation in Higher Education, 39*(8), 899–915. https://doi.org/10.1080/02602938.2013.875985

Black, P., Harrison, C., Lee, C., Marshall, B., & Wiliam, D. (2003). *Assessment for learning: Putting it into practice.* Open University Press.

Black, P., & Wiliam, D. (1998). Assessment and classroom learning. *Assessment in Education: Principles, Policy and Practice, 5*(1), 7–74. https://doi.org/10.1080/0969595980050102

Black, P., & Wiliam, D. (2009). Developing the theory of formative assessment. *Educational Assessment, Evaluation and Accountability, 21*(1), 5–31. https://doi.org/10.1007/s11092-008-9068-5

Boston, C. (2002). The concept of formative assessment. *Practical Assessment, Research, and Evaluation, 8*(9). https://doi.org/10.7275/kmcq-dj31

Bourke, R. (2016). Liberating the learner through self-assessment. *Cambridge Journal of Education, 46*(1), 97–111. https://doi.org/10.1080/0305764X.2015.1015963

Brookfield, S. D. (2017). *Becoming a critically reflective teacher* (2nd ed.). Jossey-Bass.

Brown, G. T. L. (2004). Teachers' conceptions of assessment: Implications for policy and professional development. *Assessment in Education: Principles, Policy & Practice, 11*(3), 301–318. https://doi.org/10.1080/0969594042000304609

Brown, S., & Knight, P. (1994). *Assessing learners in higher education*. Rout-ledge.

Bruton, A. (2007). Vocabulary learning from dictionary referencing and language feedback in EFL translational writing. *Language Teaching Research, 11*(4), 413–431. https://doi.org/10.1177/1362168807080961

Cimpian, A., Arce, H. M., Markman, E. M., & Dweck, C. S. (2007). Subtle linguistic cues affect children's motivation. *Psychological Science, 18*(4), 314–316. https://doi.org/10.1111/j.1467-9280.2007.01896.x

Ellis, R. (2009). Corrective feedback and teacher development. *L2 Journal, 1*(1), 3–18. https://doi.org/10.5070/l2.v1i1.9054

Fowler, Y. (2007). Formative assessment: Using peer and self-assessment in interpreter training. In C. Wadensjo, B. E. Dimitrova, & A.-L. Nilsson (Eds.), *The critical link 4: Professionalisation of interpreting in the community* (pp. 253–262). John Benjamins.

Handley, K., Price, M., & Millar, J. (2011). Beyond 'doing time': Investi-gating the concept of student engagement with feedback. *Oxford Review of Education, 37*(4), 543–560. https://doi.org/10.1080/03054985.2011.604951

Harris, M. (1997). Self-assessment of language learning in formal settings. *ELT Journal, 51*(1), 12–20. https://doi.org/10.1093/elt/51.1.12

Hatfield, S. R., & Gorman, K. L. (2000). Assessment in education—The past, present, and future. In J. Rucker (Ed.), *Assessment in business education* (pp. 1–10). National Business Education Association. https://eric.ed.gov/?id=ED441080

Hattie, J. (1992). Measuring the effects of schooling. *Australian Journal of Education, 36*(1), 5–13. https://doi.org/10.1177/000494419203600102

Hattie, J. (2012). *Visible learning for teachers: Maximizing impact on learning*. Routledge.

James, M., & Gipps, C. (1998). Broadening the basis of assessment to prevent the narrowing of learning. *The Curriculum Journal, 9*(3), 285–297. https://doi.org/10.1080/0958517970090303

Maki, P. L. (2002). Developing an assessment plan to learn about student learning. *The Journal of Academic Librarianship, 28*(1), 8–13. https://doi.org/10.1016/S0099-1333(01)00295-6

Mundrake, G. A. (2000). The evolution of assessment, testing, and evaluation. In J. Rucker (Ed.), *Assessment in business education* (pp. 39–47). National Business Education Association. https://eric.ed.gov/?id=ED441080

Perkins, D. (2003). *King Arthur's round table: How collaborative conversations create smart organizations*. Wiley.

Sadler, D. R. (2010). Beyond feedback: Developing student capability in complex appraisal. *Assessment & Evaluation in Higher Education, 35*(5), 535–550. https://doi.org/10.1080/02602930903541015

Selvaraj, A. M., & Azman, H. (2020). Reframing the effectiveness of feedback in improving teaching and learning achievement. *International Journal of Evaluation and Research in Education (IJERE), 9*(4), 1055–1062. https://doi.org/10.11591/ijere.v9i4.20654

Sheen, Y., & Ellis, R. (2011). Corrective feedback in language teaching. In E. Hinkel (Ed.), *Handbook of research in second language teaching and learning* (pp. 593–610). Routledge.

Shute, V. J. (2008). Focus on formative feedback. *Review of Educational Research, 78*(1), 153–189. https://doi.org/10.3102/0034654307313795

Steadman, M. (1998). Using classroom assessment to change both teaching and learning. *New Directions for Teaching and Learning, 75*, 23–35. https://doi.org/10.1002/tl.7503

Stiggins, R. J. (2002). Assessment crisis: The absence of assessment for learning. *PhiDelta Kappan, 83*(10), 758–765. https://doi.org/10.1177/003172170208301010

Tsagari, D. (2019). Interface between feedback, assessment and distance learning written assignments. *Research Papers in Language Teaching and Learning, 10*(1), 72–99. https://rpltl.eap.gr/images/2019/10-01-072-TSAGARI.pdf

Washbourne, K. (2014). Beyond error marking: Written corrective feedback for a dialogic pedagogy in translator training. *The Interpreter and Translator Trainer, 8*(2), 240–256. https://doi.org/10.1080/1750399X.2014.908554

Wiliam, D. (2010). An integrative summary of the research literature and implications for a new theory of formative assessment. In H. L. Andrade & G. J. Cizek (Eds.), *Handbook of formative assessment* (pp. 18–40). Routledge.

Yu, S., Zhang, Y., Zheng, Y., Yuan, K., & Zhang, L. (2019). Understanding student engagement with peer feedback on master's theses: A Macau study. *Assessment and Evaluation in Higher Education, 44*(1), 50–65. https://doi.org/10.1080/02602938.2018.1467879

Zheng, Y., & Yu, S. (2018). Student engagement with teacher written corrective feedback in EFL writing: A case study of Chinese lower-proficiency students. *Assessing Writing, 37*, 13–24. https://doi.org/10.1016/j.asw.2018.03.001

Part II

Translanguaging in Foreign Language Learning

11

Mapping Research on Translanguaging in Language Assessment

Liubov Darzhinova and David Singleton

11.1 Introduction

Deriving from the Welsh term "trawsieithu" coined by C. Williams, the initial definition of *translanguaging* referred to the routine of reading in one language and writing in another, representing bilingual education practices in Wales (Baker, 2001). Translanguaging was also defined as the "use of a home/community language during a lesson, ... or code-switching [that] can be considered as a strategic means to improve message comprehension" (Marsh et al., 2001, p. 25). Ferguson (2003,

L. Darzhinova (✉)
Graduate School, The Education University of Hong Kong, Hong Kong, China
e-mail: liubovdarzh@eduhk.hk

D. Singleton
School of Linguistic, Speech and Communication Sciences, Trinity College Dublin, University of Dublin, Dublin, Ireland
e-mail: dsnglton@tcd.ie

D. Coulson and C. Denman (eds.), *Translation, Translanguaging and Machine Translation in Foreign Language Education*,
https://doi.org/10.1007/978-3-031-82174-5_11

p. 48) described translanguaging as "having input in one language and output (speaking and writing) in another". These three definitions foreshadow the contemporary integrated model of translanguaging (MacSwan, 2017), which views code-switching as a part of translanguaging, assuming there is a distinction between the cognitive linguistic systems.

Translanguaging was then conceptualised by some as going beyond dominant languages: "The teacher introduces a topic in the majority language and then makes some remarks in the minority language, or … hand-outs and work sheets are in one language and class activities are carried out in the other language" (Bourguet, 2006, p. 643). The multimodal nature of communication was also a part of the early understanding of translanguaging:

> [It is] a language teaching technique where the input of a lesson is in one language and the output is in another. For example, the teacher teaches science concepts through ASL [American Sign Language] then the students write a summary of the lesson in English. Or the students read a passage in English, then engage in a discussion in ASL. (Li, 2005, p. xix)

Having evolved since its emergence in academic literature in 2001, translanguaging is now defined by some as the fluid and dynamic use of the various linguistic resources available to construct meaning and communicate, whether those resources are languages other than the dominant or target language (Cenoz & Gorter, 2017). Some studies (e.g., Charamba, 2020; Yasar Yuzlu & Dikilitas, 2022) argue that translanguaging positively affects language learning by involving the use of multiple languages and promoting more effective communication. Others point to the adverse effects of translanguaging: it may weaken academic performance due to increased cognitive load (Wang, 2021) or threaten language revitalisation (Leonet et al., 2017). Hence, translanguaging does not appear to be conceived as a straightforwardly positive or negative phenomenon (Singleton & Flynn, 2022).

Given the continuously increasing body of work on translanguaging, it is necessary to review it to clarify the trajectory of future research endeavours and practical applications. Adopting a systematic review approach, a recent study (Özkaynak, 2023) examined translanguaging research published between 2008 and 2022. The study found that translanguaging practices are employed for educational purposes, such as supporting language and content learning in multilingual classrooms, and have also been observed to contribute to constructing social identities and fostering inclusive classroom environments. Additionally, translanguaging is seen as a socio-political practice, challenging monolingual ideologies and promoting linguistic and social justice.

As for research methodologies, Özkaynak's (2023) review found that various qualitative and quantitative research methods, including ethnographic observations, interviews, surveys, and classroom interventions, are employed in the extant research. Theoretical frameworks, such as sociocultural theory, ecological perspectives, and critical pedagogy, are often used to analyse and interpret the data. Regarding linguistic diversity, the studies cover various languages and linguistic combinations, reflecting the multilingual nature of the educational settings examined. Participants included students, teachers, and other stakeholders from diverse linguistic backgrounds. The review argues that future research needs to move away from viewing translanguaging solely as a language-learning strategy and focus on more varied contexts and uses of translanguaging.

One such context is the domain of language assessment, wherein the utilisation of translanguaging enables test-takers to leverage the full range of their linguistic and extralinguistic resources for effective communication and meaning-making, thereby contributing to a more accurate and comprehensive evaluation of abilities. Accordingly, we have conducted this study as a scoping review (Munn et al., 2018) to identify, map, report, and discuss the existing research on translanguaging in language assessment. A scoping review is a pertinent methodological approach when addressing a research area that has yet to be comprehensively examined (Pham et al., 2014), as is arguably the case with translanguaging in language assessment.

The scoping approach is similar to the systematic approach in that both follow a structured protocol to guide the review process. However, scoping reviews do not aim to confirm or refute relevant evidence-based practices, their feasibility, appropriateness, meaningfulness, or effectiveness, as is the central goal of systematic reviews. Instead, scoping reviews are conducted to pinpoint any trends and knowledge gaps which may inform future research directions. A scoping review often serves as a basis for forthcoming systematic reviews, which have the potential to address specific research questions and examine the topic more narrowly than a scoping review (Munn et al., 2018).

Thus, our scoping review study tackled various dimensions of translanguaging in language assessment; that is, its research foci, manifestations, and geographical and learning contexts. In addition, primary research data, such as author affiliation, source type, title, and citation data, were analysed to determine the most influential studies of translanguaging in language assessment. The following guiding questions were raised:

> **RQ1:** What are the research foci in empirical studies on translanguaging in language assessment?
> **RQ2:** What methods are used to elicit translanguaging in language assessment?
> **RQ3:** In what geographical and learning contexts has translanguaging been used in language assessment?
> **RQ4:** What are the most influential empirical studies on translanguaging in language assessment based on author affiliation, source type, title, place of study, and citation data?

11.2 Method

This study followed the four-step protocol suggested for scoping reviews in second language (L2) research (e.g., Darzhinova & Zou, 2023; Jabbari & Eslami, 2019): (1) determining the search procedure; (2) identifying the search terms; (3) specifying the inclusion criteria; and (4) developing the coding scheme.

11.2.1   Search Procedure

Existing scoping reviews related to multilingualism and language education were checked for their choice of research databases. We found that the typically used databases are Scopus, Web of Science Core Collection, and the Education Resource Information Centre (ERIC) (see Gilanyi et al., 2023, for a scoping review on English as a medium of instruction and Content and Language Integrated Learning (CLIL), and Burner & Carlsen, 2023, for a scoping review on multilingualism in the classroom). These databases were deemed most suitable for identifying empirical studies on translanguaging in language assessment.

11.2.2   Search Terms

The search terms (*assessment*, OR *evaluation*, OR *test*, OR *exam*) AND *translanguaging* were keyed into the search bars of each database. The choice of these very broad terms was premeditated, given that we intended to elicit various types of language assessment. Relevant studies may not explicitly employ the term *language assessment* [*evaluation/ test/exam*] and instead utilise alternative descriptors, such as *formative assessment, assessment of writing*, among others.

11.2.3   Inclusion Criteria

The focus of this scoping review was on studies published during the past ten years, i.e., between 2013 and 2023. The choice of a ten-year period was deliberate for two reasons. First, our initial examination of the literature revealed that empirical research on translanguaging has burgeoned during the past decade. Second, ten years is a substantial yet manageable timeframe that guarantees a representative number of studies for consolidating existing findings (Alsowat, 2017).

This scoping review concentrated on peer-reviewed empirical research published as journal articles and book chapters. Other source types, such as position papers, preprints, or conference papers, were not included, given that they may not have undergone a formal peer-review process.

Whole-length books and dissertations were also not considered, as they are generally more extensive in their scope than articles and chapters.

139 records (as of December 2023) were pinpointed and subjected to the operation of Zotero® referencing software. 13 records were eliminated because of their duplication across the databases. Of the 126 records screened by abstracts and keywords, 44 were excluded on the grounds of not containing empirical research. Additionally, 60 records were removed, owing to their lack of focus on language assessment. Among the 22 records intended for inclusion, one was removed because of the unavailability of its full text. As a result, 21 research outputs from the pool of the retrieved records were retained for the scoping review (see Fig. 11.1).

11.2.4 Coding Scheme

Following Cannon and Marx (2024), we developed a coding scheme consisting of categories or variables of interest that correspond to our guiding questions. The coding scheme development followed a recursive approach, i.e., continuously refining categories based on content- and data-based considerations. Content-based considerations included the research foci addressed (RQ1), data elicitation methods employed (RQ2), and the learning and geographical contexts involved (RQ3). Data-based considerations encompassed the identification of author affiliations, source types, titles, where the study was published, and citation data (RQ4).

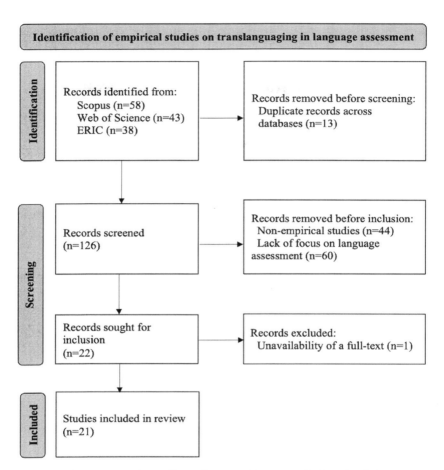

Fig. 11.1 The PRISMA 2020 flow diagram (Page et al., 2021) of the scoping review delineates the study identification, screening, and inclusion procedure

11.3 Results

11.3.1 What Are the Research Foci in Empirical Studies on Translanguaging in Language Assessment?

The papers were grouped on the basis of their primary focus of investigation, as indicated by keywords, research questions, measurable variables, and findings. We coded the papers into five areas of research focus (see Fig. 11.2). These areas represent various types of language assessments, which aim to evaluate language skills: reading, writing, listening, speaking, or several skills.

As Fig. 11.2 indicates, writing assessment attracted the most research attention in our sample. Chen et al. (2019) examined how multilingual students draw upon diverse linguistic resources, including target and home languages, together with online tools, to enhance the quality of their writing. Gómez and Lewis (2022) analysed the written responses of emergent bilingual students about their use of translanguaging and diverse discourse patterns. Heugh et al. (2017) designed and employed

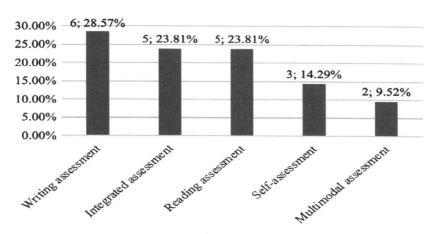

Fig. 11.2 Research foci of the studies included in the scoping review

a diagnostic instrument to capture translanguaging in students' hand-written texts, focusing on the correlation between their primary and target languages and metalinguistic expertise in translation. Schissel et al. (2021) examined the perspectives on translanguaging in classroom assessment of culturally and linguistically diverse students through written reflections of language teachers. Tsai (2022) explored the effectiveness of Google Translate in writing, gauging students' attitudes towards writing, vocabulary usage, content enrichment, and writing performance. Wang and East (2023) investigated the integration of translanguaging into L2 learning assessment, evaluating the performance and perceptions of ab initio L2 learners on online writing tests designed on the basis of the notion of translanguaging. Thus, this first research cluster underscores the rich potential of translanguaging in writing assessment, reflecting a paradigm shift towards more inclusive and effective evaluation practices.

The second cluster of studies focuses on assessing integrated language skills, such as speaking-reading (Bauer et al., 2020), reading-speaking-writing (Mbirimi-Hungwe, 2021), reading-writing (Rafi, 2023), and reading-writing-speaking (Rafi, 2022), in addition to the integration of all these skills (Baker & Hope, 2019). Four studies (Bauer et al., 2020; Mbirimi-Hungwe, 2021; Rafi, 2022, 2023) explored how translanguaging incorporated into language assessment promotes comprehension and meaning-making abilities among English as a second/foreign language (L2/FL) students with diverse proficiency levels in the target language. Baker and Hope (2019) delved into the challenges of integrating translanguaging into language assessments oriented towards university professors, highlighting the vital role of educators in facilitating translanguaging pedagogies. Overall, the studies in the cluster collectively contribute to understanding how translanguaging can be leveraged in integrated language assessment practices, promote inclusivity, and address challenges associated with dominant language ideologies.

The third research cluster collectively investigates the complexities of language use and linguistic resources in the reading assessment of emergent bilingual students. García and Godina (2017) explored cross-linguistic transfer and the correlation between reading levels, oral language proficiencies, and general and bilingual reading strategies. Similarly, Briceño (2021) focused on the influence of language backgrounds on reading behaviours, specifically syntax use, punctuation management, and strategies for complex sentence comprehension. Adding to this body of research, Noguerón-Liu et al. (2020) delved into linguistic strategies, particularly L2 approximations and code-switching observed during bilingual retelling tasks, while López-Velásquez and García (2017) drew attention to code-switching, translation, and paraphrasing practices. Standing apart in this line of research are Ascenzi-Moreno and Seltzer (2021), who analysed teachers' discourse to identify any ideological structures and reading behaviours that shape the reading assessment process of emergent bilinguals.

The common theme woven through the studies in the fourth research cluster is the exploration and implementation of tools for self-assessment. Adamson and Coulson (2015) delved into students' self-assessment of attitudes towards and perceptions of translanguaging policy during course instruction and written assignments. Cavazos and Karaman (2023) developed and validated a questionnaire that measures metalinguistic awareness and translingual dispositions among linguistically diverse students. Wong et al. (2023) explored the development of teacher candidates' translanguaging stances and design knowledge by promoting self-assessment through weekly assignments, self-assessment videos, and collaborative activities throughout the semester.

Turning to the fifth research cluster, the studies in this category concentrate on multimodal language assessment, which involves using different communication modes and resources to help learners showcase their skills in the assessment process. Test-takers may be asked to analyse and interpret such materials as written texts, recordings, videos, visuals, and readings, as part of their receptive skills (reading and listening) evaluation. By combining multiple modalities in language assessment, educators can foster an emotionally engaging and inclusive design that caters to students' diverse learning styles and linguistic abilities (Morales et al., 2020). As for productive skills (speaking and writing), Burgess and Rowsell (2020) advocate a shift from prescriptive and punitive assessment models towards more holistic and agentive methods that consider learners' identities, affect, and embodiment in meaning-making.

By producing written and spoken language, visual images, and digital media, learners can explore and communicate their experiences in ways that extend beyond traditional language skills and assessments.

11.3.2 What Methods Are Used to Elicit Translanguaging in Language Assessment?

As for the choice of data elicitation methods or techniques in the studies included in the scoping review, we established that most ($n =$ 13; 61.90%) employed analyses of written language samples. The most popular method for collecting data involved written reflections or opinions (Baker & Hope, 2019; Gómez & Lewis, 2022; Rafi, 2022, 2023; Schissel et al., 2021; Wong et al., 2023). Other methods used more sparsely were a summarisation task (Mbirimi-Hungwe, 2021), a digital storybook (Burgess & Rowsell, 2020), a written report (Adamson & Coulson, 2015), and a digital composition (Wang & East, 2023). Some studies employed a combination of such methods; for example, in Heugh et al. (2017), students were given four written assignments, as follows: (1) explain and summarise language-learning needs and objectives; (2) write a reflection as a response to a video and reading material; (3) write a film review; and (4) develop interview questions and write a biography. In two studies (Chen et al., 2019; Tsai, 2022), students drafted reflective essays in languages at their disposal, translated them using Google Translate, and revised the translations.

The second most frequently used data elicitation methods were found to be tasks for testing receptive skills ($n = 9$; 42.86%). Out of the nine studies in this category, all but one adopted elicitation via passage reading and associated sub-tasks, e.g., multiple choice and reordering paragraphs (Baker & Hope, 2019; García & Godina, 2017; López-Velásquez & García, 2017; Mbirimi-Hungwe, 2021; Morales et al., 2020; Noguerón-Liu et al., 2020; Rafi, 2022, 2023). Other approaches included the use of video-watching (Morales et al., 2020; Tsai, 2022) and listening (Baker & Hope, 2019) tasks.

The third most frequent data elicitation method used oral language and interaction sample analyses ($n = 7$; 33.33%); for example, story-retelling tasks (Bauer et al., 2020; Burgess & Rowsell, 2020; Noguerón-Liu et al., 2020), classroom interactions and group discussions (Burgess & Rowsell, 2020; Mbirimi-Hungwe, 2021; Schissel et al., 2021) were commonly employed by researchers. Other methods included audio-recordings of interactions between children and their parents (Noguerón-Liu et al., 2020), picture-based oral story construction tasks (Bauer et al., 2020), and oral answering of multiple-choice questions (Rafi, 2022).

Interviews and focus groups were equally popular for sampling oral language and interaction samples. Individual interviews with students constituted the most popular of these methods (Briceño, 2021; Burgess & Rowsell, 2020; Noguerón-Liu et al., 2020). Other data-sources included think-aloud protocols (López-Velásquez & García, 2017; Schissel et al., 2021), semi-structured interviews with teachers (Ascenzi-Moreno & Seltzer, 2021; Baker & Hope, 2019), and focus groups (Schissel et al., 2021).

Six studies (28.57%) featured surveys as data elicitation instruments, e.g., questionnaires distributed to students (Adamson & Coulson, 2015; Cavazos & Caramaz, 2023; Tsai, 2022; Wang & East, 2023), and surveys of teachers (Schissel et al., 2021) and faculty deans and decision-makers (Baker & Hope, 2019). Another set of six studies included observations in the form of field-notes (Burgess & Rowsell, 2020; Noguerón-Liu et al., 2020; Wong et al., 2023), reading inventories (Briceño, 2021), naturalistic observation (López-Velásquez & García, 2017), home visits (Noguerón-Liu et al., 2020), and think-aloud observation (García & Godina, 2017).

11.3.3 In What Geographical and Learning Contexts Has Translanguaging Been Used in Language Assessment?

Out of the total number of studies reviewed, six (28.57%) specifically focused on emergent bilingual students, who were primary and middle school students, and their parents. The participants in these studies came from diverse backgrounds, including Hispanic and Latin

American (Bauer et al., 2020; Briceño, 2021; García & Godina, 2017; Gómez & Lewis, 2022; López-Velásquez & García, 2017; Noguerón-Liu et al., 2020), African American and Biracial (Bauer et al., 2020). It is noteworthy that all of these studies were based in the United States.

There is a comparable level of research interest in teaching professionals, both pre-service (Morales et al., 2020; Rafi, 2022; Wong et al., 2023) and in-service (Ascenzi-Moreno & Seltzer, 2021; Baker & Hope, 2019; Schissel et al., 2021). Regarding pre-service teachers, these were all university students with specialisations in Teaching English to Speakers of Other Languages (Morales et al., 2020), English as a New Language (Wong et al., 2023), and English Language Teaching (ELT) (Rafi, 2022). The studies in question took place in universities in Bangladesh (Rafi, 2022), Mexico (Morales et al., 2020), and the United States (Wong et al., 2023). In-service teacher participants were school teachers in the United States and Mexico (Ascenzi-Moreno & Seltzer, 2021; Schissel et al., 2021) and university professors in Canada (Baker & Hope, 2019). This set of studies explored translanguaging in language assessment from various angles. Some studies focused on examining the perceptions of teaching professionals regarding translanguaging and its integration into their assessment methods, while one study conducted tests assessing their own use of translanguaging.

There is a comparable level of research interest in CLIL students. Collectively, the target population of these studies is heterogeneous, encompassing various learner groups, including Japanese-speaking learners of English (Adamson & Coulson, 2015), L2 English speakers whose L1 is one of the 12 South African official languages (Mbirimi-Hungwe, 2021), Bangla-speaking learners of English (Rafi, 2023), beginner learners of Chinese (Wang & East, 2023), alongside students who identify as monolinguals, bilinguals, and multilinguals with no specific languages defined (Cavazos & Karaman, 2023). The studies included in this category were conducted in colleges or universities (or both, as in Cavazos & Karaman, 2023) located in various countries, namely Bangladesh (Rafi, 2023), Japan (Adamson & Coulson, 2015), New Zealand (Wang & East, 2023), South Africa (Mbirimi-Hungwe, 2021), and the United States (Cavazos & Karaman, 2023).

English language learners (ELLs) comprise the other researched learner group in our sample, accounting for 19.05% of the studies. The studies in question involve ELLs with different language-learning goals, such as learning English as an additional language (Burgess & Rowsell, 2020; Heugh et al., 2017), EFL (Tsai, 2022) and English for specific purposes (Chen et al., 2019). The target populations in these studies are college-level (Chen et al., 2019) and university-level (Heugh et al., 2017; Tsai, 2022) students of various years, and adults (Burgess & Rowsell, 2020). The studies were conducted in Taiwan (Chen et al., 2019; Tsai, 2022), Australia (Heugh et al., 2017), and Canada (Burgess & Rowsell, 2020).

11.3.4   What Are the Most Influential Empirical Studies on Translanguaging in Language Assessment Based on Author Affiliation, Source Type, Title, Place of Study, and Citation Data?

A total of 12 countries have contributed to empirical research on translanguaging in language assessment. Most studies are authored by researchers and teaching professionals affiliated to universities and schools in the United States (11 studies), Australia (3 studies), Mexico, Taiwan, and Canada (2 studies each). Studies on translanguaging in language assessment were also conducted in Bangladesh, Japan, New Zealand, Norway, South Africa, Turkey, and the United Kingdom, yielding one study each. The top three cited studies are authored by researchers affiliated to institutions in Japan (Adamson & Coulson, 2015), the United States, Norway, Mexico (Schissel et al., 2021), and Taiwan (Tsai, 2022). These studies are published in Routledge Taylor & Francis Group research outlets and are collectively cited by 263 outputs.

As shown in Fig. 11.3, the citation count for U.S.-affiliated studies is considerably higher compared to other countries, primarily due to the active involvement of researchers concerned in cross-national research collaborations. Studies from researchers affiliated with Japan and Taiwan have more than 100 citations each. The United Kingdom, Canada, Mexico, Norway, and Australia exhibit moderate research influence, with citations ranging from 34 to 92. Studies with minimal citation counts (under ten each) are authored by researchers affiliated to South African, Bangladeshi, Turkish, and New Zealand institutions.

The studies published by Routledge Taylor & Francis Group have the highest number of citations, whereas SAGE and Springer Nature are more moderately represented, with 118 and 101 citations, respectively (see Fig. 11.4).

Concerning the places where the reviewed studies appeared, Routledge Taylor & Francis Group published ten items in its research outlets,

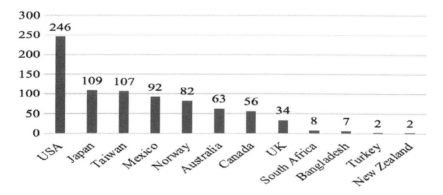

Fig. 11.3 Author countries of affiliation of the reviewed studies ranked by number of citations

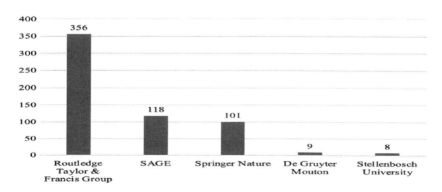

Fig. 11.4 The publishers of the reviewed studies ranked by number of citations

focusing on pedagogical practices, bilingualism, literacy development, the sociocultural aspects of language, assessment methodologies, and the use of technology in language learning and teaching. In addition, SAGE published four studies in its journals specialising in literacy research, encompassing diverse age groups and racial backgrounds. Parts of the larger Springer Nature group, namely Springer and Springer Nature Switzerland, published another set of four outputs in edited collections and a journal covering various aspects of ELT. Stellenbosch University and De Gruyter Mouton have the fewest citations, with 8 and 9, respectively.

11.4 Discussion and Conclusion

Many previous reviews of translanguaging (e.g., Beres, 2015; Özkaynak, 2023) have taken a generalised approach and have predominantly focused on ELT (e.g., Huang & Chalmers, 2023; Kim & Weng, 2022). Our study took a more focused view on its use in language assessment, illuminating research trends, patterns, and developments.

In answer to our first question, we established that writing assessment is the most researched area, with research on integrated assessment and reading assessment studies ranking next in frequency. Studies on integrated assessment prioritise reading as a focal area, emphasising its fundamental role in language acquisition and comprehension. Speaking ranks lowest, perhaps owing to the harder-to-measure nature of spoken language skills. In reading assessment, there is a predominant focus on understanding bilingual reading strategies and behaviours, e.g., cross-linguistic transfer and code-switching. The least attention was given to self-assessment and multimodal assessment, suggesting these are less established areas in language assessment. In the studies of self-assessment, there is a tendency to focus on student perceptions and attitudes towards translanguaging. The pattern of research foci in the reviewed studies aligns with the expected distribution: writing assessment and integrated assessment are overrepresented, while self-assessment and multimodal assessment are underrepresented. The traditional focus on assessments of writing and integrated skills overshadows the importance of multi-modal assessment, no doubt because the latter necessitates more intricate methodologies and tools to capture and evaluate diverse modes of expression comprehensively. The underrepresentation of self-assessment may be attributed to its perceived subjectivity and lower reliability than external assessments.

Regarding our second research question, we found that using written language samples is a choice of data elicitation method in over half the studies. It is unsurprising that this method is widely used, given that written language samples are one form of objective data that is convenient for data collection and systematic analysis. Such samples are often collected via reflections, reports, or digital compositions. Other elicitation methods include testing receptive skills, prompting oral language, interaction sample analyses, interviews, focus groups, surveys, and observations. Testing receptive skills is realised via passage reading, video-watching, and listening, while for oral language and interaction analyses, researchers deploy group discussion and story-retelling tasks. Interview methods range from individual student interviews to semi-structured teacher interviews, and surveys are commonly distributed to students and faculty members. Observations include naturalistic observation, home visits, and think-aloud observations. Almost all the studies in our sample used multiple complementary data elicitation methods. Another notable finding is that the think-aloud approach may be used as an interview protocol and observation method. The crucial difference lies in the level of interaction and engagement with participants in the process: while think-aloud observation entails passive observation and note-taking on the part of the researcher, the think-aloud protocol involves researchers' asking follow-up questions as participants navigate the task.

Regarding our third research question, we noted that the extant research on translanguaging in language assessment encompassed diverse participants, including emergent bilingual students, college/university-level students, and aspiring and current teaching professionals from various linguacultural and racial backgrounds. The studies recruited teaching professionals categorised as pre-service and in-service from the United States, Mexico, and Canada, alongside CLIL students from Japan, Bangladesh, New Zealand, South Africa, and the United States.

The studies also attracted ELLs comprising young adults and adult learners from Taiwan, Australia, and Canada. Interestingly, the emergent bilingual students, who represent African American, Biracial, Hispanic, and Latin American backgrounds, are all from the United States.

In answer to our fourth research question, we established that the highest number of citations is received by the study authored by Japan-affiliated researchers and suggests a significant contribution to research conversation on translanguaging in the domain of language assessment. While the relevant empirical work is globally distributed, with entries from Asia, Europe, North America, Oceania, and Southern Africa, U.S.-affiliated researchers consistently show a considerable number of citations across journals and edited collections. The Routledge Taylor & Francis Group has the most frequent representation, thanks to its substantial role of publishing highly impactful studies. Arguably, its publications have higher visibility and citation rates owing to its status as a commercial publisher. Thanks to this, it has larger budgets for promotion and advertising and access to a broader pool of high-profile researchers compared to university publishers.

Based on the findings of our scoping review, we would also like to provide suggestions for further empirical research on the topic. Since there is a significant gap in understanding how translanguaging is applied in self-assessment and multimodal assessment, future studies might prioritise these areas. We also suggest that researchers explore similarities and differences in applying translanguaging in language assessment between various learner types, learning approaches, and geographical contexts. This scoping review is intended to assist researchers in making informed decisions regarding data elicitation methods for their studies of translanguaging in language assessment. Moreover, educators across all teaching levels are encouraged to employ this scoping review as a reference point to inform their assessment practices.

Acknowledgements This work has been fully supported by a fellowship award from the Research Grants Council of the Hong Kong Special Administrative Region, China (EdUHK PDFS2223-8H01).

References

Note: References marked with an asterisk indicate their inclusion in the scoping review.

*Adamson, J., & Coulson, D. (2015). Translanguaging in English academic writing preparation. *International Journal of Pedagogies and Learning, 10*(1), 24–37. https://doi.org/10.1080/22040552.2015.1084674

Alsowat, H. H. (2017). A systematic review of research on teaching English language skills for Saudi EFL students. *Advances in Language and Literary Studies, 8*(5), 30–45. https://doi.org/10.7575/aiac.alls.v.8n.5p.30

*Ascenzi-Moreno, L., & Seltzer, K. (2021). Always at the bottom: Ideologies in assessment of emergent bilinguals. *Journal of Literacy Research, 53*(4), 468–490. https://doi.org/10.1177/1086296X211052255

*Baker, B., & Hope, A. (2019). Incorporating translanguaging in language assessment: The case of a test for university professors. *Language Assessment Quarterly, 16*(4–5), 408–425. https://doi.org/10.1080/15434303.2019.1671392

Baker, C. (2001). *Foundations of bilingual education and bilingualism* (3rd ed.). Multilingual Matters.

*Bauer, E. B., Colomer, S. E., & Wiemelt, J. (2020). Biliteracy of African American and Latinx kindergarten students in a dual-language program: Understanding students' translanguaging practices across informal assessments. *Urban Education, 55*(3), 331–361. https://doi.org/10.1177/0042085918789743

Beres, A. M. (2015). An overview of translanguaging: 20 years of 'giving voice to those who do not speak.' *Translation and Translanguaging in Multilingual Contexts, 1*(1), 103–118. https://doi.org/10.1075/ttmc.1.1.05ber

Bourguet, M. -L. (2006). Introducing strong forms of bilingual education in the mainstream classroom: A case for technology. In Kinshuk, R. Koper, P. Kommers, P. Kirschner, D. G. Sampson, & W. Didderen (Eds.), *Proceedings of the 6th IEEE International Conference on Advanced Learning Technologies* (pp. 642–646). IEEE. https://doi.org/10.1109/ICALT.2006.1652523

*Briceño, A. (2021). Influence of sequential and simultaneous bilingualism on second grade dual language students' use of syntax in reading. *Reading Psychology, 42*(2), 150–176. https://doi.org/10.1080/02702711.2021.1888345

*Burgess, J., & Rowsell, J. (2020). Transcultural-affective flows and multimodal engagements: Reimagining pedagogy and assessment with adult language

learners. *Language and Education, 34*(2), 173–191. https://doi.org/10.1080/09500782.2020.1720226

Burner, T., & Carlsen, C. (2023). Teachers' multilingual beliefs and practices in English classrooms: A scoping review. *Review of Education, 11*(2), 1–29. https://doi.org/10.1002/rev3.3407

Cannon, J., & Marx, N. (2024). Scoping review of research methodologies across language studies with deaf and hard-of-hearing multilingual learners. *International Review of Applied Linguistics in Language Teaching, 62*(2), 1009–1037. https://doi.org/10.1515/iral-2022-0206

*Cavazos, A. G., & Karaman, M. A. (2023). A preliminary development and validation of the Translingual Disposition Questionnaire with Latinx students. *Language Awareness, 32*(1), 58–73. https://doi.org/10.1080/09658416.2021.1960557

Cenoz, J., & Gorter, D. (2017). Translanguaging as a pedagogical tool in multilingual education. In J. Cenoz, D. Gorter, & S. May (Eds.), *Language awareness and multilingualism. Encyclopedia of language and education* (pp. 309–321). Springer. https://doi.org/10.1007/978-3-319-02240-6_20

Charamba, E. (2020). Translanguaging: Developing scientific scholarship in a multilingual classroom. *Journal of Multilingual and Multicultural Development, 41*(8), 655–672.

*Chen, F., Tsai, S.-C., & Tsou, W. (2019). The application of translanguaging in an English for Specific Purposes writing course. *English Teaching and Learning, 43*(1), 65–83. https://doi.org/10.1007/s42321-018-0018-0

Darzhinova, L., & Zou, D. (2023). Self-paced reading as a computer-based methodology for L2 assessment: A scoping review. *International Journal of Mobile Learning and Organisation, 17*(3), 368–387. https://doi.org/10.1504/IJMLO.2023.131861

Ferguson, G. (2003). Classroom code-switching in post-colonial contexts: Functions, attitudes and policies. *AILA Review, 16*(1), 38–51. https://doi.org/10.1075/aila.16.05fer

*García, G. E., & Godina, H. (2017). A window into bilingual reading: The bilingual reading practices of fourth-grade, Mexican American children who are emergent bilinguals. *Journal of Literacy Research, 49*(2), 273–301. https://doi.org/10.1177/1086296X17703727

Gilanyi, L., Gao, X. A., & Wang, S. (2023). EMI and CLIL in Asian schools: A scoping review of empirical research between 2015 and 2022. *Heliyon, 9*(6), 1–12. https://doi.org/10.1016/j.heliyon.2023.e16365

*Gómez, M., & Lewis, M. A. (2022). Identifying the assets of emergent bilingual middle school students' writing: Opportunities to validate students' linguistic repertoires and identities. *International Journal of Bilingual Education and Bilingualism, 25*(10), 3791–3803. https://doi.org/10.1080/136 70050.2022.2079371

*Heugh, K., Li, X., & Song, Y. (2017). Multilingualism and translanguaging in the teaching of and through English: Rethinking linguistic boundaries in an Australian university. In B. Fenton-Smith, P. Humphreys, & I. Walkinshaw (Eds.), *English medium instruction in higher education in Asia-Pacific: From policy to pedagogy* (pp. 259–279). Springer. https://doi.org/10.1007/978-3-319-51976-0_14

Huang, X., & Chalmers, H. (2023). Implementation and effects of pedagogical translanguaging in EFL classrooms: A systematic review. *Languages, 8*(3), 1–20. https://doi.org/10.3390/languages8030194

Jabbari, N., & Eslami, Z. R. (2019). Second language learning in the context of massively multiplayer online games: A scoping review. *ReCALL, 31*(1), 92–113. https://doi.org/10.1017/S0958344018000058

Kim, G. J. Y., & Weng, Z. (2022). A systematic review on pedagogical translanguaging in TESOL. *TESL-EJ, 26*(3), 1–20. https://doi.org/10.55593/ej.261 03a4

Leonet, O., Cenoz, J., & Gorter, D. (2017). Challenging minority language isolation: Translanguaging in a trilingual school in the Basque Country. *Journal of Language, Identity & Education, 16*(4), 216–227. https://doi.org/10.1080/15348458.2017.1328281

Li, Y. (2005). *The effects of the bilingual strategy—Preview-view-review—On the comprehension of science concepts by deaf ASL/English and hearing Mexican-American Spanish/English bilingual students* (Publication No. 305381982) (Doctoral dissertation, Lamar University, USA). ProQuest Dissertations & Theses Database.

*López-Velásquez, A. M., & García, G. E. (2017). The bilingual reading practices and performance of two Hispanic first graders. *Bilingual Research Journal, 40*(3), 246–261. https://doi.org/10.1080/15235882.2017. 1351008

MacSwan, J. (2017). A multilingual perspective on translanguaging. *American Educational Research Journal, 54*(1), 167–201. https://doi.org/10.3102/000 2831216683935

Marsh, D., Ontero, A., & Shikongo, T. (Eds.). (2001). *Enhancing English-medium education in Namibia*. University of Jyväskylä. https://www.content-english.org/data/namibia.pdf

*Mbirimi-Hungwe, V. (2021). Translanguaging as an act of emancipation: Rethinking assessment tools in multilingual pedagogy in South Africa. *Per Linguam, 37*(1), 97–108. https://doi.org/10.5785/37-1-930

*Morales, J., Schissel, J. L., & López-Gopar, M. (2020). Pedagogical sismo: Translanguaging approaches for English language instruction and assessment in Oaxaca, Mexico. In Z. Tian, L. Aghai, P. Sayer, & J. L. Schissel (Eds.), *Envisioning TESOL through a translanguaging lens* (pp. 161–183). Springer. https://doi.org/10.1007/978-3-030-47031-9_8

Munn, Z., Peters, M. D., Stern, C., Tufanaru, C., McArthur, A., & Aromataris, E. (2018). Systematic review or scoping review? Guidance for authors when choosing between a systematic or scoping review approach. *BMC Medical Research Methodology, 18*, 1–7. https://doi.org/10.1186/s12874-018-0611-x

*Noguerón-Liu, S., Shimek, C. H., & Bahlmann Bollinger, C. (2020). 'Dime de que se trató/Tell me what it was about': Exploring emergent bilinguals' linguistic resources in reading assessments with parent participation. *Journal of Early Childhood Literacy, 20*(2), 411–433. https://doi.org/10.1177/146 8798418770708

Özkaynak, O. (2023). Translanguaging in applied linguistics: A comprehensive systematic review. *L2 Journal: An Electronic Refereed Journal for Foreign and Second Language Educators, 15*(1), 1–23. https://doi.org/10.5070/L2.2460

Page, M. J., Moher, D., Bossuyt, P. M., Boutron, I., Hoffmann, T. C., Mulrow, C. D., et al. (2021). PRISMA 2020 explanation and elaboration: Updated guidance and exemplars for reporting systematic reviews. *British Medical Journal, 372*, 1–9. https://doi.org/10.1136/bmj.n160

Pham, M. T., Rajić, A., Greig, J. D., Sargeant, J. M., Papadopoulos, A., & McEwen, S. A. (2014). A scoping review of scoping reviews: Advancing the approach and enhancing the consistency. *Research Synthesis Methods, 5*(4), 371–385. https://doi.org/10.1002/jrsm.1123

*Rafi, A. S. M. (2022). Students' uptake of translanguaging pedagogies and translanguaging-oriented assessment in an ELT classroom at a Bangladeshi university. In R. Khan, A. Bashir, L. B. Basu, & E. Uddin (Eds.), *Local research and glocal perspectives in English language teaching: Teaching in changing times* (pp. 31–45). Springer. https://doi.org/10.1007/978-981-19-6458-9_3

*Rafi, A. S. M. (2023). Creativity, criticality and translanguaging in assessment design: Perspectives from Bangladeshi higher education. *Applied Linguistics Review.* https://doi.org/10.1515/applirev-2023-0086

*Schissel, J. L., De Korne, H., & López-Gopar, M. (2021). Grappling with translanguaging for teaching and assessment in culturally and linguistically

diverse contexts: Teacher perspectives from Oaxaca, Mexico. *International Journal of Bilingual Education and Bilingualism, 24*(3), 340–356. https:// doi.org/10.1080/13670050.2018.1463965

Singleton, D., & Flynn, C. J. (2022). Translanguaging: A pedagogical concept that went wandering. *International Multilingual Research Journal, 16*(2), 136–147. https://doi.org/10.1080/19313152.2021.1985692

*Tsai, S.-C. (2022). Chinese students' perceptions of using Google Translate as a translingual CALL tool in EFL writing. *Computer Assisted Language Learning, 35*(5–6), 1250–1272. https://doi.org/10.1080/09588221.2020. 1799412

*Wang, D., & East, M. (2023). Integrating translanguaging into assessment: Students' responses and perceptions. *Applied Linguistics Review*. https://doi. org/10.1515/applirev-2023-0087

Wang, X. (2021). An analysis of note-taking strategies: The effect of translanguaging on content comprehension and knowledge retention. *Journal of Language Teaching, 1*(3), 1–20. https://doi.org/10.54475/jlt.2021.020

*Wong, C.-Y., Du, X., & Estudillo, A. G. (2023). 'I've grown so much more confidence in my actual instruction': Examining teacher candidates' pedagogical knowledge growth in translanguaging. *Language and Education, 37*(6), 820–835. https://doi.org/10.1080/09500782.2023.2205839

Yasar Yuzlu, M., & Dikilitas, K. (2022). Translanguaging in the development of EFL learners' foreign language skills in Turkish context. *Innovation in Language Learning and Teaching, 16*(2), 176–190. https://doi.org/10.1080/ 17501229.2021.1892698

12

Translanguaging at the Heart of Language Education: A Systematic Review

Abbas Ali Rezaee ⓘ, Haniye Seyri,
and Mohammad Hussein Norouzi

12.1 Introduction

By nature, people look for ways to facilitate all aspects of everyday life, and enhancing communication is no exception. For bilinguals, switching from one language to another is now taken as a common practice (Wei & Lin, 2019). Pedagogical translanguaging, which is mainly planned and led by teachers, constitutes an indispensable part of modern education and everyday life for many, and aims to enhance people's linguistic and

---

A. A. Rezaee (✉)
Department of English Language and Literature, Faculty of Foreign
Languages and Literatures, University of Tehran, Tehran, Iran
e-mail: aarezaee@ut.ac.ir

H. Seyri · M. H. Norouzi
University of Tehran, Tehran, Iran
e-mail: haniye.seyri@ut.ac.ir

M. H. Norouzi
e-mail: mhnorouzi@ut.ac.ir

© The Author(s), under exclusive license to Springer Nature
Switzerland AG 2025
D. Coulson and C. Denman (eds.), *Translation, Translanguaging and Machine
Translation in Foreign Language Education*,
https://doi.org/10.1007/978-3-031-82174-5_12

235

academic development. It has been confirmed through a large number of studies that, within the English as a Foreign or Second Language (EFL/ESL) classroom, when neither teachers nor students are native speakers of the language, code-switching (CS), as a common feature of translanguaging, is very facilitative of learning (e.g., Li & García, 2022; Wei, 2022; Wei & Lin, 2019). Despite this, students and teachers might have contradictory perspectives towards the employment of the mother tongue or first language (L1) in teaching a second language (L2). The investigation of such perspectives can therefore shed light on paths towards the success or failure of language teaching and learning.

The current systematic review examines a number of studies on translanguaging to discover more about teacher and student perspectives. For teachers, these perspectives have an important impact on their actual practice of English instruction in multilingual contexts, while, for learners, they can influence their ideas of the effectiveness of teaching practices. Through further examination of this area, a more in-depth understanding of classroom, and even out-of-class, practice will become apparent. Finally, if the systematic review reveals widespread support for translanguaging to a reasonable degree among both teachers and students, then these results can be used to call into question why shifting from one language to another, at a controlled level, should be forbidden by policies and practices in numerous English language institutions around the world.

12.2 Literature Review

12.2.1 The Value of Mother Tongue

Panagiotopoulou et al. (2020, p. 1) reported the response of a Spanish girl upon receiving her math instruction using translanguaging: "The Spanish word makes it easier to understand it in English!" With this testimony, it becomes clear that translingual practices were welcome in her lessons and, furthermore, that this was a pedagogical strategy. It also indicated that the teacher acted as a translingual and, thus, as a multilingual role model for the children. In this way, social justice in education is promoted.

Aliakbari and Khosravian (2014) found that, for bilingual Iranians whose mother tongue is not the official language of Persian, the choice of language to communicate depends upon age, gender, educational level/attainment, occupation, field of study, and place of residency, among others, with gender perhaps playing the most significant role. They conclude that EFL teachers' awareness of the factors affecting the linguistic medium learners prefer to express information in would equip them with a better understanding of classroom dynamics, thus helping to create a more efficient learning environment. As an example, the authors detail how the use and learning of Kurdish as a heritage language may result in a positive experience and serve as motivation for future engagement in learning, for male students in particular.

Bahrami et al. (2020) build upon the factors offered by Aliakbari and Khosravian (2014) by describing how education in a mother tongue in a context prescribing an L2 as the official language is affected by a range of variables. These include students' socio-professional identity formation, their growth, and the degree of culture and custom preservation in their societies.

12.2.2 Translanguaging and Code-Switching

Translanguaging is a relatively recent concept used along with CS in the literature. It is similar to CS in that it refers to multilingual speakers' switching between their languages in a spontaneous manner. Translanguaging can assist multilingual speakers in making meaning, shaping experiences, and gaining deeper understandings and knowledge of the languages in use, and even of the content being taught. To achieve this, however, strategic language planning, in which two or more languages are combined systematically within the classroom, is required.

Williams first used the Welsh term 'trawsieithu' in 1994 to refer to a pedagogical practice where students in bilingual Welsh/English classrooms were asked to alternate languages for the purposes of receptive or productive use. Since then, translanguaging as a term has, according to García and Lin (2016, p. 117), "been increasingly used in the scholarly literature to refer to both the complex and fluid language practices of bilinguals, as well as the pedagogical approaches that leverage those practices".

With specific reference to translanguaging, Bolkvadze (2023) discusses the problem of human relations throughout history, and asserts that language has always attracted attention both in terms of a tool of communication and in relation to issues of its mastery. A large number of methods have been proposed in pursuit of these. With reference to the latter point, English as a lingua franca is actively taught around the world. However, despite this, the development of productive skills remains a problem in non-English-speaking countries where learners have fewer opportunities to communicate in the target language outside the classroom (Li & Chan, 2024). Translanguaging, therefore, appears to offer an opportunity to address these issues, even when it is viewed in a narrow sense as an EFL 'teaching method'.

People can employ various cognitive resources and mental processes to enhance language learning. The use of more cognitive resources, such as attention and noticing, cognitive flexibility, and cognitive strategies (Gass & Selinker, 2008), naturally enhances and improves learning and cognitive functioning. Due to the unified and holistic nature of human cognition, learning and using a new language will always benefit from available cognitive resources regardless of the positive or negative attitudes of learners or teachers. However, the attitude can greatly influence the ways they are used during the learning of a new language. Some of the aspects of the new language that benefit from the use of L1 include accuracy, fluency, and the willingness to communicate of L2 users (Noorbar & Jafarpour Mamaghani, 2016). Similarly, Zohrabi et al.'s study (2014) suggests the use of L1 as facilitative in learning English vocabulary, while Namzidost et al. (2019) concluded that upper-intermediate students of English benefitted from CS as an effective technique in learning lexis.

The use of the mother tongue, which can be in the form of translation from L2 into L1 (Cook, 2001), depends on a number of factors, including learners' proficiency, the issue of equivalent lexical concepts between the two languages involved, learners' backgrounds, and the cultural gaps that naturally exist between the two languages. This, in turn, makes the process of conveying ideas accurately arduous (Wang & Shen, 2023). The use of L1 in teaching is the mainstream in state institutions in many countries around the world, Iran being no exception, while private language institutions are more inclined to restrict themselves to the use of L2 in the language classroom. This practice becomes more focused and commonly practised as learners' proficiency level rises.

Referring to Grosjean (1989), Cook (2001, p. 408) holds that, "Code-switching is a highly skilled activity – the 'bilingual mode' of language in which L1 and L2 are used simultaneously, rather than the 'monolingual mode' in which they are used separately". This mode has long been ignored in traditional L2 instruction where the students' target and native languages are clearly divided, with the target language acting as the 'official' language in the classroom. Reyes' (2004) research counters the view that children use CS due to a lack of proficiency in their L2 and presents evidence to "support the view that it is used as a strategy to extend their communicative competence during peer interaction" (p. 77). Such an approach may have been due to the belief that switching to an alternate language is the result of having incomplete knowledge of the language in which the utterance was first made. However, more recently, a growing number of researchers maintain that CS commonly takes place in multilingual contexts, not because of a lack of knowledge in a particular language, but for different communicative functions. In addition, CS has an interpersonal, social function; multilingual speakers consistently monitor and attempt to accommodate their interlocutors' language use.

12.2.3 Attitudes Towards Code-Switching

Despite the levels of support offered above, CS continues to be widely considered as a controversial issue in language pedagogy. There have been a number of negative attitudes towards the use of the L1 in language teaching expressed in the literature among scholars and practitioners.

However, a number of recent studies have indicated the positive potential of utilizing existing linguistic and cognitive resources based on L1 in education in general, and in language pedagogy more particularly (Maftoon & Amjadiparvar, 2023).

There is a growing understanding that it would be an injustice to CS to consider it as a sign of a defect or shortcoming in teachers' linguistic or communicative abilities (Hamidi & Najafi Sarem, 2012; Rezvani & Eslami Rasekh, 2011). ELT practitioners may switch linguistic codes in the classroom to explain new grammar structures or lexis, help students relax, implement classroom discipline, provide task instructions, or even for other pedagogical purposes. It can, however, be considered a compensatory strategy for learners, and for those at lower proficiency levels in particular, to facilitate interaction and manage affective challenges. CS or L1 use is utilised in classroom instructor-learner interaction for either the same functions, i.e., facilitating communication, ensuring/enhancing or assessing comprehension or as a resort to enhance learning or compensate for shortcomings in linguistic competence (Nazeri et al., 2020).

According to Rezvani and Eslami Rasekh (2011), the judicious and informed use of L1 in the classroom is a valuable strategy to boost teaching quality while also serving pedagogical and social functions that facilitate teacher-learner interactions. As such, it further contributes to better classroom management practice. In this study, the high proficiency levels of teachers employing the L1 in their instruction suggested that its classroom use was a professionally informed strategy rather than a case of avoiding the L2.

Considering the issue of teachers' CS, students' perspectives are especially revealing as they can be conceived as recipients of their instructors' language use. A survey of the attitudes of EFL learners and teachers towards teacher CS in the classroom across language proficiency levels by Rezaee and Fathi (2016) revealed a higher tendency for teacher CS at the elementary proficiency level, and towards English-only instruction at intermediate and upper-intermediate levels. Similarly, Abdolmanafi Rokni and Khonakdar (2016) concluded that learners express a positive attitude towards teachers' CS on the grounds that EFL content can be challenging to comprehend, and teachers' use of L1 in explaining this content assists them in better comprehending and learning what is being taught.

In their study in a university context, Hashemi and Khalili Sabet (2013) investigated the perceptions of EFL students and instructors of the use of their L1 in General English Language classrooms in Iran. The authors reported a greater desire on the part of students to use Persian in the classroom while instructors were more inclined to use English and avoid their L1 on the grounds that the medium of instruction must be English. However, these findings suggested affective considerations as teachers' incentive behind their approval for the judicious and selective use of L1 to help deal with learners' psychological challenges, such as anxiety, nervousness, fear, unwillingness, and low self-esteem. The researchers conclude that an approach that is inclusive of student and instructor views would support serious consideration of L1 use in different aspects and phases of English instruction and assessment at the university level in Iran.

12.3 Present Study

Building upon the literature presented above, the current study attempts to gain a clearer understanding of EFL and ESL teachers' and students' perceptions and attitudes towards translanguaging.

12.3.1 Method

12.3.1.1 Databases and Search Keywords

To locate and gather relevant papers, theses, and book chapters, a thorough electronic search was conducted in ten widely used databases: ERIC, Google Scholar, PsycINFO, MEDLINE, JSTOR, Web of Science, Wiley Online Library, Science Direct, SCOPUS, and ProQuest. This electronic search was performed using the following key terms: *Translanguaging*, *Attitudes*, *Perceptions*, *EFL/ESL Teachers*, *EFL/ESL Students*.

12.3.1.2 Inclusion and Exclusion Criteria

The following inclusion and exclusion criteria were applied to select the most relevant papers for the current review:

- Publication date: Papers published during the last decade (2015–2024).
- Language: English.
- Context: Research studies conducted in EFL and ESL contexts.
- Participants: Teachers, students, or both.
- Outcome: Research studies that identified EFL/ESL teachers' and students' perceptions of translanguaging.

Exclusion criteria taken into consideration were:

- Context: Studies were excluded when conducted in general or mainstream education settings.
- Outcome: Studies that did not evaluate teachers' and students' attitudes towards translanguaging.

12.3.2 Selection Process

The PRISMA flow diagram was employed to identify the most applicable and relevant papers. As stated by Page et al. (2021), PRISMA is an "evidence-based minimum set of items for reporting in systematic reviews and meta-analyses" (p. 2). Following the PRISMA guidelines, manuscripts for review were first identified. In the second stage, all identified manuscripts were screened before being assessed for eligibility or appropriateness in the third stage. During the final stage, the list of manuscripts to be included in this systematic review were finalized. Figure 12.1 displays the four stages of PRISMA in addition to the number of documents processed at each.

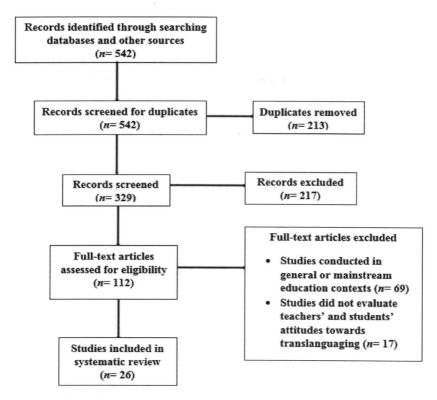

Fig. 12.1 The selection process based on the PRISMA guidelines

12.3.3 Data Extraction

As shown in Table 12.1, following the removal of duplicates and irrelevant manuscripts, a total of 26 manuscripts remained for further analysis. The remaining manuscripts were coded across six different categories (see Table 12.1). These were: (a) publication type; (b) research context; (c) participants; (d) methodology; (e) data collection instruments; and (f) major findings. As the coding process was conducted by two people, the intercoder reliability (ICR) was estimated using Cohen's Kappa (κ). The resultant Cohen's Kappa coefficient was calculated as 0.92, which indicates very high levels of agreement.

Table 12.1 Studies examining EFL/ESL teachers' and students' perceptions of translanguaging

No	Study	Publication type	Research context	Participants	Methodology	Data collection instruments	Major findings
1	Aliakbari and Fadaeian (2023)	Article	EFL context	207 Iranian teachers	Quantitative	Questionnaire	Participants maintained that using Persian to teach English is beneficial for learners
2	Canli and Canli (2023)	Article	EFL context	100 Turkish students	Mixed-methods	Questionnaire; semi-structured interviews	Students employed translanguaging variously, and had positive attitudes towards translanguaging
3	Cvilikaitė-Mačiulskienė et al. (2023)	Article	EFL context	48 Ukrainian students, 19 Ukrainian teachers	Mixed-method	Open-ended and close-ended questionnaires	Both teachers and students viewed translanguaging as an effective strategy
4	Burton and Rajendram (2019)	Article	ESL context	Five Canadian teachers	Qualitative	Semi-structured interviews	Translanguaging was seen as slowing down students' English learning rather than as a resource for deepening and expanding their knowledge
5	Doiz and Lasagabaster (2017)	Book chapter	EFL context	13 Spanish teachers	Qualitative	Group discussions	Most participants believed that L1 should be excluded from everyday teaching practices
6	Gorter and Arocena (2020)	Article	EFL context	124 Spanish teachers	Quantitative	Questionnaire	Participants had unfavorable attitudes towards multilingualism and translanguaging

No	Study	Publication type	Research context	Participants	Methodology	Data collection instruments	Major findings
7	Khairunnisa and Lukmana (2020)	Article	EFL context	50 Indonesian teachers	Quantitative	Questionnaire	The majority of participants thought it advantageous for EFL teachers and learners to combine their local language with English
8	Kucukali and Koçbaş (2021)	Article	EFL context	27 Turkish students	Qualitative	Focus group interviews; graphic elicitation tasks	Translanguaging pedagogy was found to be beneficial for student engagement
9	Liu (2021)	Thesis	EFL context	153 Thai students	Mixed-methods	Questionnaire; interviews	Results indicated that most participants considered translanguaging to be helpful in EFL classes
10	Liu et al. (2022)	Article	EFL context	1008 Chinese students	Mixed-methods	Questionnaires; follow-up interviews	Results demonstrated that translanguagingpractices can greatly contribute to students' understanding and learning, classroom communication, and learning motivation
11	Madkur et al. (2022)	Article	EFL context	Six Indonesian teachers	Qualitative	In-depth semi-structured interviews; observations	Results demonstrated that participants had favorable attitudes towards translanguaging
12	Memari (2023)	Article	EFL context	120 Iranian students	Mixed-methods	Language proficiency tests; semi-structured interviews	Almost all students had positive beliefs and attitudes towards translanguaging pedagogy

(continued)

Table 12.1 (continued)

No	Study	Publication type	Research context	Participants	Methodology	Data collection instruments	Major findings
13	Putrawan and Sinaga (2022)	Article	EFL context	Eight Indonesian teachers	Qualitative	Interviews	Participants had divergent attitudes towards translanguaging in EFL classrooms. Most participants had negative beliefs and attitudes towards this concept
14	Putri and Rifai (2021)	Article	EFL context	Four Indonesian teachers	Qualitative	Individual depth interviews (IDI)	Results showed that teachers had positive attitudes towards translanguaging and only used translanguaging pedagogy to instruct grammar
15	Raja et al. (2021)	Article	EFL context	Indonesian students	Qualitative	Questionnaires	Students had negative feelings about translanguaging and experienced some important challenges while using this educational approach
16	Raja et al. (2022)	Article	EFL context	Four Indonesian teachers	Mixed-methods	Questionnaires; semi-structured interviews	Participants expressed different feelings towards translanguaging. Participants implemented translanguaging in their instructional practices
17	Santoso (2020)	Article	EFL context	Five Indonesian students	Mixed-methods	Observations; semi-structured interviews	Students had positive perceptions of translanguaging

No	Study	Publication type	Research context	Participants	Methodology	Data collection instruments	Major findings
18	Scopich (2018)	Thesis	EFL context	225 Croatian and Italian teachers, four Croatian and Italian students	Mixed-methods	Questionnaires; classroom observations	Participants had positive perspectives towards translanguaging
19	Stihi (2021)	Article	EFL context	10 Algerian teachers	Qualitative	Semi-structured interviews	Participants reported that they are interested in using translanguaging pedagogy
20	Turnbull (2018)	Article	EFL context	373 Japanese students, 261 Japanese teachers	Quantitative	Questionnaires	Translanguaging was perceived to be an appropriate approach for teaching English
21	Tuskeyeva (2022)	Thesis	EFL context	10 Russian and Kazakh teachers	Qualitative	Individual semi-structured interviews	Both Russian and Kazakh teachers had positive attitudes towards translanguaging

(continued)

Table 12.1 (continued)

No	Study	Publication type	Research context	Participants	Methodology	Data collection instruments	Major findings
22	Wang and Shen (2023)	Article	EFL context	33 Chinese teachers	Mixed-methods	In-class observations; online questionnaire; in-depth semi-structured interviews	Students expressed positive attitudes toward translanguaging employed by instructors
23	Witari and Sukamto (2023)	Article	EFL context	Four Indonesian teachers	Qualitative	Interviews	Translanguaging was perceived to be encouraging
24	Yusri et al. (2022)	Article	EFL context	Three Malaysian teachers	Qualitative	Semi-structured interviews	Malaysian teachers had positive perceptions and attitudes towards translanguaging

No	Study	Publication type	Research context	Participants	Methodology	Data collection instruments	Major findings
25	Yuvayapan (2019)	Article	EFL context	50 Turkish teachers	Mixed-methods	Questionnaire; Classroom observations; semi-structured interviews	Participants held favorable views about translanguaging
26	Yuzlu and Dikilitas (2022)	Article	EFL context	120 Turkish students	Mixed-methods	Skills test; semi-structured interviews	Outcomes indicated that translanguaging has different constructive, cognitive, interactive and affective benefits

12.4 Findings

Findings are reported across the five categories of publication type, research context, participants, methodology, data collection instruments, and major findings below.

12.4.1 Publication Type

As the review of the pertinent literature revealed, the majority of manuscripts included in this systematic review were journal articles (81%), with the remainder (19%) being theses and book chapters.

12.4.2 Research Context

Almost all studies (96%) were conducted in EFL settings; i.e., in those countries where English is not the dominant language. Findings further showed that only one study (4%) was undertaken in an ESL context.

12.4.3 Participants

Of the 26 manuscripts included in the review, 15 (58%) evaluated the position and value of translanguaging in English courses from the standpoint of teachers. Eight studies (31%) assessed the significance of translanguaging from the perspective of students, and the remaining three (12%)[1] examined this issue from both teachers' and students' viewpoints.

12.4.4 Research Methods

11 studies (42%) adopted a mixed-methods approach to clarify EFL/ ESL teachers' and students' attitudes towards translanguaging. A further 11 (42%) only employed qualitative methods, while four (15%) used

---

[1] Rounding error means not all percentages reported in the Findings tally to exactly 100%.

quantitative approaches to assess teachers' and students' perceptions of translanguaging.

12.4.5 Data Collection Instruments

Seven (32%) of the studies included used only structured/semi-structured interviews for data collection. Six (27%) employed both open-ended and close-ended questionnaires and structured or semi-structured interviews, while five (23%) only used open-ended or close-ended questionnaires. The remaining papers (18%) utilized other data-gathering instruments, including observations, language proficiency tests, skills tests, group discussions, and graphic elicitation tasks.

12.4.6 Major Findings

12.4.6.1 Teachers' Viewpoints

One of the primary concerns of the study was with EFL/ESL teachers' attitudes towards translanguaging. Of the 18 studies focused on teachers' perceptions of translanguaging, 16 (89%) reported positive attitudes towards this pedagogical approach. The two remaining studies (11%) found that teachers had negative perspectives towards employing it.

12.4.6.2 Students' Viewpoints

The second major goal was ascertaining students' perceptions. The review revealed that, of the 11 studies which addressed students' attitudes towards translanguaging, ten (91%) reported positive perspectives and only one (9%) found that students had unfavourable beliefs and ideas.

12.5 Discussion

This study was an attempt to reveal teacher and student perceptions of translanguaging in EFL and ESL classrooms in order to determine their stance and attitudes. In addition, this review study attempted to take stock of recent advances in research on translanguaging pedagogy in EFL and ESL settings and to offer some directions for future research.

Concerning the main purpose of the review, a thorough examination of the pertinent literature revealed that the majority of English teachers and students held positive beliefs and attitudes towards translanguaging and its implementation in EFL and ESL classrooms. A potential explanation for the positive attitudes of students might be that translanguaging pedagogy allows them to use their full linguistic potential to generate and negotiate meaning (Cenoz & Gorter, 2020; Poza, 2017). Similarly, it may be that using their mother tongue helps students feel more comfortable and at ease (Huang & Chalmers, 2023; Ossa Parra & Proctor, 2021). Further, the positive perceptions of teachers regarding translanguaging may be related to the fact that it helps them to facilitate the language acquisition process by providing support to learners in a language that they readily understand (Oliver et al., 2021; Seals, 2021). Another reason could be that this pedagogical approach allows instructors to involve their pupils in the language acquisition process (Tejano, 2022). In other words, this instructional method empowers English teachers to lead their learners to higher levels of classroom engagement (Kwihangana, 2021).

Finally, a number of caveats and shortcomings need to be noted regarding the reviewed manuscripts. First, the majority of papers included in the present review were journal articles. To offer a more comprehensive picture of translanguaging and its applications in EFL and ESL classes, more theses, books, and book chapters need to be included and examined in future research. Second, almost all the reviewed studies were conducted in EFL classrooms. Since the outcomes of these studies might not be transferable to ESL classes, future research should explore ESL teachers' and students' attitudes towards translanguaging. Third, most of the reviewed studies assessed the value and significance of translanguaging from teachers' standpoints.

Further research should examine the importance of translanguaging from students' viewpoints. Fourth, the reviewed studies employed qualitative, quantitative, or mixed-methods approach to explore teachers' and students' standpoints. To reach more reliable and accurate outcomes, future investigations into translanguaging should also make use of emerging and innovative research methods.

One possibility for extending the innovative reach of research in this area is to employ the idiodynamic method, ecological approaches, and Q-methodology as a combination of quantitative and qualitative approaches to study participants' subjectivity or shared opinions. This would yield collective views on translanguaging in a rigorous and systematic way, drawing on the richness of qualitative data with the rigour of statistical analysis. The final shortcoming of the reviewed studies concerns the predominant data-gathering instruments employed. As the findings revealed, most of the research utilized questionnaires and interviews to gauge participants' perceptions and attitudes. It is thus recommended that future research uses a more diverse range of data collection instruments, including observations, focus groups, narrative writings, and so on.

12.6 Conclusion

This systematic review was undertaken to identify the position of translanguaging in EFL and ESL classrooms by reviewing previous studies conducted on teachers' and students' perspectives. Based on the results obtained from evaluating the pertinent literature, it can be concluded that translanguaging has the potential to be an effective pedagogical approach, facilitating the language acquisition process. This may have some valuable and practical implications for EFL/ESL teachers and teacher trainers. For example, teachers can refrain from viewing translanguaging as a detrimental activity, and rather include it in their classes to further facilitate language acquisition for learners. Furthermore, teacher trainers can implement programmes during which different approaches to translanguaging are taught to teachers so that they can employ such strategies based on the context.

Given the potential value of translanguaging in English classrooms, EFL and ESL teachers could employ this pedagogical approach to facilitate the language learning process. Teacher trainers should also be prepared to instruct both pre- and in-service teachers on how to implement this instructional method in EFL and ESL classes.

To conclude the findings of this chapter, the misconceptions regarding the use of translanguaging in L2 classes should be reconsidered since the findings revealed the potential benefits of translanguaging from the perspectives of both learners and teachers as the main stakeholders. Consistent with our findings, future studies should be conducted on different strategies by which translanguaging can be included in actual teaching practices.

References

Abdolmanafi Rokni, S. J., & Khonakdar, M. (2016). Investigating Iranian EFL learners' attitudes toward teachers' code switching. *International Journal for 21st Century Education, 13*(1), 5–14. https://doi.org/10.21071/ij21ce.v3i1. 5643

Aliakbari, M., & Fadaeian, F. (2023). The relationship between translanguaging perceptions and language teacher immunity. *Journal of Modern Research in English Language Studies, 11*(1), 147–168. https://doi.org/10.30479/jmrels. 2023.18225.2163

Aliakbari, M., & Khosravian, F. (2014). Linguistic capital in Iran: Using official language or mother tongue. *Procedia—Social and Behavioral Sciences, 98*, 190–199. https://doi.org/10.1016/j.sbspro.2014.03.406

Bahrami, F., Ghaderi, M., & Talebi, B. (2020). Explaining the basics and logic of mother tongue education, a way for educational justice in bilingual primary school students. *Iranian Journal of Educational Sociology, 3*(4), 43–53. https://doi.org/10.52547/ijes.3.4.43

Bolkvadze, L. (2023). Translanguaging as EFL teaching method. *Creative Education, 14*(2), 270–287. https://doi.org/10.4236/ce.2023.142019

Burton, J., & Rajendram, S. (2019). Translanguaging-as-resource: University ESL instructors' language orientations and attitudes toward translanguaging. *TESL Canada Journal, 36*(1), 21–47. https://doi.org/10.18806/tesl.v36i1. 1301

Canli, B., & Canli, Z. (2023). Translanguaging in online foreign language classrooms: Students' perceptions. *Erciyes Akademi, 37*(3), 1162–1181. https://doi.org/10.48070/erciyesakademi.1324480

Cenoz, J., & Gorter, D. (2020). Pedagogical translanguaging: An Introduction. *System, 92*, 102269. https://doi.org/10.1016/j.system.2020.102269

Cook, V. (2001). Using the first language in the classroom. *Canadian Modern Language Review, 57*(3), 402–423. https://doi.org/10.3138/cmlr.57.3.402

Cvilikaitė-Mačiulskienė, J., Daukšaitė-Kolpakovienė, A., Gvazdikaitė, G., & Linkevičiūtė, E. (2023). Translanguaging in teaching and learning of English at university level: The perspectives of Ukrainian students and their teachers. *Sustainable Multilingualism, 23*(1), 25–62. https://doi.org/10.2478/sm-2023-0012

Doiz, A., & Lasagabaster, D. (2017). Teachers' beliefs about translanguaging practices. In C. M. Mazak & K. S. Carroll (Eds.), *Translanguaging in higher education: Beyond monolingual ideologies* (pp.157–176). Multilingual Matters.

García, O., & Lin, A. M. Y. (2016). Translanguaging in bilingual education. In O. García, A. M. Y. Lin, & S. May (Eds.), *Bilingual and multilingual education* (pp. 117–130). Springer.

Gass, M., & Selinker, L. (2008). *Second language acquisition: An introductory course.* Routledge.

Gorter, D., & Arocena, E. (2020). Teachers' beliefs about multilingualism in a course on translanguaging. *System, 92*, 102272. https://doi.org/10.1016/j.system.2020.102272

Hamidi, H., & Najafi Sarem, S. (2012). A closer look at some reasons behind code-switching: A case of Iranian EFL classrooms. *ELT Voices – India, 2*(5), 89–102.

Hashemi, S. M., & Khalili Sabet, M. (2013). The Iranian EFL students' and teachers' perception of using Persian in general English classes. *International Journal of Applied Linguistics & English Literature, 2*(2), 142–152.

Huang, X., & Chalmers, H. (2023). Implementation and effects of pedagogical translanguaging in EFL classrooms: A systematic review. *Languages, 8*(3), 194. https://doi.org/10.3390/languages8030194

Khairunnisa, K., & Lukmana, I. (2020). Teachers' attitudes towards translanguaging in Indonesian EFL classrooms. *Jurnal Penelitian Pendidikan, 20*(2), 254–266. https://doi.org/10.17509/jpp.v20i2.27046

Kucukali, E., & Koçbaş, D. (2021). Benefits and issues of translanguaging pedagogies on language learning: Students' perspective. *Turkish Online Journal of English Language Teaching, 6*(1), 55–85.

Kwihangana, F. (2021). Enhancing EFL students' participation through translanguaging. *ELT Journal, 75*(1), 87–96. https://doi.org/10.1093/elt/cca a058

Li, Q., & Chan, K. K. (2024). Test takers' attitudes of using exam-oriented mobile application as a tool to adapt in a high-stakes speaking test. *Education and Information Technologies, 29*(1), 219–237. https://doi.org/10.1007/s10639-023-12297-0

Li, W., & García, O. (2022). Not a first language but one repertoire: Translanguaging as a decolonizing project. *RELC Journal, 53*(2), 313–324.

Liu, D. (2021). *A study of graduate students' perceptions towards pedagogical translanguaging at an international university* (Unpublished master's thesis). Assumption University. https://repository.au.edu/handle/662300 4553/24818

Liu, D., Deng, Y., & Wimpenny, K. (2022). Students' perceptions and experiences of translanguaging pedagogy in teaching English for academic purposes in China. *Teaching in Higher Education, 29*(5), 1234–1252. https://doi.org/10.1080/13562517.2022.2129961

Madkur, A., Friska, Y., & Lisnawati, L. (2022). Translanguaging pedagogy in ELT practices: Experiences of teachers in Indonesian pesantren-based schools. *VELES (Voices of English Language Education Society), 6*(1), 130–143. https://doi.org/10.29408/veles.v6i1.5136

Maftoon, P., & Amjadiparvar, A. (2023). Teachers' code-switching in EFL classes in Iran. *Journal of Linguistic Studies Theory and Practice, 1*(1), 15–31. https://doi.org/10.22034/jls.2023.60798

Memari, M. (2023). Language skills development via translanguaging: A case of EFL context. *Teaching English Language, 1*, 39–66. https://doi.org/10.22132/tel.2023.392066.1458

Namzidost, E., Neisi, L., & Banari, R. (2019). The impact of code-switching on vocabulary learning among Iranian upper-intermediate EFL learners. *International Journal of Linguistics, Literature and Translation, 2*(5), 309–318. https://doi.org/10.32996/ijllt.2019.2.5.35

Nazeri, S., Amini, D., & Salahshoor, F. (2020). Motivational determinants of code-switching in Iranian EFL classrooms. *The Journal of Applied Linguistics and Applied Literature: Dynamics and Advances, 8*(1), 151–173. https://doi.org/10.22049/jalda.2020.26812.1171

Noorbar, S., & Jafarpour Mamaghani, H. (2016). The effect of code-switching on Iranian elementary EFL learners' oral fluency, accuracy, and willingness to communicate. *Journal of Modern Research in Language Studies, 3*(4), 75–103.

Oliver, R., Wigglesworth, G., Angelo, D., & Steele, C. (2021). Translating translanguaging into our classrooms: Possibilities and challenges. *Language Teaching Research, 25*(1), 134–150. https://doi.org/10.1177/136216882093 8822

Ossa Parra, M., & Proctor, C. P. (2021). Translanguaging to understand language. *TESOL Quarterly, 55*(3), 766–794. https://doi.org/10.1002/tesq. 3011

Page, M. J., McKenzie, J. E., Bossuyt, P. M., Boutron, I., Hoffmann, T. C., Mulrow, C. D., et al. (2021). The PRISMA 2020 statement: An updated guideline for reporting systematic reviews. *International Journal of Surgery, 88*, 105906. https://doi.org/10.1016/j.ijsu.2021.105906

Panagiotopoulou, J. A., Rosen, L., & Jenna Strzykala, J. (Eds.). (2020). *Inclusion, education and translanguaging: How to promote social justice in (teacher) education?* Springer.

Poza, L. (2017). Translanguaging: Definitions, implications, and further needs in burgeoning inquiry. *Berkeley Review of Education, 6*(2), 101–128. https://doi.org/10.5070/B86110060

Putrawan, G. E., & Sinaga, T. (2022). Bilinguals' linguistic repertoire and foreign language instruction: What do teachers say about teaching EFL through translanguaging. *Journal of Language, 4*(1), 166–172. https://doi.org/10.30743/jol.v4i1.5489

Putri, F. I., & Rifai, I. (2021). Translanguaging practices in EFL classrooms: Teachers' perspective. *English Journal Literacy Utama, 6*(1), 460–470. https://doi.org/10.33197/ejlutama.v6i1.155

Raja, F. D., Suparno, S., & Ngadiso, N. (2021). Indonesian students' perception on translanguaging challenges in the EFL class. *ICOTEL Proceeding MPBING, 2*(1), 162–167. https://proceeding.icotel.org/index.php/mpbing/article/view/23/21

Raja, F. D., Suparno, S., & Ngadiso, N. (2022). Teachers' attitude towards translanguaging practice and its implication in Indonesian EFL classroom. *Indonesian Journal of Applied Linguistics, 11*(3), 567–576. https://doi.org/10.17509/ijal.v11i3.38371

Reyes, I. (2004). Functions of code switching in schoolchildren's conversations. *Bilingual Research Journal, 28*(1), 77–98. https://doi.org/10.1080/152 35882.2004.10162613

Rezaee, A. A., & Fathi, S. (2016). The perceptions of language learners across various proficiency levels of teachers' code-switching. *Issues in Language Teaching, 5*(2), 233–254. https://doi.org/10.22054/ilt.2017.8060

Rezvani, E., & Eslami Rasekh, A. (2011). Code-switching in Iranian Elementary EFL classrooms: An exploratory investigation. *English Language Teaching, 4*(1), 18–25. https://doi.org/10.5539/elt.v4n1p18

Santoso, W. (2020). Translanguaging through the lens of sociocultural approach: Students' attitudes and practices. *Jurnal Pendidikan Bahasa, 9*(1), 1–19. https://doi.org/10.31571/bahasa.v9i1.1707

Scopich, D. (2018). *Translanguaging in an EEL classroom: Attitudes and practice* (Unpublished doctoral dissertation). University of Rijeka. https://core.ac.uk/download/pdf/198155836.pdf

Seals, C. A. (2021). Benefits of translanguaging pedagogy and practice. *Scottish Languages Review, 36*, 1–8. https://scilt.org.uk/Portals/24/Library/slr/issues/36/36-01%20Seals.pdf

Stihi, O. (2021). Ecological approaches to language education: Translanguaging in the Algerian EFL classroom. *Revue Traduction et Langues, 20*(1), 294–308.

Tejano, L. D. (2022). Increasing multilingual first-grade learners' online engagement through pedagogical translanguaging. *International Journal of Social Science and Education Research Studies, 2*(7), 308–315. https://doi.org/10.55677/ijssers/V02I07Y2022-11

Turnbull, B. (2018). Is there a potential for a translanguaging approach to English education in Japan? Perspectives of tertiary learners and teachers. *JALT Journal, 40*(2), 101–134. https://jalt-publications.org/sites/default/files/pdf-article/jj2018b-art2.pdf

Tuskeyeva, A. (2022). *Perceptions on translanguaging from EFL teachers with different linguistic backgrounds in Kazakhstan* (Unpublished master's thesis). Nazarbayev University.

Wang, Z., & Shen, B. (2023). 'I think I am bilingual, but…': Teachers' practices of and students' attitudes toward translanguaging in a Chinese intercultural communication class. *International Journal of Applied Linguistics, 34*(1), 242–260. https://doi.org/10.1111/ijal.12491

Wei, L. (2022). Translanguaging as method. *Research Methods in Applied Linguistics, 1*(3), 100026. https://doi.org/10.1016/j.rmal.2022.100026

Wei, L., & Lin, A. M. Y. (2019). Translanguaging classroom discourse: Pushing limits, Breaking boundaries. *Classroom Discourse, 10*(3–4), 209–215. https://doi.org/10.1080/19463014.2019.1635032

Williams, C. (1994). *Arfarniad o ddulliau dysgu ac addysgu yng nghyd-destun addysg uwchradd ddwyieithog* [An evaluation of teaching and learning methods in the context of bilingual secondary education] (Unpublished doctoral dissertation) University of Bangor.

Witari, P. S., & Sukamto, K. E. (2023). Pedagogical issues of translanguaging practice in Indonesia: The voice of four EFL teachers. *IJIET: International Journal of Indonesian Education and Teaching, 7*(2), 204–220. https://doi.org/10.24071/ijiet.v7i2.5814

Yusri, N. S., Huzaimi, N. H. A., & Sulaiman, N. A. (2022). Translanguaging in Malaysian ESL classroom: Teachers' perceptions. *International Journal of Academic Research in Business and Social Sciences, 12*(9), 607–619. https://doi.org/10.6007/IJARBSS/v12-i9/14542

Yuvayapan, F. (2019). Translanguaging in EFL classrooms: Teachers' perceptions and practices. *Journal of Language and Linguistic Studies, 15*(2), 678–694. https://doi.org/10.17263/jlls.586811

Yuzlu, Y. M., & Dikilitas, K. (2022). Translanguaging in the development of EFL learners' foreign language skills in Turkish context. *Innovation in Language Learning and Teaching, 16*(2), 176–190. https://doi.org/10.1080/17501229.2021.1892698

Zohrabi, M., Yaghoubi-Notash, M., & Khodadadi, A. (2014). The facilitating role of Iranian learners' first language in learning English vocabulary. *International Journal on Studies in English Language and Literature, 2*(8), 44–57.

13

Iranian EFL Teachers' Beliefs on Pedagogical Translanguaging

Hamid Allami⬤ and Shadi Shivakhah

13.1 Introduction

Over the past decade, there has been a growing number of publications focusing on a dynamic bilingual model, which has resulted in the advancement of the term translanguaging (García & Li, 2014). However, translanguaging is not a new concept. Baker (2001) translated Williams' (1994) coinage "trawsieithu" to "translanguaging", which refers to the pedagogical practices Williams experienced in bilingual Welsh-English educational programs where learners received input in Welsh but mainly answered in English. Unlike most teachers of the time who had a negative attitude toward the practice of actively using two languages in lessons, Williams considered it a chance to enhance learning as it utilized learners' and teachers' whole linguistic repertoire to promote the

H. Allami (✉) · S. Shivakhah
Department of English Language Teaching, Faculty of Humanities, Tarbiat Modares University, Tehran, Iran
e-mail: h.allami@modares.ac.ir

© The Author(s), under exclusive license to Springer Nature Switzerland AG 2025
D. Coulson and C. Denman (eds.), *Translation, Translanguaging and Machine Translation in Foreign Language Education*,
https://doi.org/10.1007/978-3-031-82174-5_13

261

processes of learning and building problem-solving skills. That is, this form of classroom management was implemented as a teaching approach to take advantage of both languages methodically to enhance teaching and learning processes (Lewis et al., 2012). In sum, translanguaging is not merely the use of the first language (L1) to make lessons more comprehensible. Rather, it involves cognitive processes that are relevant to "retaining and developing bilingualism" (García & Li, 2014, p. 64). As a result, translanguaging can be a more effective approach for learners due to the remapping of cross-language semantics (Lewis et al., 2012).

Recent studies (e.g., Cenoz & Gorter, 2020; Yüzlü & Dikilitas, 2022) have confirmed the effectiveness of translanguaging as a pedagogical strategy in teaching and learning a foreign language. However, evidence suggests that many policymakers, practitioners, and even students still maintain favorable attitudes toward monolingual ideologies in many countries, including Iran. Therefore, teachers need to acquire in-depth knowledge about the significance of supporting students' native languages and cultures through well-organized teacher education programs (García et al., 2017). It is within this context that this paper explores Iranian English as a Foreign Language (EFL) teachers' beliefs about the advantages of pedagogical translanguaging in four dimensions: constructive, cognitive, interactive, and effective.

13.2 Literature Review

Translanguaging was originally used as a pedagogical approach in bilingual contexts as a means of developing the second language with the support of the L1, thus eventually enabling students to alternate between languages and become more proficient in both receptive and productive language skills (e.g., Williams, 1994). This fluid practice of language switching has been the focus of much attention over the past decade, specifically in the field of bilingual and multilingual education (e.g., Cenoz & Gorter, 2020, 2021; Li & García, 2022; Seltzer & García, 2020).

In pedagogical translanguaging, language learning involves discursive practices where teachers activate learners' access to their entire linguistic repertoire. To do so, teachers encourage students to employ planned alternations between languages for input and output. Hence, pedagogical translanguaging is different from spontaneous translanguaging in that it is a planned approach to teaching a language or content in a new language (Cenoz & Gorter, 2020). Specifically, teachers aim to: "1) introduce learners to a large variety of resources to support their learning, 2) increase subject understanding by encouraging deep analysis of the content and 3) scaffold the weaker language by supporting the stronger language" (Thomas et al., 2022, p. 19).

Research largely supports the view that, in addition to content learning, translanguaging can have positive effects on learning a second or a foreign language. Several studies endorse the use of two languages in EFL programs, focusing on scaffolding in the classroom and its benefits. For instance, after having employed classroom translanguaging practices with the support of scaffolding, Daniel et al. (2019) reported that learners enjoy the benefits of translanguaging once they realize that it is both recognized and valued. This cannot be achieved, however, unless teachers design and implement the required scaffolding tools and prompts at two levels: designed-in or macro-scaffolding, which includes identifying and organizing classroom goals in addition to selecting and sequencing classroom tasks and interactional or micro-scaffolding.

Pedagogical translanguaging can accelerate language learners' linguistic and communicative competencies. For example, Yüzlü and Dikilitas (2022) investigated the potential impact of translanguaging pedagogy on high-school students of English in Turkey. The researchers assigned half of each group of 60 pre-intermediate and 60 upper-intermediate students into experimental and control groups. The former received instruction incorporating translanguaging pedagogy and the latter were taught through grammar-translation methods (control group 1) or a communicative language approach (control group 2). Pre- and post-test proficiency tests complemented by semi-structured interviews indicated that translanguaging pedagogy was associated with improvements in students' core language skills, and that they experienced a range of cognitive, affective, constructive, and interactive benefits. The researchers conclude that the implementation of pedagogical translanguaging has a favorable impact on learning processes in terms of overcoming the limitations of monolingual practices and the separation of languages.

In addition to enhancing metalinguistic awareness, students' pragmatic and discourse competence can also develop as a result of pedagogical translanguaging. Aoyama (2020) reported that high-proficiency students in the third grade of a Japanese high-school English class exposed to communicative language methods used their whole linguistic repertoire as a communication strategy for completing communicative tasks. More specifically, translanguaging was employed for communicative purposes, such as fillers, backchannelling, asking for help and metalanguage. This reflected the students' abilities to use translanguaging as a communication skill to adjust their speaking strategies based on responses received from interlocutors. The students' translanguaging practice underscored active multilingual communication initiated from the classroom discourse. These results indicate that interaction between languages through translanguaging can enhance learners' communicative competence due to their access to different language practices in different contexts, which is the essence of pragmatic competence.

Despite the positive impacts of the implementation of translanguaging on students' learning potential, there is still hesitation on the part of some teachers to use it as a pedagogical approach. One possible constraint may be the persistence of educational policymakers on language separation and monolingual ideologies in many countries. This is an issue which might result in the "teacher guilt" described by Rabbidge (2019) as experienced by some EFL instructors when the L1 is used in the classroom. Teachers who believe in multilingual education, but are prohibited from using their L1, might experience this feeling when alternating between languages.

Although education institutions in various countries still largely insist on language separation, the recent spread of new trends in multilingual education cannot be ignored. Therefore, more and more weight has been given to language teachers' beliefs and perceptions regarding the notion of multilingualism in applied linguistics and sociolinguistics.

The current literature paints a picture where the acceptance of bilingual education by language teachers, accompanied by positive beliefs about its significance, exists alongside the continuing presence of monolingual practices in language teaching and learning (Yuvayapan, 2019). Opponents perceive bilingual education programs as detrimental to cognitive development and academic success in individuals. Indeed, some maintain that the use of two languages as mediums of instruction hinders the acquisition of aspects of both, especially in terms of vocabulary. Still, others claim that bilingual education creates a sense of divisiveness in society rather than maintaining national identity, of which a shared mother tongue has historically been viewed as fundamental.

It is within this framework that Gorter and Arocena (2020) designed and conducted a teacher training course for the professional development of in-service teachers at the University of Basque Country, Spain. It was offered in English, but participants had the opportunity to participate in either Spanish or Basque. The course introduced new trends in multilingual education by encouraging language teachers to apply a multilingual curriculum in elementary or secondary schools. Theoretical perspectives on the application of strategies to integrate different languages were discussed. The researchers concluded that instructors' beliefs about translanguaging can become more positive and open when teacher trainers are exposed to the principles of translanguaging during professional development programs.

Gorter and Arocena (2020) further reported cases where teachers admitted how relieved they felt when receiving approval for doing what they already practiced, i.e., covertly using Spanish or Basque in class. Some teachers, however, reported avoiding the use of these languages due to institutional and contextual constraints. This potential disparity between teachers' beliefs about the potential value of translanguaging practices and actual practices is apparent elsewhere in the literature. For example, Doiz and Lasagabaster (2017) reported that even the teachers who seek to maintain a strict monolingual environment tend to use their L1 when faced with difficult concepts or unfamiliar words.

The friction between different viewpoints on the use of translanguaging in multilingual contexts versus traditional language separation approaches can be encountered in many nations. Iran is not an exception. In the country's language institutes, there is still generally reported uncertainty about whether EFL teachers agree or disagree with the practice of translanguaging and, if they do support the practice, the areas in which they believe it can be beneficial. Therefore, the current study aims to investigate Iranian EFL in-service teachers' beliefs about practicing translanguaging as a pedagogical strategy to enhance L2 learning. More specifically, it aims to address the following research question: What do Iranian in-service EFL teachers believe about translanguaging as a pedagogical strategy?

13.3 Method

The current research investigated in-service EFL teachers' beliefs about the practice of translanguaging as an intentional approach to teaching English in Iranian language schools. A questionnaire was administered to 55 in-service teachers in several language schools across Iran while semi-structured interviews were conducted with four of these participants.

13.3.1 Participants and Data Collection

A total number of 120 in-service teachers were invited through email to participate in the study. In the invitation, potential participants were informed of the purpose of the study, their right of participation/non-participation, and the anonymity of their responses. 55 of the contacted teachers agreed to participate in the questionnaire phase of the research. Participants were EFL teachers in several language schools in different cities in Iran and included 12 novice and 43 experienced teachers. Novice teachers were defined as those within their first two years of teaching experience, while experienced instructors had taught for at least five years.

The semi-structured interviews involved four volunteer participants—two novice and two experienced teachers. Interviewees were again informed about the nature of the study, that their responses would be recorded, and of efforts made by the researchers to ensure their anonymity. Interviewees consisted of one EFL MA student, two MA holders, and one PhD candidate. The interviews were conducted online on Google Meet and were digitally recorded and later transcribed verbatim for analysis. Each interview lasted approximately 20 minutes.

13.3.2 Instruments

An online questionnaire was devised, based on Yüzlü and Dikilitas (2022), about students' attitudes toward translanguaging pedagogy. After the initial version was constructed, the researchers submitted it to two academics in the field of linguistics to help ensure face and content validity, clarity, and ease of use. As a result of this process, a brief overview of translanguaging was added to ensure participants shared a clear understanding of this key concept.

Items were translated into the participants' native language, Persian (or Farsi), to help avoid any misunderstanding or confusion. Response options on a 5-point Likert scale were: (1) strongly disagree; (2) disagree; (3) neither agree nor disagree; (4) agree; and (5) strongly agree. The final version of the questionnaire contained 15 items across the following four areas: (1) constructive dimension (2 items); (2) cognitive dimension (4 items); (3) interactive dimension (3 items); and (4) affective dimension (6 items). The English-language version of the questionnaire is featured in Appendix.

Semi-structured interviews were conducted with two novice and two experienced teachers to examine their beliefs about translanguaging practices in EFL classrooms. The guiding interview questions, which were adapted from Liu and Fang (2022), were:

- Are you familiar with the term "translanguaging"? If yes, how do you define it?
- What do you think of the practice of translanguaging in an EFL class?
- Do you switch between English and Persian purposefully or unconsciously?
- When do you find translanguaging helpful in class?
- Do you have any concerns about switching between languages in class?
- Do you allow students to use their L1 in class? And why?

13.3.3 Data Analysis

13.3.3.1 Quantitative Data

In the quantitative phase of the study, the analysis was carried out using the factor analyzer 0.4.0 library in Python. The first step involved examining correlations between potential variables to see if any were either irrelevant or very highly correlated with the others. The Kaiser–Meyer–Olkin (KMO) test was used to evaluate the adequacy of data for factor analysis. The adequacy of each separate variable and the overall adequacy rate were measured by KMO, with a KMO value lower than 0.6 taken as unacceptable and 1 considered perfect.

The next step involved selecting several factors which we conducted through the use of a scree plot, which is based on eigenvalues. Eigenvalues are used to examine how much variance is accounted for by a specific factor, thereby helping determine the ideal number of factors to extract. In creating the resultant scree plot, we plotted the eigenvalues for each factor and looked for a point where there is a noticeable drop. For the Factor Analyzer function, in which the desired number of factors and the type of rotation is specified, varimax rotation was used to make the best use of the totality of the variance of squared loadings and to confirm that the factors generated were not interconnected (orthogonality).

13.3.3.2 Qualitative Data

For the qualitative stage of the study, thematic analysis via MAXQDA Analytics Pro 2020 was used. All interviewees were assigned a random pseudonym to help protect their identities. We first read the transcripts and prepared the data for coding. Once we had coded all relevant segments, we started to define themes for each group of similar codes. Eventually, similar and redundant themes were grouped to make a list of smaller and more convenient themes that we believed fully and accurately represented the interview data.

13.4 Results

13.4.1 Quantitative Data

Factor analysis revealed that there was a considerable correlation between some themes. Specifically, the following three pairs of themes were highly correlated:

- Theme 1 (Making meaning), Theme 5 (Bilingual awareness raising)— $r = 0.785$;
- Theme 5 (Bilingual awareness raising), Theme 14 (Experiencing enjoyment of learning)—$r = 0.730$;
- Theme 6 (Facilitating learning), Theme 13 (Volunteering in-class participation)—$r = 0.740$.

KMO values fluctuated between 0 and 1. Any factor with a KMO value below 0.6 was rejected. The total KMO value for our data was 0.88, which is very strong and supports our implementation of the planned factor analysis.

Only three factors were selected to perform the factor analysis due to the drastic fall in eigenvalue after the third factor (see Fig. 13.1). These factors have eigenvalues of 8.7, 1.3, and 1.2, indicating that they describe the variance of about 11.2 variables.

Variable factor loadings are presented in Table 13.1. The interpretation of the variables resulted in the formation of the following factors:

- Effectiveness: Making meaning, promoting autonomous learning, realizing the language system, and accelerating learning.
- Enjoyment: Relishing learning, assuring a comfortable learning experience, building a secure learning environment, and promoting communicative competence.
- Self-confidence: Bilingual awareness, learning the language in a real context, voluntary class participation, and encouraging speaking.

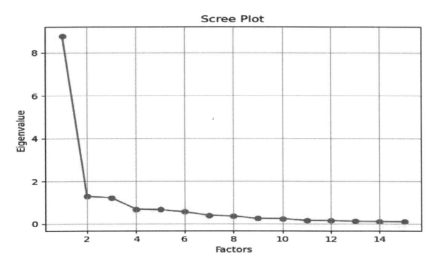

Fig. 13.1 Eigenvalue of factors

13.4.2 Qualitative Data

Semi-structured interviews revealed that only one of the four participants was familiar with the term translanguaging, while one other was familiar with the concept but did not know the terminology associated with it. The first participant, Neda, a novice teacher and PhD TEFL candidate, stated that she was aware of the concept through her higher-level studies:

> I am a PhD candidate for TEFL and we learned about it recently. I know that it is using all the linguistic repertoire to maximize understanding. The teacher chooses when to use or allow students to use their first language to exchange ideas, share opinions, etc.

However, the other novice teacher, Parsa, who is an MA student in TEFL, stated:

> I first heard it [translanguaging] in your questionnaire, and I have no idea what it exactly is in terms of pedagogical strategies. ... (I didn't know the terminology, but) I encountered this sort of method before. I believe it was CLIL [content and language integrated learning] and yes, I can see

Table 13.1 Variable factor loadings

Themes	Factor 1: effectiveness	Factor 2: enjoyment	Factor 3: self-confidence
Making meaning	0.70	0.16	0.13
Promoting autonomous learning	0.75	0.36	0.19
Utilizing all language resources	0.57	0.28	0.62
Realizing the language system	0.66	0.15	0.54
Fostering bilingual awareness	0.19	0.09	0.74
Accelerating learning	0.60	0.30	0.29
Maximizing interaction	0.53	0.53	0.23
Utilizing meaningful learning	0.58	0.34	0.42
Promoting competence	0.36	0.63	0.36
Building a secure learning environment	0.14	0.86	0.25
Assuring a comfortable learning experience	0.34	0.72	0.25
Encouraging speaking	0.37	0.45	0.61
Encouraging voluntary participation	0.72	0.42	0.62
Relishing learning	0.50	0.72	0.17
Learning the language in a real context	0.34	0.31	0.72

the implementation of translanguaging there, where the teacher presents the content using both first and second or foreign languages.

One of the experienced teachers, Bahram, with an MA in English Language Literature, stated, "What I understood from your question-naire is that it means using Persian [first language] in an English class". The final participant, Roya, an experienced teacher with an MA in TEFL, commented, "Well, as you had clarified in your questionnaire, it is a tech-nique for teaching concepts or ideas with the help of the students' first language".

When teachers' positions on translanguaging pedagogy were exam-ined, both novice teachers had favorable perceptions of the practice, while the experienced instructors were either neutral or negative in this regard. In terms of the former, Parsa stated, "It can boost or accelerate the efficiency of learning. It has a positive impact on how efficiently you deal with the content and your students… so, yes, I am all for it". Concerning this point, Neda added, "I am totally in favor of this pedagogical strategy as it enhances the learning process…. It also makes learning sweet and memorable".

Representing a contrasting point of view, Bahram replied that:

I have to disagree. Why do students spend time and money going to English classes? To learn English! And you know the classroom is the only chance they have to practice English. I think when you speak English you have to think in English; therefore, Farsi must be eliminated.

Roya was somewhat neutral in her response:

To be honest, I haven't done it myself in all years of my teaching, but I was just thinking that it could have some positive effects on students, because they feel less nervous and they can understand some points in depth. I am sure that when I teach my intermediate students a passage about extreme sports, they leave the class with some doubt about the exact meaning of some words or sentences. But, this is what we were taught to do in our TTC [teacher training courses] and what the observers insist we must do. So, I don't think I can do it in my classes.

The next set of questions was concerned with teachers' awareness of switching between languages. It can be concluded that three of four teachers were aware of their language choices and only Bahram, who had a very strict monolingual ideology, agreed that he speaks English without fail in his classes:

> I do not switch between languages, let alone purposefully or unconsciously. Even when unexpected incidents take place... I remember before the pandemic sometimes we had a blackout, or even once there was a mouse in my class. I spoke English all the time. I should say when I step into the classroom I speak English unconsciously, without thinking about it.

Roya claimed that she does not switch between languages while teaching, but that she sometimes speaks Farsi to her students purposefully:

> To tell the truth, I sometimes speak Farsi to my students not to teach them the lessons from their books but to teach them lessons about life. Sometimes, there is a situation [in] which students show a bad reaction to one student, or hurt her with their words. Then, I stop teaching and talk to them in Farsi for a few minutes to teach them a lesson about life. I do it purposefully... I tell them before being a good student with a high score you have to learn to be a good human being.

Developing this theme, Parsa added that:

> I have purposefully switched to Persian in some areas whenever I got the feeling that they could not understand the concept, no matter how much time I spent explaining it, the number of videos, and pictures that I showed them, and some subjects are just intangible for them.

Neda elaborated on how she applies translanguaging as an enhancing educational tool in her reply, "I switch between languages purposefully. I am fully aware of what I am doing and I also have my students switch to Farsi when I have a good reason for it".

When examining concerns about the implementation of translanguaging pedagogy, all four interviewees agreed to different extents that there are drawbacks that must be taken into account when using associated practices. For example, Bahram strongly opposed the whole concept:

> This new trend must not be implemented in any language school. It is destructive. I am sure many teachers will like it because it makes their job easier. But, I am sure it is bad for students. They will never learn English properly. So, I hope that you researchers let us do our job the way we know and we are sure of its efficiency.

Roya had similar opinions to Bahram in terms of switching between languages while teaching:

> Farsi and English don't have much in common… if students think in Farsi and write in English, the outcome will be only a translation and it won't be authentic…. I am sure if students are given options, they will all choose their mother tongue for interaction with peers and it reduces their chances of developing their speaking skills… If I explain only one thing in Farsi, it forms a bad habit in my students to expect me to translate even the simplest concepts to Farsi.

Parsa added that:

> I can see some major drawbacks to it and I can understand why most institutes ban using L1 in classes. Some teachers might get addicted to using and even over-using Persian because it is the easiest and quickest way. And, another drawback is about students. They get used to knowing the Farsi equivalent of every concept even though they completely understand it in English. Also, it can harm their speaking skill development if it is not controlled.

Neda has no personal concerns as she claimed to be fully aware of her translanguaging practice. However, she insisted that pre- and in-service teachers need to be trained before implementing this pedagogy:

> I don't have any concerns because I know how to apply it, but some teachers might have a mistaken understanding and use translation, or teach everything in Farsi. So, I believe that before teachers go to the

classroom, they should be trained by expert teacher trainers and know about the concept and also how it should be implemented in class. If a teacher doesn't practice translanguaging correctly, it can have serious negative impacts on students' learning process.

When asked about their beliefs about their students' language learning through translanguaging, all four teachers agreed that students will feel more comfortable, thus offering support for Factor 2 in the quantitative phase. Roya, Neda, and Parsa agreed that translanguaging positively impacts students' self-confidence, which is in agreement with Factor 3. Moreover, both novice teachers believed that students will make meaning and understand the topic better, and will be more effectively helped in the learning process, through translanguaging, which directly supports Factor 1.

13.5 Discussion

The current study aimed to investigate Iranian EFL teachers' beliefs about the implementation of translanguaging pedagogy in the current English-only dominated education system of Iran by drawing on the benefits that Iranian learners might potentially experience in a bilingual context. The findings in the quantitative phase of the study mainly revealed the areas in which teachers find translanguaging practices beneficial for their learners. In the qualitative phase, we tried to provide an in-depth understanding of EFL teachers' position on translanguaging pedagogy, their familiarity with the concept, their beliefs, and concerns about such practices, as well as their awareness of their current code-switching between languages if and when using Persian in their classrooms.

The most significant finding from the analysis of the quantitative data is that, in defiance of the monolingual policies implemented in almost all language schools in Iran, there are neutral to positive beliefs among EFL teachers about the potential value of translanguaging practices in at least three areas: improving the efficiency of teaching/learning; promoting students' enjoyment of the learning process; and developing self-confidence in learners. These findings are closely related to students' attitudes toward their learning practices through translanguaging in a large number of areas. These include, but are not limited to, the following factors: making meaning, promoting autonomous learning, discovering the language system, facilitating learning, enjoying learning, promoting a comfortable learning environment, promoting communicative abilities and bilingual awareness, developing a sense of real language learning, and sustaining motivation to speak (Yüzlü & Dikilitas, 2022).

However, as noted by Horwitz (2001), despite foreign language teachers' awareness of the importance of encouraging students' self-confidence, many instructors are not sure about how to help them achieve this. Hence, the implementation of translanguaging as a systematic approach can enable language teachers to promote learners' self-confidence and experience a stress-free environment. This outcome conforms to the findings of Yuvayapan (2019) regarding teachers' perceptions of the use of L1 in translanguaging practices in the Turkish EFL context. That is, while Yuvayapan reported that most teachers found it essential to allow students to use their L1 to facilitate the participation of less proficient students and build rapport, they nonetheless kept the use of L1 to a minimum.

Another important finding was that, generally, novice teachers had more positive beliefs about the value and utility of translanguaging than their more experienced colleagues. Surprisingly, however, even those teachers who had negative attitudes toward translanguaging agreed that students can experience a more peaceful and stress-free environment if this approach is employed. Novice teachers generally have a more open mindset about learning new notions and skills for professional development, but they often turn to experienced teachers for advice in their new profession (Hargreaves, 2005). Therefore, considering the fact that more experienced teachers tend to have less flexible mindsets, professional development programs must be carefully designed to refresh these instructors' knowledge and keep them up to date with new teaching and learning trends.

The fact that experienced teachers are less likely to be open to change shows how instructors, who are often settled in one institution early in their careers, and are exposed to certain ideas and limited approaches, may remain unaware of the practices applied in other educational institutions. This may lead to fixed mindsets, making it difficult for them to open up to change (Zilka et al., 2019). Also to address this issue, it is crucial to include new teaching trends in teacher education programs for pre-service teachers and to provide novice teachers with meaningful opportunities for ongoing professional development.

The findings further revealed that all the participants, even those in agreement with translanguaging pedagogy, had concerns regarding teachers' and students' overuse of their L1. This is contrary to Wang's (2019) study which suggests that teachers do not have concerns about students' use of their mother tongue in learning a foreign language due to their high levels of motivation and belief in the investment value of language learning. This also leads us to advocate for the implementation of professional development courses to familiarize teachers with the principles of translanguaging pedagogy and to teach them strategies to successfully implement this approach in their classrooms.

Moreover, we clarified how many teachers may not be familiar with the term translanguaging, even though some have already practiced the use of the L1 in their classrooms either for instructional or class management purposes. Thereby, teacher educators must aid the development of teachers' understanding and implementation of translanguaging practices (García et al., 2017).

With these caveats in mind, the results reported here are nonetheless encouraging, for they portend a bright future for translanguaging by Iranian EFL teachers, moving from strict monolingual policies to more flexible types of education (García & Li, 2014).

13.6   Conclusion

The systematic use of translanguaging in EFL contexts has received increasing attention from scholars in the field of bilingual foreign language teaching. The purpose of the current study was to explore EFL teachers' beliefs about the implementation of this pedagogy in the current monolingual education system of Iran. Before drawing conclusions, however, it is important to note some of the study's limitations.

We utilized convenience rather than random sampling, while the sample size, especially for the semi-structured interviews, was quite small. Consequently, the findings may not represent the beliefs and perceptions of the majority of Iranian EFL teachers, let alone their international colleagues. Considering these limitations, a more extensive survey will be required to investigate EFL teachers' ideologies and beliefs toward translanguaging practices.

With these limitations acknowledged, findings nonetheless can be interpreted as suggesting that Iranian EFL teachers have the potential, with appropriate levels of training and support, to implement translanguaging pedagogy to enhance their students' learning within constructive, cognitive, interactive, and affective dimensions. Despite this, using the L1 in EFL teaching is traditionally considered a hindrance to successful foreign language learning achievement among many Iranian EFL teachers and decision-makers, while the institutional emphasis on monolingual policies has promoted English-only contexts that consequently inhibit the use of translanguaging in lessons. Therefore, the full potential of translanguaging cannot be achieved unless there is a change in educational policies, in addition to a concerted effort to design and conduct professional development programs for in-service and pre-service teachers to introduce them to the benefits of implementing translanguaging as a pedagogical practice.

Overall, we are quite confident in arguing that carefully designed teacher training courses will lead to desirable outcomes in building a language learning context that fully welcomes the dynamic cultural and linguistic repertoires of all students, in Iran and around the world (Tian & Shepard-Carey, 2020). Furthermore, this investigation lays the groundwork for similar studies to explore Iranian student, parent, and policymaker awareness and acceptance of the relatively new notion of translanguaging.

Acknowledgements An early version of this paper was presented at the Association of English Language Teacher Educators Conference AELTE 2022 in Ankara, Turkey, 27–29 May 2022.

Appendix

Teachers' Perceptions Toward Language Learning Through Translanguaging

	1	2	3	4	5
Translanguaging enables students to make meaning and understand the topics, as well as convey messages verbally and in writing					
Students have the autonomy to decide the language to use and learn more by using both languages					
Students can realize their potential by accessing their full linguistic knowledge including their L1					
Translanguaging plays a crucial role in discovering and implementing the language system					
Students feel more powerful as they become aware of their bilingualism					
Students have positive experiences and are facilitated in the learning process through translanguaging					
Students can enjoy developing interactional language use by putting into practice what they learn both in their L1 and the L2					
Using authentic language helps students understand real-world communication and leads them to understand language as a whole					
Translanguaging improves communication by simplifying understanding and conveying messages					
Translanguaging practices make students feel more secure about expressing ideas in English only, through the freedom to use either language					
Students experience a sense of comfort and relief during translanguaging practices					
Translanguaging increases motivation and creates a genuine interest in foreign language learners					
Translanguaging helps students develop voluntary participation and engagement					
Being able to understand the teacher and peers and to talk in English lets students enjoy learning					
Unlike the non-authentic mode of course materials that gives students a sense of artificiality in learning, translanguaging makes them feel honest about themselves					

Note 1: strongly disagree 2: disagree 3: neutral 4: agree 5: strongly agree

References

Aoyama, R. (2020). Exploring Japanese high school students' L1 use in translanguaging in the communicative EFL classroom. *TESL-EJ, 23*(4). https://tesl-ej.org/wordpress/issues/volume23/ej92/ej92a12/

Baker, C. (2001). *Foundations in bilingual education and bilingualism* (3rd ed.). Multilingual Matters.

Cenoz, J., & Gorter, D. (2020). Pedagogical translanguaging: An introduction. *System, 92*, 102269. https://doi.org/10.1016/j.system.2020.102269

Cenoz, J., & Gorter, D. (2021). *Pedagogical translanguaging*. Cambridge University Press.

Daniel, S. M., Jiménez, R. T., Pray, L., & Pacheco, M. B. (2019). Scaffolding to make translanguaging a classroom norm. *TESOL Journal, 10*(1), 1–14. https://doi.org/10.1002/tesj.361

Doiz, A., & Lasagabaster, D. (2017). Teachers' beliefs about translanguaging practices. In C. M. Mazak & K. S. Carroll (Eds.), *Translanguaging in higher education: Beyond monolingual ideologies* (pp. 157–176). Multilingual Matters.

García, O., Johnson, S. I., Seltzer, K., & Valdés, G. (2017). *The translanguaging classroom: Leveraging student bilingualism for learning*. Brookes Publishing.

García, O., & Li, W. (2014). *Language, bilingualism and education*. Palgrave Macmillan.

Gorter, D., & Arocena, E. (2020). Teachers' beliefs about multilingualism in a course on translanguaging. *System, 92*. https://doi.org/10.1016/j.system.2020.102272

Hargreaves, A. (2005). The emotions of teaching and education change. In A. Hargreaves (Ed.), *Extending educational change: International handbook of educational change* (pp. 278–295). Springer.

Horwitz, E. (2001). Language anxiety and achievement. *Annual Review of Applied Linguistics, 21*, 112–126.

Lewis, G., Jones, B., & Baker, C. (2012). Translanguaging: Developing its conceptualisation and contextualisation. *Educational Research and Evaluation, 18*(7), 655–670. https://doi.org/10.1080/13803611.2012.718490

Li, W., & García, O. (2022). Not a first language but one repertoire: Translanguaging as a decolonizing project. *RELC Journal, 53*(2), 313–324. https://doi.org/10.1177/00336882221092840

Liu, Y., & Fang, F. (2022). Translanguaging theory and practice: How stakeholders perceive translanguaging as a practical theory of language. *RELC Journal, 53*(2), 391–399. https://doi.org/10.1177/0033688220939222

Rabbidge, M. (2019). *Translanguaging in EFL contexts: A call for change.* Routledge.

Seltzer, K., & García, O. (2020). Broadening the view: Taking up a translanguaging pedagogy with all language-minoritized students. In Z. Tian, L. Aghai, P. Sayer, & J. L. Schissel (Eds.), *Envisioning TESOL through a translanguaging lens: Global perspectives* (pp. 23–42). Springer.

Thomas, E. M., Siôn, C. G., Jones. B., Dafydd, M., Lloyd-Williams, S. W., Tomos, R., et al. (2022). *Translanguaging in the classroom: A quick reference guide for educators: National collaborative resources.* National Collaborative Resources: Aberystwyth University and Bangor University. https://hwb.gov.wales/api/storage/c0e59e12-c1b7-48d4-b6f1-7354f6170ab5/translanguaging-in-the-classroom.pdf

Tian, Z., & Shepard-Carey, L. (2020). (Re)imagining the future of translanguaging pedagogies in TESOL through teacher-researcher collaboration. *TESOL Quarterly, 54*(4), 1131–1143. https://doi.org/10.1002/tesq.614

Wang, D. (2019). Translanguaging in Chinese foreign language classrooms: Students and teachers' attitudes and practices. *International Journal of Bilingual Education and Bilingualism, 22*(2), 138–149. https://doi.org/10.1080/13670050.2016.1231773

Williams, C. (1994). *An evaluation of teaching and learning methods in the context of bilingual secondary education* (Unpublished doctoral dissertation). University of Bangor.

Yuvayapan, F. (2019). Translanguaging in EFL classrooms: Teachers' perceptions and practices. *Journal of Language and Linguistic Studies, 15*(2), 678–694.

Yüzlü, M., & Dikilitas, K. (2022). Translanguaging in the development of EFL learners' foreign language skills in Turkish context. *Innovation in Language Learning and Teaching, 16*(2), 176–190. https://doi.org/10.1080/17501229.2021.1892698

Zilka, A., Grinshtain, Y., & Bogler, R. (2019). Fixed or growth: Teacher perceptions of factors that shape mindset. *Professional Development in Education, 48*(1), 149–165. https://doi.org/10.1080/19415257.2019.1689524

14

Unveiling the Efficacy of Translanguaging in English Language Teaching: Insights from Turkish Teachers

Kaveh Jalilzadeh, Christine Coombe, and Adel Dastgoshadeh🆔

14.1 Introduction

The landscape of language education has witnessed a transformative paradigm shift with the emergence of translanguaging—a term coined by Williams (1996) in a bilingual context in Wales. The evolution of

K. Jalilzadeh (✉)
School of Foreign Languages, Istanbul University-Cerrahpasa, Istanbul, Turkey
e-mail: kaveh.j@iuc.edu.tr

C. Coombe
Dubai Men's College, Higher Colleges of Technology, Abu Dhabi, United Arab Emirates
e-mail: ccoombe@hct.ac.ae

A. Dastgoshadeh
Department of English, Islamic Azad University, Sanandaj, Iran

D. Coulson and C. Denman (eds.), *Translation, Translanguaging and Machine Translation in Foreign Language Education*,
https://doi.org/10.1007/978-3-031-82174-5_14

translanguaging, as illuminated by García and Kano (2014), encompasses pedagogic and ideological dimensions, challenging the monolingual view by building on a theoretical foundation of multilingual ideologies and dynamic bilingualism (Cenoz & Gorter, 2020; García & Li, 2014). In today's multilingual classrooms, the rise of individuals proficient in more than one language has given birth to the teaching methodology known as translanguaging, urging the incorporation of translanguaging methodologies in the teaching of English to speakers of other languages (García, 2009; Kleyn & García, 2019). The term "translanguaging" refers to treating one's native language not only as a fluid repertory but also as a structured system, influencing social and political judgments (García & Li, 2018). This linguistic and pedagogical approach challenges conventional views on bilingualism, treating the languages of bilingual speakers as an integrated system with distinct features (Grosjean, 1982; Li & García, 2016).

Translanguaging pedagogies, highlighted in previous research, concretely incorporate multiple languages and cultures in teaching, reflecting a dynamic and inclusive approach (Council of Europe, 2020; García & Li, 2018). For English language learners, translanguaging becomes a valuable tool for referencing and utilizing primary language abilities, facilitating effective interaction and meaning negotiation (Canagarajah, 2011; Cenoz & Gorter, 2011; Creese & Blackledge, 2010). Baker (2001, 2011) outlines four educational benefits of translanguaging, emphasizing its potential to encourage cooperation, deepen comprehension, facilitate integration, and aid in the evolution of less dominant languages. Teachers leverage translanguaging for various objectives, ranging from differentiation and metalinguistic awareness to fostering identity investment and examining linguistic inequality (García & Leiva, 2014).

Utilizing translanguaging in the classroom can facilitate collaboration between native speakers of the first language (L1) and second language (L2) learners with diverse proficiency levels (Maillat & Serra, 2009). When both languages are strategically employed, students have the opportunity to enhance their L2 skills and deepen their understanding of academic topics simultaneously (Maillat & Serra, 2009). This strategic use of both languages not only contributes to language development but also promotes subject-matter learning. The implementation of translanguaging in the classroom addresses language gaps and reduces the risk of alienation, especially for minority students (García et al., 2012). Collaborative group work within homogeneous language groups, situated in the zone of proximal development, enables students to learn from one another (García & Li, 2014). Drawing upon background knowledge from both the native language and the target language, students engage in a symbiotic relationship between their L1 practices and the acquisition of the L2, leading to the emergence of new language practices (Celic & Seltzer, 2013).

This approach allows students to communicate effectively with peers proficient in both their primary and target languages, fostering an understanding among students who do not share a common native tongue. Interactions with peers who speak a different home language prompt students to recognize that language hierarchies are self-imposed and not necessarily reflective of the classroom reality. Translanguaging is described as transformative, aiming to eliminate hierarchies in linguistic practices, particularly in classrooms with students from language minority communities, thereby serving as a mechanism for social justice (García & Leiva, 2014).

In the context of English as a Foreign Language (EFL) classrooms in Turkey, this phenomenological study endeavors to delve into the perceptions and applications of ten EFL teachers regarding translanguaging. Recognizing the significance of teachers' perceptions as part of the hidden curriculum, the study aims to provide crucial insights for curriculum developers, teacher trainers, and macro-policy makers, echoing the assertion made by Borg (2006) that teachers' cognition, which builds up teachers' beliefs and perceptions, plays a significant role in practice. The exploration of translanguaging in this setting promises to contribute to the development of inclusive language education environments that cater to diverse linguistic needs. The study reported in this paper specifically delves into the following research questions:

1. In what ways do teachers envision the application of translanguaging in English language classes?

2. How do teachers perceive the impact of translanguaging on the enhancement of their EFL learners' literacies?

14.2 Literature Review

The literature on translanguaging in language learning encompasses a diverse range of studies that explore its implications for pedagogy and student interaction. Rasman (2018) conducted a qualitative case study in Indonesia, focusing on the impact of the political and social context on students' translingual interactions. Analyzing an EFL classroom, Rasman found that students' use of their L1 did not hinder target language acquisition; instead, it demonstrated the potential for constructing individual repertoires through scaffolding during student–student interaction. Pacheco (2016) investigated how students use different languages for conceptualization, revealing instances of translanguaging between teachers and students that enhance comprehension of L2 concepts. In Hong Kong, a study by Wang (2019) on learners in Chinese as a Second Language classrooms who displayed positive attitudes toward English-Chinese translanguaging found that both teachers and students reported translanguaging fostered comprehension, learning efficiency, and motivation, thereby creating a bridge among students of different nationalities. Ebe and Chapman-Santiago's (2016) exploration of translanguaging in a New York City English classroom highlighted positive responses from students, emphasizing its potential to enhance comfort and engagement through strategies such as scaffolding and shared reading.

Nambisan's (2014) research on educators' attitudes toward translanguaging in English as a Second Language (ESL) classrooms reported that a high value was placed on this method for L2 learners. However, a noted discrepancy existed between teachers' positive perceptions and the actual frequency of classroom translanguaging use. Horasan's (2014) quantitative study explored the extent of translanguaging in EFL settings, finding numerous instances of translanguaging by both instructors and learners, with general agreement that L1 use is appropriate at lower levels but should be reduced at higher levels.

In an exploration by Hoffman (2014), translanguaging strategies during reading, under both explicit and non-explicit instructions, were investigated. This involved the translation of English text into American Sign Language (ASL). The study included five prelingually deaf adults proficient in both English and ASL, with participants employing various translanguaging strategies such as translations, ASL expansions, non-manual ASL features, integration of additional information, omission and miscues, fingerspelling, utilization of context clues, reflective thinking and pausing, and referencing the preceding sentence.

Mazak and Herbas-Donoso (2014) conducted research observing translanguaging phenomena in a science class at a university in Puerto Rico. Despite instruction being in Spanish, an English textbook was used. The case study focused on an upper-level science class and spanned 11 observations over a 15-week semester. The findings indicated that translanguaging facilitated comprehension among these Spanish-speaking students, leading to a shift away from English as the dominant language. Despite involving adults in a content-focused class, students employed translanguaging to grasp scientific concepts in the target language. Sayer (2013) investigated translanguaging as a dynamic movement. The author's ethnographic study explored how teachers and students used their home language—a local vernacular known as TexMex—in an academic context as a medium for content mediation. The classroom environment examined often witnessed code-switching among students, a practice commonly perceived as negative and thus discouraged. Sayer reported that this tendency emerged as a prevalent behavior among emergent bilingual students.

Daryai-Hansen et al.'s (2017) examination of translanguaging outcomes at Roskilde University in Denmark revealed encouraging student attitudes in addition to teacher's desire to employ translanguaging, particularly when the other languages spoken were Danish and/or English. Torpsten's (2018) study highlighted the potential of translanguaging for multilingual individuals to effectively expand their repertoires. The practice of translanguaging, as explored by García and Kleyn (2016), was also found to positively influence language development and transform language teaching. Creese and Blackledge's (2010) investigation focused on the pedagogical function of translanguaging, showing that Gujarati and English could effectively function in various ways in the classroom setting.

Findings offered by Sali (2014) indicated teachers' favorable views on using Turkish to instruct students on grammatical concepts. Kim and Petraki's survey (2009) found that having teachers clarify English grammar in Korean was beneficial for students. Mahmoudi and Amirkhiz's (2011) study revealed that students perceived the use of L1 by teachers during grammar teaching as helpful for improving their English grammar skills.

Despite conflicting results in recent studies (e.g., Charalambous et al., 2016; Guerrero, 2021), translanguaging has shown positive outcomes, particularly in grammar instruction and classroom management. Ho and Tai's (2020) research not only revealed opportunities for teacher professional development but also highlighted avenues for student empowerment. Their study, centered on online teaching videos, brought forth visible language attitudes, such as YouTube comments discussing different English varieties. These insights became a catalyst for educator discussions, fostering an understanding of macro-level discourses surrounding "standard" language varieties and prompting reflections on the typical contextual occurrences and the diverse domains applying these language standards.

Ho (2022) conducted a study on how English for Academic Purposes (EAP) students grapple with artificial constraints inherent in registers, genre conventions, and modalities. The students endeavored to produce instructional videos as a component of their course evaluation unveiling their proactive stance in (re)shaping novel genre conventions. This portrayal casts them not only as rapidly developing EAP writers striving to transcend sociohistorical and ideological boundaries within academic genres. They are also depicted as proficient experts adept at conveying disciplinary knowledge. Tian and Zhang-Wu's (2022) study focused on the translanguaging challenges encountered by content area educators within a graduate-level teacher education setting undertaking a course designed from a translanguaging perspective. Their investigation aimed to uncover how educators navigated the intricacies of translanguaging practices within their teaching contexts.

In an important discovery, Hamman (2018) observed that students adeptly harnessed their entire linguistic arsenal to articulate diverse facets of a message. In reaching this conclusion within the domain of Dual Language Bilingual Education (DLBE), a linguistic ethnographic exploration was carried out by observing the classroom with approximately 30 hours of video data. Various participation patterns were recorded, focusing on translanguaging practices, and the teacher was interviewed formally at the beginning and end, and informally during the study. The researcher reported that students actively used both Spanish and English for social and academic purposes, adjusting based on their peers' dominant language. For instance, during a Spanish lesson, students creatively engaged in dialogue, demonstrating their understanding of concepts in both languages. This authentic communication highlighted their attention to the intended audience and ability to test hypotheses about language use. Hamman's report of the intricate language dynamics within the microcosm of the classroom thereby helps reveal wider macro-level disparities between English and Spanish.

Khote and Tian (2019) investigated the crossroads where translanguaging intertwines with other critical theories in education, such as critical literacy, culturally sustaining systemic functional linguistics (SFL), and feminist post-structuralism. Their investigation aimed to expand the understanding of translanguaging by integrating insights from these critical perspectives to address the educational and societal challenges faced by language-minoritized students. By combining Halliday's SFL theory with García's concept of translanguaging, the researchers utilized culturally sustaining SFL as an integrative framework to create meaningful learning environments that embrace linguistic diversity and support multiliteracies among multilingual learners.

Mendoza's investigations (2022, 2023) focused on two secondary English classes in Hawai'i. Each class was distinctly marked by a prevailing linguistic majority, with one predominantly communicating in Ilokano and the other in Filipino. Despite the intentional promotion of translanguaging within both educational settings, Mendoza reported a noteworthy influence exerted by the translanguaging practices of the predominant linguistic group in each class. This influence was particularly pronounced among students who spoke languages divergent from the prevailing linguistic majority, including, but not limited to, Cantonese, Chuukese, Mandarin, Marshallese, Samoan, or Vietnamese. The intricate dynamics of translanguaging within these classrooms highlighted the nuanced impact that the dominant language practices within a given group can have on the linguistic experiences of students from diverse language backgrounds.

As this brief overview of the literature suggests, it remains imperative for forthcoming research to persistently probe into translanguaging as an innovative and transformative pedagogical approach (Sánchez & García, 2022), challenging and disrupting the prevailing oppressive norms surrounding language and literacy within both educational institutions and society at large. It is within this framework that the current research took place.

14.3 Methodology

14.3.1 Participants

The study involved a cohort of ten EFL teachers recruited from state and private high schools in Turkey using a combination of purposive and convenience sampling methods. Purposive sampling involves selecting participants based on specific criteria relevant to the research aims, while convenience sampling involves selecting those who are readily available or easily accessible. Participation in the study was entirely voluntary, with respondents providing written informed consent after being given a detailed explanation of the study's purpose, the expected nature of participant involvement, and the handling of their data, particularly with respect to safeguarding their identity. They were assured that their responses would be kept anonymous and were informed of their right to withdraw from the study at any time without penalty. Moreover, participants were informed of the possibility of findings being shared in academic fora, with the necessary precautions taken to protect their privacy and confidentiality. The resultant participant group included both male ($n = 4$) and female ($n = 6$) teachers with ages ranging from 24 to 53.

14.3.2 Instruments

Data were collected from two distinct sources: narrative framing and cognitive interviews. We positioned narrative frames within the context of teachers' utilization of translanguaging and their perceptions of translanguaging in educational settings. Specifically, narrative frames were selected due to their ability to "provide guidance and support in terms of both the structure and content of what is to be written" (Barkhuizen & Wette, 2008, p. 376). This approach involved creating customized prompts (narrative frames) for teachers to reflect on their experiences with translanguaging, covering both positive and negative aspects. These prompts explored why and how they used translanguaging in the classroom and their beliefs about its impact on teaching and student learning. Available in both Turkish and English, all participants preferred to respond in the former. By collecting these reflections before interviews, we aimed to enhance our understanding of teachers' perceptions of translanguaging. It afforded teachers ample time to reflect on and recollect their experiences with applying translanguaging and their perceptions of it.

To further explore teachers' narratives, cognitive interviews were implemented to gain a more comprehensive understanding of how they incorporate translanguaging in classrooms. These one-on-one, face-to-face interviews, averaging 20 minutes per teacher and conducted in English, aimed to delve into the intricacies of teachers' perceptions of ways of utilizing translanguaging and translanguaging practices. A comprehensive review of relevant literature informed the development of a semi-structured interview guide, from which specific questions were derived. To help ensure their validity, three experts in applied linguistics critically reviewed the interview questions and suggested minor revisions where necessary.

14.3.3 Data Analysis

MAXQDA social sciences analysis software was used to analyze data collected during the research. The three-week data analysis phase involved the transcription and inputting of data from narrative frames and interviews into the software. Following the framework proposed by Corbin and Strauss (1990), the researchers engaged in open coding, axial coding, and selective coding across three successive stages. The reflectivity feature of the software facilitated the generation of open codes through iterative examination of the data. Subsequently, the second stage involved the comparison and integration of open codes, leading to the development of more comprehensive codes. The final step encompassed the organization of identified themes into broader categories, thereby aligning with Creswell's (2008) guidelines.

To bolster the rigor and validity of data analysis, the process of member checking involved instructors thoroughly reviewing and scrutinizing both the extracted codes/themes and the researchers' interpretations. Additionally, to assess inter-coder reliability, 20% of the codes/themes were assigned to a second coder, resulting in a Cohen's Kappa coefficient of 0.92. This step further ensured the robustness and consistency of the coding process.

14.4 Results and Discussion

14.4.1 Research Question 1: Implementation of Translanguaging

The primary focus of the initial research question was how EFL teachers view the different applications of translanguaging in the classroom. As per the information provided in Table 14.1, teachers believe that translanguaging can be effectively utilized in different aspects of the classroom, such as tasks and activities, collaborative work, enhancing both L1 and L2 knowledge, incorporating teaching content and materials, and employing it as a feedback mechanism.

The first subtheme addressed tasks and activities ($f = 8$), encompassing codes such as reviewing lessons in L1 by the teacher/class ($f = 3$), encouraging L1 conversations ($f = 2$), promoting the creation of multilingual character stories ($f = 1$), students generating ideas in L1 or a mix of L1 and L2 ($f = 1$), and students completing assignments

Table 14.1 Teachers' perceptions of applications of translanguaging in classroom

	Frequency
Tasks & activities	8
– Reviewing lessons in L1 by the teacher/class	3
– Encouraging L1 conversations	2
– Promoting the creation of multilingual character stories	1
– Students generating ideas in L1 or a mix of L1 and L2	1
– Students completing assignments in L1 while explaining thoughts in L2	1
Collaborative work	6
– Students using multiple languages in groups	3
– Seeking clarification in L1 while collaborating on assignments	2
– One student providing the L2 equivalent for an L1 word	1
Utilizing and improving both L1 and L2 knowledge	5
– Using L1 words for unknown concepts in L2	3
– Students' imparting knowledge to one another in their L1	2
Teaching content and materials	1
– Teachers' showing video/audio clips, providing supplementary materials in students' L1	1
Translanguaging as a feedback mechanism	1
– Teachers resort to L1 to foster a supportive environment	1

in L1 while explaining thoughts in L2 ($f = 1$). Teacher participants provided the following insights:

– *"The instructor or class reviews the entire lesson in the native language".*
– *"Students predominantly generate initial ideas, plans, and drafts in their native language or a combination of their native language and English".*
– *"Students have the option to finish assignments in their native language, even if the task is in English, and then articulate their thoughts in English".*

The second subtheme focused on collaborative work ($f = 6$), featuring codes including students using multiple languages in groups ($f = 3$), seeking clarification in L1 while collaborating on assignments ($f = 2$), and a student providing the L2 equivalent for an L1 word ($f = 1$). The EFL teachers shared the following observations:

- *"Translanguaging is evident when students express themselves in groups using multiple languages".*
- *"To clarify questions during assignments, students may use translanguaging by quietly communicating in Turkish".*
- *"A student uses the Turkish word, and their partner provides the corresponding English term".*

The third subtheme was utilizing and improving both L1 and L2 knowledge ($f = 5$), with codes including students using L1 words for unknown concepts in L2 ($f = 3$) and students sharing knowledge in L1 ($f = 2$). In relation to this point, one EFL teacher stated: *"Students exchange knowledge with each other in their native language".*

The fourth subtheme, teaching content and materials ($f = 1$), highlighted teachers showing multimedia or providing supplementary materials in students' L1. A teacher participant stated: *"Instructors may present audio and audio clips or offer texts in the native language".*

The last subtheme, translanguaging as a feedback mechanism ($f = 1$), underscores the role of teachers employing translanguaging as a strategic feedback mechanism to assess students' understanding and guide them effectively. One EFL teacher participant stated: *"Teachers use translanguaging intentionally, not only to gauge students' comprehension but also to provide guidance, making it an integral feedback mechanism in the learning process".*

14.4.2   Research Question 2: Perceptions of Translanguaging

As shown in Table 14.2, educators assert that the incorporation of translanguaging into classroom procedures yields enhancements across three distinct categories: academic advancements, teaching methodology enhancements, and teacher professional development.

The primary facet, academic advancements ($f = 11$), encompasses various dimensions which appeared in the data one time each. These include facilitating multilingual students in comprehending and communicating about diverse topics, assisting them in advancing their

Table 14.2 Teachers' perceptions of utilizing translanguaging to enhance learners' literacies

	Frequency
Academic advancements	*11*
– Facilitating multilingual students in comprehending and communicating about diverse topics	1
– Assisting the learners in advancing their proficiency in the first and second language (L2)	1
– Promoting connections between learners' native language (L1) and L2	1
– Fostering a deeper engagement with learning materials	1
– Enabling the utilization of learners' entire language repertoire	1
– Improving comprehension of intricate concepts presented in classrooms	1
– Enhancing competence in both L1 and L2	1
– Guiding students in recognizing commonalities and distinctions between languages	1
– Providing opportunities for language skill practice	1
– Promoting inclusive learning for all learners	1
– Allowing excellence in L1 proficiency	1
Teaching methodology enhancements	*4*
– Optimizing classroom procedures	1
– Serving as an effective learning resource	1
– Helping alleviate challenges faced by multilingual and bilingual students in the classroom	1
– Allowing for the adaptation of pedagogical practices	1
Teacher professional development	*3*
– Promoting the use of multiple languages during lessons	1
– Assisting teachers in overcoming barriers that hinder the integration of native languages in lessons	1
– Cultivating a language-inclusive teaching environment as part of ongoing professional development	1

proficiency in the L1 and L2, promoting connections between their native language and other languages, fostering a deeper engagement with learning materials, enabling the utilization of their entire language repertoire, improving comprehension of intricate concepts presented in core classrooms, enhancing competence in both native and other languages, guiding students in recognizing commonalities and distinctions between languages, providing opportunities for language skills practice, promoting inclusive learning for all students, and allowing excellence in L1 proficiency. These codes all appeared one time each. Selected statements from EFL teachers on this matter are shown below:

- *"Incorporating translanguaging activities and integrating students' native languages into the classroom enhances students' full engagement with educational materials"*.
- *"Educators are gearing up to employ deliberate translanguaging strategies to help students utilize their complete language repertoire"*.
- *"Utilizing translanguaging aids multilingual students in understanding and discussing topics within specific subject areas"*.

The second facet, teaching methodology enhancements ($f = 4$), encompasses codes appearing a single time each, such as optimizing classroom procedures, serving as an effective learning resource, being widely recognized as a technique to alleviate challenges faced by multilingual and bilingual students in the classroom, and allowing for the adaptation of pedagogical practices. EFL teachers expressed their perspectives on this theme through statements such as:

- *"Translanguaging optimizes classroom procedures"*.
- *"It has been empirically validated as an effective learning resource"*.
- *"Translanguaging allows for the adaptation of pedagogical practices"*.

The final aspect, teacher professional development ($f = 3$), comprises three codes: promoting the use of multiple languages during lessons, assisting teachers in overcoming barriers that hinder the integration of L1 in lessons, and cultivating a language-inclusive teaching environment as part of ongoing professional development, with these again only being apparent one time teach. EFL teachers articulated their viewpoints on this aspect through statements that included:

- *"Encourage teachers to use several languages"*.
- *"It helps teachers break down barriers that prevent students from utilizing L1 in their lessons"*.

14.5 Discussion

The comprehensive review of literature and the current study underscore the transformative nature of translanguaging in the realm of language education, particularly in EFL classrooms in Turkey. This study delved into the perspectives of EFL teachers regarding the applications of translanguaging in the classroom, employing a qualitative analysis of data gathered from narrative frames and interviews. Teachers recognized translanguaging as beneficial for various aspects of teaching and learning, including tasks, collaborative work, bolstering both L1 and L2 knowledge, seamlessly integrating teaching content, and employing it as a constructive feedback mechanism. Subthemes provided nuanced insights into specific instances, such as reviewing lessons in L1, students generating ideas in multiple languages, and applying translanguaging for collaborative assignments. Noteworthy findings underscored that the incorporation of translanguaging into classroom practices yielded positive outcomes, influencing academic advancements, enhancing teaching methodologies, and contributing to the professional development of teachers. Educators highlighted the favorable effects of translanguaging on student engagement, proficiency in both languages, and the establishment of an inclusive learning environment.

The findings from both the literature review and the study align seamlessly, reinforcing the positive impact of translanguaging on language acquisition, student interaction, and pedagogy. The studies referenced in the literature review, such as Rasman's (2018) work in Indonesia, Pacheco's (2016) research in the United States, and Wang's (2019) study in Hong Kong, have consistently demonstrated the positive effects of translanguaging. Rasman's (2018) findings regarding the facilitation of target language acquisition through scaffolding during student–student interaction resonate with the broader theme of using native languages as valuable resources in the language learning process. Pacheco (2016) and Wang (2019), operating in different cultural and linguistic settings, further substantiate the idea that translanguaging contributes to enhanced comprehension and efficiency in language learning. These parallels not only validate the global applicability of translanguaging but also emphasize its potential as a pedagogical tool that transcends cultural and contextual boundaries.

The diverse educational settings explored in the literature review—from Indonesia to Hong Kong and New York City—highlight the versatility of translanguaging strategies. The consistent theme of enhanced comfort, engagement, and literacy skills through translanguaging strategies, as revealed in Ebe and Chapman-Santiago's (2016) exploration and Nambisan's (2014) investigation, adds depth to the understanding of the method's effectiveness. The multi-faceted benefits of translanguaging, encompassing comfort, engagement, and literacy, substantiate its potential to create inclusive and supportive learning environments across different cultural and linguistic contexts. The current study contributes significantly by delving into the perceptions of EFL teachers in Turkey regarding the application of translanguaging. The alignment of teachers' visions with the broader findings in the literature review further solidifies the notion that translanguaging is perceived as a valuable asset in language classrooms. The study goes beyond general endorsements by providing specific insights into how teachers envision the practical implementation of translanguaging in various aspects of language education, including tasks and activities, collaborative work, teaching content and materials, and as a feedback mechanism.

According to the findings of García and Kano (2014), students who translanguaged in their written work expressed the belief that the practice played a significant part and inspired more self-assurance in their ability to communicate effectively via writing. This aligns with the broader benefits of translanguaging, emphasizing its role not only in spoken communication but also in enhancing written language skills and fostering student confidence in expressing themselves through writing. Creese and Blackledge (2010) contribute to the discourse by highlighting the adaptable practice of translanguaging as an educational tool for language teachers in the classroom environment. Their research underscores the versatility of translanguaging, suggesting its potential as a pedagogical strategy that can be tailored to meet the specific needs of language educators. This insight further emphasizes the practicality and relevance of translanguaging in diverse educational settings.

The findings of this study are in agreement with the research conducted by Kim and Petraki (2009) regarding teachers' and learners' perceptions of the use of translanguaging. The alignment of findings indicates that teachers held favorable attitudes toward the use of the L1 for classroom management purposes. This consistency in attitudes toward translanguaging emphasizes its acceptability among educators, reinforcing its potential as a valuable tool for various aspects of language education.

14.6 Conclusion

In conclusion, the amalgamation of evidence from the literature review and the current study results presents a compelling case for the integration of translanguaging into English language education. The potential benefits, ranging from enhanced language acquisition and student interaction to the creation of inclusive learning environments, underscore the need for a paradigm shift in language education approaches. As educators, policymakers, and curriculum developers continue to navigate the complexities of multilingual classrooms, translanguaging emerges as a promising pedagogical tool that not only respects linguistic diversity but also harnesses it for the betterment of language learners. This discussion invites further exploration and collaboration to advance the development of inclusive language education environments that prioritize the linguistic needs of diverse student populations.

The literature and findings suggest that translanguaging holds great potential for application in English language classes. Teachers envision its use in various aspects of the classroom, and they perceive it as a powerful tool for enhancing EFL learners' literacies. Translanguaging has the ability to facilitate comprehension, promote engagement, and foster inclusive learning environments. As such, it is important for teachers to continue exploring and incorporating translanguaging strategies in their English language classrooms to support their students' language development and academic success.

References

Baker, C. (2001). *Foundations of bilingual education and bilingualism*. Multilingual Matters.

Baker, C. (2011). *Foundations of bilingual education and bilingualism* (5th ed.). Multilingual Matters.

Barkhuizen, G., & Wette, R. (2008). Narrative frames for investigating the experiences of language teachers. *System, 36*(3), 372–387. https://doi.org/10.1016/j.system.2008.02.002

Borg, S. (2006). *Teacher cognition and language education: Research and practice*. Continuum.

Canagarajah, S. (2011). Translanguaging in the classroom: Emerging issues for research and pedagogy. *Applied Linguistics Review, 2*(1), 1–28.

Celic, C., & Seltzer, K. (2013). *Translanguaging: A CUNY-NYSIEB guide for educators*. CUNY-NYSIEB. https://www.cuny-nysieb.org/wp-content/uploads/2016/04/Translanguaging-Guide-March-2013.pdf

Cenoz, J., & Gorter, D. (2011). A holistic approach to multilingual education: Introduction. *The Modern Language Journal, 95*(3), 339–343. https://doi.org/10.1111/j.1540-4781.2011.01204.x

Cenoz, J., & Gorter, D. (2020). Pedagogical translanguaging: An introduction. *System, 92*. https://doi.org/10.1016/j.system.2020.102269

Charalambous, P., Charalambous, C., & Zembylas, M. (2016). Troubling translanguaging: Language ideologies, superdiversity and interethnic conflict. *Applied Linguistics Review, 7*(3), 327–352.

Corbin, J. M., & Strauss, A. (1990). Grounded theory research: Procedures, canons, and evaluative criteria. *Qualitative Sociology, 13*(1), 3–21.

Council of Europe. (2020). *Common European Framework of Reference for Languages: Learning, teaching, assessment*. https://www.coe.int/en/web/common-european-framework-reference-languages

Creese, A., & Blackledge, A. (2010). Translanguaging in the bilingual classroom: A pedagogy for learning and teaching? *The Modern Language Journal, 94*(1), 103–115. https://doi.org/10.1111/j.1540-4781.2009.00986.x

Creswell, J. (2008). *Educational research: Planning, conducting, and evaluating quantitative and qualitative research* (3rd ed.). Prentice Hall.

Daryai-Hansen, P., Barfod, S., & Schwarz, L. (2017). A call for (trans)languaging: Language profiles at Roskilde University. In C. Mazak & K. S. Carroll (Eds.), *Translanguaging in higher education: Beyond monolingual ideologies* (pp. 29–49). Multilingual Matters.

Ebe, A. E., & Chapman-Santiago, C. (2016). Student voices shining through: Exploring translanguaging as a literary device. In O. García & T. Kleyn (Eds.), *Translanguaging with multilingual students: Learning from classroom moments* (pp. 57–82). Routledge.

García, O. (2009). *Bilingual education in the 21st century: A global perspective.* Wiley-Blackwell.

García, O., Flores, N., & Woodley, H. (2012). Transgressing monolingualism and bilingual dualities: Translanguaging pedagogies. In A. Yiakoumetti (Ed.), *Harnessing linguistic variation to improve education* (pp. 45–76). Peter Lang.

García, O., & Kano, N. (2014). Translanguaging as process and pedagogy: Developing the English writing of Japanese students in the US. In J. Conteh & G. Meier (Eds.), *The multilingual turn in languages education: Opportunities and challenges* (pp. 258–277). Multilingual Matters.

García, O., & Kleyn, T. (Eds.). (2016). *Translanguaging with multilingual students: Learning from classroom moments.* Routledge.

García, O., & Leiva, C. (2014). Theorizing and enacting translanguaging for social justice. In A. Blackledge & A. Creese (Eds.), *Heteroglossia as practice and pedagogy* (pp. 199–216). Springer. https://doi.org/10.1007/978-94-007-7856-6_11

García, O., & Li, W. (2014). *Translanguaging: Language, bilingualism and education.* Palgrave Macmillan.

García, O., & Li, W. (2018). Translanguaging. In *The encyclopedia of applied linguistics.* Wiley. https://doi.org/10.1002/9781405198431.wbeal1488

Grosjean, F. (1982). *Life with two languages: An introduction to bilingualism.* Harvard University Press.

Guerrero, M. (2021). Gauging the adequacy of translanguaging allocation policy in two-way immersion programs in the U.S. *Journal of Latinos and Education, 22*(4), 1–15. https://doi.org/10.1080/15348431.2021.1971086

Hamman, L. (2018). *Reframing the language separation debate: Language, identity, and ideology in two-way immersion* (Unpublished doctoral dissertation). University of Wisconsin-Madison.

Ho, W. Y. J. (2022). 'Coming here you should speak Chinese': The multimodal construction of interculturality in YouTube videos. *Language and Intercultural Communication, 22*(6), 662–680. https://doi.org/10.1080/14708477.2022.2056610

Ho, W. Y. J., & Tai, K. W. H. (2020). Doing expertise multilingually and multimodally in online English teaching videos. *System, 94*, 1–12. https://doi.org/10.1016/j.system.2020.102340

Hoffman, D. L. (2014). *Investigating phenomenological translanguaging among deaf adult bilinguals engaging in reading tasks* (Publication No. 3670856) (Doctoral dissertation). Lamar University. ProQuest Dissertations and Theses database.

Horasan, S. (2014). Code-switching in EFL classrooms and the perceptions of the students and teachers. *Journal of Language and Linguistic Studies, 10*(1), 31–45.

Khote, N., & Tian, Z. (2019). Translanguaging in culturally sustaining systemic functional linguistics: Developing a heteroglossic space with multilingual learners. *Translation and Translanguaging in Multilingual Contexts, 5*(1), 5–28. https://doi.org/10.1075/ttmc.00022.kho

Kim, Y., & Petraki, E. (2009). Students' and teachers' use of and attitudes to L1 in the EFL classroom. *Asian EFL Journal, 11*(4), 58–89.

Kleyn, T., & García, O. (2019). Translanguaging as an act of transformation: Restructuring teaching and learning for emergent bilingual students. In L. C. de Oliveira (Ed.), *The handbook of TESOL in K-12* (pp. 69–82). Wiley.

Li, W., & García, O. (2016). Translanguaging: Language, bilingualism and education. *Palgrave Pivot*. https://doi.org/10.1057/9781137385765

Mahmoudi, L., & Amirkhiz, S. (2011). The use of Persian in the EFL classroom—The case of English teaching and learning at pre-university level in Iran. *English Language Teaching, 4*(1), 135–140. https://doi.org/10.5539/elt.v4n1p135

Maillat, D., & Serra, C. (2009). Immersion education and cognitive strategies: Can the obstacle be the advantage in a multilingual society? *International Journal of Multilingualism, 6*(2), 186–206. https://doi.org/10.1080/14790710902846731

Mazak, C. M., & Herbas-Donoso, C. (2014). Translanguaging practices at a bilingual university: A case study of a science classroom. *International Journal of Bilingual Education and Bilingualism, 18*(6), 698–714. https://doi.org/10.1080/13670050.2014.939138

Mendoza, A. (2022). What does translanguaging-for-equity really involve? An interactional analysis of a 9th grade English class. *Applied Linguistics Review, 13*(6), 1055–1075. https://doi.org/10.1515/applirev-2019-0106

Mendoza, A. (2023). *Translanguaging and English as a lingua franca in the plurilingual classroom*. Multilingual Matters.

Nambisan, K. A. (2014). *Teachers' attitudes towards and uses of translanguaging in English language classrooms in Iowa* (Unpublished master's thesis). Iowa State University.

Pacheco, M. (2016). *Translanguaging in the English-centric classroom: A communities of practice perspective* (Unpublished doctoral dissertation). Vanderbilt University.

Rasman, R. (2018). To translanguage or not to translanguage? The multilingual practice in an Indonesian EFL classroom. *Indonesian Journal of Applied Linguistics, 7*(3), 687–694. https://doi.org/10.17509/ijal.v7i3.9819

Sali, P. (2014). An analysis of the teachers' use of L1 in Turkish EFL classrooms. *System, 42*, 308–318. https://doi.org/10.1016/j.system.2013.12.021

Sánchez, M. T., & García, O. (Eds.). (2022). *Transformative translanguaging espacios: Latinx students and their teachers rompiendo fronteras sin miedo.* Multilingual Matters.

Sayer, P. (2013). Translanguaging, TexMex, and bilingual pedagogy: Emergent bilinguals learning through the vernacular. *TESOL Quarterly, 47*(1), 63–88. https://doi.org/10.1002/tesq.53

Tian, Z., & Zhang-Wu, Q. (2022). Preparing pre-service content area teachers through translanguaging. *Journal of Language, Identity & Education, 21*(3), 144–159. https://doi.org/10.1080/15348458.2022.2058512

Torpsten, A. C. (2018). Translanguaging in a Swedish multilingual classroom. *Multicultural Perspectives, 20*(2), 104–110. https://doi.org/10.1080/15210960.2018.1447100

Wang, D. (2019). *Multilingualism and translanguaging in Chinese language classrooms.* Palgrave Macmillan.

Williams, C. (1996). Secondary education: Teaching in the bilingual situation. In C. Williams, G. Lewis, & C. Baker (Eds.), *The language policy: Taking stock* (pp. 39–78). CAI.

15

Exploring the Affordances and Challenges of Translanguaging: The Context of Oman

Fatemeh Ranjbaran Madiseh[iD]

15.1 Introduction

The recent surge in research surrounding second language education across the globe has explored how translanguaging can be utilized as an inclusive pedagogical practice in the second language classroom, bringing forth equal access to learning opportunities and facilitating student engagement in educational settings (Fang et al., 2023; Jiang & Zhang, 2023; Tai & Wong, 2023). This is occurring as English Medium Instruction (EMI) is rapidly expanding in higher education worldwide, including in Oman, where policy support and financial assistance have contributed to an increase in EMI courses (Al-Bakri & Troudi, 2020). EMI is defined by Macaro (2018) as "the use of the English language to teach academic subjects (other than English itself) in countries or jurisdictions where the first language of the majority of the population is not

F. R. Madiseh (✉)
Sultan Qaboos University, Muscat, Oman
e-mail: f.madiseh@squ.edu.om

D. Coulson and C. Denman (eds.), *Translation, Translanguaging and Machine
Translation in Foreign Language Education*,
https://doi.org/10.1007/978-3-031-82174-5_15

English" (p. 37). An implicit teaching objective in the EMI classroom is suggested as learning the English language, while learning content knowledge is the explicit and major objective (Pecorari & Malmström, 2018).

However, significant language-related challenges have been noted in EMI higher education programs, especially when both lecturers and students are typically non-native English speakers and lack exposure to English-speaking environments in both social and academic settings (Richards & Pun, 2022). Students' challenges with learning content knowledge through EMI, including associated psychological stress and anxiety, in addition to lecturers' challenges with teaching content in English and their reportedly commonly-held belief that they are not in the classroom to teach language skills, add to these obstacles (Ismailov et al., 2021; Kamaşak & Sahan, 2023). In technical courses in faculties such as the sciences and engineering, students and teachers might encounter additional language-related challenges due to lesson content, which may include specialized lexico-grammatical features, a broad range of technical terms, and non-technical vocabulary with specific contextual meanings. To address these issues, translanguaging pedagogies, initially designed to bridge meaning-making gaps in bilingual education, are now widely recommended for EMI in higher education, prompting research into their implementation by EMI teachers (Jia et al., 2023; Kao, 2023; Tai & Wong, 2023).

One aspect that is investigated is EMI lecturers' "spontaneous and pedagogical" translanguaging practices, as put forth by Fuster and Bardel (2024). Studies on this component have found various functions, i.e., creating diverse spaces to motivate teacher-student and student–student interaction (Kao et al., 2021; Sahan & Rose, 2021; Tai & Li, 2021), asking higher-order questions (Back, 2020; Pun & Macaro, 2019), and strategically using translanguaging for developing academic skills (Adamson & Coulson, 2015; Barahona, 2020; Kim & Chang, 2022).

Another strand of research focuses on counterarguments about the potential utility of translanguaging practice by advancing the belief, for example, that translanguaging is a hindrance to the development of English language skills and should therefore be avoided (Karakaş, 2023; Sobkowiak, 2022; Yuan & Yang, 2023). However, while there are studies on EMI lecturers' translanguaging practices and perceptions in different regions of the world (Costley & Leung, 2020; Liu et al., 2020; Shah et al., 2019), little is known about Omani lecturers' perceptions and practices when it comes to EMI. This dearth of research is more evident for EMI university lecturers' translanguaging practices in the fields of sciences and engineering, where research remains relatively scarce in the Middle East region. Thus, it is necessary to further explore the teaching practices of EMI insxtructors in addition to their endeavors to deliver subject content while simultaneously taking into account their learners' linguistic needs (Gu et al., 2022, p. 4).

Accordingly, this study aims to address the following research questions:

1. What are EFL learners' perceived challenges with EMI in the Oman higher education context?
2. What translanguaging practices do Omani teachers employ in the EMI context and what purposes do they serve?

15.2   Literature Review

Considering the uncontested reality that huge amounts of exposure to the target language facilitate foreign language learning and subsequent policies in numerous educational contexts to ensure this exposure is achieved, some teachers have been left with a sense of uncertainty about the use of their first language (L1) in the English as a Foreign Language (EFL) classroom. Meanwhile, the theory of translanguaging has gained widespread recognition as a result of its agreement with the needs of post-multilingualism in the late twentieth century (Tai, 2021). As a result, translanguaging has been extensively explored in educational contexts across the globe (Zhou et al., 2021), with significant focus on how translanguaging pedagogy can enhance teaching and learning effectiveness (Wang & Shen, 2023). This pedagogical approach, advocating the holistic use of students' linguistic resources, has been adopted in classrooms to facilitate the shift from monolingualism to multilingualism (Fang et al., 2023; Ho & Tai, 2021; Jiang et al., 2022). Extensive discussion on pedagogical translanguaging over the past decade has evidenced interest in language learning, especially in EFL and English as a Second Language (ESL) contexts (Ismailov et al., 2021). Translanguaging provides for flexible pedagogical practices, allowing for a deeper understanding of learning content (Gu et al., 2022), enhancing students' participation in the classroom (Rabbidge, 2019; Sahan & Rose, 2021), and supporting the bilingual identities of students (Tai & Wong, 2023).

Previous research on teachers' translanguaging practices has indicated their potential to facilitate teaching and learning in diverse educational settings. For instance, Kao et al. (2021) explored how two instructional and interactional strategies were used to assist in content delivery, students' comprehension, and teacher-student interaction in Taiwan. Jiang and Zhang (2023) revealed that teachers' monologic lectures in the Chinese context included four translanguaging practices: cross-language labeling, recapping, code-mixing, and using multimodal resources. Similarly, Yuan and Yang (2023) found that a teacher educator used three translanguaging strategies: blending academic and everyday discourse, connecting verbal and other semiotic resources, and using students' first language to create a translanguaging space in EMI classrooms.

In their study, Fuster and Bardel (2024) discussed the distinction between spontaneous and pedagogical translanguaging and noted the very understated role pedagogical translanguaging plays in Sweden. In the same vein, research by Sobkowiak (2022) in the Polish context found that teachers claimed to prioritize exclusive English use in the classroom, but actually adopted a pragmatic approach toward using the L1.

Results from Muguruza et al.'s (2023) exploration of student and teacher responses to the use of a flexible language policy in the Basque Country indicated the positive role of translanguaging in developing comprehension in EMI classes balanced by its potential to limit learners' production skills. In the Arab world, Jaafarawi (2023) noted students' utilization of translanguaging in note-taking and summarizing. This, however, requires teachers to explicitly guide students in employing their full range of linguistic abilities to mediate understanding and provide translanguaging spaces where they are encouraged to communicate naturally.

In content-specific courses, it has been found that translanguaging can integrate students' out-of-school experiences into content knowledge to facilitate learning (Tai & Wong, 2023). Tai and Li (2021) investigated translanguaging in Hong Kong mathematics classes, with results indicating that teachers can better utilize multilingual resources to convey meaning, build knowledge, and enhance student participation.

While translanguaging offers potential new and flexible ways of responding to the needs of students, many educators have encountered difficulties in addressing the gaps between policy and classroom realities (Costley & Leung, 2020). Thus, there is a need to explore actual language practices in EMI settings through a translanguaging lens, considering the relative deficiencies in EMI programs in Oman and challenges students face in learning the language subskills.

15.3 Methodology

This study employed an exploratory research design through a two-phase sequential mixed-methods approach. The rationale for this approach is grounded in the fact that neither quantitative nor qualitative methods alone are sufficient to explore so potentially complex an area. Therefore, to collect data from both students and teachers, both methods were combined for a more robust analysis, leveraging their strengths in each phase. To this end, a closed-ended survey was used to gather data in the quantitative phase, while focus group discussions were conducted in the qualitative phase.

15.3.1 Instrument and Participants

Quantitative data was collected through a structured survey composed of two main parts. The survey was in both English and Arabic to help prevent any ambiguities for students and obtain more accurate responses. The first part focused on participant demographic information, including gender, age, academic level, year of study, and study program. The second part involved participants rating the difficulty of various English language subskills on a scale of 1 (indicating high levels of difficulty) to 7 (high levels of ease). Table 15.1 indicates that survey participants included 118 students from a public university in Oman, consisting of 91 females and 27 males, with the majority between 20 and 25 years of age. Students were selected randomly from across four majors. Ethical approval for both study phases was obtained through formal approval from the university ethics committee. Students were assured of anonymity, confidentiality, and their right to participate and withdraw at any time.

In the second research phase, two focus group discussions were held in English with nine instructors teaching across four majors at the university. Participants were teaching on EMI courses that included Entrepreneurship, International Human Resources Management, Introduction to Information Security, Principles of Accounting, Financial Management and Business Ethics, Computing Skills, Digital Media, Introduction to Communication, and Introduction to Advertising (see Table 15.2). They volunteered after being informed about the nature of the research and their ethical rights, and were asked to offer explicit

Table 15.1 Participants' demographic data

Item	Category	Frequency	Percent
Gender	Male	27	22.9
	Female	91	77.1
Age	17–19	3	2.5
	20–22	71	60.2
	23–25	41	34.7
	Above 25	3	2.5
Level	Bachelor's	33	28
	Advanced diploma	36	30.5
	Diploma	49	41.5
Year	1st	31	26.3
	2nd	36	30.5
	3rd	49	41.5
	4th	2	1.7
Program	Business studies	31	28.4
	Information technology	39	34.5
	Engineering	33	29.2
	Mass communication	15	7.9

Note Due to a rounding error, not all rows tally to exactly 100%

Table 15.2 Focus group participants

Number	Gender	Age	Education level	Department
9	Female (n = 5)	31–35 (n = 6)	Master's (n = 8)	Business (n = 2)
	Male (n = 4)	36–40 (n = 3)	PhD (n = 1)	Engineering (n = 3)
				Information technology (n = 2)
				Communications (n = 2)

consent to be digitally recorded. To help satisfy assurances of participant anonymity and confidentiality of information, the focus groups were held on MS Teams with only the presence of the researcher and participants. The two focus groups lasted for 45 and 47 minutes, respectively.

Focus groups were selected for this phase as they serve as a means of efficiently gathering data and enable participants to share and expand upon each other's perspectives. Described as an effective method by Rabiee (2004) for gaining insight into the meanings, beliefs, and cultures that shape individuals' feelings, attitudes, and behaviors, they offer the opportunity for participants to discuss their perceptions, ideas, opinions, and thoughts (Krueger & Casey, 2015). As such, they allow participants to express their views on the research topics in their own words, with minimal intervention from the researcher.

15.3.2 Data Analysis

For the quantitative data collected through the survey, the difficulty ratings for each subskill were analyzed using descriptive statistics, including means and standard deviations. For qualitative focus group data, transcriptions of both discussions were utilized to conduct emergent-systematic analysis. In this type of qualitative analysis, the term "emergent" refers to the group that is used for exploratory purposes, and "systematic" refers to the other group which is used for verification purposes. In the case of the current study, data from the first focus group was transcribed to identify emergent themes. The data from the second focus group was then transcribed and used as additional sampling to assess the significance of the themes and to refine them.

For the thematic analysis of the first group, the framework put forth by Braun and Clarke (2006), with a six-phase process, was used: (1) becoming familiar with the data; (2) generating initial codes from the data; (3) identifying emergent themes; (4) reviewing and refining the themes; (5) defining and labeling themes; and (6) compiling the final report. This initial phase was followed by an investigation of the recurring themes in the second focus group for verification and theme refinement. Adhering to this method facilitated a rigorous examination of the data.

15.4 Findings and Discussion

15.4.1 Survey Data: English Subskill Variations

The subsequent sections elaborate on the distinct subskills associated with each skill and offer a detailed exploration of the diverse challenges students face in studying through EMI.

15.4.1.1 Listening Subskills

As shown in Table 15.3, students found comprehending their lecturers' main ideas, organization, and key vocabulary moderately difficult, while note-taking was easier. Identifying supporting ideas and examples posed average difficulty. Understanding their lecturers' accents and different views was moderately challenging, but classmates' accents were easier to understand, highlighting variations in perceived difficulty across listening contexts.

Table 15.3 Listening subskills

Subskills	Mean	Std. deviation
Understanding the main ideas of lectures	4.81	1.597
Understanding the overall organization of lectures	4.94	1.560
Understanding key vocabulary	4.97	1.561
Taking brief, clear notes	5.00	1.664
Identifying supporting ideas and examples	4.92	1.542
Understanding lecturers' accents	4.69	1.544
Identifying different views and ideas	4.59	1.391
Understanding questions	4.81	1.467
Understanding classmates' accents	5.73	1.667

15.4.1.2 Speaking Subskills

Students' self-reported assessments of their speaking skills are shown in Table 15.4. Participants indicated challenges in speaking accuracy, while pronunciation also presented a moderate level of difficulty. Students further reported moderate difficulty in presenting information, participating in discussions, and answering questions. They also faced challenges in communicating fluently, speaking from notes, asking questions, and communicating confidently. However, using visual aids like Power-Point was perceived as somewhat easier.

Table 15.4 Speaking subskills

Subskills	Mean	Std. deviation
Speaking accurately (grammar)	3.85	1.363
Speaking clearly (pronunciation)	4.19	1.485
Presenting information/ideas	4.25	1.385
Participating actively in discussions	4.22	1.474
Communicating ideas fluently	3.89	1.495
Speaking from notes	4.50	1.673
Asking questions	4.64	1.550
Answering questions	4.49	1.478
Communicating ideas confidently	4.15	1.652
Using visual aids (e.g., PowerPoint)	5.02	1.649

Table 15.5 Reading subskills

Subskills	Mean	Std. deviation
Understanding specific vocabulary	4.42	1.482
Comprehending the meaning of difficult words	4.08	1.514
Reading carefully to understand a text	4.75	1.547
Reading quickly to find specific information	4.17	1.571
Identifying supporting ideas and examples	4.42	1.458
Reading quickly to get the overall meaning	4.22	1.715
Identifying the key ideas of a text	4.49	1.578
Taking brief, relevant notes	4.30	1.592
Using one's own words when taking notes	4.84	1.679

15.4.1.3 Reading Subskills

As shown in Table 15.5, students found understanding specific vocabulary, comprehending the meaning of difficult words, and reading comprehension to be moderately difficult. Challenges included understanding texts, identifying supporting ideas, reading quickly for specific information, and reading quickly to grasp overall text meaning. Participants also struggled with identifying key ideas, taking relevant notes, and paraphrasing in notes.

15.4.1.4 Writing Subskills

Table 15.6 shows participants' self-reported assessment of their writing skills. Students indicated a moderate level of difficulty in planning for written assignments and revising written work, suggesting that these tasks require careful consideration and effort. Likewise, expressing ideas in correct English and using an appropriate academic style were perceived as moderately challenging. Respondents also reported challenges in proofreading written work. Referring to sources in written work and summarizing/paraphrasing ideas from sources were identified as moderately challenging aspects of incorporating information. Additionally, organizing ideas in coherent paragraphs, expressing ideas clearly and logically, and linking ideas from different sources were acknowledged as areas requiring attention and improvement. Students found writing specific sections of an assignment (e.g., introduction, body, and conclusion) to be

Table 15.6 Writing subskills

Subskills	Mean	Std. deviation
Planning written assignments	4.58	1.554
Expressing ideas in correct English	4.15	1.539
Revising written work	4.71	1.451
Using an appropriate academic style	4.36	1.454
Writing a bibliography/references section	4.80	1.771
Proofreading written work	4.08	1.459
Referring to sources in written work	4.58	1.646
Summarizing/paraphrasing ideas in sources	4.42	1.560
Organizing ideas in coherent paragraphs	4.51	1.478
Expressing ideas clearly and logically	4.42	1.482
Linking ideas from different sources	4.39	1.536
Writing the introduction to an assignment	4.89	1.668
Writing the body of an assignment	4.58	1.609
Writing the conclusion to an assignment	4.95	1.622
Linking sentences smoothly	4.75	1.503

relatively easier. Furthermore, linking sentences smoothly was perceived as a moderately challenging yet manageable aspect of writing.

15.4.2 Focus Group Results

The results of focus group discussions indicate the following four translanguaging strategies used by teachers in the classroom: active learning, attention-raising, explanatory, and rapport-building strategies.

15.4.2.1 Active Learning Strategies

The focus group discussions revealed that active learning played a crucial role as a translanguaging strategy in Omani EMI classrooms. Teachers utilized various methods, such as incorporating YouTube videos in Arabic, to clarify complex concepts, and assigning semester-long group projects. These projects required students to collaborate for 14 weeks, using their L1 to transfer ideas and share content. This approach aligns with the findings of Mbirimi-Hungwe and McCabe (2020) and Kandu-boda (2020), which emphasize the effectiveness of collaborative learning and the Interaction for Learning Framework (ILF) in fostering active student engagement and enhancing understanding through translanguaging.

15.4.2.2   Attention-Raising Strategies

Teachers found that maintaining students' focus and interest was challenging when instruction was exclusively in English. To address this, they strategically shifted to Arabic to highlight key points and facilitate instructional clarity. This proactive attention-raising strategy helped maintain the flow of the lesson and ensured that students remained engaged. The use of Arabic for emphasizing important content was reported to be effective in keeping students attentive and involved in the learning process.

15.4.2.3   Explanatory Strategies

The explanatory strategy involved teachers using a mix of English and Arabic to explain textbook-related content, particularly in technical courses. This bilingual approach was essential for conveying specific content knowledge and ensuring that students comprehend fundamental concepts. Teachers reported that explanations and definitions in Arabic were frequently necessary to overcome obstacles in students' understanding, a practice corroborated by the student surveys indicating challenges in the four subskills. This strategy is consistent with instructional explanations designed to teach and convey specific aspects of the material (Leinhardt, 2010), ensuring that students fully grasp the lesson before progressing to practice and activities.

15.4.2.4   Rapport-Building Strategies

Rapport-building strategies were prominent in teacher-student interactions. Teachers used Arabic to maintain natural communication flow and avoid discouraging students who struggled to express themselves in English. During group discussions, students often relied on Arabic to tackle complex ideas, with teachers initially participating in L1 before gradually shifting to English. This approach facilitated a smooth transition to English while respecting the course objectives of enhancing speaking skills. The strategy aligns with findings by Thongwichit and Ulla (2024), which highlight translanguaging pedagogy as a scaffolding mechanism that leverages students' linguistic and cultural backgrounds to improve English proficiency. This approach creates a safe and inclusive classroom environment, promoting language skill development without disrupting the flow of discussion.

15.5 Discussion

RQ1: What are EFL learners' perceived challenges with EMI in the Oman higher education context?

The first research question was addressed by analysis of the survey data, which indicated significant challenges for students across all four subskills in their EMI classes. For example, for the listening subskill, students reported experiencing moderate difficulties in comprehending the main ideas of lectures, understanding their overall organization, and understanding key vocabulary. Understanding lecturers' accents posed a moderate challenge, while identifying different views and ideas was perceived as moderately difficult. For reading, the results of student surveys indicated a moderate level of difficulty in understanding specific vocabulary and comprehending the meaning of difficult words. In terms of reading comprehension, students indicated challenges in reading carefully to understand a text and identifying supporting ideas and examples. Reading quickly to find specific information and get the overall meaning of a text was also perceived as moderately difficult. Furthermore, students reported a moderate level of difficulty in identifying the key ideas of a text, taking brief, relevant notes, and taking notes using their own lexical knowledge. These results in Oman's higher education context could potentially lead to a growth in negative outcomes, similar to claims made by other researchers, such as Al-Mahrooqi and Denman (2017) and Sinha et al. (2018), who reported high attrition rates in the country's EMI programs.

Students reported challenges with grammatical accuracy in speaking and moderate difficulty with pronunciation. Presenting information, participating in discussions, and answering questions also posed moderate challenges, along with general communication difficulties. Further, their reported writing challenges align with the results of studies by Al-Bakri and Troudi (2020) and Al-Hashami (2022). That is, participants found planning and revising assignments moderately to highly difficult, requiring careful effort. Expressing ideas correctly and using an appropriate academic style were also moderately challenging. Proofreading presented additional difficulties, emphasizing the need for attention to detail. Graham et al. (2021) have reported similar challenges associated with the application of monolingual EMI approaches.

RQ2: What translanguaging practices do Omani teachers employ and what purposes do they serve?

The second research question was addressed in focus group discussions from which emerged, somewhat similar to results offered by Zhou and Mann (2021) and Wang and Shen (2023), four translanguaging strategies used by teachers in the classroom, i.e., active learning, attention-raising, explanatory, and rapport-building strategies.

Analysis revealed that active learning is crucial in the Omani context, with examples of this offered by teacher participants including the use of Arabic YouTube videos for conveying complex concepts and group projects enhancing teamwork and research skills. Teachers stated that shifting to Arabic helped maintain student focus and interest in lessons and that the language's strategic use allowed them to effectively highlight important points and preserve lesson flow.

The explanatory strategy occurred when teachers used a combination of English and Arabic to explain textbook-related content. This was mostly performed to convey specific content knowledge in technical courses. Explanatory support for learning includes instructional explanations designed to teach and convey specific aspects of the classroom material (Leinhardt, 2010). When students do not understand the fundamental concepts of their lessons, it becomes an obstacle for continuing with practice and activities. As a result, teachers reported seeking to ensure their learners' understanding by offering explanations and definitions in Arabic. The need for all teacher participants to use translanguaging for explanations finds support in the survey results of learner challenges across all four subskills.

Teachers used rapport-building strategies in interactions with students by incorporating Arabic to maintain communication flow and avoid discouragement. In group discussions, students relied on Arabic for complex ideas. Teachers started with technical concepts in L1 and gradually shifted to English to enhance speaking skills, guiding students toward accurate English use while maintaining smooth discussions. This approach has also been described by Thongwichit and Ulla (2024), who found that translanguaging pedagogy can act as a scaffolding mechanism, allowing students to use their existing language skills to improve their English proficiency. Such an approach prioritizes students' linguistic and cultural backgrounds, creating a safe and inclusive classroom. It also highlights the importance of language teachers acknowledging and embracing translanguaging pedagogy in English-only classrooms.

Overall, however, the focus group discussions indicated that these translanguaging strategies were not uniformly applied by all teachers, which suggests a need for awareness-raising sessions and training workshops to ensure more consistent implementation across the board.

15.6 Implications and Conclusion

Although the study reported here was conducted in Oman, involving the perspectives of 118 students and nine lecturers, the findings have implications for scholars and practitioners in a wide range of educational contexts. To begin, higher education instructors need to acknowledge the potential benefits of promoting students' L1 use, as this can effectively enhance the quality of classroom interactions and improve learning outcomes. This, however, requires the provision of higher levels of professional support for teachers to develop translanguaging pedagogy, which necessitates teacher training on the affordances of various translanguaging strategies in EMI settings. Teachers need awareness of the potential benefits of integrating students' L1 in order to facilitate a more seamless progression in the development of their English language skills, with this being especially the case for students with lower English language proficiency.

Based on student survey responses, it is evident that significant challenges exist across various language skills in their EMI classes. These results underscore the urgent need for targeted interventions and support mechanisms to address learner difficulties, thereby helping them overcome communication barriers in both general English and EAP courses. In addition, teachers need to encourage students to take part in collaborative language activities to effectively communicate their thoughts and promote substantial interactions as a means of improving their language proficiency. This approach could be readily placed under the active learning initiative put forth by Oman's Ministry of Higher Education, Research and Innovation, and is an area that will greatly benefit from further research.

Finally, findings emphasize the importance of moving beyond the rigid beliefs underpinning monolingual (i.e., English-only) institutional policies, with a focus on transitioning to translanguaging pedagogy. Hence, it is essential that teachers and policymakers re-evaluate existing rules and incorporate translanguaging to support program content and language learning objectives. Among potentially effective strategies to achieve this is encouraging teachers of English for Academic Purposes to critically reflect on their beliefs about translanguaging through involvement in researcher-teacher collaboration (Liu et al., 2020). This obviously necessitates access to more collaborative professional development programs for researchers and teachers, which is an aspect that is, at the time of writing, generally neglected in Oman. Once introduced, however, these programs will enable meaningful discussions with teachers about the principles of valuing multilingual speakers' full linguistic repertoires in teaching and learning, while also providing fuller explorations of how these can be put into action in local contexts.

References

Adamson, J., & Coulson, D. (2015). Translanguaging in English academic writing preparation. *International Journal of Pedagogies and Learning, 10*(1), 24–37. https://doi.org/10.1080/22040552.2015.1084674

Al-Bakri, S., & Troudi, S. (2020). Effects of the English medium instruction policy on students' writing experiences in content courses in a public college in Oman. In S. Troudi (Ed.), *Critical issues in teaching English and language education* (pp. 11–40). Palgrave Macmillan.

Al Hashami, A. S. M. (2022). *Exploring the complexity and controversy of code-switching practices in the EFL and EMI classrooms at a higher education institute in the Sultanate of Oman* (Unpublished doctoral dissertation). University of Exeter.

Al-Mahrooqi, R., & Denman, C. J. (2017). Investigating FL attrition among Omani teachers of English: Implications for educational reform in Oman and the Arab Gulf. In A. Mahboob & T. Elyas (Eds.), *Challenges to education in the GCC during the 21st century* (pp. 19–43). Gulf Research Centre Cambridge.

Back, M. (2020). 'It is a village': Translanguaging pedagogies and collective responsibility in a rural school district. *TESOL Quarterly, 54*(4), 900–924. https://doi.org/10.1002/tesq.562

Barahona, M. (2020). The potential of translanguaging as a core teaching practice in an EFL context. *System, 95*, 102368. https://doi.org/10.1016/j.system.2020.102368

Braun, V., & Clarke, V. (2006). Using thematic analysis in psychology. *Qualitative Research in Psychology, 3*(2), 77–101. https://doi.org/10.1191/1478088706qp063oa

Costley, T., & Leung, C. (2020). Putting translanguaging into practice: A view from England. *System, 92*, 102270. https://doi.org/10.1016/j.system.2020.102270

Fang, F., Jiang, L., & Yang, J. (2023). To impart knowledge or to adhere to policy: Unpacking language ideologies and practices in Chinese EMI courses through a translanguaging lens. *Language Teaching Research*, 1–30. https://doi.org/10.1177/13621688231183771

Fuster, C., & Bardel, C. (2024). Translanguaging in Sweden: A critical review from an International perspective. *System, 121*, 103241. https://doi.org/10.1016/j.system.2024.103241

Graham, K. M., Eslami, Z. R., & Hillman, S. (2021). From English as the medium to English as a medium: Perspectives of EMI students in Qatar. *System, 99*, 102508. https://doi.org/10.1016/j.system.2021.102508

Gu, M. M., Lee, C.-K. J., & Jin, T. (2022). A translanguaging and trans-semiotizing perspective on subject teachers' linguistic and pedagogical practices in EMI program. *Applied Linguistics Review, 14*(6), 1589–1615. https://doi.org/10.1515/applirev-2022-0036

Ho, W. Y. J., & Tai, K. W. H. (2021). Translanguaging in digital learning: the making of Translanguaging spaces in online English teaching videos. *International Journal of Bilingual Education and Bilingualism*, 1–22. https://doi.org/10.1080/13670050.2021.2001427

Ismailov, M., Chiu, T. K., Dearden, J., Yamamoto, Y., & Djalilova, N. (2021). Challenges to internationalisation of university programmes: A systematic thematic synthesis of qualitative research on learner-centred English Medium Instruction (EMI) pedagogy. *Sustainability, 13*(22), 12642. https://doi.org/10.3390/su132212642

Jaafarawi, N. (2023). Current discussions on plurilingual pedagogy: Language learning implications in the Arabian Peninsula. In D. Coelho & T. G. Steinhagen (Eds.), *Plurilingual pedagogy in the Arabian Peninsula: Transforming and empowering students and teachers* (pp. 24–38). Routledge.

Jia, W., Fu, X., & Pun, J. (2023). How do EMI lecturers' translanguaging perceptions translate into their practice? A multi-case study of three Chinese tertiary EMI classes. *Sustainability, 15*(6), 4895. https://doi.org/10.3390/su15064895

Jiang, A. L., & Zhang, L. J. (2023). Understanding knowledge construction in a Chinese university EMI classroom: A translanguaging perspective. *System, 114*, 103024. https://doi.org/10.1016/j.system.2023.103024

Jiang, Z. W., Zhang, L. J., & Mohamed, N. (2022). Researching translanguaging as a feasible pedagogical practice: Evidence from Chinese English-as-a-Foreign-Language students' perceptions. *RELC Journal, 53*(2), 371–390. https://doi.org/10.1177/00336882221113653

Kamaşak, R., & Sahan, K. (2023). Academic success in English medium courses: Exploring student challenges, opinions, language proficiency and L2 use. *RELC Journal*. https://doi.org/10.1177/00336882231167611

Kanduboda, P. B. (2020). Fostering active interaction and engagement among students via translanguaging: The case of students in Japanese universities from diverse cultural backgrounds. *Journal of the Asia-Japan Research Institute of Ritsumeikan University, 2*, 151–165. https://doi.org/10.34389/asiajapan.2.0_151

Kao, S. M., Tsou, W., & Chen, F. (2021). Translanguaging strategies for EMI Instruction in Taiwanese higher education. In W. Tsou & W. Baker (Eds.), *English-medium instruction translanguaging practices in Asia: Theories, frameworks and implementation in higher education* (pp. 81–99). Springer.

Kao, Y. T. (2023). Exploring translanguaging in Taiwanese CLIL classes: An analysis of teachers' perceptions and practices. *Language, Culture and Curriculum, 36*(1), 100–121. https://doi.org/10.1080/07908318.2022.203 3762

Karakaş, A. (2023). Translanguaging in content-based EMI classes through the lens of Turkish students: Self-reported practices, functions and orientations. *Linguistics and Education, 77*, 101221. https://doi.org/10.1016/j.linged.2023.101221

Kim, S., & Chang, C.-H. (2022). Japanese L2 learners' translanguaging practice in written peer feedback. *International Journal of Bilingual Education and Bilingualism, 25*(4), 1363–1376. https://doi.org/10.1080/13670050.2020.1760201

Krueger, R. A., & Casey, M. A. (2015). *Focus groups: A practical guide for applied research.* Sage.

Leinhardt, G. (2010). Introduction: Explaining instructional explanations. In M. K. Stein & L. Kucan (Eds.), *Instructional explanations in the disciplines* (pp. 1–5). Springer.

Liu, J. E., Lo, Y. Y., & Lin, A. M. (2020). Translanguaging pedagogy in teaching English for Academic Purposes: Researcher-teacher collaboration as a professional development model. *System, 92*, 102276. https://doi.org/10.1016/j.system.2020.102276

Macaro, E. (2018). *English medium instruction: Content and language in policy and practice.* Oxford University Press.

Mbirimi-Hungwe, V., & McCabe, R.-M. (2020). Translanguaging during collaborative learning: A 'transcollab' model of teaching. *Southern African Linguistics and Applied Language Studies, 38*(3), 244–259. https://doi.org/10.2989/16073614.2020.1847670

Muguruza, B., Cenoz, J., & Gorter, D. (2023). Implementing translanguaging pedagogies in an English medium instruction course. *International Journal of Multilingualism, 20*(2), 540–555. https://doi.org/10.1080/14790718.2020.1822848

Pecorari, D., & Malmström, H. (2018). At the crossroads of TESOL and English medium instruction. *TESOL Quarterly, 52*(3), 497–515. http://www.jstor.org/stable/44987078

Pun, J., & Macaro, E. (2019). The effect of first and second language use on question types in English medium instruction science classrooms in Hong Kong. *International Journal of Bilingual Education and Bilingualism, 22*(1), 64–77. https://doi.org/10.1080/13670050.2018.1510368

Rabbidge, M. (2019). The effects of translanguaging on participation in EFL classrooms. *Journal of Asia TEFL, 16*(4), 1305–1322. https://doi.org/10.18823/asiatefl.2019.16.4.15.1305

Rabiee, F. (2004). Focus-group interview and data analysis. *Proceedings of the Nutrition Society, 63*(4), 655–660.

Richards, J. C., & Pun, J. (2022). Teacher strategies in implementing English medium instruction. *ELT Journal, 76*(2), 227–237. https://doi.org/10.1093/elt/ccab081

Sahan, K., & Rose, H. (2021). Translanguaging or code-switching? Re-examining the functions of language in EMI classrooms. In B. Di Sabato & B. Hughes (Eds.), *Multilingual perspectives from Europe and beyond on language policy and practice* (pp. 348–356). Routledge.

Shah, M., Pillai, S., & Sinayah, M. (2019). Translanguaging in an academic setting. *Lingua, 225*, 16–31. https://doi.org/10.1016/j.lingua.2019.05.001

Sinha, Y., Roche, T., & Sinha, M. (2018). Understanding higher education attrition in English-medium programs in the Arab Gulf States: Identifying push, pull and fallout factors at an Omani University. In R. Al-Mahrooqi & C. J. Denman (Eds.), *English education in Oman. Current scenarios and future trajectories* (pp. 195–230). Springer.

Sobkowiak, P. (2022). Translanguaging practices in the EFL classroom—The Polish context. *Linguistics and Education, 69*, 101020. https://doi.org/10.1016/j.linged.2022.101020

Tai, K. W. (2021). Researching translanguaging in EMI classrooms. In J. K. H. Pun & S. M. Curle (Eds.), *Research methods in English medium instruction* (pp. 119–132). Routledge.

Tai, K. W., & Li, W. (2021). Constructing playful talk through translanguaging in English Medium instruction mathematics classrooms. *Applied Linguistics, 42*(4), 607–640. https://doi.org/10.1093/applin/amaa043

Tai, K. W., & Wong, C. Y. (2023). Empowering students through the construction of a translanguaging space in an English as a first language classroom. *Applied Linguistics, 44*(6), 1100–1151. https://doi.org/10.1093/applin/amac069

Thongwichit, N., & Ulla, M. B. (2024). Translanguaging pedagogy in Thailand's English medium of instruction classrooms: Teachers' perspectives and practices. *The Electronic Journal for English as a Second Language (TESL-EJ)*, *27*(4). https://doi.org/10.55593/ej.27108a7

Wang, Z., & Shen, B. (2023). 'I think I am bilingual, but...': Teachers' practices of and students' attitudes toward translanguaging in a Chinese intercultural communication class. *International Journal of Applied Linguistics, 34*(1), 242–260. https://doi-org.squ.idm.oclc.org/10.1111/ijal.12491

Yuan, R., & Yang, M. (2023). Towards an understanding of translanguaging in EMI teacher education classrooms. *Language Teaching Research, 27*(4), 884–906. https://doi.org/10.1177/1362168820964123

Zhou, X., Li, C., & Gao, X. A. (2021). Towards a sustainable classroom ecology: Translanguaging in English as a medium of instruction (EMI) in a finance course at an international school in Shanghai. *Sustainability, 13*(19), 10719. https://doi.org/10.3390/su131910719

Zhou, X., & Mann, S. (2021). Translanguaging in a Chinese university CLIL classroom: Teacher strategies and student attitudes. *Studies in Second Language Learning and Teaching, 11*(2), 265–289. https://doi.org/10.14746/ssllt.2021.11.2.5

Part III

Machine Translation in Foreign Language Learning

16

College-Level Language Education in the Machine-Translation Era: A Metacognitive Approach

Yoko Hasegawa, Kiyono Fujinaga-Gordon, Eri Nakagawa, and Jun Kanazawa

16.1 Introduction

The stunning improvement in machine translation (MT) engines based on large language models (e.g., ChatGPT, DeepL, Google Translate) and their ubiquitous accessibility in recent years has begun to alter college-level foreign language curricula. Rote memorization of vocabulary and grammatical constructions is being deprived of its raison d'être when simple sentences can be machine-translated with increasing speed and accuracy. Lively and attractive learning materials—including anime,

Y. Hasegawa (✉)
Department of East Asian Languages and Cultures, University of California, Berkeley, CA, USA
e-mail: hasegawa@berkeley.edu

K. Fujinaga-Gordon
Department of Languages, Cultures & Applied Linguistics, Carnegie Mellon University, Pittsburgh, PA, USA
e-mail: kfujinag@andrew.cmu.edu

© The Author(s), under exclusive license to Springer Nature Switzerland AG 2025
D. Coulson and C. Denman (eds.), *Translation, Translanguaging and Machine Translation in Foreign Language Education*,
https://doi.org/10.1007/978-3-031-82174-5_16

329

manga, mobile language apps, and YouTube videos—are readily available, and many people are acquiring a foreign language independently through these non-traditional modalities. Reflecting this state of affairs, an increasing number of students have been enrolling directly in intermediate Japanese courses, skipping the elementary level (e.g., Ikeda, 2023).[1]

Some educators consider that the advent of MT, together with the popularity of non-traditional learning methods, exacerbates the declining enthusiasm for college-level foreign language courses. According to the Modern Language Association, average college student enrollment in foreign languages dropped by 16.6% between 2016 and 2021 (Lusin et al., 2023).

This tendency was epitomized by the recent upheaval at West Virginia University (see Anderson, 2023). Despite a fierce nationwide outcry, the university decided to relinquish its entire World Languages, Literatures, and Linguistics department against a background of ebbing financial support from the state government (Svrluga & Anderson, 2023). Its president declared that foreign languages are "not a high priority nationally" (*Gee speaks on the budget deficit*, 2023, para. 1) and that the number of language majors and minors accounts for less than 1% of the university's entire student body (Schackner, 2023).

E. Nakagawa
College of Arts and Sciences, The University of Tokyo, Komaba, Meguro City, Japan
e-mail: erinakagawa@g.ecc.u-tokyo.ac.jp

J. Kanazawa
Department of Political Sciences, Faculty of Law, Daito Bunka University, Itabashi City, Japan
e-mail: jun-kanazawa@ic.daito.ac.jp

[1] Naturally, significant regional variability exists. A joint survey in 2016 by Dentsu Inc. and the Japan Foundation reports that the number of Japanese language learners in Hong Kong, South Korea, and Taiwan was about eight million, compared with the 2015 Japan Foundation survey's figure of about 800,000 learning at educational institutions in the same region. That is, in these locations, only 10% study Japanese formally. In the present work, we limit our scope to the U.S., of which we have firsthand knowledge.

This is a far-reaching opinion that must be scrutinized meticulously. To counter such a claim, it is frequently stated that foreign language education enables students to develop critical thinking, problem solving, and analytic and interpretive capacities. However, those discussions tend to remain abstract, leaving opponents to wonder how such rebuttals can be justified as these skills are commonly taught in most liberal arts disciplines and are not unique to foreign language education. This study examines the merits of taking Japanese language courses in higher education more concretely with tangible examples. Although we concentrate on the case of Japanese education in the U.S., we believe our discussion will also shed new light on the circumstances of other languages.

The structure of this chapter is as follows: after examining language learners' motivation and objectives in Sect. 16.2, it deliberates on the possible impacts of the emergence of potent MT in Sect. 16.3. If information exchange is the primary goal, the relevance of foreign language learning will inevitably be lessened as the popularity of MT surges. However, language is not solely for communication; its other significant function is as a vehicle for thought. Shifting the curriculum focus from a communication-based to a thinking-based design will likely preserve the vital relevance of foreign language education. Section 16.4 discusses four topics selected from Japanese that are particularly suitable for a thinking-based curriculum. Section 16.5 demonstrates the current advancement of ChatGPT and considers how its use can be incorporated into the curriculum before Sect. 16.6 concludes the chapter.

16.2 Motivations for Studying Japanese

The Japan Foundation (2021) indicates the following to be the top ten motivations of students of Japanese in the U.S. and Canada:

1. Interest in Japanese pop culture (e.g., anime, manga, J-Pop, fashion)   92.1%
2. Interest in the Japanese language itself   82.2%
3. Interest in traditional Japanese culture (e.g., history, literature, art)   81.9%
4. Travel in Japan   66.7%

5.	Current or future work in the U.S. or Canada	60.6%
6.	Native or heritage language	55.2%
7.	Future work in Japan	48.9%
8.	Interest in international understanding and rapport, intercultural exchange	46.4%
9.	Study abroad in Japan	34.9%
10.	To gain access to higher education in the U.S. or Canada	30.4%

These motives can be categorized into a desire to (i) talk with speakers of Japanese, (ii) acquire information that cannot be readily learned if one remains monolingual, and (iii) a hybrid of both. Category (i) includes Response (8), while (ii) includes Responses (1, 3, 4). Response (2) merely alludes to a vague interest in Japan. Respondents are unlikely to be interested in the Japanese language at face value, e.g., the typological properties of the language itself.

Regarding (i), learners' primary objective mainly is to enjoy verbal interaction per se while making use of a foreign language (an innate pleasure for human verbal communication). It focuses on the phatic function of language (e.g., greetings, building rapport) to establish and maintain social relations and bonds, while the exchange of meaningful information is secondary. For this type, the advent of MT is simply irrelevant; they will likely continue to take courses if available.

If, by contrast, the primary motivation is (ii), a desire for information, the relevance of foreign language courses will inevitably be lessened with the enhancement of MT. Understandably, for example, fewer students will take courses if traveling in Japan (i.e., Response (4)) is a driving force because gathering information that travelers need is one of MT's most triumphant arenas.

The ten points mentioned above suggest that the majority of learners aim at a hybrid of (i) and (ii), which encompasses (5, 7, 9, 10), and possibly (6). That is, the purpose of learning is to live in a community where the target language serves the requirement for predominant social and information exchange, and smooth verbal interactions in Japanese are necessary or beneficial for achieving ultimate objectives (e.g., business, study, or personal matters).

From an educator's perspective, this group can be the most crucial and fruitful. Tohsaku (2014, p. 8), for example, asserts that the goal of Japanese language education is "the acquisition of social and networking abilities; that is, abilities to engage in social activities, to connect with others to develop new communities and societies, and improve quality of life by using the Japanese language." In other words, the goal is to become a full-fledged member of the speech community. However, this group constitutes only a tiny portion of the total number of students. The overwhelming majority discontinue college courses after the first year, and some even after one semester, which is inadequate to accomplish this goal.

These points imply that the advent of MT has the greatest impact on the L2 learner population pursuing broader information, perspectives, and knowledge.

16.3 A Quest for a Post-Communicative Paradigm

16.3.1 The Metacognitive Approach

Since Hymes' (1971) influential proposal of *communicative competence*, foreign language curricula have shifted the focus from the rote memorization of vocabulary and grammatical rules to the ability to use the foreign language in a socially appropriate way to accomplish specific communicative goals. This paradigm shift emphasizes information-gathering skills and highly values the ability to express intended meanings rather than grammatical accuracy.

As discussed above, communication-oriented curricula may be negatively susceptible to the impact of the pervasive use of MT. We anticipate that programs prioritizing information exchange via communication will be unable to stem the decline in student enrollments. What can we do, then, to prevent another case similar to West Virginia University from happening?

We must recognize that language is not solely for communication. Its other significant function is as a vehicle for thought. If the currently prevailing communicative method is likely to lose attractiveness and, consequently, student enrollment rates fall, a paradigm shift is called for. We consider that a promising post-communicative candidate will emphasize language as a means of thinking. We call it the *metacognitive approach*.

Metacognition is the awareness of cognitive processes. The American Psychology Association (2024) defines *cognition* as "all forms of knowing and awareness, such as perceiving, conceiving, remembering, reasoning, judging, imagining, and problem solving." In these terms, metacognition is conceived of as recognizing and understanding what we know, how we acquire such knowledge (learn), and what we do with such knowledge (think).

Some cognition-based approaches have been proposed in awareness of the shortcomings of the communicative method. For example, Tyler (2012) argues that L2 learners have well-developed sets of conceptual categories, and describes how they are linked to their L1 linguistic forms (expressions) depending on their perception and categorization of the surrounding world. Therefore, she continues, learning an L2 enables learners to re-categorize many aspects of reality, i.e., to see "familiar landscapes through new eyes" (p. 62).

We agree with Tyler. However, we consider what she advocates to be *meta*cognitive, not at the cognitive level proper. In order to re-establish the network of form-meaning pairs in L2, learners must bring compatible pairs from their L1 into consciousness, a process which is likely to be tacit in the monolingual brain. In other words, seeing familiar landscapes through new eyes necessarily accompanies examining one's preexisting cognitive structure. Therefore, we hold that L2 learning is unique in that it is the paramount means to improve one's metacognition. This advantage could be employed as a most powerful defense of foreign language education when a budget crisis arises. It needs to compete with other liberal arts disciplines because metacognition is most effectively cultivated in foreign language courses, whereas other liberal arts disciplines may emphasize cognitive skills proper, such as critical thinking.

16.3.2 Learner-Centered Curricula

Regarding the changing composition of the student body, we foresee that the current practice of assigning students a course level by placement tests will become progressively impractical. When students learn Japanese by taking college courses, their linguistic knowledge can be accurately assessed because grammatical constructions are typically introduced in academic curricula following common patterns. However, when students acquire the language via non-traditional paths, their ability to employ a complex grammatical construction does not necessarily guarantee the knowledge of other constructions customarily taught prior to it. If the order of introduction of grammatical constructions is no longer a reliable indicator of learners' knowledge, forming homogeneous classes will become elusive.

Moreover, the current practice of strict division of students according to their proficiency levels can hardly be sustainable if student enrollment declines further. For example, in the past, the Japanese program at the University of California, Berkeley offered five levels of instruction. However, it was forced to close the highest (5th) level due to insufficient enrollment, which was followed by the closure of the 4th level. The 3rd level had three sections but now offers only two. If the 3rd level is the most advanced instruction a curriculum can offer, it must accommodate all fluency levels above the second. Moreover, what if the closure of the 3rd level is unavoidable? The second level then must accommodate all eager students who are above the first.

Hence, we anticipate another paradigm shift will become inevitable. The new one is likely to be a learner-centered methodology to an extreme extent. Currently, the common practice is teacher-centered in the sense that syllabi designers and instructors determine what should be taught and learned at each level. However, when multiple levels of learners must be taught in a single class (possibly due to a shrinking academic budget), we cannot regulate what should be learned. Rather, instructors are required to prepare materials that can provide different aspects of the L2 to multiple levels of learners, and they help students learn whatever is suitable and beneficial for their level from given materials.

For this purpose, MT becomes an invaluable aid because its incorporation into a course design permits the accommodation of students with diverse levels of fluency. Students with low fluency can nevertheless read and grasp the content of the assigned material with the help of MT. The class can then spend the time on more sophisticated discussions (e.g., text organization, background presupposition(s), the effect of an eloquent expression, comparison of an articulation technique between L2 and L1) rather than checking the accuracy of text comprehension (e.g., who/what is the subject of a specific sentence, when and where the event took place), which can be done by MT.

The flexibility of accommodating multiple levels of students allows the creation of courses with narrowly focused topics that are usually unfeasible due to enrollment limitations. One of the co-authors of this chapter has taught a translation course, which used to require a high-intermediate level of fluency (the N2 level of the Japanese Language Proficiency Test) as a prerequisite.[2] As the entire Japanese language learner population has shrunk, enrollment has dropped. It now accommodates students with a lower intermediate (N3) level, allowing them to use MT. Students sometimes just copy what MT engines supply, but more frequently, they try to understand the original text (with the help of MT) and create their own translations.

An example of appropriate materials to be used in such a course is provided in (1a), which was derived from the Wikipedia article "Triangular eating." This eating pattern was developed post-World War II when skimmed milk donated by the U.S. was served at school lunch. ChatGPT-3.5 rendered the translation in (1b).

---

[2] The Japanese Language Proficiency Test is a standardized test to evaluate a person's Japanese language proficiency given under the auspices of the Japan Foundation and Japan Educational Exchanges and Services.

(1) a.

Ichijū	issai	ni okeru	dentōtekina	washoku	de wa
one.soup	one.side.dish	in	traditional	Japanese.meal	In

shokujichū	wa	misoshiru	mata wa	cha	o	nomu
during.eating	TOP	miso.soup	or	tea	ACC	drink

no	gakkō	kyūshoku	de wa,	pan-shoku	to	kawarazu	ga,
GEN	school	meal.service	in	bread.eating	to	different.not	but

gyūnyū	ga	inryō	ni	kyōsareta	with	beihan	to
milk	NOM	drink	in	served	with	rice	and

to iu	isasaka	washoku	to iu	gainen	tame,	tōji
such.as	a.little	Japanese.meal	such.as	concept	because	then

toriawase	to	natta.³	such.as	kara	hazureta	gyūnyū
combination	to	became	such.as	from	deviated	milk

b. In traditional Japanese cuisine, particularly in the context of "one soup, one dish" meals, it is customary to drink miso soup or tea during the meal. However, in school lunches at that time, milk was served as a beverage just like with bread, deviating from the concept of a somewhat traditional Japanese meal with the combination of rice and milk.

---

³ ACC: accusative; COP: copula; EVID: evidential; GEN: genitive; Lit: literally; LOC: locative; NMLZ: nominalizer; NOM: nominative; QUOT: quotative; SFP: sentence-final particle; TOP: topic.

The most challenging part of this passage is *panshoku to kawarazu* 'not different from the bread-based meal.' The best student translation in the class was (1c).

(1)   c.   In traditional Japanese meals, which typically consist of rice, soup, and one side dish, it is common to drink miso soup or tea during the meal. However, in the school lunch program at that time, milk was served as **the** beverage, similar to a Western-style meal with bread, which created a somewhat unconventional combination of rice and milk, departing from the concept of traditional Japanese cuisine.

This student was at the highest level of proficiency in the class, and his translation surpassed ChatGPT, which rendered "milk was served as **a** beverage." By contrast, the student's translation utilizes "the," which is more accurate because the original text conveys that milk was always served regardless of the main dish.

A lower-level student created a slightly inaccurate translation, marked in bold in (1d):

(1)   d.   Moreover, in the traditional Japanese diet of one soup and one dish, miso soup or tea is served during the meal, but in school lunches at that time, milk was served as a beverage **as well as bread**, and the combination of rice and milk was somewhat out of keeping with the Japanese concept of a Japanese meal.

Her translation of the entire text shows that she clearly consulted ChatGPT, and this mistranslation is likely due to the misunderstanding of ChatGPT's phrase "milk was served as a beverage just like with bread." By acknowledging this error, she can learn that *pan-shoku to kawarazu* 'not different from the bread-based meal' is an additional piece of information suitable to express with a non-restrictive relative clause: i.e., milk was served as the beverage, which did not differ from the bread-based meal. The basic grammar of this type of adverbial phrase can be taught here with similar examples.

Another erroneous translation is shown in (1e), created by a student whose proficiency level is even lower than the second student. This translation indicates that the student did not comprehend the passage thoroughly; the original text does not indicate that bread was served *previously*. Letting the student explain why this rendering was created will make her realize her unconscious parsing strategies.

(1) e.   When eating a traditional Japanese meal (*ichijū-issai*) which contains a bowl of rice, one soup/broth, and one side dish, people usually drink miso soup or tea during their meal. However, school meals at that time kept offering milk as the beverage, just like they did **previously** for school meals with bread, which created a combination of a rice bowl and milk that did not follow the usual concept of *washoku*, or Japanese cuisine.

Until two years ago, when the entry requirement to the course was the JLPT N2 level, this student would not have been allowed to enroll. However, she completed the course satisfactorily, demonstrating impressive progress in proficiency.

16.4 A Metacognitive Approach in Japanese Language Curricula

This section provides some embodiment possibilities with discussion topics using linguistic contrasts between English and Japanese. Languages grammaticalize concepts that their speech communities value. *Grammaticalization* refers to historical language changes in which a certain expression becomes part of grammar: i.e., "a sign is grammaticalized to the extent that it is devoid of concrete lexical meaning and takes part in obligatory grammatical rules" (Lehmann, 1992, p. 6). For example, the Latin demonstrative *ille* 'that' with strong deictic function became the obligatory definite article of French (e.g., *le livre 'the book,' la lampe 'the lamp'*), where its function is to mark the noun phrase as definite.

European languages commonly distinguish singular and plural noun forms. As monolingual native Japanese speakers, we were shocked when we learned this fact in middle school English classes. The amount of countables—whether one owns one car or two—is significant, but we had never thought that the distinction between one and more than one is so essential that we must mention it every time we use a countable noun. In Japanese, nouns do not have singular-plural distinction; when the amount is relevant, we specify the number.

Gendered personal pronouns are another example. Sex and gender are significant in both cultures, but, again, the obligatoriness of specifying a person's gender every time he/she is referred to may appear excessive. The recent prevalence of the singular *they* is well understood. Indeed, "[l]anguages differ essentially in what they *must* convey and not in what they *may* convey" (Jakobson, 1959/2000, p. 116).

Some grammaticalized elements in foreign languages are very idiosyncratic. L2 education is frequently said to embrace and respect other people's beliefs, opinions, viewpoints, and behavior. Recognizing highly alien concepts promotes learning diversity in human thoughts and deeds. This precious lesson, indispensable for humans to coexist in an ever-shrinking world, cannot be learned effectively by reading machine-translated foreign texts; rather, one needs to be immersed in another culture via an understanding of its linguistic system. In what follows, we provide four topics adaptable to multi-level Japanese language classes.

16.4.1 Mandatory Evaluation of a Conveyed Event

One of the salient differences between Japanese and English language use occurs in expressing speakers' subjective evaluations of an event they are involved in. Such expressions are sometimes mandatory in Japanese but never in English. For example, the speaker of (2a) sounds indifferent, and the utterance may be deemed socially inappropriate. On the other hand, its English translation exhibits neither of these negative qualities.

(2) a. Haha   wa   watashi ni   sētā   o   okutta.
         mother   TOP   I   to   sweater   ACC   sent
         'Mother sent me a
          sweater.'

If the speaker is grateful for the mother's sending a sweater, adding the auxiliary verb *kureru* 'give' habitually expresses this feeling of gratefulness.

(2) b. Haha   wa   watashi   ni   sētā   o   okutte   **kureta.**
         mother   TOP   I   to   sweater   ACC   sending   gave
         [Lit.] 'Mother did the favor
         of sending me a sweater.'

Why such a subjective evaluation of the depicted event is so significant is a thought-provoking discussion topic. Does this linguistic feature
possibly influence the speech community's style of communication? That
is, would people communicate differently when the prevailing social
norm mandates such a speech style vis-à-vis when it allows them to
express the situation more objectively, in a matter-of-fact way? These can
be natural questions that students may want to pause and discuss.

16.4.2 Adversity Passive Constructions

Japanese has so-called *adversity passive constructions*. The quintessential
distinction between the active and passive voices in the world's languages
is that the direct object of the active clause appears as the subject in
the corresponding passive clause, while the subject of the active clause
is optionally encoded as an incidental agentive phrase (e.g., a *by*-phrase
in English) in the passive clause. As a rule, English passive clauses must
have corresponding active clauses, as in (3).

(3) a. The company fired her.   [Active]
     b. She was fired (by the company).   [Passive]

The Japanese passive that corresponds to the English passive is referred
to as the *direct passive*.

(4) a. Kaisha   wa   kanojo   o   kaikoshita.   [Active]
         company   TOP   she   ACC   fired
         'The company fired her.'
     b. Kanojo   wa   kaisha   ni   kaiko-sareta.   [Passive]
         she   TOP   company   by   fired.PASSIVE
         'She was fired by the company.'

Japanese additionally permits two types of *indirect passive* (vis-à-vis direct passive) constructions unavailable in English. Because such sentences are routinely used to describe negative incidents, they are called *adversity passives*. The first type contains the passive form of an intransitive verb, as exemplified by (5).

(5) a. Shigeru   no   hahaoya   ga   shinda.   [Active]
                GEN   mother   NOM   died
         'Shigeru's mother died.'
     b. Shigeru   wa   hahaoya   ni   shinareta.   [Passive]
                TOP   mother   by   died.PASSIVE
         [Lit.] 'Shigeru was died by his mother.'
         'Shigeru was adversely affected by his mother dying.'

The second type of indirect passive involves a transitive verb, but unlike the common direct passive, the direct object of the active clause remains the direct object of its passive variation, as in (6b).

(6) a. Dareka   ga   Shigeru no   **jitensha**   o   nusunda. [Active]
        someone NOM   GEN   bicycle   ACC stole
        'Someone stole Shigeru's bicycle.'
    b. Shigeru   wa   **jitensha o**   nusumareta.   [Indirect
                                                                 Passive]
               TOP   bicycle   ACC   stole.PASSIVE
        [Lit.] 'Shigeru was stolen his bicycle.'
        'Shigeru was adversely affected by someone stealing his bicycle.'

A typical difference between the active and the passive is that a sentient being intentionally brings about some event in the former, while in the latter, the event occurs spontaneously. Wierzbicka (1979/1988, pp. 257–292) argues that this might reflect the speech community's perception of the reality they live in. Spontaneous events that humans have no control over are often adverse. This can be another topic conducive to understanding when adversity passives are compared to the dative of misfortune in European languages or the adverse *on me* construction, as exemplified in (7).

(7) Ihm   ist   die   Frau   gestorben. (German)
     to.him   is   the   wife   died
     'His wife died **on him**.'

16.4.3 Evidentiality and the Territory of Information

Epistemic modality signifies the speaker's judgment regarding the statement's truth, falsity, or probability, typically using modals (e.g., *may, might, must*) or adverbials (e.g., *possibly, perhaps, necessarily*), but the basis for such judgment is not identified. When the speaker's epistemic stance is expressed by mentioning evidence, it is referred to as *evidentiality*. Japanese is well known for its rich array of evidential markers, e.g., (8).

(8) Kotoshi   no   kaze   wa,   onaka   ga   itaku naru [sō]   da.
     this.year GEN   flu   TOP   stomach   NOM   hurt   [EVID]   COP
     '(I hear) this year's flu can
      cause abdominal pain.'

Among such markers, the hearsay evidential is particularly consequential. English also provides hearsay expressions (e.g., *I hear, they say, it is said*), but the information gained by hearsay is treated differently in Japanese and English.

Kamio (1995) posits two conceptual categories involving information: the speaker's and the addressee's territory of information. A piece of information is said to fall into one's territory if one of the following contingencies applies:

(9) a. The information is obtained through one's internal direct
         experience, e.g., pain, emotions, beliefs.
     b. The information falls into one's professional or other areas of
         expertise.
     c. The information is obtained by direct experience through the five
         senses.
     d. The information is about persons, objects, events, and facts close
         to oneself, e.g., one's own birthday or that of one's spouse.

To support Condition (9d), Kamio (1995, p. 241) provides this example:

(10)   John, a company president, and Tom, his business associate, are talking in John's office. Susan, John's secretary, informs John, "You have a meeting at three." When three o'clock approaches, John can say, "I have a meeting at three." However, it would sound odd for Tom to say, "You have a meeting at three." Instead, he must say, "I guess/believe/understand you have a meeting at three."

Both John and Tom have obtained the information simultaneously from the same source. However, because it is about John's schedule, i.e., in John's information territory, Tom must employ a hedged, indirect statement.

This constraint also applies to Japanese; one must utilize a hearsay marker. However, English and Japanese differ drastically regarding newly acquired information. In Japanese, it is not considered to belong to the speaker's territory of information, whereas in English, it is if the information source is deemed reliable. Consider this scenario: Jack, a friend of the Clark family, phones Jane Clark and says he will visit them soon. Then Jane's mother asks her, "What did Jack say?" Jane can respond, "He's coming to visit us soon," without a hearsay marker.

In contrast, such an exchange is untenable in Japanese. Hearsay information falls outside one's territory until it has been thoroughly processed and absorbed into one's knowledge. Therefore, in the Clark family case, the use of a hearsay marker is obligatory in Japanese, as in (11).

(11)   Kondo   asobi ni   kuru   tte.
        soon   play.for   come   [EVID]
        'I hear (he) will
        visit (us) soon.'

Indeed, native Japanese speakers faithfully mark most hearsay information with evidentials even when they trust the information sources. This difference in linguistic behavior may cause cross-cultural misunderstanding. Native English speakers may think Japanese speakers are overtly vague and indecisive, whereas Japanese speakers may determine that English speakers are too decisive and even arrogant (Trent, 1998, p. 11).

16.4.4 Gendered Language

Japanese is well known for its conspicuous linguistic differentiation by gender, which originated in ancient times. Nevertheless, it is commonly understood that in those early periods, the Japanese language had far fewer morphosyntactic differentiations than in modern times (Mashimo, 1969). Prevalent ways to express femininity in those days were not initiating a conversation, not completing sentences, and muttering rather than clearly articulating (Sato, 2006, pp. 110–111). The distinction between masculine and feminine forms became more apparent in the Muromachi period (1392–1568). Furthermore, women started using honorifics more frequently than men would, e.g., the verbal politeness auxiliary *masu* (Mashimo, 1969, pp. 9–10). The so-called *nyōbō kotoba* 'court ladies' language' was also developed during this period, e.g., *ohiya* 'ice water,' *ogushi* 'hair,' *otsumu* 'head.'

Although the tradition of differentiating men's and women's languages has ancient roots, most of the stylistic characteristics, as we know them today, emerged in the Meiji period (1868–1912) (Komatsu, 1988). A female utterance in modern times is exemplified in (12a).

(12)	a.	Sanka suru	no	wa	**watashi**	dake	kashira	[Female]
		participate	NMLZ	TOP	I	only	SFP	
		'I'm the only one who participates, I wonder.'						
	b.	Sanka suru	no	wa	**ore**	dake	kana.	[Male]
		participate	NMLZ	TOP	I	only	SFP	
		'I'm the only one who participates, I wonder.'						

Although male speakers can utilize the first-person pronoun *watashi* in (12a), its use is restricted to a formal register. In casual conversations, males do not use *watashi*. *Ore* in (12b) is another first-person pronoun, which is traditionally used exclusively by male speakers in most dialects. *Kashira* in (12a) is a sentence-final particle to indicate one's uncertainty; it is a prescriptive female expression that is becoming obsolete. *Kana* in (12b) is another sentence-final particle for uncertainty, but it is gender-neutral.

In her experimental study on soliloquy, Hasegawa (2010, Ch. 4) discovered that women do not use female expressions, except for female first-person pronouns, in soliloquy. That is, females do not speak femininely when free from social pressure because they are not heard by anyone. By contrast, male speakers employ masculine expressions frequently in their soliloquy.

Gendered language in Japanese is so clearly discernible that when a conversation is transcribed, the reader can easily identify the speaker's gender. English, by contrast, does not have a clear distinction between female and male speech. Therefore, we can hardly tell the speaker's gender from a transcribed conversation. This fact, however, does not attest that gender difference does not exist in English. It is only that the cues are much subtler. Incorporating this material in a course design may trigger a lively discussion during lessons.

16.5 The Current Capacity of ChatGPT-4

The final topic to discuss in this chapter is whether or not taking a course (formal learning) and self-study utilizing MT, specifically with ChatGPT, are equally effective. First, let us examine ChatGPT's current capability. Consider the following transcription of a spoken chat session, where C stands for ChatGPT, and U the user:

(13)   U: Konnichiwa.
            'Hello.'
       C: Konnichiwa. Dōitta goshitsumon-ya sapōto-ga hitsuyō desu-ka? Okigaru-ni otazunekudasai.
            'Hello. What kind of questions or support are you looking for? Please feel free to ask me.'
       U: Watashi-wa ima nihongo-o benkyō-shiteimasu. Isshoni hanashite kudasai.
            'I'm learning Japanese now. Please chat with me.'
       C: Mochiron desu! Donna topikku-ni-tsuite hanashimashō-ka? Mata-wa, nihongo-gakushū-ni kansuru shitsumon-ga arimasu-ka?
            'Of course! What topics should we discuss? Or do you have any questions about studying Japanese?'
       U: Machigaetara naoshite kudasai.
            'Please correct me if I make a mistake.'

C: Mochiron, machigai-ga areba teisei itashimasu. Nanika hanashitai
     topikku-ya shitsumon-wa arimasuka?
     'Sure, I'll correct it if there are any. Do you have any topic or
     question you want to talk about?'
U: Kinō okāsan-ga watashi-ni kēki-o agemashita.
     'Yesterday, mother gave me a cake.'
C: Subarashii bun desu-ne. Tada, sukoshi shūsei-ga hitsuyō-kamo
     shiremasen. "Kinō okāsan-ga watashi-ni kēki-o agemashita" wa
     "Kinō okāsan-ga watashi-ni kēki-o kuremashita" to suruhō-ga
     shizen desu. Nihongo-dewa, hokanohito-ga jibun-ni nanika-o
     suru baai, "kureru" o tsukaimasu. Hokanohito-ni nanika-o
     ageru toki-niwa "ageru" o tsukaimasu. Donna kēki deshita-ka?
     Oishikattadesu-ka?
     'Superb sentence! But you might want to revise it a little. It is
     more natural to say, "Mother gave [*kuremashita*, the past tense
     of *kureru*] me a cake," instead of "Mother gave [*agemashita*,
     the past tense of *ageru*] me a cake." In Japanese, when
     someone else does something to you, you use *kureru*. When
     you give something to someone, you use *ageru*. What kind of a
     cake? Was it delicious?'

This is a remarkable piece of real-time conversation between a human
and a machine. ChatGPT produced not only grammatical and colloquial
sentences but also delivered them in a pragmatically appropriate way.
When the user mistakenly selected a verb, it first praised her effort. Only
then did it point out the error very gently and correct it. Moreover, it
prompts how to respond to this utterance ('Was it delicious?').

However, ChatGPT is designed for realistic verbal exchanges with
fluent language speakers. Therefore, its sentences are frequently unsuit-
able for a conversation with a learner. The final utterance in (13) is too
complex, beyond the reach of elementary learners. On the other hand, if
users are at an intermediate level, they may be able to clarify when some
sentences or words are incomprehensible.

Our experimental sessions suggest that ChatGPT can make self-study
as natural as learning with a human teacher. However, it has not learned
non-native speakers' language capabilities, such as limited vocabulary
and grammatical constructions as well as common error patterns. Therefore, at present, beginners are unlikely to be able to learn the language
effectively through this method.

As mentioned earlier, most learners take college courses for only one year, or even one semester. Therefore, teaching how to use ChatGPT judiciously in elementary courses is necessary. A key concept in such an approach is *prompting*, i.e., providing necessary guidance, which can be done in English. Examples of such prompts are:

(14)   a.   I want to chat with you in Japanese.
       b.   I want to talk about my summer plans.
       c.   Please limit each of your utterances to 100 Japanese characters.
       d.   Please restrict your utterances only to your opinions, not to mention encyclopedic information.

Examples (14c–d) are important because ChatGPT tends to start providing relevant, but not solicited, information.

16.6 Conclusion

This study has scrutinized the ongoing and seemingly amplifying downtrend of student enrollment in college-level Japanese language courses—a phenomenon likely instigated by the surging advancement of MT engines. It was argued that the population whose primary aim is to gather information to enrich knowledge is most susceptible to not enroll when real-time translation of text and speech is ubiquitously available. Therefore, the currently prevailing communicative method must be adjusted in order to maintain college course offerings and make them more attractive.

Consequently, we have proposed a metacognitive approach, which emphasizes how we think rather than how we communicate. Such cogitation becomes more attainable when material for comparison is available. Foreign languages excel as comparison tools. Whenever learners encounter expressions that deviate from their routine ways, they can delve into the difference and thereby cultivate an intellectual habit.

As advocates for the raison d'être of college-level foreign language education, we must unequivocally assert the effectiveness of college courses over self-study. Our experiments with ChatGPT suggest that, while beginners are unlikely to be able to utilize it effectively for self-study, intermediate learners will enhance their self-study immensely. Given that most students do not continue to take college-level courses after the first year, it is proper and considerate to prepare them in elementary courses to become proficient in using ChatGPT, namely techniques in prompting.

References

American Psychology Association. (2024). Cognition. In *APA dictionary of psychology*. Retrieved February 29, 2024, from https://dictionary.apa.org/cognition

Anderson, N. (2023, August 18). WVU's plan to cut foreign languages, other programs draws disbelief. *The Washington Post*. https://www.washingtonpost.com/education/2023/08/18/west-virginia-university-academic-cuts/

Gee speaks on the budget deficit, academic transformation and Huggins. (2023, August 25). *The DA*. https://www.thedaonline.com/news/university/gee-speaks-on-the-budget-deficit-academic-transformation-and-huggins/article_5600875c-4059-11ee-81d2-dffc69b12c86.html

Hasegawa, Y. (2010). *Soliloquy in Japanese and English*. John Benjamins.

Hymes, D. (1971). *On communicative competence*. University of Pennsylvania Press.

Ikeda, T. (2023). Dokugaku de nihongo o manabu hitotachi kara manabu koto [What can be learned from self-taught students of Japanese]. *Montreal Academy Club*. https://www.montreal-academy.com/single-post/

Jakobson, R. (2000). On linguistic aspects of translation. In L. Venuti (Ed.), *The translation studies reader* (pp. 113–118). Routledge. (Original work published 1959)

Japan Foundation. (2021). *Survey report on Japanese-language education abroad 2021*. https://www.jpf.go.jp/e/project/japanese/survey/result/dl/survey2021/All_contents_r2.pdf

Kamio, A. (1995). Territory of information in English and Japanese and psychological utterances. *Journal of Pragmatics, 24*(3), 235–264. https://doi.org/10.1016/0378-2166(94)00064-L

Komatsu, H. (1988). Tōkyōgo ni okeru danjosa no keisei: Shūjoshi o chūshin to shite [The emergence of gendered variations in the Tokyo dialect: A study focusing on sentence-final particles]. *Kokugo to Kokubungaku, 65*, 94–106.

Lehmann, W. P. (1992). *Historical linguistics: An introduction* (3rd ed.). Routledge.

Lusin, N., Peterson, T., Sulewski, C., & Zafer, R. (2023). *Enrollments in languages other than English in US Institutions of higher education, Fall 2021.* Modern Language Association of America. https://www.mla.org/content/download/191324/file/Enrollments-in-Languages-Other-Than-English-in-US-Institutions-of-Higher-Education-Fall-2021.pdf

Mashimo, S. (1969). *Fujingo no kenkyū* [A study of women's language]. Tokyodo.

Sato, S. (2006). Genji monogatari to jendā: Sukuse o iwanu onna-gimi [The tale of Genji and gender: Princess who does not talk about her past life]. In M. Sasaki (Ed.), *Nihongo to jendā* (pp. 109–120). Hituzi Syobo.

Schackner, B. (2023, August 28). WVU President E. Gordon Gee defends cuts, despite growing dissent and potential no-confidence vote. *TRIB Live.* https://triblive.com/local/regional/betting-that-he-is-right-west-virginia-uni versitys-e-gordon-gee-is-determined-to-make-cuts-despite-growing-dissent-and-potential-no-confidence-vote/

Svrluga, S., & Anderson, N. (2023, September 15). WVU board approves cuts in academic programs. *The Washington Post.* https://www.washingtonpost.com/education/2023/09/15/west-virginia-board-approves-academic-cuts/

Tohsaku, Y. (2014). Japanese language education in the global age: New perspectives and advocacy. *National Symposium on Japanese Language Education Proceedings*, 3–13.

Trent, N. (1998). Cross-cultural discourse pragmatics: Speaking about hearsay in English and Japanese. *Texas Papers in Foreign Language Education, 3*(2), 1–31.

Tyler, A. (2012). *Cognitive linguistics and second language learning: Theoretical basics and experimental evidence.* Routledge.

Wierzbicka, A. (1988). *The semantics of grammar.* John Benjamins. (Original work published 1979)

17

Machine Translation and Language Learning: Teachers' Perspectives and Practices

Louise Ohashi(ID)

17.1 Introduction

Machine translation (MT) has become embedded into many facets of daily life. For example, social media posts give us the option to "see translation," and whole websites can be translated in a single click. Tools like Google Translate can be used not only with what we type or paste in, but also what we say, photograph or show through our smartphone's lens. MT's accuracy is not guaranteed, but it has improved dramatically since neural network technology was adopted in 2016. The recent development of advanced natural language processing chatbots such as ChatGPT has driven MT even further ahead. As these tools can provide multiple versions of each translation and produce text in our target language based on our instructions—translating content that we have not even created ourselves—we are entering a new realm that can only be described as

L. Ohashi (✉)
Gakushuin University, Tokyo, Japan
e-mail: ohashijalt@gmail.com

© The Author(s), under exclusive license to Springer Nature Switzerland AG 2025
D. Coulson and C. Denman (eds.), *Translation, Translanguaging and Machine Translation in Foreign Language Education*,
https://doi.org/10.1007/978-3-031-82174-5_17

351

a paradigm shift. MT is, and will be further, adopted at many levels of society, so it is essential that teachers consider its role in language education.

This chapter aims to provide teachers and educational institutions with insights into the MT-related beliefs and practices of language teachers. Both teacher cognition, defined as "what teachers know, believe, and think" (Borg, 2003, p. 81), and their experiences in and out of educational settings can have a powerful effect on teaching practices. Therefore, the following three research questions were investigated:

RQ1: How do language teachers use MT, both personally and in their courses?
RQ2: What are teachers' views on the use of MT in the context of L2 education?
RQ3: Do teachers feel they have enough knowledge to help students use MT effectively to develop their L2 skills and/or do they want to learn more about this?

These research questions were investigated with 153 foreign language teachers at Japanese universities. This type of empirical research has the potential to inform and promote change, but only if it is read, and one potential obstacle is the way results are shared. Researchers have found that the "inaccessible way in which research findings are presented" can deter teachers from reading it (Kostoulas et al., 2019, p. 319), so effort has been made to present the current study in a simple, engaging way without deviating from ethical reporting standards. With engagement in mind, I use first person "I" to tell the story of my research journey and quote extensively to share the stories of my participants in their own words.

17.2 Method

This research was conducted online in 2022 with teachers who taught foreign languages at universities in Japan. I used snowball sampling, which means participants helped me recruit more participants. This sampling method is recognised as an effective approach for accessing participants beyond the researchers' network (Leighton et al., 2021).

Phase One was an anonymous online survey[1] that mainly collected quantitative data. It was initially posted in Facebook groups for Japan-based teachers, with participants sharing it further. All 153 participants taught at least one foreign language, with most (98%) teaching English.[2] Phase Two was a follow-up interview with a sub-sample. Twenty-four English teachers volunteered to participate and all were interviewed after being informed of the study's nature and signing a consent form. The semi-structured interviews took approximately 20 minutes and elaborated on key areas investigated in the survey, primarily through open questions. For example, they were asked, "As a teacher, how do you feel about MT?", and, "In your view, what would be acceptable and unacceptable use of MT by students in your courses?".

The interviews were transcribed and uploaded to Taguette, where they were open coded. During the coding process, initial codes were refined and transcripts that had already been coded were updated. To create a coherent "story" for readers, it was necessary to be selective in presenting quotes. Omissions (indicated by three dots) were made to ensure readability when participants deviated from the topic, and when a truncated version could faithfully convey their message, I shortened quotes to leave space for other important points. I also wanted to include quotes from all interviewees, so when multiple quotes made similar points, I gave preference to participants who had not had their voices heard elsewhere.

17.3 Results and Discussion

Before sharing the findings, it is important to note that the survey results have been reported in a short open-access paper (Ohashi, 2022) so this chapter mainly focuses on the interview data. Tables and graphs are not reproduced here, so interested readers are encouraged to refer to that

---

[1] The full survey was published in Ohashi (2022).

[2] 147 taught English only, three taught English and another language (French, Spanish, Italian), and three taught other languages (Indonesian, Spanish, German).

article. In this chapter, the key points of the survey are summarised and extended upon, with interview data providing deeper insights into the areas investigated.

17.3.1 RQ1: How Do Language Teachers Use MT, Both Personally and in Their Courses?

17.3.1.1 Teachers' Personal Use of MT

The survey revealed that many teachers had used MT regularly in the previous year. This was particularly true for reading (37% daily/most days, 27% at least weekly, 15% several times a month, 11% once a month or less frequently, 10% never) and writing (22% daily/most days, 22% at least weekly, 25% several times a month, 21% once a month or less frequently, 10% never). In contrast, very few used it for listening or speaking. Perhaps unsurprisingly, adoption of MT in their courses reflected the same pattern, with more using it to provide support to students for reading and writing development than for listening or speaking. However, it should be noted that course integration fell far below personal usage rates. While 90% of teachers had used MT to assist with their own L2 reading and writing in the previous year, 56% had not taught any of their students how to use it for writing development and 69% had not guided any of them to use it for reading development. Course integration rates for other skills were even lower, with no guidance offered in any courses for speaking (87%) or listening (88%). This large gap between teachers' personal use and course integration echoes findings from Delorme Benites et al. (2021).

Interview data from my study provide a more nuanced understanding of how teachers used MT themselves, how they supported students' use of it, and why some chose not to bring it into their courses. When considering MT as a tool for personal use, teachers were generally positive. They viewed it as a real-world tool that offered many benefits. Some referred to it through the use of job titles, calling it "my little robot assistant" (T6) and "an interpreter who helps me out" (T7). Others credited it with life enhancement, saying it "facilitates my life" (T22) and "adds a dimension to my life, whether social or working" (T10). Increased efficiency was noted by many, with some explaining that technological advancements had made it possible to rely on MT more heavily:

It saves me a tonne of time, that's the main thing. And it definitely has gotten better, because say, 10 years ago, I don't think I could have really relied on it in the way that I do now. (T7)

I'm a translator as well as the teacher, and I used to hate MT ... [but more recently] I have found that DeepL can give me an approximation of sentences and sometimes in pretty good English ... It often does not come up with something that's really good English. However, it's usable as a start-off point for me. (T23)

Increased trust was not extended to all languages, with T2 noting, "For Thai, it's just not there yet," and T8 explaining MT "is not good for Hungarian." There was also awareness of the need to choose the right tool for different language combinations:

It depends on the machine. DeepL is good. Google Translate is usually pretty good ... [Japanese] translated into English through Facebook MT comes out as really gobbledygook. Between Japanese and Korean, because their grammar is so similar you get very good translations, even on Facebook, but I think with the difference in syntax between English and Japanese, it tends to be more difficult. (T15)

The interviews elicited a wide range of experiences with MT for language learning. For instance, T5 used the Google Chrome extension Language Reactor to learn vocabulary while watching movies, explaining, "You're able to hover across the word and get a translation or definition of that word. And it will just basically slow down the video until you unhover." T18 used MT for speaking development, noting, "If I know I'm going to practice using one of the target languages I'm learning, then I might take something that I want to say in English, translate that into the target language, and then use that to speak." T16 used it to learn Italian vocabulary and pronunciation, and T7 used it as a support tool when building Indonesian reading skills. At times, teachers made positive connections between their own use and their recommendations for students:

> I'll do what I tell my students to do. I start it in German, then translate back to English to make sure that it reads okay, then back translate to make sure that it reads okay in German again. (T24)

Other times, they admitted they used MT as a way to "cheat" rather than using it to learn:

> I sort of use it a bit like a cheat. In particular, it increases my efficiency in reading second language emails and things like that are sort of time sensitive. (T6)

> For French, I cheat. Actually, I am quite fluent in French, but when I have to write a paper in French, it's so much easier for me to write it in English, and then have it translated with the software into French, and then go through it and just check the French. (T8)

These experiences did not necessarily mean teachers suspected their students of cheating, with survey results of these two teachers confirming that neither expressed strong concerns about cheating, and both strongly disagreed with MT being heavily restricted or banned. However, negative experiences could shape pedagogical practice, as excerpts from T3's interview show:

> I can read some Japanese ... but I can't read some of the kanji [characters], it's too difficult ... And I'm sometimes too lazy ... And my wife often tells me, 'You can read this, come on!' You know? I think machines are making us a little lazy.
> When [my students] are reading something in English, words or phrases, I kind of put a limit there, because if they look up the entire paragraph in a MT device or whatever, they would ... it kind of makes them lazier, I feel.

17.3.1.2 MT Use in Language Courses

While survey results showed MT support was seldom included in courses, interviews provided valuable insights into teaching practices and reasons for MT avoidance. For instance, some teachers covered the importance of pre-editing, telling students "they had to write in a different way in Japanese if they wanted to have good results in English" (T8). The advice included adding pronouns that are often dropped in Japanese, as MT needs them for accurate English translations and, without training, students may not realise this. There were also examples of post-editing training and activities that pushed students to challenge the accuracy of output:

> I teach my students how to use it and then I stress, for example, the importance of editing after you've translated something. It's a tool much like a dictionary. It's not something you can ... just translate and send. (T21)

> [We looked] at the process of writing directly into English, but then using DeepL to translate back into Japanese and see how it went. We did a few activities on awareness, raising [the point] that the same sentence or slightly tweaked sentences produced very different output from MT, that different MT platforms will translate differently. So, some awareness activities like that ... then checking at the end. (T6)

> I send them to Google Translate or something like that and I ask them to find examples where Google makes a mistake. And I ask them to explain the mistake because I want them to be comfortable knowing that they shouldn't just blindly copy the output of the translation system and use it. They should understand that it could be wrong, and to think about the kinds of mistakes that it could make, and to know what to look for, to know that basically they're responsible for the text. (T9)

The practices these teachers incorporated into their courses have been shown to be important in empirical studies. For example, Loock et al. (2022) called attention to the need to question output after most students in their study indicated they could identify MT output errors but generally failed to do so. Furthermore, Chang (2022) found that students were better equipped to judge MT output when they used a range of tools, such as multiple MT tools, dictionaries and search engines.

The majority of examples teachers shared were about writing, but some did offer support for other skills. For instance, T2 guided students to skim read and identify words and phrases they couldn't understand and then check them with MT. That participant also demonstrated how to scaffold listening tasks by using transcription software and transferring the output to MT. However, the latter led to problems with colleagues:

> It created a big thing at my university because the teachers were furious that I taught the students how to do that, because they're like, 'You just taught them how to make all of our listening tests worthless if they're online'. Like now the students know how to just turn on the translator and they can get captions as they listen to any English test. (T2)

Fears of cheating and misuse were partly responsible for MT not being integrated into classes, both by individual teachers and at the institutional level. When teachers worked in institutions where students were expressly prohibited from using MT, it sometimes aligned with their own beliefs:

> As a representative of the university, I think it's not my position to tell them [to use it]. I don't want to encourage them to use it as well, because there might be that small group, say 15%, that aren't using it, wouldn't intend to use it, because it's not in the rules, and will actually try to improve their writing without it and see that as a beneficial skill. I don't want to encourage that section to give up that idea and just resort to machine learning. (T13)

If the teacher felt MT was beneficial though, such restrictions could reduce teacher agency and limit the guidance provided:

> Our university explicitly prohibits using MT. I [will] read it, 'Using translator software to write a report is plagiarism'. I have to explain this to my students at the beginning of the semester, so I cannot encourage them to

use it in my course. However, when I think of my students using English after they graduate from university, I'm sure they want to use it. And if they don't know how to use it, and if they use it wrongly, then I think it's a pity, so in the last lesson … I gave a short workshop to my students. (T19)

Some teachers also used MT themselves in their courses. The following examples show how teachers from different language backgrounds used MT to scaffold their own L2 output:

I'm an English teacher, so I don't want to write messy English to students and I don't want my students to think that my English is not perfect, so I try to write as perfect English as possible … I kind of translate it in English in my mind in parallel so that if anything is wrong on MT, I can know this … so if there is a big gap between my translation and DeepL's or MT's translation, I can notice, then I spend more time checking. (T19, L1 Japanese)

I also have used it also for making posts [in Japanese] that I've put up on the university LMS [Learning Management System] for students, so that I can tell them important information that I think they need some help with in terms of things like say coronavirus information … I thought those things were a little bit too important just for them to try to read through it in English and maybe misunderstand. (T20, L1 English)

The interview data built on the survey data by providing more nuanced insights, illustrating the complexity that exists behind decisions related to the adoption of MT within language education settings.

17.3.2 RQ2: What Are Teachers' Views on the Use of MT in the Context of L2 Education?

As intimated above, teachers saw MT as a tool that could be used or abused in language education. Viewed positively, survey results showed acknowledgement of MT's potential as a learning tool, with many agreeing it could be effective for developing L2 skills for writing (71%) and reading (67%), and some recognising its potential for speaking

(37%) and listening (36%). There was evidence of teachers' own positive experiences influencing their acceptance of use by students:

> If the students' goal is to learn the language, I think MT can be very, very valuable. Just like I said, for me, it's very valuable in Japanese. It can be valuable for them, too. (T3)

> It's such a useful tool that I, of course, use myself extensively, so I find it would be a bit hypocritical to not allow my students to use it. (T21)

However, there was also wariness over integrating these increasingly accurate translation tools into formal education. The survey found that 81% of teachers suspected their students were using MT in ways that could be considered cheating. Although only 15% thought it was widespread (i.e. among all/most of their students), it raised deep concerns over fairness and loss of learning opportunities:

> I see it as a problem in the sense that students who don't do as much work could get better grades than the students who have tried really hard to write things, to earnestly write in English. (T20)

> If I have recorded lectures on YouTube, or whatever, and I have students listening and using that recorded material to take notes ... the biggest problem is that they'll put the translator on into Japanese, right? And then that defeats the whole purpose to me. (T5)

> Especially with the first-year students who are really doing their first serious writing to any extent in English, I ask them, 'Please don't use MT'. ... I think at that level, it's kind of important for them to at least have that experience of really trying to write it themselves without the support of the MT software. (T7)

Despite concerns over cheating, the survey revealed that very few teachers felt MT should be heavily restricted or banned (strongly agree 1%, agree 16%). Here again, teachers' own experiences with MT had an influence:

It has to be in some way that they work with the students to show them that it can help their writing. Because you know what, in the real world, people are going to use MT to help their writing if they're not a native speaker. I mean, it's an important skill to have. I'm telling you, I'm a professional literary translator, I have been working for over 15 years, and I'm finding it useful. It's unrealistic to have this, 'Oh, my students are cheating' attitude … Every educator has to come to terms with the fact that it exists and start thinking about how to integrate it into their courses. (T23)

Rather than banning it, there was a preference for teacher guidance, with the majority believing that MT usage guidelines are essential in all language courses (48% strongly agree, 39% agree). However, only 21% provided guidelines in all of their courses and 28% did not provide guidelines in any courses. This was partly because teachers did not have enough guidance on this themselves, were concerned about causing problems, or saw MT guidelines as writing-related and they didn't teach writing courses:

I don't want to get into the situation where I'm giving sort of rules, which are then contradicted by somebody else, or potentially creating a problem. (T7)

Because I don't have writing [courses], I don't present any guidelines for usage of MT. But in the speaking [course], because I don't see it really as an issue if you're using MT, I haven't given guidelines. (T18)

Others shared how they guided students towards acceptable MT use, with the teacher below also making recommendations for others:

I try to make it really clear for each assignment or each project or each thing that we're working on … I like to prescribe when they can and cannot use it. I want to make sure that they have the translation skills they need to be a good human translator, but I also want them to realise that there are situations in which MT can really help them and be a useful tool … I think the very best thing any teacher can do at the beginning of the semester is have an open conversation about MT. Like when you're going through the syllabus, it's the first day of class … have an open conversation about MT with students so that they know what the expectations are from that particular teacher. (T14)

Although there were concerns about misuse, most teachers (95%) felt their students used MT for L2 learning, with 35% envisaging widespread adoption for this purpose (all students 11%, most students 24%). Due to this, teachers were generally open to students using MT, but it depended on the way it was used:

> I think it's an important tool for anyone who's working in a second language or learning a second language. I think it's something that they should be using. It's all about really how they use it. (T16)

> [Former students did] an international virtual exchange project. They really, really wanted to communicate with students in Colombia and they were using the translation tools, and I didn't have a problem with that, because I was like, 'This is real life, this is what we do. If we connect with people, we'll find a way'. So, in this context, for me that wasn't problematic. However, now I'm in a kind of English-only environment and lower level, I just turn a blind eye to it and just go, 'Okay, if you're trying to be authentic and meaningful, that's okay'. At higher levels, when it kind of goes into plagiarism, then I'm like, 'Sorry, that's not on'. That's my line. (T12)

Defining the line between acceptable and unacceptable use proved challenging for teachers, and the interviews gave insights into this:

> Between acceptable and unacceptable, the lines can blur very quickly. (T17)

> Acceptable use would be using MT, I suppose, like I do, just to check it to see if your English is correct. (T15)

> Cheating would be composing complete sentences, and beyond that, even paragraphs. (T22)

> I don't mind it if students do use it to check a word or check a phrase or try to understand it, but I really dislike the use of it to replace their own

learning or their own cognitive tasks, like where they should just try to make an effort to write a paragraph. (T11)

Some teachers believed they could easily identify misuse of MT through issues such as misuse of pronouns, but others were unsure:

When they write in Japanese, it's very normal to omit subjects, and MT always adds subjects which are often inappropriate. And so, the student will be writing about, say, somebody born in the 19th century, and then suddenly will say, 'I was born in 1880'. (T1)

I don't know how to monitor it, specifically how to monitor when students take Japanese text, and translate it into English on Google Translate. (T11)

To avoid misuse, there was some acknowledgement that students need to be an active part of the process, with one teacher calling for "an honour system" (T23) and another discussing the importance of actively involving students in decision making:

I don't try to control what the students do with the technology, but I think we need to talk with our learners about it, about how it can be used and how it can be abused ... get them thinking about, 'When is this going to be helping me to learn English? And when is this going to be me just cutting corners and not learning anything?' Autonomy is sort of my main focus now so I want them to be aware of what they're doing and why they're doing it and reflecting on the choices that they make. (T4)

Viewing these findings in relation to other studies helps to provide some recommendations. First, teachers who mentioned length of translated text tended to see shorter lengths as more acceptable. Ata and Debreli (2022) found students' views on ethical use of MT and their self-reports favoured word-level and phrase-level translation, with sentence-level or longer translations less common and viewed as less ethical. This suggests student recognition of the value of targeted use, so opening up discussions between teachers and students may lead them to find common ground and prevent potential misuse. This is particularly important as teachers' perceptions of students' MT practices have been shown not to align well (Alm & Watanabe, 2022). Furthermore, the present study found that many teachers offered limited or no MT training in their classes, echoing Delorme Benites et al.'s (2021) findings. However, offering training would not only help address cheating, it would also provide greater opportunities for skilled use by students for their language development.

Students of the current study's participants were not involved in this investigation, but Ata and Debreli's results (2022) revealed that only 58% of the 462 university students they surveyed felt proficient in using MT for language learning, so we cannot automatically assume students know what to do. Guiding students towards optimal use is recommended, but to do this, teachers themselves need adequate knowledge. Their preparedness for this is explored in the final research question below.

17.3.3 RQ3: Do Teachers Feel They Have Enough Knowledge to Help Students Use MT Effectively to Develop Their L2 Skills and/ or Do They Want to Learn More About This?

The survey revealed that only 31% of participants felt they had enough knowledge to help students use MT effectively to develop their L2 skills and most (84%) wanted to learn more. Existing MT skills and knowledge came from many sources. Teachers recounted experiences of teaching themselves how to use it, teacher-teacher learning, and learning with, and from, their students:

> I also do a lot of testing of MT in preparation for using it in class with my students. (T14)

> One of the teachers … came to my office, and he asked me about translation software … I showed him DeepL, and he was so happy. I could show him in ten minutes how it worked. (T8)

I just want to keep experimenting with it with my students and see what we can come up with in terms of making it a useful tool for learning. (T4)

Students seem to know more than I do about MT, so I often learn more than I teach when it comes to that particular field. (T22)

Teachers identified some specific areas they needed support with to help develop students' L2 skills:

For English teachers who are teaching the language, teaching writing ... trying to figure out a way to teach it that links to the students developing actual writing skills for themselves. So not only learning how to write Japanese sentences that translate well, but to figure out a way to use that tool to bridge to actually being able to write directly into English would be really nice. It'd be nice if there was some resource or something. (T1)

I've mostly encouraged or discussed its use in terms of writing assignments. But what possibilities does it offer for other [skills], for speaking, or reading or listening for that matter? Those are areas I'd be interested in exploring. (T4)

For higher level students, I'd like to learn how you teach translation using MT, because once they start working, I think this is a very strong tool, a very effective tool for them. (T19)

To effectively help students, teachers not only need practical skills, but also knowledge on what constitutes fair use and how to guide students towards it. Excerpts below show teachers' desire for such support from universities:

I think people need to know what it is, what it does, what it doesn't do, and what teachers need to do. (T24)

From the university side, setting guidelines and encouraging teachers to interact with the technology is probably the way to go. (T21)

A policy on fair usage and unfair usage would be extremely helpful. (T22)

Some put the onus for training on universities and pointed out it was lacking:

> Universities should have a broader space for MT, and there should be a global system of teachers' training about it. Some teachers are very comfortable, because they are tech savvy, but then there are teachers who want to use it, but there is not enough support. (T17)

> Unfortunately, a lot of universities have part-time staff doing a lot of their courses, or even most of their courses, and then don't include part-time teachers in faculty development [sessions]. (T9)

If universities provide training, should it be optional or required? Teachers who are already knowledgeable do not need basic training and some prefer to learn through other channels. For example, T13 had "a network of close friends who are teachers in the same course to swap ideas with" so didn't feel the need for training sessions. This points towards optional training as most beneficial. However, if it is not compulsory, those who would rather avoid MT may not attend, widening the gap between students of teachers with different levels of knowledge, a problem alluded to below:

> Every university has these people that are just like technophobes. And they're, you know, 'This is not the way we did it in [the past]'. I think they also just need training. And they just need to see how it could be used, because actually, there are a lot of lazy teachers who would let students do it irresponsibly. (T2)

Therefore, universities have difficult decisions to make and it is worth spending time investigating the needs and attitudes of their staff. By providing guidelines and training, universities could equip teachers with the skills required to deal with language education in a world where MT exists, and foster greater understanding between colleagues by reducing the likelihood of situations like the following:

> I had a colleague say that I was using the computers to teach the students instead of doing the work myself. 'The computer isn't really teaching,

it's cheating, you're not doing the work'. So, you would need education about what MT is, what it does and doesn't do. (T24)

This study did not collect quantitative data on MT training for teachers, and this is a limitation that should be covered in future research about the Japanese context. Delorme Benites et al. (2021) found that under 10% of the 666 university teachers they surveyed said their universities in Switzerland provided official guidelines, training or instructions for MT use. This low rate may be behind the finding that almost 80% of the teachers in that study did not even mention MT in their courses, let alone provide student training. If Japanese universities want students to learn to use MT effectively and fairly, providing adequate guidance to teachers would be advisable.

Educators facing time constraints can start building knowledge by reading systematic literature reviews, such as Lee's (2023) review of 87 articles from 2000 to 2019 and my review of 14 articles from 2020 to 2022 (Ohashi, 2024). Such reviews introduce the work of many researchers, so can help shape ideas for classroom practice and teacher training.

17.4 Conclusion

This chapter has provided insights into Japan-based foreign language teachers' MT-related views and practices. Despite limited generalisability, the findings may play a role in shaping discussions, training and policies in this and other foreign language education contexts. Data were collected in 2022, just before ChatGPT and other highly-capable chatbots were publicly released. Rather than this being a limitation, the findings offer a useful starting point for future studies that encompass these new technologies. With the rapid rate of change, it is essential that teachers understand MT and guide students towards optimal use, and universities should play their part by providing guidelines and training. Teachers' views and experiences are not uniform, so the path ahead will be winding. Hopefully this chapter has provided some insights that will spark thoughts and actions that will carry teachers and institutions forward.

References

Alm, A., & Watanabe, Y. (2022). Online machine translation for L2 writing across languages and proficiency levels. *Australian Journal of Applied Linguistics, 5*(3), 135–157. https://doi.org/10.29140/ajal.v5n3.53si3

Ata, M., & Debreli, M. (2022). Machine translation in the language classroom: Turkish EFL learners' and instructors' perceptions and use. *IAFOR Journal of Education: Technology in Education, 9*(4), 103–122. https://files.eric.ed.gov/fulltext/EJ1318690.pdf

Borg, S. (2003). Teacher cognition in language teaching: A review of research on what language teachers think, know, believe, and do. *Language Teaching, 36*(2), 81–109. https://doi.org/10.1017/S0261444803001903

Chang, L.-C. (2022). Chinese language learners evaluating machine translation accuracy. *The JALT CALL Journal, 18*(1), 110–136. https://doi.org/10.29140/jaltcall.v18n1.592

Delorme Benites, A., Cotelli Kureth, S., Lehr, C., & Steele, E. (2021). Machine translation literacy: A panorama of practices at Swiss universities and implications for language teaching. In N. Zoghlami, C. Brudermann, C. Sarré, M. Grosbois, L. Bradley, & S. Thouësny (Eds.), *CALL and professionalisation: Short papers from EUROCALL 2021* (pp. 80–87). Research-publishing.net. https://doi.org/10.14705/rpnet.2021.54.1313

Kostoulas, A., Babić, S., Glettler, C., Karner, A., Mercer, S., & Seidl, E. (2019). Lost in research: Educators' attitudes towards research and professional development. *Teacher Development, 23*(3), 307–324. https://doi.org/10.1080/13664530.2019.1614655

Lee, S.-M. (2023). The effectiveness of machine translation in foreign language education: A systematic review and meta-analysis. *Computer Assisted Language Learning, 36*(1–2), 103–125. https://doi.org/10.1080/09588221.2021.1901745

Leighton, K., Kardong-Edgren, S., Schneidereith, T., & Foisy-Doll, C. (2021). Using social media and snowball sampling as an alternative recruitment strategy for research. *Clinical Simulation in Nursing, 55*, 37–42. https://doi.org/10.1016/j.ecns.2021.03.006

Loock, R., Lechauguette, S., & Holt, B. (2022). Dealing with the 'elephant in the classroom': Developing language students' machine translation literacy. *Australian Journal of Applied Linguistics, 5*(3), 118–134. https://doi.org/10.29140/ajal.v5n3.53si2

Ohashi, L. (2022). The use of machine translation in L2 education: Japanese university teachers' views and practices. In B. Arnbjörnsdóttir, B. Bédi, L. Bradley, K. Friðriksdóttir, H. Garðarsdóttir, S. Thouësny, & M. J. Whelpton (Eds.), *Intelligent CALL, granular systems, and learner data: Short papers from EUROCALL 2022* (pp. 308–314). Research-publishing.net. https://doi.org/10.14705/rpnet.2022.61.1476

Ohashi, L. (2024). Machine translation in language education: A systematic review of open access articles. *Kenkyu Nenpou: The Annual Collection of Essays and Studies, 70*, 105–125. https://www.gakushuin.ac.jp/univ/let/top/publication/KE_70/KE_70_008.pdf

18

How Can Machine Translation Help Chinese Students in an English Academic Writing Task?

Yu Huiwen and David Coulson[iD]

18.1 Introduction: The Place of Machine Translation in Second-Language Education

Since their inception, machine translation (MT) websites have undergone significant development. For example, DeepL Translator was officially released in 2017 and, in 2024, began to offer support for 30 languages, including Chinese. These websites are popular among language learners for their speed and ability to handle complex texts, and the cognitive, linguistic, and affective benefits they offer (Rushton, 2022).

Y. Huiwen · D. Coulson (✉)
Ritsumeikan University, Kyoto, Japan
e-mail: coulson@fc.ritsumei.ac.jp

Y. Huiwen
e-mail: hyr23177@fc.ritsumei.ac.jp

© The Author(s), under exclusive license to Springer Nature
Switzerland AG 2025
D. Coulson and C. Denman (eds.), *Translation, Translanguaging and Machine Translation in Foreign Language Education*,
https://doi.org/10.1007/978-3-031-82174-5_18

371

Nevertheless, MT is viewed with skepticism by many teachers (Lee, 2021), especially in terms of ongoing concerns about passive learning (Crossley, 2018). Additionally, the use of MT in classrooms has been perceived by some scholars and educators as contrary to established pedagogical norms (Paterson, 2023), and has been criticized for producing erroneous sentences and inaccurate grammar (Bahri & Mahadi, 2016).

The research reported in this chapter seeks to explore the benefits of integrating MT into the language learning process, with a particular focus on second-language (L2) writing. The study examines how encouraging learners to write an initial draft before utilizing MT can aid them in critically assessing and enhancing their work, from word choice to overall textual coherence. The research involved guiding students in comparing MT output with their own drafts, with the aim of making significant improvements in their writing. This approach not only supports the development of lexical and syntactic features but also encourages the process of noticing, which is crucial for language learning.

18.2 Literature Review

During the process of writing, the use of the first language (L1) has been demonstrated by Bayless (2023) as helping language learners generate ideas, improve the efficiency of writing in an L2, and better monitor output. Even advanced learners benefit from detailed feedback on, and careful revision of, their writing (Lee, 2020). However, teachers are not always available, and learners equally do not always have access to native speakers for grammar correction or more suitable word suggestions. Therefore, many learners, especially those of lower English proficiency, seek help from MT.

Although frowned upon in many learning contexts, the effectiveness of using MT while learning a new language has gradually been confirmed. While translation may not be well regarded by many language teachers, it is a natural part of the language learning and usage process (Cook, 2010). MT has also been shown to enhance the overall quality of students' writing (Stapleton & Ka Kin, 2019) and, as stated above, can provide feedback when teachers are not readily accessible (Ducar & Schocket, 2018).

Feedback and revision are crucial for producing high-quality writing and have been shown to improve students' writing ability (Ferris, 2011). Concerning this, MT provides individualized feedback, allowing students to focus more on the content of their writing and produce more lexically accurate and complex texts (Lee, 2020). MT has been shown to create a supportive learning environment and reduce cognitive load (Baraniello et al., 2016). This leads to decreased anxiety, particularly among learners of lower proficiency (Bahri & Mahadi, 2016), and increased confidence, motivation, and linguistic awareness (Niño, 2008). By fostering learning autonomy through the use of independent learning strategies and self-directed learning processes, the use of MT can facilitate language learning (Kim, 2011). Research has shown that it is beneficial for learners to compare their writing drafts in L2 with output from MT on the linguistic characteristics that form the same ideas in their L1 (Lee & Briggs, 2021).

In terms of learner ability, Lee (2021) illustrated how MT can be used effectively with English learners of low-proficiency. Conversely, Murtisari (2021) focused on advanced learners, showing that, although translation may be employed less as proficiency increases, advanced learners still make use of it. The main benefit to appear in her research was the support provided to learners for expressing complex ideas and ensuring progress in their writing. For these reasons, Murtisari advocates that translation be accepted as a pedagogical strategy from elementary to advanced levels. Supporting this conclusion, research by Lee (2020) showed how pedagogic use of MT positively influenced the English writing of Korean L1 intermediate- and high-intermediate-level students.

Researchers have investigated how learners make use of MT from various perspectives, especially in which aspects (syntactic, lexical, etc.) they make progress. For example, Xu's (2022) investigation with four Japanese learners found many differences in the scope and types of revisions. Specifically concerning scope, one intermediate and two mid-advanced learners made more changes at the word level, while Xu's lowest-proficiency participant revised mostly at the sentence level. There was no change at the paragraph level among participants. Further, those with higher Japanese proficiency levels made a smaller number of changes.

Overall, these studies suggest that writing instruction incorporating translation has a positive impact on students at different levels of proficiency, and offer new insights into learners' L2 writing strategies. Importantly, however, compared to learners at lower and intermediate levels of proficiency, there is less research about more advanced learners. This is a concerning oversight as these learners are better prepared linguistically to evaluate output from MT. Indeed, a comparison of two English versions of a text can stimulate moments of noticing, which is an essential process, even for advanced learners (Murtisari, 2021).

Moreover, although MT strategies, such as back translation, have been introduced to learners in some research, no further specific instructions from teachers on the use of MT have been reported. Consequently, further pedagogical and instructional research and analysis is warranted to clarify the possible incorporation of MT in second-language instruction and to provide guidance to teachers on its effective use. Further, the existing literature does not indicate whether what is learnt from modifications made through the use of MT output has a positive influence on participants' future writing. To address these issues, the research reported here seeks to answer the following questions:

1. Does MT contribute to improvements in the English proficiency levels of advanced and intermediate EFL students? If yes, is there a difference in the level of improvement between intermediate and advanced learners?
2. To what extent are learners able to recall MT-inspired changes to their writing and how does this recollection influence their future written work?
3. What are the perceptions of advanced and intermediate English learners on the use of MT before and after revisions?

18.3 Methodology

18.3.1 Sample and Sampling

After being informed of the nature of the study, their rights of participation/non-participation and withdrawal, and steps taken to ensure anonymity and confidentiality, 12 Chinese students (five males and seven females, aged 23–32) joined the research. Nine were enrolled in a postgraduate linguistics program, and two were in undergraduate courses, in Japan. The other was a full-time university student in the USA. Participants' proficiency levels were: CEFR C1 (advanced; $n = 5$), B2 (upper-intermediate; $n = 5$), and B1 (intermediate; $n = 2$). All students had over ten years of English-learning experience at school in China, and seven had majored in English during their undergraduate or master's degrees.

18.3.2 Research Plan and Data Collection

The eight steps in the research plan based on Xu (2022) are shown in Table 18.1.

In Step 1, participants wrote an English essay without the use of MT based on the topic of a Chinese newspaper article. In Step 2, they were interviewed about their prior MT experiences. In Step 3, three strategies were provided to help students write the second drafts of their essays:

(1) Back translation and editing of the Chinese from DeepL. This involves putting Draft 1 (English) into DeepL and checking the Chinese translation. Next, use the reverse button to switch the English to Chinese and then edit the Chinese output from DeepL to make the meaning more precise. Participants were advised to make additions and deletions at this stage.
(2) Check the DeepL in-built dictionary. Click on English words of uncertain meaning to check the L1 Chinese translation supplied by DeepL's in-built dictionary.

Table 18.1 The research process

Steps	Procedures
1	[Essay-writing] English without help from MT (Draft 1)
	Participants are asked to read an article from a Chinese newspaper about alcohol consumption and use the information to write an English essay
	Requirement: Write 180 words in an academic style within 30 minutes
2	[Interview 1]
	Participants talk about their previous experience with MT
3	[Instructions on how to use DeepL]
	Participants receive instructions on how best to use DeepL
4	[Essay-writing] Writing in English with help from MT (Draft 2; video-recorded)
	Use DeepL to revise Draft 1 and write Draft 2
5	[Submit Draft 1 and 2]
6	[Interview 2]
	Based on their experience thus far, participants were asked about the benefits, challenges, and possible future use of MT
7	[Post-test 1] Essay-writing (Draft 3) one week later
	Participants write another essay on the same topic in English
8	[Post-test 2] Translation post-test one month after Draft 3
	Participants translate phrases and sentences from Chinese into English

(3) Check synonyms. DeepL Translator provides synonyms for words clicked on. Participants were advised to judge which synonym is most appropriate in each case.

In Step 4, in order to write Draft 2, students wrote revised versions of their first draft on their PCs based on feedback from DeepL. With their consent, this process was recorded through screen share to investigate the effect of MT on learners' writing. The time allowed for revision was 30 minutes. While revising, students were requested not to use any other online or paper resources than DeepL. Both Drafts 1 and 2 were submitted in Step 5. In Step 6, students were interviewed about the benefits, challenges, and their possible future use, of MT.

In Step 7, participants were told there would be follow-up interviews one week later. In fact, a post-test had been planned, and the aim was to prevent participants reviewing their earlier drafts in advance in order to reliably examine the longitudinal effect of use of MT on their L2 learning gains. In the test, participants were asked to write a new version of their essay on the same topic as before. Again, they were requested not to use MT or dictionaries or check their previous drafts.

Finally, in Step 8, one month later, based on the changes participants had made in Draft 2, further unannounced Chinese-English translation tests (individualized for each student) were given. These consisted of phrase and sentence-level translations of expressions which had appeared earlier in this process. The purpose was to check whether the changes that had been made during the revision process to write Draft 2 were reflected in their answers. The first author of this chapter (a Mandarin Chinese L1 speaker) created the test based on the changes participants had made in Draft 2.

The two interviews (Step 2 & 6) were conducted in Chinese before and after the revision process to clarify eight issues:

Before the revision process:

1. When writing, do you usually make a first draft and a second draft after that? How do you make revisions?
2. Have you ever used MT to help with your English writing before?
3. How often do you use MT?
4. What are the pros and cons of using MT?

After the revision process:

1. What do you think are DeepL's pros and cons? Give some examples.
2. Did you use all the strategies that were introduced to you?
3. What difficulties did you encounter during the revision process?
4. Will you continue using DeepL in your future writing?

18.3.3 Data Analysis

Post-test 1 (Draft 3, written in Step 7) was analyzed by comparing it to participants' Draft 2. Analysis focused on whether changes made in Draft 2 were retained in Draft 3, thereby indicating if participants had internalized their revisions. Post-test 2 focused more on whether the changes that participants had made also appeared in other English phrase- or sentence-level answers (Step 8). As stated above, post-test 2 was individualized according to each student's previous modifications.

Semi-structured interview data was analyzed using the SCAT (Steps for Coding and Theorization) method. This involved systematically coding interview responses to identify recurring themes and patterns, allowing for a thorough examination of participants' experiences and perceptions regarding the use of MT in their language learning process.

18.4 Results

18.4.1 Pre-revision Interviews

Interview 1 results indicated that all participants had previously revised during, or after, their writing prior to taking part in this study. However, their revisions depended on whether it was necessary to carry these out within fixed time limits, or whether a score would be given. Concerning the purpose of using MT, three of the 12 participants, including two at C1 level, had never used MT for writing, but had done so for reading academic articles. The B1 group had consistently used MT both in writing and reading. Altogether, nine participants across various proficiency levels had used MT for writing.

Participants cited various benefits of MT, including convenience, the ability to search for words and expressions, and avoidance of errors. They claimed to usually search for a suitable L2 word in MT by writing a sentence in Chinese in which the intended meaning appears, rather than just using a dictionary. Respondents further reported that MT aids in quickly organizing words into coherent sentences. Additionally, some participants reported that the frequent use of MT may improve memorization of words and expressions.

Table 18.2   The characteristics of Draft 2 texts

Participant	1	2	3	4	5	6	7	8	9	10	11	12
CEFR	C1	C1	C1	C1	C1	B2	B2	B2	B2	B2	B1	B1
○ = participants who revised Draft 1 based on DeepL suggestions ● = participants who used DeepL's version as their Draft 2 albeit with small changes	●	○	○	●	●	●	●	○	○	○	●	○
Changes	35	9	33	45	25	21	42	22	35	18	42	14
DeepL influence	33	9	30	45	25	21	42	21	32	18	40	14

18.4.2   Draft 2 Revision

Most participants used all 30 minutes available to make modifications to their initial drafts in English when writing Draft 2. This was unrelated to English proficiency. While revising, half the participants referred back to the original Chinese newspaper article, checking words and expressions that they did not know when writing the first draft. Additionally, while editing the Chinese text, some included adverbs to make the context more specific and precise (e.g., *It is [prohibitively] expensive*). Additionally, some participants edited the Chinese which DeepL had translated into more academic expressions (e.g., *shi* to *zuowei*). Concerning how participants edited their essays, half revised their first drafts based on suggestions from DeepL (with these individuals shown as ○ in Table 18.2). This means they used DeepL's suggestions as a guide to their amendments. The other half directly used DeepL's version to make their Draft 2, albeit with slight changes added after (shown as ● in Table 18.2).

18.4.3   Analysis of Draft 1 and 2

Following the completion of Draft 2, quantitative analysis began with a comparison of all participants' first and second drafts. These changes were categorized as positive, neutral, or negative. These mean: (a) improved accuracy, (b) no change in accuracy, and (c) decreased accuracy. Two native-English university faculty members helped with identifying the types of changes. These were categorized into 11 types: words, phrases, sentence formation, additions, deletions, articles, prepositions, single/plural forms, parts of speech, tense, and linkers. During the process of evaluating the kinds of changes by examining the video recordings made during the revision process (whether these were positive, negative, or neutral), only those changes prompted by output from DeepL were included in the analysis. The two native speakers' judgments were found to be largely consistent, with a 78% agreement rate.

The number of changes among the 12 participants ranged from 9 to 45 (see Table 18.2). Overall, there were 341 changes, of which 96.7% were in response to feedback from DeepL. The average number of changes per individual based on DeepL feedback was 27.5 ($SD = 11.42$). The average number of changes, based on DeepL for C1-level participants, was 28.4 ($SD = 13.11$), 26.8 ($SD = 10.03$) for B2, and 27.0 ($SD = 18.38$) for B1. These results show that participants who made changes to DeepL's English version after back translation made more changes compared to those who revised their first drafts with output from DeepL.

Overall, participants in each proficiency level made by far the largest number of changes in the phrasal category, and then the word category (Fig. 18.1). Next were additions, sentence formation, prepositions, single/plural forms, linkers, articles, part of speech, verb tense, and deletions. B1-level participants made fewer phrasal changes than the other two groups. C1-level participants made more changes in sentence formation, while B2 respondents made relatively fewer changes and B1 participants made no changes in this respect.

18.4.4 Interviews After the Revision Process

In the interviews in Step 6, all the participants evaluated DeepL positively. Benefits such as "filling gaps in my vocabulary" and "reminding me of forgotten words" were among the most commonly highlighted. Notably, DeepL suggested substitutions, native-like expressions, and

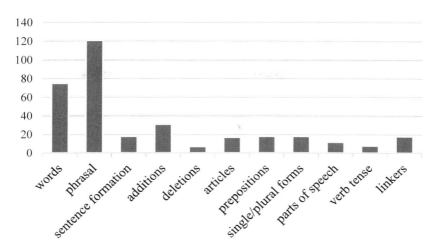

Fig. 18.1 Numbers of types of changes across the three groups

precise academic phrases for the topic of alcohol consumption. These included *tax revenue* for *tax income* and *revitalize* for *make…popular*.

Most participants utilized all recommended strategies, with back translation being particularly popular, even among those unfamiliar with MT. Particularly, back translation provided students with chances to check meanings in Chinese. Most importantly, several C1 and B2 participants reordered some sentences and even paragraphs, or added sentences and paragraphs to make their meanings clearer and more precise after checking the Chinese translation.

However, all participants faced difficulties with revision, particularly in choosing the most academic synonyms amid uncertainty about the naturalness of DeepL's suggestions. Higher-proficiency participants stated that, besides DeepL, they wanted to check a dictionary, a corpus, or other websites to confirm particular word usages and collocations. Finally, when asked about their future use of DeepL, three participants, including two at the C1 level, expressed reluctance to continue using it in their English writing, citing preferences for existing methods and tools such as Grammarly for quick and effective checks. While acknowledging MT's benefits, they were not convincing enough to change these respondents' learning habits. However, the other nine participants, including those who had never previously tried using DeepL for editing drafts, said they would continue using it.

18.4.5 Post-test 1

In post-test 1, participants' recall of the changes made in Draft 2 with the help of DeepL was assessed. Figure 18.2 shows three measures: the number of changes made in Draft 2, recall of modifications in Draft 2, and recall of the changes which were categorized as positive (see Sect. 18.4.3).

Figure 18.2 shows that participants made a diverse number of changes in Draft 2. In Draft 3 (post-test 1), some participants could recall their revisions in their previous versions, although some of the recalled phrasal expressions and words were rated as neutral changes. The average recall rate was 30.6%, with the highest 71.4% and the lowest 7.1% (see Table 18.3). Participants who revised their first drafts to make Draft 2 based on the suggestions given by DeepL (as above, shown as ○ in Table 18.3) exhibited a higher recall rate (37.51%) in Draft 3 than those who directly used DeepL's English version to make Draft 2 (23.7%).

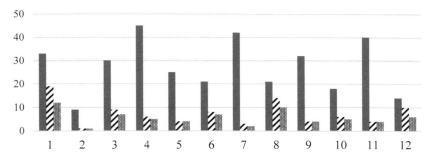

■ the number of changes by comparing Drafts 1 and 2 (influenced by MT)
◿ the number of words/phrases recalled by comparing Draft 2 and Draft 3
▩ recall of positive changes

Fig. 18.2 The number of changes, recall, and positive recall in post-test 1

Table 18.3 The number of changes in Draft 2 and the percentage recalled in Draft 3

Participant	1	2	3	4	5	6	7	8	9	10	11	12
○ = participants who revised Draft 1 based on DeepL suggestions ● = participants who used DeepL's version as their Draft 2 albeit with small changes	●	○	○	●	●	●	●	○	○	○	●	○
Changes	33	9	30	45	25	21	42	21	32	18	40	14
Recall	19	1	9	6	4	8	3	14	4	6	4	10
Recall Percentage	57.6	11.1	30.0	13.3	16.0	38.1	7.1	66.7	12.5	33.3	10.0	71.4

18.4.6 Post-test 2

The results of the translation test—post-test 2—conducted one month after the initial draft was written, are shown in Fig. 18.3. From a total of 55 Chinese-to-English translations, five were phrasal and the remainder were sentences. Each sentence included at least one change made by participants in their Draft 2. Among the changes selected, all participants successfully recalled and used 58% of the changes they had made in their Draft 2 in this post-test.

18.5 Discussion

18.5.1 Research Question 1

The first research question concerned whether MT improves English proficiency in advanced and intermediate EFL students and, if so, whether the improvement differs between these groups. The results indicated that both advanced and intermediate-proficiency students benefitted, to varying degrees, from MT feedback. Most changes made by participants occurred at the phrasal and word level, reflecting MT's capacity to provide substitutions and suggestions to fill lexical gaps. Further, the two native speaker raters agreed that the second drafts were

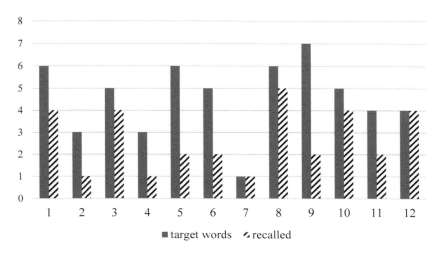

Fig. 18.3 Results of translation post-tests by participants

much better than the first, indicating that MT had supplied more precise and appropriate words or expressions.

Participants also made improvements to syntax. That is, they wrote more detailed, formal, and native-like sentences with DeepL's help. Therefore, the results from the writing of English drafts clearly show that DeepL assists with both lexical and syntactic aspects. While these findings align with those reported by scholars such as Y. J. Lee (2021), evidence reported here that MT can assist learners of both intermediate and high proficiency levels beyond the construction of sentences challenges claims by researchers including M. W. Lee (2018) and S.-M. Lee (2020) that MT's efficacy is limited to the sentence level.

Before the revision process, participants were introduced to the three strategies described in Sect. 18.3.2. Based on the output in Chinese from DeepL, students were able to notice deficiencies in their initial drafts. They made additions and deletions, and other changes including the reordering of sentences and paragraphs in subsequent drafts. For example, participants added adverbs and phrases, changed words, sometimes changed the sequence of sentences, wrote new sentences, or even, exceptionally, added longer sections to refine their intended meanings. Back translation was a particularly useful strategy, helping participants to organize their thoughts, enhance coherence, and achieve clearer expressions in their writing. This allowed participants to identify areas lacking cohesion, and add details to improve clarity. This contrasts with M. W. Lee's (2018) findings and may stem from participants' proficiency levels and the absence of instructions for using MT strategies.

Evaluation by the two native-English-speaker raters confirmed that drafts produced with the help of DeepL feedback were superior to those written without it across all participant levels. Conversely, negative changes (i.e., changing correct into incorrect English), although fewer, appeared at each level, including for some C1-level participants. Some of these negative changes were due to participants mistakenly choosing alternative synonyms provided by DeepL. This matches M. W. Lee's (2018) findings that changes made with the assistance of MT are not always correct, including for advanced-level students. This further supports Murtisari's (2021) findings that, although learners at advanced levels are more competent language users, they still have gaps in their L2 for which support is needed.

In addition, participants at different levels of proficiency occasionally wrote unnatural collocations even with the output from DeepL. This illustrates that relying solely on MT may not suffice, and the integration of additional resources, such as corpora, online thesauruses, and advice from teachers or native speakers, is desirable. This fully aligns with M. W. Lee's (2018) recommendation that teachers should guide students to use various online resources for accurate writing.

Further, participants of higher proficiency made more revisions at the sentence level. This result contradicts Xu's (2022) finding that mid-advanced learners made more changes at the word level, while the single participant at the lowest level of Japanese proficiency in that study made more changes at the sentence level. This difference may be caused by the number of participants and the language (Japanese) used in Xu's research. The finding in this research, however, supports Im's (2017) assertion that lower-proficiency individuals may face challenges in evaluating complex grammatical nuances. More advanced individuals may also feel more confident in editing at the sentence level.

18.5.2   Research Question 2

As discussed above, all participants recalled some of the changes made during the revision process in both Draft 3 (post-test 1, conducted one week later), and the translation post-test (post-test 2, conducted one month later). Notably, participants with the strongest post-test results attributed their success to DeepL. These learners stressed that it helped with their uncertainties and improved the quality of expressions in Draft 1 during the editing process. Additionally, frequent encounters with specific words such as *tax revenue* and *alcoholic beverages* apparently promoted implicit learning.

The results of this study also show that suggestions from DeepL may be inadequate, even for C1-level learners. As Niño (2009) described, advanced learners were aware of errors, corrected them, and produced more accurate and coherent writing. Our results supported this, but suggested that advanced English learners cannot always recognize more suitable words to use in different contexts. For example, one C1 participant struggled in the translation post-test with the words *event* and *campaign*. The participant recalled that he had changed *event* to *campaign* in his second draft following DeepL's suggestion but had no idea which one was better in which situation.

Likewise, in one B2 participant's translation post-test, the student stated that she had difficulty in choosing between *revive* and *revitalize*. She could not remember which suggestion DeepL had given, as the word only appeared once. This phenomenon also occurred with B1-level participants. This highlights the fragile nature of new vocabulary knowledge (Webb, 2007), and the fact that MT does not necessarily guarantee progress.

Lastly, based on results reported in Table 18.3, the ability to recall the changes made was unrelated to the timing of the revision process and was linked, rather, with participants' efforts. It can be inferred from this that revisions on self-written versions may be associated more with implicit learning.

18.5.3 Research Question 3

All participants responded positively to the use of MT for draft revisions, even those who had initially given a negative response about MT for English essay writing. The post-tests and interviews conducted after the study revealed that participants across English proficiency levels had unconsciously learned new words and expressions through the editing process with DeepL. This finding again suggests the possibility of implicit learning.

During the composition of Draft 1, participants identified deficiencies in their English knowledge and noticed a lack of vocabulary, expressions, and/or sentence structure. The incorporation of new information observed in participants' Draft 2 texts confirmed this awareness. The revision process with MT also involved cognitive engagement, as respondents compared their own drafts with DeepL's suggestions, thereby making judgments to determine the better option.

Some participants commented in interviews that they were unsure of the academic appropriateness of their writing and used DeepL as a guide. Although two C1 participants confirmed the benefits of MT in interviews, they expressed their intention not to continue using it in their future English writing as it differed from their usual editing practices. This highlights the possibility of incorporating MT editing into earlier stages of English learning. In this way, English language learners may be able to develop an additional writing strategy.

18.6 Implications for Second-Language Education

The results from this study offer an alternative perspective on the widely held view of students copying and pasting from MT among teachers and administrators. They indicate that, with appropriate guidance, learners are willing to try, and benefit from, writing an initial draft before using MT. This approach helps learners to critically assess their writing in different respects, ranging from words to textual coherence. Such a practice complements previous research (e.g., Lee, 2021), in that the comparison by learners of the output from MT into L2, and their own writing directly in L2, is useful.

Participants in this study successfully edited their drafts after carefully comparing and considering the suggestions given by MT with their own drafts. This provides a source of noticing, which is a highly valuable process in language learning (Schmidt, 2010). The research reported here has thus described a method for implementing this dynamic through the use of MT.

Further, participants' production of words and sentences can act as a scaffold for the further development of lexical and syntactic features (Godwin-Jones, 2015). Findings offered above thus reflect the potentially positive contribution of DeepL as a learning strategy for students' L2 development. This study further questions results from previous investigations that MT cannot help beyond the sentence level.

18.7 Conclusion

Before considering the implications of these results for future research and teaching practice, a number of limitations must be taken into account. First, it is important to note that this study was conducted with 12 learners across three proficiency levels. Increasing the sample size to conduct more in-depth analysis of a wider range of L2 students would be a useful next step. Further, the changes made by participants in Draft 2 were evaluated by only two native-English-speaking raters, who, despite relatively high levels of agreement, had divergent opinions on some changes. It would, therefore, be beneficial to employ a larger number of raters.

In addition, instead of just relying on one single MT application, the English output from different applications could provide useful points of comparison and contrast in participants' writing revision process. Finally, the post-tests, including the writing of Draft 3 one week after the second draft and translation post-tests conducted one month later, did not provide conclusive evidence about whether participants could effectively utilize the positive changes made during the revision process in their future writing. A more extensive examination of subsequent English essays written by participants could help clarify this issue.

With these limitations and potential future research areas acknowledged, the results here offer a number of valuable insights about the impact of MT use on the revision process of advanced and intermediate-level English-L2 participants, the potential influence of MT on their subsequent writing assignments, and their perceptions before and after the use of MT. The results showed that, although some participants had no prior experience with MT in editing English essays, they recognized its potential effectiveness during the revision process and in follow-up writing tasks. Participants made most changes at the word and phrasal levels, with fewer changes appearing at the sentence level, especially for those of lower proficiency. This research confirms that MT can assist participants beyond these levels if compensatory MT strategies are effectively applied.

This study also illustrates how MT can be a valuable tool for classroom practice as a means of refining learners' essays and supporting their English learning. While it is important to recognize the limitations of MT and emphasize the necessity of teacher guidance, it is crucial to increase understanding among instructors and second-language learners that MT should not be underestimated or neglected as a learning resource.

References

Bahri, H., & Mahadi, T. S. T. (2016). Google Translate as a supplementary tool for learning Malay: A case study at Universiti Sains Malaysia. *Advances in Language and Literary Studies, 7*(3), 161–167. https://doi.org/10.7575/aiac.alls.v.7n.3p.161

Baraniello, V., Degano, C., Laura, L., Zahonero, M. L., Naldi, M., & Petroni, S. (2016). A wiki-based approach to computer-assisted translation for collaborative language learning. In Y. Li, M. Chang, M. Kravcik, E. Popescu, R. Huang, Kinshuk, & N.-S. Chen (Eds.), *State-of-the-art and future directions of smart learning* (pp. 369–379). Springer. https://doi.org/10.1007/978-981-287-868-7_45

Bayless, C. (2023). *L1 use in the L2 composition process: An empirical study of Philippine ESL writers* [Unpublished doctoral dissertation]. University of British Columbia. https://open.library.ubc.ca/soa/cIRcle/collections/ubcthe ses/24/items/1.0431102

Cook, G. (2010). *Translation in language teaching: An argument for reassessment.* Oxford University Press.

Crossley, S. A. (2018). Technological disruption in foreign language teaching: The rise of simultaneous machine translation. *Language Teaching, 51*(4), 541–552. https://doi.org/10.1017/S0261444818000253

Ducar, C., & Schocket, D. H. (2018). Machine translation and the L2 class-room: Pedagogical solutions for making peace with Google Translate. *Foreign Language Annals, 51*(4), 779–795. https://doi.org/10.1111/flan.12366

Ferris, D. R. (2011). *Treatment of error in second language student writing* (2nd ed.). University of Michigan Press. https://doi.org/10.3998/mpub.2173290

Godwin-Jones, R. (2015). Contributing, creating, curating: Digital literacies for language learners. *Language Learning & Technology, 19*(3), 8–20. http://dx.doi.org/10125/44427

Im, H.-J. (2017). The university students' perceptions or attitudes on the use of the English automatic translation in a general English class: Based on English writing lessons. *Korean Journal of General Education, 11*(6), 727–751. https://j-kagedu.or.kr/journal/view.php?number=629

Kim, E. Y. (2011). Using translation exercises in the communicative EFL writing classroom. *ELT Journal, 65*(2), 154–160. https://doi.org/10.1093/elt/ccq039

Lee, M. W. (2018). Translation revisited for low-proficiency EFL writers. *ELT Journal, 72*(4), 365–373. https://doi.org/10.1093/elt/ccy007

Lee, S.-M. (2020). The impact of using machine translation on EFL students' writing. *Computer Assisted Language Learning, 33*(3), 157–175. https://doi.org/10.1080/09588221.2018.1553186

Lee, S.-M., & Briggs, N. (2021). Effects of using machine translation to mediate the revision process of Korean university students' academic writing. *ReCALL, 33*(1), 18–33. https://doi.org/10.1017/S0958344020000191

Lee, Y. J. (2021). Still taboo? Using machine translation for low-level EFL writers. *ELT Journal, 75*(4), 432–441. https://doi.org/10.1093/elt/ccab018

Murtisari, E. T. (2021). Use of translation strategies in writing: Advanced EFL students. *LLT Journal: A Journal on Language and Language Teaching, 24*(1), 228–239. https://doi.org/10.24071/llt.v24i1.2663

Niño, A. (2008). Evaluating the use of machine translation post-editing in the foreign language class. *Computer Assisted Language Learning, 21*(1), 29–49. https://doi.org/10.1080/09588220701865482

Niño, A. (2009). Machine translation in foreign language learning: Language learners' and tutors' perceptions of its advantages and disadvantages. *ReCALL, 21*(2), 241–258. https://doi.org/10.1017/S0958344009000172

Paterson, K. (2023). Machine translation in higher education: Perceptions, policy, and pedagogy. *TESOL Journal, 14*(2), e690. https://doi.org/10.1002/tesj.690

Rushton, A. (2022). Motivating Japanese university EFL learners to produce longer speaking turns with web-based machine translation: A pilot study. *Kobe Kaisei Jogakuin University Research Bulletin, 66*, 73–81. https://www.kaisei.ac.jp/wp-content/uploads/2022/60_9.pdf

Schmidt, R. (2010). Attention, awareness, and individual differences in language learning. In W. M. Chan, S. Chi, K. N. Cin, J. Istanto, M. Nagami, J. W. Sew, T., et al. (Eds.), *Proceedings of CLaSIC 2010* (pp. 721–737). National University of Singapore, Centre for Language Studies.

Stapleton, P., & Ka Kin, B. L. (2019). Assessing the accuracy and teachers' impressions of Google Translate: A study of primary L2 writers in Hong Kong. *English for Specific Purposes, 56*, 18–34. https://doi.org/10.1016/j.esp.2019.07.001

Webb, S. (2007). The effects of repetition on vocabulary knowledge. *Applied Linguistics, 28*(1), 46–65. https://doi.org/10.1093/applin/aml048

Xu, J. (2022). Proficiency and the use of machine translation: A case study of four Japanese learners. *L2 Journal, 14*(1), 77–104. https://doi.org/10.5070/L214151328

19

Integrating Machine Translation in Language Learning in the Age of Artificial Intelligence: A SWOT Analysis

María del Mar Sánchez Ramos(iD)

19.1 Introduction

Technology-mediated learning has matured over the past decades, and a range of tools are currently widely used in language learning to enhance, for example, collaborative learning or vocabulary acquisition (Ziegler & González-Lloret, 2022). Along with the rapid advances in artificial intelligence (AI), the quality of machine translation (MT) has improved greatly in the last decade, largely due to the development of neural machine translation (NMT) systems.

The speed of technological change has prompted professionals in applied linguistics and language teaching to explore how best to incorporate these tools into their curricula. While MT can benefit language learning, it is also important to consider its limitations. MT is not a

M. M. Sánchez Ramos (✉)

Department of Modern Philology, University of Alcalá, Alcalá de Henares, Madrid, Spain

e-mail: mar.sanchezr@uah.es

© The Author(s), under exclusive license to Springer Nature Switzerland AG 2025

D. Coulson and C. Denman (eds.), *Translation, Translanguaging and Machine Translation in Foreign Language Education*,

https://doi.org/10.1007/978-3-031-82174-5_19

393

"magical" process; nor is it (yet) performed by a machine with the ability to reason. Rather, it is an efficient data processing system that can be usefully implemented in different environments, but only if its benefits and limitations are fully understood.

This chapter investigates how a group of English as a Second Language (ESL) teachers at the University of Alcalá in Madrid, Spain, use MT and AI tools (grouped together in this chapter as "MT tools") when teaching modules in an undergraduate degree in Modern Languages and Translation, and their attitudes toward these resources. A non-experimental mixed methods design was employed to address the following research questions:

RQ1: How do Spanish university-level ESL teachers use MT tools in their classroom?
RQ2: How do Spanish university-level ESL teachers view the positive and negative qualities of MT tools in their classroom?

19.2 Literature Review: Machine Translation in Language Learning

The use of MT in language learning is not new, with various authors having charted its development over more than three decades now (Anderson, 1995; Niño, 2008; Zhang & Torres-Hostench, 2022). However, despite MT showing great potential to transform language learning, its pedagogical uses remain controversial (Tasdemir et al., 2023). Although a complete overview of the relevant literature is not feasible here due to space constraints, Jolley and Maimone's (2022) comprehensive survey offers five interconnected research strands in MT in language education, with two of these—MT in Language Teaching and Learning and MT Use and Perceptions—being of direct relevance to the current study.

With regard to the use of MT in language teaching, a number of studies have reported that ESL teachers and students can benefit from it in a number of ways. For example, researchers have investigated the incorporation of MT in ESL settings as a tool to enhance grammatical accuracy (Lee, 2020); to improve writing and communication skills (Polakova & Klimova, 2023); and to support vocabulary acquisition (Clifford et al., 2013; Garcia & Pena, 2011; Niño, 2008; Resende & Way, 2020). Other studies have found that incorporating MT in the ESL curriculum has the potential to empower students to use these technologies in responsible ways, while also developing their MT literacy (e.g., Alm, 2022). Further, Torres-Hostench (2023) reported how MT can help ESL students become more autonomous and self-directed in their language learning and even begin to appreciate the complexities of translation.

Despite these potential advantages, a number of studies have focused on the limitations and challenges MT can pose for ESL teachers and students (Niño, 2009). MT can, for example, produce inaccurate translations, especially when translating idiomatic expressions, and students' over-reliance on it can hinder both their learning progress and ability to think critically and creatively in the target language. Another key issue is the ethical implications of MT use. That is, students need to be explicitly taught how to use MT responsibly and ethically in order to avoid plagiarism and inappropriate uses of the raw machine output (Ducar & Schocket, 2018).

Given these potential pitfalls, it is perhaps not surprising that some scholars have discouraged MT's use as a language learning resource. These include Garcia and Pena (2011) who found that using MT was detrimental to learning because students became too dependent on the technology. Moreover, Fredholm (2015) reported that MT was useful for advanced students but counterproductive for those at the beginner and intermediate levels. Despite these warnings, Torres-Hostench (2023) counters that these and similar studies date from a time when MT output merely relied on linguistic or statistical systems. As such, their results may no longer be valid during a time of rapid advances in AI translation tools and NMT in which the quality of the translations has improved enormously.

Beginning in 2016, NMT represents a new paradigm in MT that is the result of the combination of AI, big data, and neuroscience (Klimova et al., 2023). Unlike linguistic- and statistical-based MT models, NMT employs deep learning and artificial neural networks to predict the likelihood of a sequence of words. Klimova et al. (2023) maintain that, due to its development, nowadays "hardly anyone working in the field of foreign language teaching and learning can imagine life without machine translation (MT) tools" (p. 663). However, this claim may not accurately reflect developments across the world or, indeed, within a single institution. For example, in their study of Swiss universities, Delorme Benites et al. (2021) found that even teachers who were quite familiar with MT rarely used it in their teaching, which leaves MT's potential, even in a country often lauded for the quality of its education system, largely untapped.

As Delorme Benites et al.'s (2021) research implies, with regard to ESL teachers' perceptions, a relatively small but growing number of studies currently available suggest different levels of acceptance, and even a certain degree of contradiction, in attitudes toward MT tools as language learning resources. Some authors argue that MT has a place in the ESL and/or foreign language classroom and that both instructors and students would benefit from training in how to introduce MT as a language learning resource (Stapleton & Ka Kin, 2019). Others, however, continue to emphasize the dangers and pitfalls of integrating MT into ESL classrooms.

Returning to Jolley and Maimone's (2022) systematic review of the literature, the authors summarize the situation by stating:

> Both instructors and learners hold nuanced and often conflicting views on the suitability of MT in the L2 classroom and, although many instructors object to student use of MT, some see a pedagogical role for it, supporting additional MT training for themselves and their students. (p. 39)

In order to contribute to this discussion and improve our understanding of the place of MT tools in ESL teaching, the research detailed in this chapter explores how a group of Spanish university-level ESL teachers used MT tools in their classroom, and their perceptions of the positive and negative qualities of these technologies.

19.3 Methods

19.3.1 Data Collection and Analysis

The study reported here adopted a mixed methods design to address the two research questions stated above. The first objective was to discover if and how a group of language teachers at the University of Alcalá used MT tools as teaching resources with students enrolled in the university's Modern Languages and Translation undergraduate degree. The second aim was to identify the most prominent positive and negative aspects of using MT tools as language learning tools.

Quantitative data were collected through a Spanish language questionnaire designed to gauge the degree of knowledge and awareness that participating teachers had of MT tools as language learning resources. The data collection instrument was designed by the researcher and validated by three professional language teachers to detect and remove any ambiguities in terms of content and terminology.

The questionnaire included 16 questions across two sections (reproduced in English in the Appendix). The first section collected teacher demographics while the second elicited information about the MT tools participants used in their ESL classrooms. A variety of question formats were employed, including single-answer questions, multiple-choice questions, and open-ended questions. Following Mellinger and Hanson's (2021) recommendation, the single-answer and multiple-choice questions featured Likert-type scales with response options from 1 (total disagreement) to 5 (total agreement). As the structure of some questions followed the logic of exclusion (Zaretzkaya et al., 2018), the questionnaire was adjusted based on responses to previous questions offered by respondents. For example, teachers who stated that they did not use MT tools in the classroom were not required to respond to questions about what MT tools they did employ.

Descriptive analysis, with a focus on frequency counts, was applied to data collected from items using predetermined response scales. Responses to open-ended questions and free comments were analyzed using thematic analysis, including by being grouped according to the identified themes (Bryman, 2012).

Further qualitative data were obtained through a SWOT analysis of questionnaire results that sought to determine the strengths, weaknesses, opportunities, and threats of using MT tools as ESL resources (Gil Zafra, 2001; Plaza Lara, 2019; Plaza Lara & Bobadilla-Perez, 2024). For the SWOT analysis, a three-stage methodology was implemented following an approach that has been successfully employed in previous studies (e.g., Moral López et al., 2010; Sánchez Ramos, 2022). The first stage involved *planning*, which consists of defining the main SWOT factors. The second stage was *analysis*, which examines both internal (weaknesses and strengths) and external (threats and opportunities) perspectives. Finally, a matrix was constructed to analyze findings and suggest strategies for improvement.

For the first stage, the four factors of the SWOT analysis were defined thus:

- *Strengths*: resources or capabilities that help to achieve desired goals.
- *Weaknesses*: barriers that hinder the chance of progress toward desired goals.
- *Opportunities*: factors that can offer a competitive advantage.
- *Threats*: potential obstacles that could affect a project.

For the second and third SWOT analysis stages, the aim was to draw conclusions from the survey results and propose strategies for improvement. To achieve this, and as part of the third stage, the SWOT questions in Table 19.1 were used by the researcher as an ad hoc matrix.

19.3.2 Sample

Eight ESL instructors teaching English I and English II—two first-year compulsory modules of the Modern Languages and Translation undergraduate degree at the University of Alcalá—were recruited for the study. In the 2023–2024 academic year, the teachers taught both modules: one in each semester to a group of 74 students (51 for English I and 23 for English II). The main aim of these modules is to provide students with basic English written and oral skills.

Table 19.1 Observation items for the SWOT analysis checklist

Strengths	– What is done well? – What elements facilitate the use of MT and other AI resources in the ESL classroom? – What resources facilitate the use of MT and AI tools?
Weaknesses	– What do language teachers perceive as weaknesses? – What could be done better? – What factors could potentially reduce the success of incorporating MT and other AI resources in the ESL classroom?
Opportunities	– What technology-related changes are occurring? – Is the situation within the ESL classroom appropriate for addressing improvement opportunities? – What changes are emerging in ESL in terms of technologies?
Threats	– What obstacles hinder the use of MT and other AI resources in the ESL classroom? – What type of problems are observed within the ESL classroom? – Are individuals perceived as responsible for the lack of use of MT and AI resources in the ESL classroom?

Prospective participants were informed about the research by email and asked to volunteer. Those who expressed interest were sent a consent form which assured participants of the confidentiality of their information, their right to withdraw, etc. Once consent was obtained in writing, each participant was sent a link to the electronic questionnaire, which was administered through the EncuestaFacil platform and made available from February 2024 to mid-April 2024.

19.4 Results

19.4.1 Initial Questionnaire Analysis

The first part of the questionnaire elicited participants' background information (Questions 1–9). Table 19.2 indicates that most participants were female (87.5%) and around 21–35 years old (50%). Their level of experience in ESL teaching varied, with 37.5% having 1–3 years of experience, and 25% teaching ESL for the first time. Over half of the participants were PhD students, with 25% enrolled in Translation and 37.5% in English Studies.

Table 19.3 shows that the majority of participants (62.5%) stated they had a strong interest in technology as determined by responses to Question 6 which asked them to rank their level of interest from none to high. In response to Question 7 about the importance that participants attached to the different syllabus content areas, teachers rated grammar, writing, and vocabulary as their main areas of instruction when teaching the English I and English II modules.

Table 19.2 ESL teachers' demographic information

Variable	%
Gender	
Male	12.5
Female	87.5
Age	
21–35	50
36–45	25
46–55	0
56–65	25
Years of Experience	
Less than 1	25
1–3	37.5
4–6	12.5
7–9	25
10 or more	0
Qualification	
Holder of doctorate in English Studies	37.5
PhD student in Translation	25
PhD student in English Studies	37.5

Table 19.3 ESL teachers' interest in technology

Level of interest in technology	Frequency
1—None	0
2	0
3	1 (12.5%)
4	2 (25%)
5—High interest	5 (62.5%)

Questions 8 and 9 aimed to establish how familiar participants were with the use of MT tools as language learning resources, and whether they used these in their classrooms. In response to Question 8, "Do you use MT or any AI system as resources when teaching the subject?", most participants claimed that they largely avoided using these tools, with 75% stating they did not use any MT tools whatsoever. This was somewhat unexpected given that most respondents were young and female with 1–3 years of experience and a strong interest in technology.

Participants stating that they do not use MT or AI systems in the classroom were asked to briefly explain the main reasons for this in response to Question 9. Thematic analysis of responses to this open-ended question revealed the primary reasons as including a lack of knowledge about MT and AI as teaching resources, and lack of training in their use. Other participants' comments here focused on the belief that MT was not an appropriate tool for ESL instruction.

The specific objective of Questions 10–16 was to obtain information about the use of MT tools and AI as language learning resources. As stated above, in response to Question 8, only two participants (25%) employed these tools in their classrooms. These participants were asked, "In general, what percentage of your time do you spend on using these tools when teaching ESL?" (Question 10). The two participants reported using MT between 51 and 75%, and AI tools around 26–50%, of the time while teaching. They further stated that the MT tools they used most often in the classroom (Question 11) included Google Translate and DeepL, while one respondent offered ChatGPT as an example of generative AI tool.

These two teachers' responses to Question 12, which asked them to specify the main tasks they used MT and AI tools for, revealed that MT and AI tools were mostly employed as linguistic and pedagogical resources, with participants considering them useful for grammatical correction, translation tasks, and designing ESL classroom activities. When next asked to rate their use of MT and other AI systems across the core language skills (Question 13), respondents claimed that they generally used these more often to develop their learners' reading and writing skills.

Responses to Questions 14–16 reflected the increasing influence of MT tools on ESL teaching. A key advantage of these technologies identified by participants in response to Question 14 (concerning the main advantages of including MT and AI tools as resources in the ESL classroom) was related to "optimiz[ing] time". One participant stated, "MT and other AI systems can help to optimize time as we can use them to design learning tasks". Demonstrating awareness of large language models, like ChatGPT, that can produce a wide range of vocabulary lesson plans, participants considered MT tools to be very useful for designing language tasks to be used in the ESL classroom. One participant also highlighted how these resources can help develop students' critical awareness and their responsible use of technologies, by stating: "I believe that openly using MT and AI systems can help develop critical thinking skills and help students use them responsibly".

In response to Question 15 about the main disadvantages of including MT and AI tools in teaching, one participant identified the importance of setting limits on their use:

> We also have to be aware of the limitations of MT. In my opinion, these tools have to be used as ESL resources, but we also need to set limits, or our students will use them for every activity in class. We also need to make them aware that MT and other AI tools are resources that can be used in class.

Participants also identified lack of training as a key challenge when using MT tools as pedagogical resources in the ESL classroom, with one stating:

> I think it's of paramount importance to provide training for ESL teachers. Ultimately, we, as teachers, try to teach what we know.... We need to know how to use [MT tools] as resources for ESL, get to know more examples and best practices, and situations where their use is not recommended, etc.

Finally, regarding issues that hinder the usefulness of MT tools as resources in the ESL classroom (Question 16), participants believed that teachers should be cautious in their use of them, but also stay aware of their usefulness. Early familiarization with MT tools, participants suggested, could improve students' awareness of the need to use them responsibly and ethically. It was also highlighted that teachers needed to familiarize themselves with technological advances as part of their own professional development and to explore them as potentially innovative approaches in ESL classrooms.

19.4.2 SWOT Analysis

19.4.2.1 Internal Analysis: Strengths and Weaknesses

Participants perceived a key strength of MT tools as ESL resources as being their methodologically innovative nature, with this finding supporting results by Borsatti and Blanco Riess (2021) and Mahardika (2017). Another strength was related to the use of MT tools as a means of increasing and developing students' interest in specific topics. Participants explicitly stated that becoming familiar with MT tools helped their students understand the ethical issues of using these technologies, which is a finding echoed by Torres-Hostench (2023).

Respondents had an overall positive attitude toward MT tools and believed that they provide opportunities to design activities specifically adapted to the proficiency level of their classes, which again reinforces the findings of Torres-Hostench (2023). Another important strength of these technologies is that they aid not only students' comprehension levels but also their understanding of linguistic nuances and cultural issues.

In terms of weaknesses, most participants reported that overuse of MT tools could result in students becoming overly dependent on them, which could have a negative impact on the language learning process. This finding is corroborated by various other studies that have explored the impact of MT as a language learning tool (e.g., Ata & Debreli, 2021). A further weakness highlighted by participants was related to the lack of personalized feedback when students use MT tools for assessing their own writing.

19.4.2.2 External Analysis: Opportunities and Threats

Regarding the opportunities and threats associated with using MT tools in ESL classrooms, a number of studies have reported that technological advances are driving change—both positive and negative—in the classroom (Niño, 2020; Polakova & Klimova et al., 2023; Torres-Hostench, 2023). In terms of opportunities, some participants felt that knowing how to use MT tools opens up innovative teaching paths and makes it easier to adapt to new curricular changes. Nevertheless, participants who were not confident enough to use these technologies in their own classrooms were concerned that they would have to change their whole methodological approach. All participants agreed that effective training in MT tools is essential, especially as teachers' effective use of these tools will increase their positive impact on students.

Respondents further suggested that students should receive training in MT tools as soon as possible in their Modern Languages and Translation degree to successfully prepare them for the job market. Use of these technologies can also be seen as an opportunity to introduce or develop other skills, such as critical thinking and reflective practice.

The main threats identified by participants were the perceived unstoppable advance of technology in the ESL classroom, and what this might mean for their own job security. Some participants had noticed reticence among their colleagues to incorporate MT tools in their classrooms. Indeed, the low number of participants currently using MT tools in their classrooms as reported here reflects a general reluctance to explore new technologies and pedagogical approaches that could benefit language learners. Teachers' lack of application of new technologies in their pedagogical practice revealed in the questionnaire responses above, combined with an over-dependence on traditional language learning methodologies and resources, could potentially have a negative impact on translation students' careers in our increasingly digitalized world.

The SWOT analysis led to the development of improvement strategies that address negative aspects (i.e., weaknesses and threats) and consolidate positive aspects (strengths and opportunities) of the phenomenon under study (Table 19.4).

Table 19.4 Results of the SWOT analysis

SWOT analysis	Internal factors	External factors
Negative qualities	**Weaknesses** – High dependence on MT and AI tools – Lack of personalized feedback	**Threats** – High dependence on traditional methodology and resources – Lack of pedagogical innovation
Positive qualities	**Strengths** – Innovative methodologies – Additional language resources	**Opportunities** – Effective training – Early skill introduction and development

Four different types of strategies can be developed from the SWOT analysis: defensive, guidance, offensive, and survival. First, by considering strengths together with threats, defensive strategies are proposed. These are commonly employed to react against threats by utilizing identified strengths. Thus, one strength of MT tools described by participants in this study is their potential for methodological innovation. Closely related to this is the threat that some teachers were reluctant to incorporate new technologies in their classroom for various reasons. One approach to dealing with this reluctance would be, therefore, to focus professional development on the opportunities for methodological innovation offered by MT tools.

Second, by considering weaknesses with opportunities, guidance strategies can also be proposed. These strategies aim to turn weaknesses into opportunities. One such strategy involves establishing coordinated pedagogical and collaborative networks for ESL teachers to encourage reflection and raise their interest in using these tools in the classroom. This would enable students to gain a deeper understanding of the appropriate uses of MT tools while, simultaneously, preventing learners from becoming overly dependent on them.

Third, by taking strengths and opportunities together, offensive strategies can also be developed. For example, the already strong undergraduate degree at the university could be strengthened further, including by designing and promoting innovative pedagogical projects focused on the integration of MT tools in its ESL classrooms. This would involve offering training courses and activities on MT tools as resources for reflection and development of critical thinking in students.

Finally, by focusing on weaknesses and threats, survival strategies can also be proposed. These strategies place the internal and external negative points at the core of the analysis. As a means of ensuring best practices are followed, weaknesses and threats could be periodically reviewed and updated, and networks or coordinated teaching groups could be created to focus on lines of improvement in response to these.

19.5 Discussion

Despite a wide range of studies investigating the use of MT tools in ESL and translation classrooms, there is very limited research on the subject in the context of ESL teaching in general, and in Spain particularly. As a step toward rectifying this situation, an exploratory mixed methods study was conducted to investigate Spanish ESL teachers' perceptions on the use of MT tools in the university classroom, including in terms of their views on the positive and negative qualities of these tools.

Findings show that most of the ESL teachers in our sample had a strong interest in technology. However, somewhat paradoxically, most did not use MT tools as resources in their teaching. This seeming contradiction arose from participants feeling like they had insufficient training in the use of MI tools—a finding echoed in a recent study by Tasdemir et al. (2023). The mostly young teachers in the current research were not familiar with these technologies in terms of training, knowledge, or incorporation in the ESL classroom. Thematic analysis of the open-ended questions also revealed that some respondents were reluctant to use these technologies because they believed they could potentially have a negative impact on their students' learning.

When SWOT analysis results are considered, in terms of positive qualities (i.e., strengths and opportunities), the introduction of MT tools opens up new pathways in ESL pedagogy, including the creation of more specific resources for language learning and curricular design (Chen, 2020). Most respondents foregrounded training as a key element for the successful inclusion of MT tools in the ESL classroom, a finding also highlighted by other studies (e.g., Klimova et al., 2023; Torres-Hostench, 2023).

With regard to negative qualities (i.e., weaknesses and threats), participants felt that the risk of students becoming overly dependent on MT tools and the lack of personalized feedback these technologies offer were problematic. In terms of the impact on students' learning, however, teachers' lack of interest in MT tools and excessive dependence on traditional methodologies can be identified as threats to their learners' preparedness for the job market. As noted in the previous section, effective training in MT tools for ESL teachers can be argued to be essential for their future workplace readiness.

19.6 Conclusion

Like all research, the current study is not without limitations. To begin, the above findings have limited external validity due to the quite small sample size, with this being especially the case for the sub-sample of only two participants who reported actually using MT and AI tools in their teaching practice. The small number of volunteers participating in the study means that self-selection bias is also a concern, with it being quite feasible that those teachers who did not participate may have significantly different behaviors and opinions than those who did. Finally, the fact that the researcher was also one of the respondents' colleagues means that issues of potential self-response bias cannot be ruled out.

Nevertheless, with these limitations acknowledged, this exploratory research presents a snapshot of the use of, and attitudes toward, MT tools in ESL teaching in a Spanish undergraduate translation degree program. In addition, it offers strategies for improvement in view of the relentless advance of technology. The hope is that this study will act as a starting point for subsequent research exploring the use of MT in undergraduate translation training both in Spain and beyond.

Acknowledgements This article was developed within the framework of the following research projects: "Multidimensional analysis of machine translation in the third sector" (PIUAH23/AH-11), funded by the University of Alcalá

(Madrid, Spain), and "Training app for post-editing neural machine translation using gamification in professional settings" (GAMETRAPP) (TED2021-129789B-I00), funded by the Spanish Ministry of Science and Innovation and the European Union (NextGenerationEU/PRTR).

Appendix: Questionnaire

Machine Translation in Language Learning (Undergraduate Degree in Modern Languages and Translation)

[Translated from the Original Spanish]

Section 1. Profile

1. Age
2. Gender
3. Nationality
4. Level of formal education or training
5. Indicate the number of years teaching this subject
6. Rate the interest you have in technology
   No interest (1) ←-----→ High interest (5)
7. Rate in order of importance the main content areas (i.e., vocabulary, grammar, culture, etc.) you teach as part of the syllabus:
   The least important (1) ←-----→ The most important (5)
8. Do you use MT or any AI system as resources when teaching the subject?
9. If your answer was "No", explain briefly why you do not use them as language learning resources.

Section 2. Machine Translation in the ESL Classroom

10. In general, what percentage of your time do you spend on using these tools when teaching ESL?

MT?	0–25%	26–50%	51–75%	76–100%
Other AI systems?	0–25%	26–50%	51–75%	76–100%

11. Which MT or AI systems do you use when teaching in your ESL classroom?
    Google Translate
    DeepL
    Systran
    Bing
    ChatGPT
    Gaby-T
    Gemini
    Other (Please, specify)

12. Specify the main tasks you use MT and AI tools for:
    To generate ideas (i.e., brainstorming activities)
    To translate
    To design and prepare other tasks
    To correct grammatical mistakes
    Other (please, specify)

13. Rate the use you make of MT and other AI systems in each of the four language skills:
    None (1) ←-----→ Highly used (5)
    Reading
    Listening
    Writing
    Speaking

14. In your opinion, what are the main advantages of including MT and AI tools as resources in the ESL classroom?

15. In your opinion, what are the main disadvantages of including MT and AI tools as resources in the ESL classroom?

16. Please indicate those issues that hinder the usefulness of MT and AI tools as resources in the ESL classroom in your opinion.

References

Alm, A. (2022). Actualizing the affordances of machine translation tools for language learning. In J. Colpaert, Y. Wang, & G. Stockwell (Eds.), *Proceedings of the XXIst International CALL Research Conference* (pp. 1–6). Castledown Publishers. https://doi.org/10.29140/9781914291050-1

Anderson, D. (1995). Machine translation as a tool in second language learning. *CALICO Journal, 13*(1), 68–97.

Ata, M., & Debreli, E. (2021). Machine translation in the language classroom: Turkish EFL learners' and instructors' perceptions and use. *IAFOR Journal of Education, 9*(4), 103–122. https://doi.org/10.22492/ije.9.4.06

Borsatti, D., & Blanco Riess, A. (2021). Using machine translator as a pedagogical resource in English for specific purposes courses in the academic context. *Revista de Estudos da Linguagem, 29*(22), 829–858.

Bryman, A. (2012). *Social research methods*. Oxford University Press.

Chen, W. (2020). Using Google Translate in an authentic translation task: The process, refinement efforts, and student perceptions. *Current Trends in Translation Teaching and Learning E, 7*, 213–238.

Clifford, J., Merschel, L., & Munné, J. (2013). Surveying the landscape: What is the role of machine translation in language learning? *@tic: Revista d'Innovació Educativa, 10*, 108–121.

Delorme Benites, A., Cotelli Kureth, S., Lehr, C., & Steele, E. (2021). Machine translation literacy: A panorama of practices at Swiss universities and implications for language teaching. In N. Zoghlami, C. Brudermann, C. Sarré, M. Grosbois, L. Bradley, & S. Thouësny (Eds.), *CALL and professionalisation: Short papers from EUROCALL 2021* (pp. 80–87). Research-publishing.net.

Ducar, C., & Schocket, D. H. (2018). Machine translation and the L2 classroom: Pedagogical solutions for making peace with Google Translate. *Foreign Language Annals, 51*(4), 779–795.

Fredholm, K. (2015). Online translation use in Spanish as a foreign language essay writing: Effects on fluency, complexity and accuracy. *Revista Nebrija de Lingüística Aplicada a la Enseñanza de las Lenguas, 18*, 7–24. https://doi.org/10.26378/rnlael918248

Garcia, I., & Pena, M. I. (2011). Machine translation-assisted language learning: Writing for beginners. *Computer Assisted Language Learning, 25*(5), 471–487. https://doi.org/10.1080/09588221.2011.582687

Gil Zafra, M. Á. (2001). Planificación estratégica: 'Método DAFO.' In T. R. Villasante, M. M. Serrano, & P. M. Gutiérrez (Eds.), *Prácticas locales de creatividad social* (pp. 123–136). El Viejo Topo.

Jolley, J. R., & Maimone, L. (2022). Thirty years of machine translation in language teaching and learning: A review of literature. *L2 Journal, 14*(1), 26–44. https://doi.org/10.5070/L214151760

Klimova, B., Pikhart, M., Delorme Benites, A., Lehr, C., & Sanchez-Stockhammer, C. (2023). Neural machine translation in foreign language teaching and learning: A systematic review. *Education and Information Technologies, 28*(1), 663–682. https://doi.org/10.1007/s10639-022-11194-2

Lee, S.-M. (2020). The impact of using machine translation on EFL students' writing. *Computer Assisted Language Learning, 33*(3), 157–175. https://doi.org/10.1080/09588221.2018.1553186

Mahardika, R. (2017). The use of translation tools in EFL learning? Do[1] machine translation give positive impact in language learning? *Pedagogy: Journal of English Language Teaching, 5*(1), 49–56. https://doi.org/10.32332/pedagogy.v5i1.755

Mellinger, C. D., & Hanson, T. A. (2021). Methodological considerations for survey research: Validity, reliability, and quantitative analysis. *Linguistica Antverpiensia, New Series—Themes in Translation Studies, 19*, 172–190. https://doi.org/10.52034/lanstts.v19i0.549

Moral López, A., Arrabal Gómez, J. M., & González López, I. (2010). Nuevas experiencias de evaluación estratégica en los centros educativos: La aplicación de una matriz DAFO en el centro de educación infantil y primaria 'mediterráneo' de Córdoba. *Estudios Sobre Educación, 18*, 165–200. https://doi.org/10.15581/004.18.4658

Niño, A. (2008). Evaluating the use of machine translation post-editing in the foreign language class. *Computer Assisted Language Learning, 21*(1), 29–49. https://doi.org/10.1080/09588220701865482

Niño, A. (2009). Machine translation in foreign language learning: Language learners' and tutors' perceptions of its advantages and disadvantages. *ReCALL, 21*(2), 241–258.

Niño, A. (2020). Exploring the use of online machine translation for independent language learning. *Research in Learning Technology, 28*, 1–32. https://doi.org/10.25304/rlt.v28.2402

---

[1] The published article includes this typo.

Plaza Lara, C. (2019). Análisis DAFO sobre la inclusión de la traducción automática y la posedición en los másteres de la red EMT. *JosTrans—The Journal of Specialised Translation, 31*, 260–280.

Plaza Lara, C., & Bobadilla-Perez, M. (2024). Finding spaces for improvement in the didactic use of audiovisual translation in the ESL classroom: The case of the TRADILEX project. *Parallélles, 36*(1), 217–233. https://doi.org/10.17462/PARA.2024.01.13

Polakova, P., & Klimova, B. (2023). Using DeepL translator in learning English as an applied foreign language—An empirical pilot study. *Heliyon, 9*(8), e18595. https://doi.org/10.1016/j.heliyon.2023.e18595

Resende, N., & Way, A. (2020). MTrill project: Machine translation impact on language learning. In A. Martins, H. Moniz, S. Fumega, B. Martins, F. Batista, L. Coheur, C. Parra, I. Trancoso, M. Turchi, A. Bisazza, J. Moorkens, A. Guerberof, M. Nurminen, L. Marg, & M. L. Forcada (Eds.), *Proceedings of the 22nd Annual Conference of the European Association for Machine Translation* (pp. 497–498). European Association for Machine Translation. https://aclanthology.org/2020.eamt-1.69.pdf

Sánchez Ramos, M. M. (2022). La integración de la traducción automática y la posedición en la traducción jurídica: Un análisis DAFO para su implantación en la formación de traducción e interpretación en los servicios públicos. *Revista de Llengua i Dret – Journal of Language and Law, 78*, 121–137. https://doi.org/10.2436/rld.i78.2022.3687

Stapleton, P., & Ka Kin, B. L. (2019). Assessing the accuracy and teachers' impressions of Google Translate: A study of primary L2 writers in Hong Kong. *English for Specific Purposes, 56*, 18–34. https://doi.org/10.1016/j.esp.2019.07.001

Tasdemir, S., Lopez, E., Satar, M., & Riches, N. (2023). Teachers' perceptions of machine translation as a pedagogical tool. *The JALT CALL Journal, 19*(1), 92–112. https://doi.org/10.29140/jaltcall.v19n1.24

Torres-Hostench, O. (2023). Integrating machine translation literacy skills in language learning. In Ó. Ferreiro-Vázquez, A. T. Varajão Moutinho Pereira, & S. Lima Gonçalves Araújo (Eds.), *Technological innovation put to the service of language learning, translation and interpreting: Insights from academic and professional contexts* (pp. 79–92). Peter Lang.

Zaretzkaya, A., Corpas Pastor, G., & Seghiri, M. (2018). User perspectives on translation tools: Findings of a user survey. In G. Corpas Pastor & I. Durán Muñoz (Eds.), *Trends in e-tools and resources for translators and interpreters* (pp. 37–56). Brill-Rodopi.

Zhang, H., & Torres-Hostench, O. (2022). Training in machine-translation post-editing for foreign language students. *Language Learning & Technology, 26*(1), 1–17.

Ziegler, N., & González-Lloret, M. (Eds.). (2022). *The Routledge handbook of second language acquisition and technology*. Routledge.

20

Exploring the Use and Perception of Machine Translation in Language Learning: A Study in a Japanese High School Immersion Program

Lauren Walker and Carl Vollmer

20.1 Introduction

In a globalizing world, the need to transfer messages and ideas between languages has significantly increased. This has led to extensive development of machine translation (MT) technology in terms of accessibility, quality of output, and application (Jiménez-Crespo, 2017; Jolley & Maimone, 2022; Lee, 2023). While MT has many potential uses in the language classroom, it has often been met with skepticism by teachers (Lee, 2020, 2023). As a potentially beneficial tool for language instruction, it is vital that MT be researched further so that it can be more fully understood and implemented to the greatest benefit for language learners.

L. Walker · C. Vollmer (✉)
Ritsumeikan Uji Junior and Senior High School, Uji, Japan
e-mail: cvollmer@ujc.ritsumei.ac.jp

L. Walker
e-mail: walkerl@ujc.ritsumei.ac.jp

If MT is to be further implemented in language classrooms, it is important for teachers to be willing to allow and encourage its use. However, there are valid concerns on the part of teachers about the acceptability and use of MT by their learners (Groves & Mundt, 2021; Vinall & Hellmich, 2021). Currently, MT presents a complex issue which poses more questions than answers.

For these reasons, this study explored student perceptions of MT through three stages of a study abroad program at a private high school in Japan. Three separate surveys were administered to different student cohorts, before, immediately after, and one year after study abroad. This approach provided a deeper understanding of how and why MT was utilized by students. An additional aim for this investigation was to observe if study abroad or the rigors of an English immersion environment influenced how students perceived MT. Additionally, the findings inform further recommendations for how to effectively implement MT in language learning classrooms.

20.2 Literature Review

One concern that is frequently raised by educators is the fear that learners will overuse MT, relying on the technology to do the work for them. Teachers often voice their worry that MT is used to conceal the inability of learners to correctly use the target language (Vinall & Hellmich, 2021). Such uses of MT make it difficult for teachers to know the exact level that they should be teaching to, as well as to fully trust the output of learners. Additionally, teachers worry that if learners are overusing MT, their overall development will be negatively impacted (Lee, 2023; Stapleton & Ka Kin, 2019).

Another teacher concern is that learners will use MT in a way that cannot be detected. If the teacher is not able to detect the use of MT, assignments and tasks within a course could be completed with little effort on the part of the learners. Additionally, if its use is not found, there is no consequence for learners having used MT.

Stapleton and Ka Kin (2019) found that, when asked to assess scripts, most teachers were unable to identify texts written using MT. In recent years, MT technology has improved even further, making human detection more difficult. This makes fully trusting texts produced by learners more challenging. One way that teachers can identify texts for which students have overutilized MT is by noticing advanced vocabulary or extended sections of advanced grammar with no errors. However, programs such as ChatGPT can now be instructed to write in simplified language, within the range of learners' abilities, and can also produce grammar errors if prompted to do so. This poses a further challenge to teachers' ability to detect texts that may be written using MT.

While teachers have concerns about MT, a number of studies have indicated that it can be valuable in the language learning process. Studies have shown that MT has a positive effect on learners' lexical and grammatical accuracy, as well as syntactic complexity (Lee, 2023). For example, Niño (2008) found that MT was especially valuable for helping learners in the editing process and notably found that MT benefited advanced learners. Lee (2020) also reported that learners made improvements to the quality of their writing based on MT suggestions about drafts. Furthermore, Fredholm (2019) observed that using MT helped learners to produce more varied vocabulary in their writing, although results did not show that the effects were long lasting, while O'Neill (2019) found that training learners how to use MT for their writing drafts helped to improve the quality of their writing.

Learner perceptions of MT have been the subject of several recent studies (Alm & Watanabe, 2022; Briggs, 2018). Lee (2023) reported that, while learners may use MT for studying, they are cautious about the accuracy of the output provided. Alm and Watanabe (2022) observed that learners with non-alphabetic L1s were less trusting of MT output, which aligns with Briggs (2018), who found that Korean university learners were unlikely to trust the output of MT. This lack of trust may be a relief to teachers, as it shows that learners are not solely relying on MT but, instead, are critically considering the accuracy of its output.

With regards to MT as a language learning tool, learners are more willing to accept and incorporate MT than teachers. For example, Briggs (2018) claimed that most learners believed MT did not negatively affect language learning and should be allowed for classroom use. Alm and Watanabe (2022) also argue that learners believe MT to be a useful learning tool, as many of the students in their survey reported MT was valuable for searching for vocabulary, writing, and editing. In contrast, in Stapleton and Ka Kin's (2019) survey of teacher perceptions, it was found that all respondents had concerns about the negative effect of MT on students' language development and almost half of those teachers did not consider that MT had a place in the classroom.

In line with earlier research (Alm & Watanabe, 2022; Briggs, 2018; Zhou et al., 2022), this study conducted surveys to measure students' perceptions and use of MT. While there is a growing body of research on MT, most research has been conducted within university contexts, limiting the ability of such studies to comment on the development or growth of perceptions of MT at the secondary level. Understanding how secondary students perceive MT can help develop a more comprehensive understanding of how learner perceptions of MT evolve. Therefore, this current study implemented surveys across all three years of a study abroad program, exploring how learner language proficiency, educational demands, and overall trust of MT changed before and after studying abroad in an English-speaking country. The research questions addressed are:

1. How do learners utilize MT while studying English?
2. In what ways does the academic context affect the use of MT by learners?
3. Does study abroad experience and/or the additional demands of extensive study in English impact the use of MT?

20.3 Methodology

20.3.1 Context

The data for this study were collected from a private high school in Japan. The school offers three distinct courses. First, the Japanese government curriculum in Japanese, with English as an ESL subject for most students, and elements of a "non-traditional type C" international school, as described by Hayden and Thompson (2013). There are also two courses with a greater focus on English in their curriculum, including an International Baccalaureate (IB) program and an English-medium immersion program. The focus of this study is students enrolled in the immersion program.

20.3.2 Participants

The immersion program spans three years and is designed to prepare students for a year-long study abroad program in English-speaking countries, beginning in the first year of high school and extending into the middle of the second year. The preparatory curriculum includes seven hours of EFL (English as a Foreign Language), four hours of CLIL (Content and Language Integrated Learning) classes, and 20 hours of classes taught in Japanese, adhering to the standard Japanese curriculum. Each academic year, students are divided into three groups, each participating in an 11-month study abroad experience in Canada, Australia, or New Zealand.

Upon entry into the program, a wide range of English proficiency levels is evident among students, with TOEFL scores spanning from 360 to 550. After spending the second year at schools abroad and living with local host families, students return to Japan, where most of their classes are taught in English, including subjects like history and science. The curriculum for the second year includes 16 hours of classes taught in English and 14 hours of Japanese language classes. Post-study abroad, TOEFL scores typically increase, with scores of participants in this study ranging from 423 to 590.

In the third year, the program intensifies the language immersion experience, including additional subjects taught in English, amounting to 17 hours per week, alongside 13 hours of Japanese language classes. The TOEFL scores for the third-year cohort ranged from 410 to 580, with an average of 502.

20.3.3   Instrument and Data Collection

A digital survey (see Appendix) was developed by the researchers to address the research questions. The surveys were available in both English and Japanese (the participants' L1) and was modeled on the survey used by Briggs (2018). Each survey varied slightly according to year level, comprising three sections for first-year students and four for second- and third-year students.

In the first section, students reported their highest TOEFL scores within a specified range. The second section consisted of multiple-choice questions intended to identify the MT tools participants used, their frequency and reasons for use. The third section included five Likert-style questions to assess attitudes toward MT tools. A fourth section was added to the second- and third-year student surveys and included two additional Likert-style questions to explore perceptions of changes in MT tool use throughout the program. The fourth section was not included in the first-year survey, as students had not yet experienced study abroad and were still in the initial stages of the program and therefore would not have any perceived changes to report on.

Response options for all Likert-style questions were: Strongly Agree (5), Agree (4), Neutral (3), Disagree (2), Strongly Disagree (1). The survey also included an optional open-ended, short-answer question for second- and third-year students that allowed them to explain any perceived changes in attitude.

After receiving required permission from the school, the surveys were distributed during class by the researchers with completion taking approximately ten minutes. All potential participants were told of the survey's voluntary nature, the anonymity of responses, and that results might be reported in academic fora. First-year students were surveyed before their departure for the study abroad component, second-year students upon their return to Japan, and third-year students after nine months into the curriculum. In total, 37 first years, 53 second years, and 34 third-year students completed the survey.

20.3.4 Data Analysis

The analysis of the quantitative data gathered from the survey primarily involved frequency counts to determine the prevalence of specific responses across different questions. This approach allowed the researchers to quantify the usage patterns, preferences, and attitudes toward MT tools among the students. Additionally, comparative analyses were conducted between groups, specifically comparing first-, second- and third-year students to identify any trends or significant changes in responses over the course of their academic progression. For the qualitative data collected from the short-answer questions, a thematic analysis was employed and emergent themes were identified. Responses were reviewed by the researchers to extract insights regarding students' change in attitudes toward MT.

20.4 Results

20.4.1 First-Year Students

First-year results reveal an average TOEFL score range of 400–419. In terms of MT tool usage, DeepL emerged as the most popular choice, with 64.9% of respondents using it, followed closely by Google Translate at 62.2%. ChatGPT was the third most frequently used option, with 24.3% of students using it for translation purposes.

Regarding the frequency of MT tool use in school, 51.4% of respondents utilized MT a few times a week or occasionally (see Fig. 20.1). The remaining half was divided between daily users (24.3%) and those who used the tools less than once a week (24.3%). When students were asked about their purpose for using MT tools in school, 86.5% reported using them to search for lexical meaning. Additionally, 59.5% used the tools to translate Japanese into English.

Outside of school, the primary use of MT was for searching for lexical meanings (83.3%). For school assignments, 55.6% used these tools for English reading assignments, 50.0% for English writing assignments,

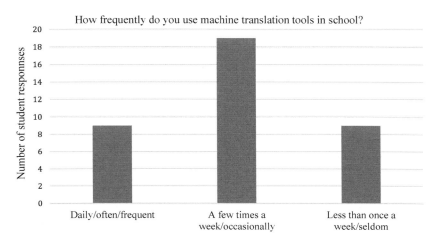

Fig. 20.1 First-year student responses on the frequency of using MT

and 36.1% for English-speaking assignments. Only 2.8% stated that they did not use MT tools for assignments.

When asked about the reasons for using MT tools in assignments, 63.9% selected "To improve the quality of my assignments". 13.9% of students cited the need to use these tools when they could not complete an assignment otherwise, and 11.1% mentioned using them to complete assignments more quickly.

A majority of students (70.3%) view electronic translation tools as valuable learning tools for English. In regards to use of MT outside of school, the majority of first-year students (70.3%) reported that they needed to use MT to complete various daily tasks a few times a week.

First-year students generally held neutral views about the output of translation tools, suggesting a balanced perspective between trust and distrust (see Fig. 20.2). The students clearly showed a negative perception of the accuracy of their own translation ability in comparison to MT. This was shown by their response to the statement "I trust the accuracy of my own Japanese-English translations more than electronic translations", with 40.5% of students reporting a "Neutral" view, while 51.3% selected either "Disagree" or "Strongly Disagree". Student experiences with electronic translators for English assignments have been generally positive, with the highest percentage of respondents (45.9%) in the "Agree" category, indicating moderate trust. More than half of students were confident that they would be able to identify errors made by translation tools, with 53.0% indicating that they were either confident, or somewhat confident, that they would notice.

When the dataset was examined for possible links between TOEFL scores and utilization of MT tools, certain tendencies were revealed. Students were categorized based on their TOEFL scores into three levels: lower level (340–399), medium level (400–419), and higher level (420–459). While the responses across these groups did not show large differences, a few distinct patterns emerged. Higher-level students demonstrated a broader array of use of MT tools, notably including using them for the comprehension of foreign websites. They also mentioned using these tools for a variety of speaking assignments, such as presentations and debates. However, lower-level students primarily focused on reading and writing assignments. Students with higher TOEFL scores also showed greater confidence overall in identifying errors in machine-generated translations. These observations suggest that, as students'

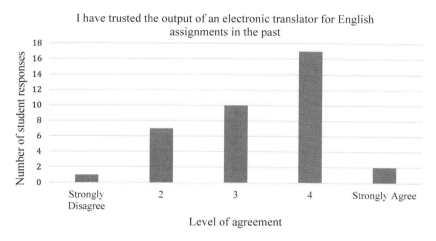

Fig. 20.2 First-year student trust of output of MT for English assignments

English proficiency increases, so does the diversity in their use of translation tools and their confidence in critically evaluating the accuracy of these tools.

20.4.2 Second-Year Students

The TOEFL score distribution among the second-year students is as follows: the largest portion (30.19%) scored between 420 and 439, followed by 20.75% scoring between 400 and 419, and 13.21% between 440 and 459.

When asked about their choice of MT tools, Google Translate, and DeepL were the most popular (see Fig. 20.3). DeepL is used by 83.0% of students, while Google Translate is used by 67.9%. A smaller percentage of students use Chat GPT (7.5%) compared to first-year students (24.3%). Other translation tool options were only used by a very small percentage of respondents, which suggests a preference for well-known, reliable translation tools among the majority of students.

The frequency of MT tool use in school for second-year students varied. A majority (64.2%) used these tools a few times a week or

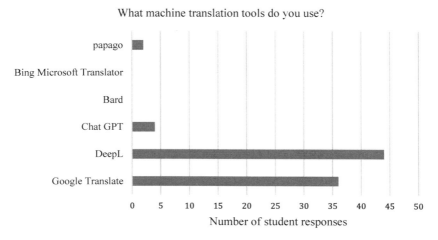

Fig. 20.3 Translation programs used by second-year students

occasionally, while 22.6% used them less than once a week or seldom, and 13.2% used them daily or often. This suggests that, while these tools were regularly used by students, daily reliance on them was not widespread.

Regarding the primary use of these tools in school, the most common response (94.2%) was searching for lexical meanings, followed by translating English to Japanese (46.2%) and translating Japanese to English (40.4%). These findings suggest a focused use of translation tools for specific language challenges rather than a broader application. The most common response fitting the broad application category was using translation tools to understand foreign websites (30.8%). The least selected category was to communicate, with only 9.6% of students using translation tools for this purpose. In terms of the types of assignments in which students utilized these tools, the majority primarily used them for English writing assignments (66.0%) and English reading assignments (62.3%) (see Fig. 20.4). Speaking assignments were less frequently seen as requiring the input of translation tools, with only 32.1% of students selecting this option.

Regarding their reasons for using MT tools, the majority of students (80.4%) reported that it was to improve the quality of their assignments.

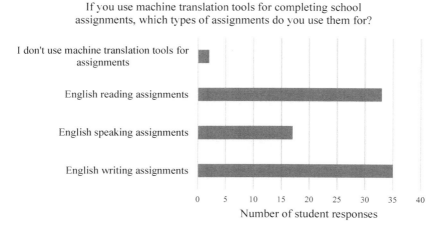

Fig. 20.4 Types of assignments that second-year students use MT to complete

The next most popular options were "to reduce the time it takes for me to complete assignments" and "because I feel like I can't complete the English assignments without using them", with 7.5% selecting these options. For this cohort, the percentage of students who use MT tools to improve their grades is higher than the first grade (80.4% second year, 63.9% first year), despite the overall English level of students being higher.

For MT tool use outside of school, almost all learners (90.6%) use them to search for lexical meanings, with the next most chosen categories being general study (37.7%) and translation (34.0%). Around 24.5% reported that they also used these tools to communicate with English speakers, which is only slightly higher than reported for first-year students prior to their study abroad (13.9%).

The majority of second-year students (75.5%) reported a neutral or slightly negative view of the statement "I trust the output of an electronic translator for English learning writing assignments". Students had similarly neutral and/or negative views in response to statements asking them to rate their trust in the accuracy of their own Japanese-English and English-Japanese translations compared to electronic translators. Overall, students had slightly less trust in their own English-Japanese translations with 43.3% either disagreeing or strongly disagreeing with the statement "I trust the accuracy of my own English-Japanese translations more than electronic translations", compared to 35.9% in response to the statement "I trust the accuracy of my own English-Japanese translations more than electronic translations" (see Fig. 20.5).

Despite this limited trust in their own translation ability compared to electronic translators, more than half of the participants (52.4%) stated that they either agree or strongly agree with the statement, "If the electronic translator makes an error, I am likely to notice".

The survey also examined changes in usage patterns after studying abroad. A notable 47.1% of respondents reported using translation tools less frequently while they were abroad than they did in Japan, while 30.2% used them to about the same degree. Those using them more frequently constituted 22.6% of the second-year sample. These findings suggest that experiences abroad may lead to decreased reliance on translation tools. In terms of attitudes and opinions, the majority (64.2%)

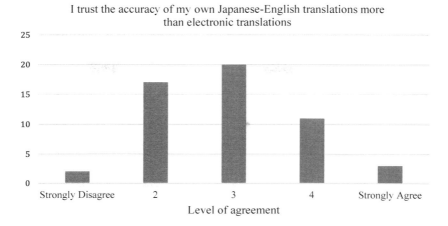

Fig. 20.5 Second-year student perception of their own translation accuracy

reported no change in their view of MT tools. However, 30.2% had a lowered opinion, and a small minority of 5.6% viewed these tools more favorably. This indicates that, while most students' perceptions remain unchanged, a significant portion may develop a critical view of these tools over time.

Thirty of the second-year students responded to the optional open-ended question, "If there has been a change in your use or opinion of MT tools, why do you think this is?" One of the more common responses here was that these participants realized that translation tools produce sentences which are not natural language, as shown in Table 20.1.

Another significant proportion of students answered that their opinion of translation tools had changed to be slightly more negative because they felt that excessive use would limit their ability to learn (see Table 20.2).

Table 20.1   Reasons for changes in perception of MT by second-year students

I learned many English words and how to use them, and realized that writing sentences using a translator often resulted in awkward sentences
I use translation tools to search the vocabulary, but native speakers don't speak sentences like translation tools
I was spending a lot of time in NZ so I could know that transition tools are not exact

Table 20.2 Negative changes in perception of MT by second-year students

If you rely on it too much, you won't grow
It would be better for me if I could speak English without using it
I didn't improve my English skills because I used too many translation tools

20.4.3 Third-Year Students

The survey of third-grade students revealed an average TOEFL score within the 500–519 range. DeepL stood out as the preferred MT tool, used by around 94.0% of the respondents, with Google Translate being the second choice at 41.0%. ChatGPT ranked third, utilized by 8.8% of students for translation. Although students were not required to give reasons for their choices, the low of ChatGPT could be due to school policy which prohibited AI usage but allowed for mainstream translation applications such as DeepL and Google Translate. Teachers in the program had particularly stressed the importance of this policy for this cohort.

A majority (67.6%) of the students used MT tools in school a few times a week or occasionally. A smaller group (14.7%) used them less than once a week, while 17.6% used them daily or often. The primary use of these tools, as indicated by 79.4% of the students, was for searching for lexical meanings. Large portions of this sample also used them for translating from English to Japanese (41.2%) and for comprehending foreign websites (44.1%), with the latter showing a notable increase compared to first- and second-year students.

Regarding assignments, the most common application of translation tools was for English writing tasks (46.9%), followed by speaking (25.0%) and reading assignments (25.0%). Interestingly, 15.6% of third-year students reported not using translation tools for assignments, which is a higher percentage than the 5.6% in the first grade and 3.8% in the second grade, possibly reflecting improved English proficiency.

Outside of school, the predominant uses for MT tools were for lexical searches (79.4%) and translations (26.5%), with 23.5% using these tools for communication with English speakers—a figure consistent with the second-year findings but higher than the first-year's 13.9%

(see Fig. 20.6). For these activities, 61.8% of students reported using translation tools a few times a week or less, with 26.5% using them less than once a week.

Shifting focus to student perspectives on translation tools, third-year students presented a wider variety of reasons for using these tools than their first- and second-year peers. The predominant motive was to improve the quality of their assignments, with time-saving during assignment completion being the second most cited reason. When asked to provide their own explanations for this, a number of respondents mentioned utilizing the tools specifically for looking up individual words in the context of school assignments.

In comparison to first and second-year students, a larger percentage of third-year students (35.3%) agreed with the idea that "Reliance upon electronic translators is a detriment to language learning". However, a large majority (86.7%) still recognized the occasional necessity of using electronic translators to complete various tasks.

Concerning trust in the accuracy of electronic translators for English learning assignments, 79.4% of third-year students expressed skepticism, reflecting either a neutral or negative stance. This result aligns with the findings of Zhou et al. (2022) that students do critically analyze the

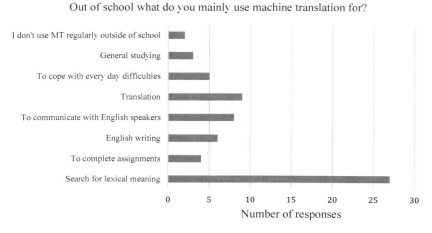

Fig. 20.6 Third-year student responses on what MT is used for outside of school

output of MT and do not just simply accept the result of the translation. Their confidence in translating Japanese to English, and vice versa, without electronic assistance was viewed neutrally to positively by 67.0% of respondents. Further, a large majority (58.8%) were confident in their ability to detect errors made by translators, with only 17.6% doubting their capability.

Reflecting on their usage over three years of an immersion course, the majority of these learners (73.5%) reported the highest usage of translation tools during their first year. A smaller segment (17.6%) felt they relied on these tools most while studying abroad, and 8.8% reported consistent use throughout the program. None of the students reported the highest use during their third year, despite it being the period with the most immersion class hours.

Twenty of the 34 third-year students who responded to the open-ended question highlighted reduced reliance on translation tools as a result of improved English proficiency. Some examples of students' comments are shown in Table 20.3.

Additionally, a significant number of students echoed sentiments from the second grade, suggesting that excessive reliance on translation tools could hinder their language learning progress, as evidenced by Table 20.4.

Table 20.3 Changes in reliance on MT by third-year students

My vocabulary has increased and I can now complete and read English sentences without having to look up vocabulary
After returning to Japan, I started using it less frequently. I feel a little more confident in my grammar skills
When you become confident in your English grammar, you will no longer need to rely on translation tools

Table 20.4 Third-year student responses about excessive reliance on MT

I thought that if I used it too much because it was convenient, it would not lead to my growth
I used it quite a bit in my first year, but I started to think that relying on it all the time wouldn't help improve my English skills

These insights demonstrate a growing awareness among students of the balance needed between tool usage and language acquisition, reflecting a nuanced understanding of the role of technology in learning.

20.5 Discussion and Implications

The data from these surveys reveal nuanced perspectives among students across different years of study regarding their use and perception of MT. These findings resonate with the broader discussion in the literature, which often portrays both benefits and challenges of integrating MT into language learning environments (Jolley & Maimone, 2022; Lee, 2023).

Firstly, the higher levels of reliance on MT, as reported by the first-year students, align with the literature that MT can support language learning, especially, as noted by Fredholm (2019), in enhancing lexical breadth in students' writing. Data revealed a gradual decrease in reliance on MT tools, as students progressed through the program and their language proficiency improved. This suggests a maturation in which students move from a more dependent use of MT to a more selective and strategic use of technology. This trajectory supports the argument for MT as a potentially beneficial tool in the language classroom, particularly when used judiciously and as part of a broader array of learning strategies (Lee, 2023; Niño, 2008).

As MT use by students has increased, so has the necessity of teachers accurately identifying its overuse. However, the burden of proof on teachers can be challenging, especially without sufficient training. Therefore, ideally, teachers should be trained on how to detect MT to support and assess their students. Studies have shown that, without training, teachers have little success in being able to detect learners' use of MT (Stapleton & Ka Kin, 2019). Additionally, in many schools, teachers must provide evidence of students' overuse of MT, which can be difficult without a student's direct admission. The challenges of detection of MT use are more difficult with highly proficient language users, like the third-year student cohort. These students sometimes used advanced vocabulary terms in essays, often a sign of MT use. However, upon further investigation, the students accurately explained the words, displaying a high level of language acquisition. Currently, the pedagogical support and research resources to assist or train teachers in MT detection are lacking. Yet, with MT technology quickly improving, it is vital that teachers develop the knowledge, skills, and resources necessary to effectively manage the complexities and benefits provided by MT.

In addition to teacher training in detection, teachers could benefit significantly from training in how to integrate MT into language teaching. The widespread use of MT among students, combined with their overall neutral level of trust toward its output, implies that learners could be amenable to learning how to engage with technology more critically. If teachers were able to learn the different capabilities of MT tools and how to design activities that encourage critical engagement with technology, this would help students to use MT as a complement to their learning rather than a substitute for it (Alm & Watanabe, 2022). This can be achieved through activities that involve comparing MT-generated texts with human translations and discussing nuances and errors that technology may introduce. It would also be beneficial for teachers to emphasize that, while MT can be useful for initial drafts or understanding complex texts, students should focus on using translation tools for individual words and phrases to better develop their language skills.

Additionally, teachers might consider tailoring their use of MT and the message they convey about it to match their students' proficiency levels. As the survey results indicate, student reliance on, and perception of, MT evolve as their language skills improve. Early-stage learners may benefit more from MT for comprehension and drafting while advanced learners may use MT more effectively for refining their use of language for specific tasks such as editing. While this study cannot conclusively argue for MT being more useful for a particular proficiency level, it does provide an additional nuance, namely that students with different levels of proficiency may find different MT functions useful. This finding may provide some of the clarity required to help reach consensus regarding the suitability of MT for various proficiency levels (Lee, 2023).

This study has several limitations that warrant consideration in future research. Firstly, its reliance on survey results as the sole method of data collection limited the depth of consideration for student experiences with MT tools. Although these types of surveys provide valuable quantitative, and even a degree of qualitative, insights into broad patterns of usage and perceptions, more extensive qualitative methods, such as interviews and focus groups could offer more detailed accounts of how students engage with MT. Additionally, the study's scope is limited to a specific educational context—a private high school in Japan with a distinct immersion program. This context, while insightful, cannot be generalized further than this specific context. Moreover, the study relied on self-reported data, which is prone to experience a certain degree of unreliability, as respondents may overestimate their proficiency or underreport their reliance on MT due to perceived expectations. Finally, due to design restraints, our study could not track changes in students' MT use and perceptions over time through a longitudinal design, which would provide insights into how these aspects evolve with continued language development and exposure to different educational experiences.

Addressing these limitations in future research would enhance understanding of the role of MT in language learning and teaching. Thus, it is recommended that further research be conducted to explore the beliefs that learners have regarding MT, and how educators can better control, monitor, and guide learners to use MT as a language learning tool.

20.6 Conclusion

In conclusion, this study highlights the interplay between secondary student use and perceptions of MT tools and their language learning development. Through examination of the survey data, it was found that most students in this context used MT as a tool in their studies. However, the extent to which MT was utilized and trusted varied, with first-year students relying on it more before studying abroad, and then students in the second and third years gradually relying on MT less as they experienced study abroad and developed their language proficiency. When aligning these insights with the existing literature, it becomes clear that there is a need for a more nuanced approach to integrating technology into language education. Teachers will inevitably play a crucial role in navigating this landscape, guiding students to use technology in ways that enhance their learning while also developing their independent language skills. By thoughtfully integrating MT into language learning classes and tailoring pedagogical strategies to match learners' levels, it may be possible to use this technology to improve language learning for the future.

Appendix

1st year survey—https://forms.gle/RNxeVwpjPQWoN9G4A
   2nd year survey—https://forms.gle/EdERQNMK8vMev4wv8
   3rd year survey—https://forms.gle/e5QsGPALFRm7Y4dy9

References

Alm, A., & Watanabe, Y. (2022). Online machine translation for L2 writing across languages and proficiency levels. *Australian Journal of Applied Linguistics, 5*(3), 135–157. https://doi.org/10.29140/ajal.v5n3.53si3

Briggs, N. (2018). Neural machine translation tools in the language learning classroom: Students' use, perceptions, and analyses. *JALT CALL Journal, 14*(1), 3–24. https://doi.org/10.29140/jaltcall.v14n1.221

Fredholm, K. (2019). Effects of Google Translate on lexical diversity: Vocabulary development among learners of Spanish as a foreign language. *Revista Nebrija de Lingüística Aplicada a la Enseñanza de las Lenguas, 13*(26), 98–117. https://doi.org/10.26378/rnlael1326300

Groves, M., & Mundt, K. (2021). A ghostwriter in the machine? Attitudes of academic staff towards machine translation use in internationalised higher education. *Journal of English for Academic Purposes, 50*, 1–11. https://doi.org/10.1016/j.jeap.2021.100957

Hayden, M., & Thompson, J. J. (2013). International schools: Antecedents, current issues and metaphors for the future. In R. Pearce (Ed.), *International education and schools: Moving beyond the first 40 years* (pp. 3–23). Bloomsbury.

Jiménez-Crespo, M. A. (2017). The role of translation technologies in Spanish language learning. *Journal of Spanish Language Teaching, 4*(2), 181–193. https://doi.org/10.1080/23247797.2017.1408949

Jolley, J. R., & Maimone, L. (2022). Thirty years of machine translation in language teaching and learning: A review of the literature. *L2 Journal, 14*(1), 26–44. https://doi.org/10.5070/L214151760

Lee, S.-M. (2020). The impact of using machine translation on EFL students' writing. *Computer Assisted Language Learning, 33*(3), 157–175. https://doi.org/10.1080/09588221.2018.1553186

Lee, S.-M. (2023). The effectiveness of machine translation in foreign language education: A systematic review and meta-analysis. *Computer Assisted Language Learning, 36*(1–2), 103–125. https://doi.org/10.1080/09588221.2021.1901745

Niño, A. (2008). Evaluating the use of machine translation post-editing in the foreign language class. *Computer Assisted Language Learning, 21*(1), 29–49. https://doi.org/10.1080/09588220701865482

O'Neill, E. M. (2019). Training students to use online translators and dictionaries: The impact on second language writing scores. *International Journal of Research Studies in Language Learning, 8*(2), 47–65. https://doi.org/10.5861/ijrsll.2019.4002

Stapleton, P., & Ka Kin, B. L. (2019). Assessing the accuracy and teachers' impressions of Google Translate: A study of primary L2 writers in Hong Kong. *English for Specific Purposes, 56*, 18–34. https://doi.org/10.1016/j.esp.2019.07.001

Vinall, K., & Hellmich, E. A. (2021). Down the rabbit hole: Machine translation, metaphor, and instructor identity and agency. *Second Language Research & Practice, 2*(1), 99–118. http://hdl.handle.net/10125/69860

Zhou, S., Zhao, S., & Groves, M. (2022). Towards a digital bilingualism? Students' use of machine translation in international higher education. *Journal of English for Academic Purposes, 60*, 101193. https://doi.org/10.1016/j.jeap.2022.101193

21

Empowering ESL Translation Studies: Integrating Machine Translation for Enhanced Language Proficiency and Productivity

Gayane R. Hovhannisyan⑩, Kristina A. Harutyunova, Hayk B. Hambardzumyan, and Srbuhi Aydinyan

21.1 Introduction

In the realm of global communication, most languages are evolving as a natural extension of local cultures alongside the prominence of English. Although the situation was markedly different a few decades ago, over time English language learning has generally overcome the need to integrate culture into its concepts, instead focusing on such specialist fields as science and professional communication and ethics. As a consequence, the juxtaposition of Global English versus Local Language transformed into a situation where Global English caters to the common communication environment while local languages maintain the ecology of cultural and linguistic diversity. Consequently, the integration of English into

G. R. Hovhannisyan (✉) · K. A. Harutyunova · H. B. Hambardzumyan · S. Aydinyan
Brusov State University, Yerevan, Armenia
e-mail: grhovhannisyan@bryusov.am

437

D. Coulson and C. Denman (eds.), *Translation, Translanguaging and Machine Translation in Foreign Language Education*,
https://doi.org/10.1007/978-3-031-82174-5_21

global communication, science, and technology has increased the importance of translation. It is the logical extension of learning English as a global language for the outer and expanding circles of communication (Al-Mutairi, 2019).

Translation has now become a highly sought-after academic program at many universities. At Brusov State Pedagogical Institute of Foreign Languages, Armenia, which has over eight decades of higher linguistic education tradition, English language teacher training was the most popular five-year program up to the end of the 1980s. Later, after joining the Bologna process, the institute grew into a University of Languages and Social Sciences, where a strong curriculum in foreign languages laid the basis for its novel bilingual and trilingual qualifications. English Language Teaching (ELT) remains one of the most in demand programs at the university, offering potential combinations with another 12 or so foreign languages, or a specialization in such areas as Public Administration, Journalism, Hospitality and Service, Tourism, Political Science.

The high level of interest in translation as a specialization in Armenian linguistics education emerged in the early 2000s when it became clearly accepted that merely knowing a foreign language was not, in fact, a profession. This was a principal reconceptualization of linguistic education, although one that was essentially in line with global trends at the time. Moreover, the emergence of Information Technology (IT) and AI technologies added new professional interest spheres to the list of foreign language and communication qualifications, with media translation and machine translation (MT) editing joining it more recently.

With Machine Learning (ML) and MT developing rapidly within the speech communication and intercultural spheres, the profession of English translation in low-resource and minority languages has acquired new features, underscoring such competencies as technology-assisted translation and MT error analysis and editing. In turn, these professions require learning, teaching, and translation resources, with the result that, in Armenia, Armenian-English bidirectional corpus development has been brought forward as a priority.

Corpus development is vital for a low-resource language, and universities have to acknowledge this demand by upgrading and offering not only programs and training in translation and interpretation, but also incorporating a strong technology component to bridge the growing gap between the global information market and local cultural communication environments. Unsurprisingly, the rise of interest in translation studies is linked with the spread of computer-assisted tools (CAT) and now there is a reason to call them MT tools. While these tools reduce the time and effort required for translation, they come with new challenges in terms of quality and relevance to human needs and contexts.

Subsequently, it would be appropriate to state that human mediation between MT and culturally and socially sensitive knowledge is emerging as a well-defined profession of "translation editor". These changes have also reshaped the content and structure of university English Communication programs, as well as various social professions including hospitality, service, journalism, education, psychology, law, economics, science, and other culture-specific social communication roles, in which English has become increasingly integral. Finding a balance between English in global communication and the necessity of maintaining the functionality of minority languages like Armenian requires innovative solutions in education in linguistics at the university level. Translation studies programs can respond to this demand through the modernization of methods and technologies.

Advances in ML, AI, and Large Language Models are associated with increasing interest in human translation (Resnik & Lin, 2010). Natural language processing technologies absorb the data produced from student language learning and translation activities to enhance their accuracy. English language programs have also recently acquired new features as they try to diversify both the content and the skills and subfields of communication offered. They incorporate translation and digital skills, in addition to specific domain purposes, to meet the demand of the professional market, which now relies heavily on digital competencies. These tools help students develop relevant skills and contribute to the digitalization industries of both the source and target languages.

Another key point is the shift in language learning motivation. If, a few decades ago, learning the English language symbolized a key to other cultures and internationalization, it now symbolizes a bidirectional bridge linking cultures through languages, including nurturing those low-resource languages that are struggling to find their way into the world of digital communication. It is within this context that the research in this chapter is an attempt to develop and combine in a meaningful way the English language learning, translation, and corpus development competencies in linguistic education at Brusov State University.

21.2 Literature Review

Earlier language teaching theories often criticized the value of translation as a tool for learning a language. These theories emphasized direct, immersive, and communicative methods as more important (Larsen-Freeman & Anderson, 2011). However, recent perspectives recognize the importance of translation in maintaining language diversity on a global scale.

Some scholars (see Hatim & Munday, 2004) argue that translation is an exercise in cross-cultural communication. It serves as a strong communication tool and motivates learners from a foreign language perspective. This perspective is also essential for utilizing findings in corpus linguistics for translation and language learning purposes. Others, such as McEnery and Wilson (2011), point out the challenges in making accurate language-wide assertions from limited data, emphasizing the necessity of reliable quantitative data for forming solid inferences. Drawing on their educational background, McEnery and Wilson prefer carefully curated smaller corpora, like the Brown or the Lancaster Spoken English Corpus. These corpora are notable for their detailed metadata which facilitates repeated and diverse analyses to yield broader linguistic insights.

As the use of corpora has become increasingly popular in Linguistics, it has enabled researchers to study language in a more empirical and data-driven way. The application of corpora in linguistic research is broad and diverse (e.g., Summers, 1993). Some of the most common uses of corpora include language description, language variation, language learning and teaching, and Translation Studies. Incorporating corpus resources into second-language writing and translation enhances traditional grammar learning (Alfuraih, 2020). It transforms grammar from a mere collection of "dictionary items + combinatory rules" to a more dynamic framework of corpora plus rules for querying and analyzing them (Zanettin, 2009).

Integrating corpus methods with translation not only improves language proficiency, but also deepens understanding of cognitive aspects and cultural nuances within languages. Language corpora play a vital role in linguistic research, language teaching, and natural language processing (Sinclair, 1997). The development of corpus-based studies provides language learners and teachers with ample access to parallel corpora, aiding in translation teaching and learning. They also help in solving practical problems, such as finding appropriate collocations (Bai, 2016).

Parallel corpora include translations of texts in two or more languages. They are valuable resources for examining cross-linguistic differences and translation-related phenomena, enriching our understanding of translation properties and features of translated language (Lefer, 2020). Additionally, utilizing parallel corpora in translation teaching enhances the effectiveness of instruction and fosters skilled translators, meeting the growing demand for MT editors (Yang et al., 2023).

Parallel corpora can be classified into different types based on the level of alignment between the translations (Gong & Cheng, 2023). Depending on the level of alignment, students are challenged with problems of different complexity, from morphological to textual and discoursal levels. Not only are ready-made corpora used as teaching materials and resources, but corpus development tasks can serve as a process-oriented method of translation skills development and deeper learning of both the source and target languages.

21.3 Context and Purpose

This chapter provides information about a research project carried out at the English Translation and Communication Chair of Brusov State University in academic year 2022–2023. The project aimed to find efficient methods for creating parallel Armenian-English language corpora by students in the Translation Studies BA program. The course and progress results of the project have been discussed at international conferences by members of the research team, with this chapter serving as the final report on pilot project takeaways.

The university has three English core programs, including the Translation Studies BA program, providing a comprehensive linguistic education over four years. The program requires CEFR B1+ English language proficiency level for admission. The first four semesters focus on intensive English language training and include reading and vocabulary, speaking and phonology, listening and comprehension, and writing and grammar. Students also learn basics in courses such as Linguistics, Intercultural Communication, and Theory of Translation Studies. In later semesters, students take professional translation courses, along with theoretical and practical English courses. These courses replace the common compulsory subjects and include a wide range of translation and interpretation activities in various fields such as literature, economics, politics, media, medicine, and children's literature. The program also includes courses on professional digital literacy, such as computer-assisted translation, translation techniques, and interpretation methodology. Students are also able to choose electives on different aspects of English and translation.

In recent years, Armenia has faced economic and geopolitical challenges, leading to a lack of progress in digital literacy initiatives, particularly in language data collection and digitalization. Online learning practices, which were implemented during the COVID pandemic, were deemed ineffective once the situation improved. Although Google and other machine translators have improved, there are still challenges in translating Armenian due to the complexity of the language and a lack of data in Armenian natural language processing.

Recognizing the need to address the gap in language data collection and digital literacy, linguists and AI professionals in Armenia turned to Translation Studies students. These students are well-suited for the task as they possess competencies in both languages, code-switching abilities, and skills in working with online applications and platforms. They also quickly learn to use corpus methods and MT, align bilingual texts in the form of parallel corpora, and compare, identify, and analyze translation errors.

Given the Translation Studies curriculum needed an upgrade to meet professional workforce demands, digital skills in MT editing became the goal of syllabus reform. The students were aware of the low-resource status of digital Armenian, and this served as a strong factor for transforming mere English as a Second Language (ESL) and translation into a product-oriented learning process. To develop high-quality bilingual datasets, the students and the teaching staff took up new roles—students as editors of Google-translated texts, and lecturers as correctors of machine-translated texts.

One of the most frequent mismatches found in MT outputs was related to syntax. Google had "learned" to correctly translate the words, but it was not resilient enough in terms of context, syntax and phraseology. Paradoxically, the flexible word order of Armenian, allowing speakers to express a range of opinion/attitude modalities more freely and to emphasize and argue facts both in written and spoken communication, yielded complications in translation. However, this free word order *was* the difficulty, not only for Google but for the students as well. Google Translate especially struggles with translating to Armenian due to the lack of syntactical and semantic data. Additionally, bilingual interference caused student editors to unconsciously distort Armenian syntax by adapting it to the less flexible word order of English when the latter is the source language of translation, and vice versa, making the English translation wordy, vague, and often grammatically wrong. The result was low-quality translation, difficult to read and comprehend.

As stated above, this mechanism of undermining the target language in translation is particularly damaging for minority, low-resource, and endangered languages. To prevent this form of language devaluation, it is crucial to raise awareness of the significance of high-quality translation and, hence, the pivotal role of proficiency in both languages of translation. Thus, the project goal and design were shaped by objective linguistic circumstances, social and contextual factors, market and global progress requirements, institutional needs and national interests.

The pilot materials revealed other linguistic challenges in MT editing, and we could predict a possible risk of negative learning results if we set very high expectations in student performance. Therefore, adjusting MT platforms and developing learning methods was possible through step-by-step planning adjustments.

21.4 Methodology and Procedure

21.4.1 Project Overview

The research team adopted an interdisciplinary approach to the project methodology by identifying several directions of research: critical analysis and selection of literature on MT, bilingual corpora, and student learning compared to ML. Along with compiling the team's library, we selected some "student-friendly" scientific books and papers as reading and reference sources to be used in term-paper writing. The books and papers mainly focus on revealing the potential of corpus linguistics and ML. The students were encouraged to do their own research as well. We also had to familiarize ourselves and the lecturers with the online platform and conduct a training workshop for lecturers. The platform enables two types of registration and usage: one for students (editor) and one for supervisors (proofreader). The training sessions were necessary to familiarize the supervisors with the functionality of the platform. The platform enables editing, proofreading, and submission of text translations.

Neither the idea of using the MT platform nor the parallel alignment methodology (i.e., making sure each syntagmatic unit is placed next to the corresponding translation) in ESL and translation were familiar to the staff and students. Thus, the interdisciplinary character of the project, besides the above-mentioned factors, was also predefined by the strong cognitive and psychological challenge staff and students were going to face. While preparing the project design, we initially hypothesized that integrating MT practice into the curriculum would create unease. However, we also believed it would have a positive and lasting impact on learning if implemented in a thoughtful and reassuring manner.

At first, adding the new corpus competence and parallel alignment techniques' requirement seemed obscure and irrelevant. For this reason, the team was prepared for the strategic interplay between process and product-oriented activities to maintain the degree of engagement and motivation in the activity. One interesting aspect of the research for both the team and students was observing linguistic transformations between similar bilingual texts. Machine-translated texts aligned with the source language paragraphs allowed for the exploration of different language units and navigating for precise translation.

This process revealed an abundance of analytical imagination, insights, and evaluation of equivalence at various linguistic levels, such as morphology, words, phrases, clauses, sentences, and paragraphs. These transformations, which would not have been discovered without MT, contributed to a bilingual learning process improving language and translation competencies in both Armenian and English (Warschauer, 2000). It also enhanced the translators' code-switching skills and raised their metalinguistic, psychological, social, cultural, and cognitive awareness, thus increasing their motivation in language learning and translation.

In the course of our research design, we discovered the Multilingual Student Translation (MUST) project (Granger & Lefer, 2020, 2023), which indirectly aligned with our study on an industry-based student learning approach. The MUST project targeted many of our objectives in its conceptual design and technical performance. It involved collaboration with the IT industry, internationalization, pedagogical communication approaches, and quantitative and qualitative methods of linguistic analysis. Chapelle (2007) highlights the effectiveness of such a complex approach in language learning research.

In our project, the term "interdisciplinary" refers to any study undertaken by scholars from multiple scientific disciplines. The research is based on a model that integrates theoretical frameworks from various disciplines, uses a study design and methodology not limited to any specific field, and incorporates the perspectives and skills of the disciplines involved throughout the research process (Tobi & Kampen, 2018).

A central concern while designing a research project in an academic context is to consider the program requirements and align research stages with the curriculum timeline and student learning outcomes. Following the timelines and working formal frameworks at the piloting stage was also part of the project success strategy. Hence, we had to factor in the time framework the students had, credit requirements for the project and the number of students that could be involved. The research targets of the project, which were framed within the university's professional educational program, included supporting the goals of enhancing students' English and Armenian proficiency, translation skills, and digital literacy. To achieve these, the team developed a new guide to writing a term-paper so that all project participants—the research team, students and instructors—could regulate, monitor, and evaluate the acquisition of bilingual translation proficiency, digital literacy for professional purposes, and parallel corpus development as the product of all the activities. The use of the text-alignment method and MT error analysis provided a language learning environment (Zhou & Waibel, 2021) through translation activities.

For academic adaptation purposes, we preferred the product-oriented strategy at this initial stage of MT component implementation, not giving much importance to the quality of the product but rather to the compilation of aligned texts. This decision was made to take and give everyone the time to understand and get used to the new learning environment, practice the novel working style, and make sense of the advantages and disadvantages of working in a new style in that innovative environment.

21.4.2 Project Phases

The first phase of the project involved preparing literature and basic knowledge in corpus development. We identified an appropriate online platform, selected scientific papers for common use, and adapted an MT development business platform for academic purposes. Simultaneously, we developed methodology and procedure documentation, as well as a guide for participating faculty members. As mentioned above, the documentation procedure was used to track progress in implementing the project into the curriculum and acted as a toolkit for regulating, monitoring, and evaluating the initiative, identifying possible risks and future directions.

The second stage involved preparing a new description of the research work, implementation procedure, and assessment methodology for students in Translation Studies. This document consisted of three main parts. It included sections introducing the research project's concept, the proposed structure of the coursework, and the expected outcomes for student learning and the evaluated product. As this activity was new to teaching staff and students, the document provided a detailed assessment description with examples and samples in the appendices. Additionally, a timeline with recommendations for strict adherence and an assessment component for timely submission of work were included. The learning outcomes focused on general knowledge of MT and parallel corpora, basic skills in bilingual text alignment, and identification of MT errors in translation.

The final project stage began in the spring semester of 2023, when approximately 100 third-year students and over 30 lecturers began to pilot parallel translation and MT evaluation. Several aspects and phases were outlined to address these objectives: raising English language learning motivation by introducing industry-based tasks to students, managing resistance and supporting faculty using corpus-based teaching methods, and integrating new research methodologies into the academic program. Enhanced language and translation skills were not the explicit objective of the project but were necessary conditions and logical impli-cations. Additionally, the technical support for translation operations was modernized, and students were familiarized with intelligent translation tools. The new coursework methodology was monitored by several pre-specified criteria and ongoing consultancy was provided to instructors and students throughout the project.

Soon after the project started, it became clear that a one-year cycle was not sufficient for full implementation of the parallel translation and alignment method, and development of any high-quality corpora. While piloting the corpus creation process was one of the project goals, the academic focus on the development of language and translation skills was the main concern. Despite these challenges, launching the process and embedding it into the academic activities was successfully done.

21.5 Skills Development

The initial project results show that participating students improved their language comprehension, translation abilities, and digital skills. This progress was revealed by comparing the students' results and knowledge before and after the project. This was completed by the supervisors who followed the grading rubrics clearly defined in the term-paper guide. Dörnyei and Ushioda (2011) suggest that these multifaceted educational initiatives help in motivating students and facilitating their overall development. In an attempt to integrate theory with practice in students' activities, learners were asked to read three to five research articles and introductory chapters in corpus linguistic and MT textbooks. This work was submitted and assessed as a component of independent research. Reading research papers in English and understanding and writing meaningful summaries was a challenge, and that is why the supervisors were given freedom to choose texts of suitable complexity for their students. Becoming familiar with professional research provides students with the basic knowledge to start the project. It also motivates and enhances research skills. A process-oriented assessment strategy was applied in the evaluation of this part of the course paper.

The next step was to familiarize students with the MT platform and corpora, which was initially developed for practical MT data collection and piloted in one of the universities of the Artsakh Republic. It did not have any of the educational components of the MUST project (Granger & Lefer, 2020, 2023), rather offering automated annotation options and part-of-speech tagging enhancing grammatical literacy via multiple choice drop-down menu bars.

The platform adapted for our students[1] had English-Armenian and Armenian-English texts, which participants were to compare, edit, and submit to the supervisor for correction and assessment. The main problem with students' translation in this case was getting used to going through several editing rounds while striving to improve the translation to a native-like text. Both in cases when Armenian or English were the target languages, students considered such issues as the conventional reader's personality, the pragmatic goal of the text, the cultural context, possible linguistic distortions, and so on. Despite the previously mentioned issue of Armenian's independent syntax when compared to English, the students gradually found the activity engaging.

---

[1] https://hayq.ican24.net/hyenmt/index.php.

The error analysis and editing activity can release students' potential in critical thinking and creativity once the translation task is understood, and participants quickly understood the role and reported enjoying improving the MT. The following examples illustrate the compare-edit-correct cycle.

Original: որուն բնակիչներուն թիւը նոյնիսկ կը զերազանցէ հայրենաբնակ Հայ

ժողովուրդին թիւը,

Google Translate: whose number of inhabitants even exceeds the number of the native Armenian people,
Student's edit: no changes to Google Translate output.
Supervisor's edit: whose number even exceeds the number of the Armenian people living in their homeland.

Feedback students received from their supervisors consistently pointed out the same outcomes in more precise and targeted forms. Paraphrasing the word-for-word MT into constructions that were more natural in the target language and speech community activates students' metalinguistic competencies. This, and similar kinds of error analysis, resulted in numerous insights and recommendations for course and curriculum amendments.

21.6 Error Analysis

We discovered that the error annotations made by students provided extremely valuable data for understanding the limitations of MT algorithms, similar to the "helpful feedback loops" reported by Saldanha and O'Brien (2013). Corpus-based translation primarily enhances students' ability to reflect on the structure and content of the texts being translated. It assists them in comprehending the interactions between different levels and units of language, leading to a more hands-on learning experience of typological differences. Understanding these differences enables students to make inferences based on language types and reassess their proficiency in both their native and foreign languages.

An important outcome of this process is the development of the ability to visually recognize quantitative distinctions between the source and target texts. The students were asked to use MT parallel translations to compare and contrast, identify, and learn the linguistic features of English and Armenian equally. Focusing on the semantic aspect of transfer and equivalence, the students became clearly aware of such quantitative features of the text as the number and length of the words in aligned texts. Initially, the students felt that Armenian was too long and uncomfortable to translate from English as the words are normally longer and often it is hard to find an exact equivalent instead of coming up with a descriptive phrase. However, they obtained similar results when translating from Armenian to English—they had to face the fact that they had not sufficiently mastered both English and their native language in order to accurately convey the connotations and details of meanings, organize their thoughts on the intentional level, and utilize the most appropriate synonyms and grammatical structures in both languages. It also revealed the correlation between proficiency in one's native language and the rate of acquiring a foreign language. This factor may be underestimated in both language teaching and Translation Studies methodologies.

Another issue that students' attention was drawn to is conducting further investigation of MT outputs where necessary. The edits by students mainly failed to correct the terms, names and acronyms when incorrectly translated by MT. Another key aspect of translation is the quality and clarity of the target text, not only in terms of grammar, but also style. Weaknesses, like wordy expressions, redundancies, repetitions, confusion between homonyms, and illogical statements, are typical of low-resource machine translators. Our examination of the students' translations uncovered a deficiency in addressing these problems too, as seen in the following examples:

Original: Այսօր «Դեբատ» մամուլի ակումբում Բորիս Նավասարդյանը կարծիք

հայտնեց՝ փորձը ցույց է տալիս, որ տվյալ լրագրողի գործունեությունը

խորհրդարանում կապվում է իր քաղաքական ուժի գործունեության հետ, ոչ թե իրենց

նախկին գործունեության.

Google Translate: Today, at the 'Debat' press club, Boris Navasardyan expressed his opinion that the experience shows that the activities of the given journalist in the parliament are connected with the activities of his political force, not with their previous activities.
Student's edit: no changes to Google Translate output.
Supervisor's edit: Today, at the 'Debate' press club, Boris Navasardyan expressed his opinion stating that judging from experience the activities of the given journalist in the parliament are connected with the activities of his political force, not with their previous activities.

The next examples exemplify the difficulty of disambiguating homonyms, which remains an unresolved problem for ML with Armenian due to the limited availability of digitalized language resources:

Original: լրատվամիջոցներ, որոնք ուղղակի տպագրվում էին ՀՅԴ-ին

պատկանող տպարանում,

Google Translate: which were directly printed in the printing house belonging to the ARF,
Student's edit: no changes to Google Translate output.
Supervisor's edit: which were just printed in the printing house belonging to the ARF.

The students failed to consider the importance of linguistic transformations. Translators commonly utilize transformations to achieve equivalence by taking into account differences in syntax, tone and style, cultural aspects, domain, and even meter. As part of the pre-translation analysis, translators delve into the writer's intentions, the overall discourse, and the pragmatic functions of the text. Based on this information, they make numerous small decisions that often involve lexical and grammatical transformations.

We impart this theoretical knowledge to our students during translation courses to prepare them for the term-paper project. However, our research revealed that they require further guidance related to what to focus on when editing MT outputs. Despite the rapid advancement of translation machines, there are still typological differences and grammatical nuances that they do not manage well, as the following example shows:

> Original: Սրա վառ ապացույցը փետրվարի 18-ին Արցախի կենտրոնական
>
> ընտրական հանձնաժողովի կողմից ընդունված որոշումն է Սահմանադրական
>
> փոփոխությունների համար կազմակերպվող ստորագրահավաքի, այնուհետև դրա
>
> արդյունքում հանրաքվե կազմակերպելու մասին.
>
> Google Translate: A vivid proof of this is the decision taken by the Central Electoral Commission of Artsakh on February 18 to organize a signature collection for constitutional amendments, and then to organize a referendum as a result of it.
> Student's edit: no changes to Google Translate output.
> Supervisor's edit: A vivid proof of this is the decision taken by the Central Electoral Commission of Artsakh on February 18 on the signature collection for constitutional amendments and the subsequent organization of a referendum as a result of it.

The sentence above contains two grammatically parallel elements, one of which is a noun (ստորագրահավաքի) and the second is an infinitive form (կազմակերպելու). The second element has been derived with the grammatical suffix "and", which makes the infinitive serve as a noun. However, this rule is apparently not included in the English grammar.

The above-mentioned case was not considered by the translation machine and the student, resulting in a confusing structure in English. Our examination of the students' translations or edits also showed that they lack consistency, which is essential in delivering a high-quality translation. It is not surprising that translation machines also do not maintain consistency, as the context is fluid and different translation variants may be considered correct by the machine.

21.7 Future Directions

We believe that the first stage of our research has proved invaluable in honing the students' translation and editing skills, as well as locating their main areas of weakness. Through the project, students developed digital skills and acquired knowledge of corpus linguistics and MT. The project helped us to find the main weaknesses of our students and address them in a systematic way. Secondly, our students developed a sense of responsibility as their translations contribute to the bilingual corpus and its quality, as well as that of MT.

From the educators' perspective, the project seemed more challenging, as the ultimate quality of the texts being imported into the systems lies with them. To make it a success, they had to work more closely with the students and make sure the objectives were duly met. Overall, supervisors' feedback on the outcomes was consistent. Students have things to learn from MT. Conversely, supervisors' editing proved invaluable in teaching students where to intervene and improve the translation.

Concerning corpus development, this fact will benefit not only MT algorithms but also future pedagogical methods in language teaching. One important direction is using MT as a teaching tool to help students improve their writing accuracy. By incorporating it into instructional design, teachers can use algorithms to detect and correct grammar mistakes, word usage errors, and stylistic issues. Another possible direction is using MT to create educational materials in multiple languages. Language programs can convert English content into different languages, making learning more inclusive for bilingual or multilingual students.

Using MT for real-time translation in interactive educational settings can enable e-learning without language barriers. Students can communicate with teachers and peers from all around the world, enriching their learning experiences. However, ethical and practical implications matter when it comes to the accuracy and reliability of output from MT. The risk of relying too heavily on MT instead of developing genuine language proficiency, and the protection of learner privacy in the use of AI in education, are crucial issues. Only by carefully managing these matters can we fully realize the potential of MT in English language education in the future.

21.8 Conclusion

The pilot project reported in this chapter highlighted the urgency of upgrading linguistic education and staying up-to-date with advancements in communication technologies and the needs of the translation profession. The integration of MT editing and corpus development studies opens up new possibilities in foreign language learning and research.

The key conclusions drawn from this project are that student translation activities contribute to the development of bilingual corpora and enhance knowledge in MT, digital literacy, and language pedagogy. Integrating corpus resources into second-language writing and translating enriches traditional language learning. In addition, introducing parallel corpus development tasks improves language learning motivation and comprehension. The use of bilingual parallel corpus methods enables students to visualize the differences between source and target texts, develop digital skills, and acquire knowledge and competencies for their future careers.

Acknowledgements The study was funded by the Brusov State University Internal Research Grant No. 1GH-22/004 for one year through August 2023. Parts of the project were presented at Dragomanov State University online conferences in 2022 and 2023, Kyiv, Ukraine.

References

Alfuraih, R. F. (2020). The undergraduate learner translator corpus: A new resource for translation studies and computational linguistics. *Language Resources and Evaluation, 54*(3), 801–830. https://doi.org/10.1007/s10579-019-09472-6

Al-Mutairi, M. A. (2019). Kachru's three concentric circles model of English language: An overview of criticism & the place of Kuwait in it. *English Language Teaching, 13*(1), 85–88. https://doi.org/10.5539/elt.v13n1p85

Bai, J. (2016). Parallel corpora and translation teaching. *Advances in Intelligent Systems Research, 130*, 689–693. https://doi.org/10.2991/mcei-16.2016.143

Chapelle, C. A. (2007). Technology and second language acquisition. *Annual Review of Applied Linguistics, 27*, 98–114. https://doi.org/10.1017/S02671 90508070050

Dörnyei, Z., & Ushioda, E. (2011). *Teaching and researching motivation* (2nd ed.). Longman/Pearson.

Gong, Y., & Cheng, L. (2023). Research on the application of translation parallel corpus in interpretation teaching. *ACM Transactions on Asian and Low-Resource Language Information Processing*. https://doi.org/10.1145/362 3270

Granger, S., & Lefer, M.-A. (2020). The multilingual student translation corpus: A resource for translation teaching and research. *Language Resources and Evaluation, 54*(4), 1183–1199. https://doi.org/10.1007/s10579-020-09485-6

Granger, S., & Lefer, M.-A. (2023). Learner translation corpora: Bridging the gap between learner corpus research and corpus-based translation studies. *International Journal of Learner Corpus Research, 9*(1), 1–28. https://doi.org/10.1075/ijlcr.00032.gra

Hatim, B., & Munday, J. (2004). *Translation: An advanced resource book*. Psychology Press.

Larsen-Freeman, D., & Anderson, M. (2011). *Techniques and principles in language teaching* (3rd ed.). Oxford University Press.

Lefer, M.-A. (2020). Parallel corpora. In M. Paquot & S. T. Gries (Eds.), *A practical handbook of corpus linguistics* (pp. 257–282). Springer. https://doi.org/10.1007/978-3-030-46216-1_12

McEnery, T., & Wilson, A. (2011). *Corpus linguistics: An introduction* (2nd ed.). Edinburgh University Press.

Resnik, P., & Lin, J. (2010). Evaluation of NLP systems. In A. Clark, C. Fox, & S. Lappin (Eds.), *The handbook of computational linguistics and natural language processing* (pp. 271–295). Wiley. https://doi.org/10.1002/9781444324044.ch11

Saldanha, G., & O'Brien, S. (2013). *Research methodologies in translation studies*. Jerome Publishing.

Sinclair, J. (1997). *Corpus, concordance, collocation* (4th ed.). Oxford University Press.

Summers, D. (1993). Longman/Lancaster English language corpus—Criteria and design. *International Journal of Lexicography, 6*(3), 181–208. https://doi.org/10.1093/ijl/6.3.181

Tobi, H., & Kampen, J. K. (2018). Research design: The methodology for interdisciplinary research framework. *Quality & Quantity, 52*(3), 1209–1225. https://doi.org/10.1007/s11135-017-0513-8

Warschauer, M. (2000). On-line learning in second language classrooms: An ethnographic study. In M. Warschauer & R. Kern (Eds.), *Network-based language teaching* (pp. 41–58). Cambridge University Press. https://doi.org/10.1017/CBO9781139524735.005

Yang, Y., Liu, R., Qian, X., & Ni, J. (2023). Performance and perception: Machine translation post-editing in Chinese-English news translation by novice translators. *Humanities and Social Sciences Communications, 10*(1), 798. https://doi.org/10.1057/s41599-023-02285-7

Zanettin, F. (2009). Corpus-based translation activities for language learners. *The Interpreter and Translator Trainer, 3*(2), 209–224. https://doi.org/10.1080/1750399X.2009.10798789

Zhou, Z., & Waibel, A. (2021). Active learning for massively parallel translation of constrained text into low resource languages. In *Proceedings of the LoResMT Workshop of the 18th Biennial Machine Translation Summit in 2021.* https://doi.org/10.48550/arXiv.2108.07127

22

Language Teaching in Transition: Educator Perspectives on Integrating Machine Translation Tools in Tertiary Contexts

Antonie Alm and Yuki Watanabe

22.1 Introduction

Machine translation (MT) tools have rapidly gained popularity among language learners in recent years due to the advances in artificial intelligence (AI). From Google Translate (GT) to generative models such as ChatGPT (Chat Generative Pre-trained Transformer), students are increasingly resorting to these technologies to assist with language learning tasks. The integration of AI-based tools to support language learning creates new pedagogical challenges. In response, instructional frameworks, such as Knowles' (2022) ADAPT model, as described below, have emerged to guide the appropriate integration of MT in the foreign and second language (L2) classroom. However, many instructors remain

A. Alm (✉) · Y. Watanabe
University of Otago, Dunedin, New Zealand
e-mail: antonie.alm@otago.ac.nz

Y. Watanabe
e-mail: yuki.watanabe@otago.ac.nz

© The Author(s), under exclusive license to Springer Nature
Switzerland AG 2025
D. Coulson and C. Denman (eds.), *Translation, Translanguaging and Machine Translation in Foreign Language Education*,
https://doi.org/10.1007/978-3-031-82174-5_22

457

ambivalent and are only beginning to address the challenges of integrating these technologies as well as devising effective ways to implement them in the curriculum. The study examines this transitional process as teachers explore integrating AI technologies in tertiary language teaching. It investigates instructors' attitudes towards these technologies and their perceived impacts on language learning. Additionally, it analyses the extent to which instructors currently incorporate AI-based applications into their teaching practices by situating them within Knowles' ADAPT framework for structured, pedagogical MT adoption.

22.2 Literature Review

22.2.1 Background on MT in Language Learning

The intersection of Machine Translation (MT) tools and second and foreign language (L2) education has expanded rapidly, enabled by advances in artificial intelligence (AI). Neural MT models used in popular applications like GT and DeepL now provide fast, high-quality translation. More recent conversational AI systems like ChatGPT have also emerged as both valuable resources and potentially disruptive influences on conventional language learning approaches (Klimova et al., 2023; Lee, 2023).

Studies over the past decade have found that guided writing revision with MT can improve accuracy, vocabulary diversity and overall quality (Garcia & Pena, 2011; Lee, 2020). For example, having Korean English as a Foreign Language (EFL) students translate first language (L1) texts into English and compare them to MT output helped reduce errors and improve expressions and quality (Lee, 2020). Analyses of Chinese EFL student essays written with MT assistance show marked improvements in vocabulary, grammatical accuracy and complexity, idea development and rhetorical structure (Tsai, 2019). Some studies point to variations in MT use and effectiveness across proficiency levels and language types (Alm & Watanabe, 2022). For example, Xu (2022) observed advanced Japanese learners focused more on stylistic editing in MT-assisted writing, while intermediate learners addressed grammar and vocabulary.

However, several studies highlight the risks of over-dependence on MT, which can compromise learning. Chung (2023) found advanced Korean EFL learners over-relied on raw MT output when reading. Knowles (2022) and Xu (2022) also note the risks of dependence without meaningful language engagement. Overall, while some over-reliance concerns persist, most literature indicates strategic MT use can support language learning.

22.2.2 Research on Instructor Attitudes Towards MT

While instructors' attitudes towards MT use in language learning vary, a predominant trend in the literature reveals a prevalence of negative perceptions. For example, Uehara (2023) interviewed university teachers and found acceptance only for limited MT use to support writing. Stapleton and Ka Kin (2019) interviewed primary school teachers, who largely disapproved of use beyond single-word lookups. Multiple studies, employing various methodologies, consistently show that most teachers view MT use as academically dishonest "cheating", posing threats to learning and their pedagogical authority (Clifford et al., 2013; Merschel & Munné, 2022; Uehara, 2023). As conceptualised by Vinall and Hellmich (2022), these prohibitive attitudes reflect a "detect-punish-prevent" perspective that focuses on limiting the use of MT in academic contexts.

Concerns arise that MT may replace traditional reading and writing habits (Tasmedir et al., 2022) and threaten language teaching as a profession (Merschel & Munné, 2022; Ohashi, 2022). However, studies also indicate that many language teachers are still unaware of recent technological developments or lack training in how to use MT effectively (Alm & Watanabe, 2022; Vinall & Hellmich, 2022), suggesting these negative perceptions may arise from insufficient familiarity with, and skills in, applying such tools educationally, thus presenting barriers to the translation of research into practice.

As the quality and accessibility of MT improves, studies suggest a shift in instructors' attitudes towards MT in language education (Alm &

Watanabe, 2022). This shift is gaining support through recommendations for the regulated integration of MT (Ducar & Schocket, 2018). Pedagogical adaptations emphasise a transition from accuracy to communication and the scaffolding of purposeful MT activities aligned with course objectives (Tasmedir et al., 2022; Uehara, 2023). These pedagogical shifts reflect an "integrate-educate" approach (Vinall & Hellmich, 2022), which recognises the increasing prevalence of AI-based tools, their potential for language learning and the need to build critical MT literacy skills.

Further studies are essential, both to develop pedagogically best practices for the use of MT and to prepare teachers to implement such frameworks through professional development focused on MT literacy. As teachers shape curriculum design and learner development, their perspectives are an essential part of ensuring the effective adoption of new technologies.

22.2.3   Instructional Models for MT Integration

Researchers have explored different approaches to integrating MT tools into the language classroom. In their systematic review, Deng and Yu (2022) identified common patterns of MT integration involving introduction, demonstration, task assignment and reflection primarily in the form of writing and translation tasks. Ryu et al. (2022) proposed the Guided Use of Machine Translation model, which involves strategically incorporating MT tools with supplementary online resources to enhance students' sociopragmatic awareness and support writing tasks. These models demonstrate the flexibility of integrating MT with interactive and collaborative work.

One comprehensive pedagogical framework is the ADAPT model developed by Knowles (2022) based on her decade-long transition from face-to-face to online Spanish teaching. The model aims to address students' increased reliance on GT by integrating it into the L2 learning environment. Its objective is to mitigate students' over-reliance on MT while fostering meaningful language learning experiences through guided integration.

The acronym encompasses five key components of the model:

1. **Amending assignments** involves adapting tasks to prevent over-reliance on MT tools by, for example, requiring the use of specific grammatical structures and vocabulary appropriate to students' language proficiency. It also emphasises the repeated use of learned language in different contexts to deepen understanding and retention.
2. **Discussing MT** involves fostering an environment where MT is openly discussed throughout the course. The aim is to set clear expectations for MT use and to promote practices that support language learning.
3. **Assessing with MT in mind** entails developing assessment strategies and rubrics that take MT use into account. The aim is to assess language comprehension and production in a way that ensures students' work reflects their understanding and skills.
4. **Practising integrity** emphasises the promotion of academic integrity. It encourages strategies that facilitate mindful engagement with MT tools, such as allowing for revision and emphasising the value of the learning process over the mere completion of tasks.
5. **Training students** encompasses providing students with the necessary guidance to use MT effectively. Training includes instruction in how to use these tools to support areas such as pronunciation, vocabulary acquisition, and the development of writing skills.

In this study, the ADAPT model serves as a conceptual lens through which to situate the interview data from language teachers. Developed from a teacher's perspective, the model offers an "adaptable" framework for addressing local teaching needs, outlining a pedagogical pathway for purposeful MT integration into language curricula. The model, thus, provides insights into the implications of such integration in the evolving landscape of language education.

Within this framework of MT use and beliefs, the following two research questions guide the current investigation:

RQ1: What are L2 educators' perspectives, experiences and attitudes regarding the integration of AI technologies, in particular MT tools into language teaching?

RQ2: To what extent do their perspectives and practices align with the ADAPT model for transitioning towards guided integration of MT tools in language curricula?

22.3 Method

Our study employs a qualitative research methodology to explore language educators' experiences and perspectives on AI-based tools, such as GT, DeepL and ChatGPT. Using a semi-structured interview format, we focus on understanding how these technologies are integrated into language teaching and the pedagogical strategies that teachers use.

22.3.1 Participants

We approached all teachers in the Languages and Cultures Department of a tertiary institution in New Zealand to participate in one-on-one interviews for this study. Consent was obtained after potential participants were informed of the study's purpose, their rights of participation/ withdrawal, and how their data would be used.

We interviewed six teachers and then purposively selected four to include in the study. This strategic selection aimed to elicit perspectives from teachers of typologically diverse languages operating in different linguistic contexts. Additionally, the inclusion of both beginner and advanced-level educators sought to capture a broader range of experiences with MT use across varied student proficiency.

The participants were Pierre, Maria, Ling and Aiko (pseudonyms), with their teaching covering French, Spanish, Chinese and Japanese— two European and two Asian languages—at levels ranging from beginner to advanced proficiency. Table 22.1 summarises key information about each participant's language teaching background and multilingual profile.

Table 22.1 Participant information

Pseudonym	Language, language teaching and learning background
Pierre	L1 French speaker and proficient L2 English speaker. Teaches French at all levels from high school through university. Also works as a freelance translator. Learning Māori
Maria	L1 Spanish speaker, grew up bilingually alongside German and proficient L2 English speaker. Teaches all levels of Spanish courses. Learning French
Ling	L1 Cantonese speaker and proficient L2 English speaker. Teaches advanced Chinese (Mandarin) language and translation courses. Learning Esperanto
Aiko	L1 Japanese speaker and proficient L2 English speaker, previously taught English in Japan. Teaches Japanese courses for beginners and intermediate learners. Learned some Chinese and Spanish

22.3.2 Data Collection and Analysis

Data was collected in May 2023 through recorded interviews conducted by one of the researchers using Otter, a digital recording and transcription tool. The transcripts were then cleaned to ensure the accuracy and completeness of the qualitative data set and exported to a word processor document.

The data analysis involved a two-stage approach:

1. Inductive thematic analysis: Initially, following Braun and Clarke's (2006) guidelines for inductive thematic analysis, we coded the transcripts to identify emergent themes related to participants' backgrounds, experiences and views of AI-based tools. Coding was carried out independently by each researcher, followed by comparison and discussion to finalise the thematic framework. This collaborative analysis ensured a comprehensive understanding of the data and incorporated multiple perspectives, informing RQ1.
2. Deductive analysis: For RQ2, we used the five components of the ADAPT model as a lens to examine how language teachers integrate AI-based tools into their pedagogical practices. This deductive approach enabled systematic categorisation of educators' responses.

This two-step process incorporated both researchers' perspectives through independent coding followed by collaborative finalisation of themes and categories.

22.4 Results

22.4.1 Language Educators' Perspectives, Experiences and Attitudes

This section addresses recurring themes that emerged from data analysis: personal use of MT tools, observed student engagement, moderate acceptance with reservations, concerns about over-reliance, confidence in detecting MT use and perspectives on ChatGPT.

22.4.1.1 Personal Use of MT Tools and ChatGPT

Participants described frequent personal use of MT tools while acknowledging their limitations. Ling reported using GT to check word meanings and synonyms. Pierre alternated between GT and DeepL in his freelance translation work, although he avoided MT when sentences were too linguistically complex, explaining, "I can predict it's going to fail". Maria was also critical of the output: "I know it's going to be a blueprint, and I will have to work on it".

In contrast to MT, most teachers had limited experience with generative AI. Pierre described ChatGPT as a "super Google" and reported using it for problem-solving across diverse applications and for writing assistance. Meanwhile, both Aiko and Maria admitted struggling with its functionality during brief explorations—with Maria stating that she and ChatGPT were not "good friends". Despite expressing curiosity, observed inaccuracies of the output, such as fake references, provoked scepticism. Overall, generative AI represented an unknown domain for most teachers compared to the more established presence of MT.

22.4.1.2   Student Use of MT Tools

Participants reported significant student MT use across courses and assignments. Aiko noted that students use MT to correct their writing. Maria noticed students using GT and Reverso to look up words, and Pierre observed a "heavy reliance" on MT as a dictionary, not just for written work but also during discussions in class. The teachers agreed that MT was widely used in their classes, as Maria concisely summed up: "It is evident that students of all levels are engaged with MT".

22.4.1.3   Moderated Acceptance of MT Use

Participants endorsed the use of MT as one learning tool among others. Aiko encourages students to first write sentences before checking them with MT. Maria described MT as "one more tool" that could support students' expression, like traditional dictionaries. However, she stressed the need to use it critically, not as an instant fix for comprehension gaps. Pierre, despite initial reluctance, claimed to have "fully accept[ed]" MT integration given its significant advancement in recent years. However, he remained circumspect about motivational impacts, expressing concern that MT dependence may undermine "pride in doing something challenging".

22.4.1.4   Concerns About Over-Reliance on MT

Participants were concerned about MT potentially interfering with students' basic writing and memorisation skills, especially in Chinese and Japanese. Aiko warned against over-reliance as it can prevent students from producing original work: "If they really heavily use it and depend on that, then they don't create… their own things". Ling expressed concerns about students losing opportunities for meaningful cognitive engagement with the target language. According to her, unrestricted access to MT threatens to undermine intrinsic motivation rooted in "experiential learning", where students may have previously felt a sense of satisfaction from working through challenges and solving linguistic problems.

Maria talked about the challenge of managing unrealistic student expectations in a generation that wants instant results:

> I realise I'm in front of a completely different generation… I found it very difficult to navigate myself with students because this is a generation that wants everything now… They're not used to wait for things to develop in their own heads.

She described instances where students would immediately turn to GT and present the expressions not yet covered in class. This reliance on tools made her reiterate the importance of working with the language at hand, and to warn students against expecting to achieve fluency in an unrealistically short time. For this reason, Maria was reluctant to introduce MT into the beginning-level classroom and highlighted the importance of encouraging novice learners to think creatively within the limits of their current language abilities, rather than immediately resorting to technological shortcuts.

22.4.1.5 Detecting MT Use

Participants were confident they could recognise when their students use MT tools in their writing. Aiko explained that her knowledge of students' language skills at specific levels helped her identify discrepancies arising from MT use. Ling pointed to similarities between students' work as an indicator. However, they emphasised that, despite these signs, they trust students to use MT sensibly, understanding that the true value of their education lies in the effort and engagement with the language itself, not just the end result. As evidenced by her comment—"My job is not to catch you"—Ling defiantly rejects the notion of policing MT use. Rather than monitoring, she seeks to promote student self-direction and internal accountability for their learning.

22.4.1.6 Perspectives on ChatGPT

Given their limited familiarity with generative AI, participants' comments about ChatGPT were sparse. However, Pierre liked the idea of using AI conversations for speaking practice and Maria suggested using ChatGPT-generated content as a springboard for in-class discussions. Their attention was primarily focused on determining appropriate strategies for the more established MT resources already prevalent among students.

22.4.2 Instructor Perspectives and Practices Situated in the ADAPT Framework

This section explores how language teachers' practices and perceptions are reflected in each of the five components of the ADAPT model. These components, defined in Sect. 22.2.3, provide a structured lens for the analysis of teaching strategies as detailed below.

22.4.2.1 Amending Assignments

Participants adapted assignments to manage student reliance on AI-based tools by using in-class pen-and-paper tests, conducting translation tasks as group activities and changing the format of oral presentations. Aiko and Ling emphasised the cognitive benefits of handwriting for language learning. Both Maria and Ling described how group translation activities create an environment that encourages discussion about the accuracy of translations, including those generated by MT. They observed that this collaborative process also promotes peer learning and critical thinking.

Oral presentations posed challenges when students read MT-generated scripts. To address this, Pierre changed the assignment format, requiring memorisation of the script to encourage students to engage more with the content they are presenting. For take-home assignments, Ling emphasised the importance of reflecting on the translation process: "It's not about what you did in the translated part. It is how you did it. I want to see the process…". This approach shifts the focus from the translated output to the articulation of learners' decision-making, methods of error correction and learning experiences. These examples illustrate the instructors' deliberate efforts to create tasks that both challenge and limit the reliance on MT.

22.4.2.2 Discussing

Pierre and Maria included the departmental guidelines for AI use in their course syllabi, openly addressing ethical use. Maria explained that the guidelines give students a little sense of "freedom" to use MT tools. However, she also stressed the importance of talking to students directly as, in her experience, many do not read the course outline.

Participants all had informal discussions about MT with their students. Ling suggested using MT for individual words for translation tasks. Aiko encouraged students to write their sentences before consulting MT. Pierre encouraged students to use GT to practise their pronunciation, explaining that "there's nothing wrong about using Google Translate", as long as students provide their own "input". He emphasised the concept of "garbage in, garbage out", a key takeaway from a training session he attended, also relating it to ChatGPT. Pierre was the only interviewee who claimed to talk about generative AI with his students. Drawing on French media sources, he discussed the tool's various applications, such as the case where ChatGPT was used to spot a legal flaw in an employment agreement during a labour dispute.

22.4.2.3 Assessing with MT in Mind

While the use of rubrics is a common practice to assess students' work, participants' emphasis appeared to be on effective learning rather than specifically addressing the use of AI-based tools. For example, Ling placed greater weight on the learning process, allocating more marks to the reflections students submit alongside their translation work. Maria recommended rubrics for beginners to assess basics such as grammar, writing and speaking within defined parameters. As students progress,

Maria stated she introduces different texts such as speeches, videos and drama to offer open-ended opportunities for skill demonstration. She believes that gradually expanding assessment types can validate students' ability to engage critically with the language.

22.4.2.4 Practicing Integrity

Participants expressed their concerns about maintaining academic integrity, while implementing strategies to support the responsible use of MT tools. Pierre was initially reluctant to endorse a tool that could be negatively perceived or banned in academic settings, fearing potential workplace conflict, stating, "I'm gonna get into trouble with my colleagues". He also acknowledged some students' reluctance to use ChatGPT due to concerns about perceived cheating and pride in their writing style. He thought this could lead to the compromise of students' motivation in assessments requiring critical thinking and problem-solving.

As recommended by Knowles (2022), measures to reduce the motivation to cheat, such as providing opportunities for revision and resubmission, find support from teachers like Aiko and Ling. Both allow students to revise their writing assignments based on feedback for higher grades and use the revised versions as scripts for subsequent oral presentations. At an advanced level, Maria adopted an open approach to MT tools, asking students to highlight or italicise words they have looked up: "I had students highlighting... words that came from the DeepL, Reverso, or Google Translate... That's a way of referencing". This aimed to foster transparency and eliminate students' sense of guilt associated with MT use. Ling advocated equal access to resources, suggesting that "everyone use the free version" as she does not want her students "to pay premium to produce better quality work", thus aiming to mitigate financial disparities. These strategies highlight the teachers' efforts to encourage technology use while upholding academic integrity in language classes.

22.4.2.5 Training Students

While our participants demonstrated proficiency in basic MT skills, they acknowledged their limited knowledge of more advanced AI functionalities. Pierre, for instance, was unsure about specific MT functionalities, particularly its "behaviour" in translating language pairs such as French and Chinese, citing challenges that arise when working with students from non-English backgrounds. Maria admitted being somewhat ignorant about the specific MT features. These reflections indicate a shared sense of unfamiliarity among participants regarding emerging AI translation technologies.

Despite feeling under-qualified as technical experts, some teachers demonstrated their working MT skills to their students. For instance, Maria facilitated basic training in reverse translation techniques to check writing accuracy. She also encouraged the strategic use of MT by guiding the comparative use of GT and DeepL, advising students to choose the tool aligning better with their specific language learning goals. Pierre taught how to use Reverso Context for precise language translations in context and demonstrated the method of "rehearsing" pronunciation by copying and pasting text into GT for pronunciation feedback.

While participants seemed comfortable with basic MT functions, they expressed uncertainty when it came to the more advanced pedagogical applications of AI tools. Pierre, drawing on his experience as a translator, stated, "I have an experience with it [GT] as a translator. But... I don't have a lot of experience with it as a teacher". Ling acknowledged her lack of research expertise and entrusted her students by stating, "I don't research how to use those machines myself much... I think they [students] should know how to use it".

However, interviewees considered asking more knowledgeable colleagues to train students, such as Pierre who suggested a demonstration for speech-to-writing applications. Echoing her earlier stance on not policing students, Ling maintained that technology training fell outside her responsibilities, stating, "I just provide the mechanism to make sure that they use it in such a way that they learned something". She suggested specialists in educational technology should provide training sessions.

22.4.3 Themes Beyond ADAPT

22.4.3.1 Core Values in Language Teaching

Participants emphasised the vital role of interpersonal relationships built through classroom interactions, seeing human connection in that context as essential to learning. As Aiko explained, her classes facilitate "things not just about Japanese, but about how to… build friendship and communication… I don't think AI can [do those things]". Maria shared this view, adding that dependence on translation tools "won't allow any meaningful relationships because you're going to be on the surface of the language". She pointed out that an over-reliance on MT could hinder not only students' interpersonal connections, but also their "cultural" development.

Some teachers predicted shifts in focus—diminished emphasis on writing but increased attention towards cultural engagement—which technology makes increasingly accessible. As Pierre maintained, "I think the writing is going to become minor. And I think culture will be all the more important". He felt this change that AI facilitates could better enable authentic learning experiences. However, Ling stressed the need to respect student agency and cautioned not to allow technology to dictate learning approaches, explaining that "whether you have technology or not, you always need to adjust. … There's always a way you can have agency to think how it should be done".

22.4.3.2 Teacher Development Needs

Participants recognised the need for their own training in the effective use of AI-based tools and wanted to be well-versed in the technology their students were using. Pierre wanted to expand his knowledge of speech tools, while Maria aimed to acquire more general, practical MT skills to demonstrate applications in specific language learning contexts, such as speaking, writing and pronunciation. Several participants advocated for the collaborative, team-based development of teaching strategies to encourage mindful MT use rather than simplistic reliance on it.

Aiko stated, "I really want to listen to what other people think". This was reinforced by Pierre, who also emphasised the need for a team-based approach, advocating the sharing of knowledge and experience among colleagues. The emphasis was not only on using these tools, but also on developing critical thinking and problem-solving skills in language learning.

22.5 Discussion

22.5.1 Key Findings

This study explored the perspectives and experiences of language teachers at the tertiary level regarding the integration of MT/AI-based technologies into their teaching practice. Several key themes emerged from the interviews with four teachers of four languages.

First, the findings indicate a general acceptance among participants of the use of MT tools. They recognised the benefits to support language learning, but also articulated concerns about over-reliance, motivation and superficial learning. Second, participants expressed limited familiarity with ChatGPT or other emergent generative AI technologies. Despite some curiosity, they remained sceptical about their capabilities and unsure of how to incorporate such tools into language pedagogy. Their attention was more focused on observed student use of MT tools.

Third, while acknowledging the prevalence of MT use at all proficiency levels, participants sought to encourage critical, complementary use through various teaching strategies. Examples included requiring in-class handwriting tasks, group translation activities, revision and modification of oral assessments. Fourth, cross-examination of instructors of four different languages reveals differences in how Asian and European language teachers engage with the ADAPT model. Notably, Asian language teachers emphasise pen-and-paper assignments as a method to address MT use, whereas their counterparts distinguish themselves by incorporating standardised AI guidelines into course syllabi and providing specific MT feature training. These distinctions may be rooted in linguistic differences between alphabet-based and non-alphabet-based languages, along with a prevailing perception that associates technological development more closely with Anglophone systems, influencing the perceived availability and quality of language resources.

Finally, the study revealed teachers' insecurities about their ability to implement pedagogical MT use. They struggled with unrealistic student expectations in a generation accustomed to instant results and expressed challenges in addressing this trend. This highlights a key dimension overlooked in existing integration frameworks such as the ADAPT model. Instead, participants expressed a preference for collaborative peer learning and open discussion with students, emphasising shared knowledge over individual expertise. The findings reflect the transitional state in which teachers are adapting their practices to the changing educational landscape. Greater support for teachers through communities of practice and institutional training could help address their uncertainty and potentially facilitate purposeful integration.

The participants' acceptance of MT integration, along with their concerns about its impact on student motivation and depth of learning, is consistent with findings from previous studies (e.g. Knowles, 2022; Tasmedir et al., 2022; Xu, 2022). The findings are also consistent with trends recently documented in the literature, indicating a move away from more prohibitive attitudes towards controlled, strategic integration (Vinall & Hellmich, 2022). Examples included scaffolding the use of MT through modified assignments, rubrics and revisions. Such adaptations conceptually mirror the principles of Knowles' (2022) ADAPT model for MT adoption.

While parallels exist between the findings of this study and the principles outlined in the ADAPT framework, new insights emerged regarding teachers' preparedness. Participants overwhelmingly expressed being inadequately equipped to train students in the use of MT tools. This confirms the gaps identified by Alm and Watanabe (2022) regarding instructor MT literacy and contrasts with the assumption in ADAPT that instructors have the requisite knowledge.

The uncertainty surrounding ChatGPT highlights the transitional state where teachers struggle to keep up with the rapidly evolving changes in language education driven by technology. For example, while the conversational features of AI open up multiple possibilities for engaging language activities, such as interactive dialogues and problem-solving scenarios, instructors predominantly remained focused on the MT applications their students were using. This suggests that the integration of technology is often reactive, responding to learners' behaviours, rather than a proactive process initiated by educators. These findings highlight the need for pedagogical frameworks and instructor support that directly address this unpreparedness to facilitate the effective integration of AI tools into teaching practices.

22.5.2 Pedagogical Implications

Using the ADAPT framework as a lens revealed partial alignment in instructor practices, such as amending assignments and discussing to manage student use of AI-based tools. However, significant variations were identified in assessment policies/procedures, student training and academic integrity practices. This confirms that participants are in a transitional phase. Despite using the tools personally and having basic knowledge of their functionality, they remain unsure about MT features and implications for language learning.

Alongside factors such as language types, proficiency level and personal preferences, the degree of involvement identified through the ADAPT model points to a context-specific approach to technology integration in language education. This suggests the need for the flexible application of adoption models to a range of languages, proficiency levels, personal preferences and institutional contexts.

The original focus of the ADAPT model on Spanish may imply that it could be more congruent with European rather than Asian language classes due to the different writing systems and the availability and accuracy of MT tools. Therefore, when adapting the model, educators can adjust it to suit the needs of non-European languages, ensuring a more comprehensive and inclusive approach to technology integration.

In addition, ADAPT does not address the needs of advanced learners—these experienced learners may use MT more independently with a stronger sense of agency. The model's original online setting also contrasts with our participants' classroom contexts, thus introducing additional collaborative factors. There are different ethical complexities online and in person that may also influence control measures.

While ADAPT provides a useful starting point, its primarily teacher-driven approach does not address the integration of student perspectives. Limited familiarity with MT functionality exacerbates the need for a two-way approach when engaging more advanced learners and their greater language proficiency and agency. Encouraging the sharing of good practices from both teachers and learners could facilitate the collaborative shaping of purposeful MT use.

Finally, participants expressed an interest in greater collaboration between teachers, reflecting a desire for more peer-based development. Despite being beyond the original scope of ADAPT, fostering communities of practice to develop integration strategies may help to address self-identified readiness limitations. Ultimately, evolving language programmes require sustaining multi-dimensional collaboration—both in terms of incorporating student input and fostering collegial teamwork—to promote technology integration that supports language education as a whole.

When considering these pedagogical implications, however, it is important to note that the study's generalisability is necessarily limited due to the small sample size of participants drawn from a single institutional context. Further research is therefore needed to investigate whether similar themes emerge with a more diverse range of participants and settings.

22.6 Conclusion

This study explored instructors' perspectives of the integration of AI-based tools and found that acceptance is limited by a lack of familiarity with their functionalities, which in turn restricts pedagogical adoption. Analysis of alignment with the ADAPT framework revealed not only commonalities in amended assignments and discussions, but also significant divergences in consciously assessing MT, training students and academic integrity.

These findings contribute empirical insights that shed light on assumptions about teacher readiness and highlight struggles in reconciling learner expectations, teaching perspectives, personal beliefs, technological capabilities and institutional culture. They also help inform calls for new pedagogical approaches that transform the teacher-centred development of technology integration models by highlighting the importance of collaboration between language teachers and students and among educators within and beyond institutions. Meaningful MT integration is likely to require flexible frameworks to address complex realities through the collective sensemaking of teachers and learners towards ethical and purposeful technology adoption.

References

Alm, A., & Watanabe, Y. (2022). Online machine translation for L2 writing across languages and proficiency levels. *Australian Journal of Applied Linguistics, 5*(3), 135–157. https://doi.org/10.29140/ajal.v5n3.53si3

Braun, V., & Clarke, V. (2006). Using thematic analysis in psychology. *Qualitative Research in Psychology, 3*(2), 77–101. https://doi.org/10.1191/1478088706qp063oa

Chung, E. S. (2023). L2 learners' use of raw machine-translated output in reading comprehension. *Computer-Assisted Language Learning Electronic Journal, 24*(3), 1–19. https://callej.org/index.php/journal/article/view/44/25

Clifford, J., Merschel, L., & Munné, J. (2013). Surveying the landscape: What is the role of machine translation in language learning? *@tic. Revista d'innovació Educativa, 10*, 108–121. https://doi.org/10.7203/attic.10.2228

Deng, X., & Yu, Z. (2022). A systematic review of machine-translation-assisted language learning for sustainable education. *Sustainability, 14*(13), 7598. https://doi.org/10.3390/su14137598

Ducar, C., & Schocket, D. H. (2018). Machine translation and the L2 classroom: Pedagogical solutions for making peace with Google Translate. *Foreign Language Annals, 51*(4), 779–795. https://doi.org/10.1111/flan.12366

Garcia, I., & Pena, M. I. (2011). Machine translation-assisted language learning: Writing for beginners. *Computer Assisted Language Learning, 24*(5), 471–487. https://doi.org/10.1080/09588221.2011.582687

Klimova, B., Pikhart, M., Benites, A. D., Lehr, C., & Sanchez-Stockhammer, C. (2023). Neural machine translation in foreign language teaching and learning: A systematic review. *Education and Information Technologies, 28*(1), 663–682. https://doi.org/10.1007/s10639-022-11194-2

Knowles, C. L. (2022). Using an ADAPT approach to integrate Google Translate into the second language classroom. *L2 Journal, 14*(1), 195–236. https://doi.org/10.5070/L214151690

Lee, S.-M. (2020). The impact of using machine translation on EFL students' writing. *Computer Assisted Language Learning, 33*(3), 157–175. https://doi.org/10.1080/09588221.2018.1553186

Lee, S.-M. (2023). The effectiveness of machine translation in foreign language education: A systematic review and meta-analysis. *Computer Assisted Language Learning, 36*(1–2), 103–125. https://doi.org/10.1080/09588221.2021.1901745

Merschel, L., & Munné, J. (2022). Perceptions and practices of machine translation among 6th-12th grade world language teachers. *L2 Journal, 14*(1), 60–76. https://doi.org/10.5070/L214154165

Ohashi, L. (2022). The use of machine translation in L2 education: Japanese university teachers' views and practices. In B. Arnbjörnsdóttir, B. Bédi, L. Bradley, K. Friðriksdóttir, H. Garðarsdóttir, S. Thouësny, & M. J. Whelpton (Eds.), *Intelligent CALL, granular systems, and learner data: Short papers from EUROCALL 2022* (pp. 308–314). Researchpublishing.net. https://doi.org/10.14705/rpnet.2022.61.1476

Ryu, J., Kim, Y., Park, S., Eum, S., Chun, S., & Yang, S. (2022). Exploring foreign language students' perceptions of the guided use of machine translation (GUMT) model for Korean writing. *L2 Journal, 14*(1), 136–165. https://doi.org/10.5070/L214151759

Stapleton, P., & Ka Kin, B. L. (2019). Assessing the accuracy and teachers' impressions of Google Translate: A study of primary L2 writers in Hong Kong. *English for Specific Purposes, 56*, 18–34. https://doi.org/10.1016/j.esp.2019.07.001

Tasmedir, S., Lopez, E., Satar, M., & Riches, N. G. (2022). Teachers' perceptions of machine translation as a pedagogical tool. *JALT CALL Journal, 19*(1), 92–113. https://doi.org/10.29140/jaltcall.v19n1.24

Tsai, S. C. (2019). Using Google Translate in EFL drafts: A preliminary investigation. *Computer Assisted Language Learning, 32*(5–6), 510–526. https://doi.org/10.1080/09588221.2018.1527361

Uehara, S. (2023). Teacher perspectives of machine translation in the EFL writing classroom. In P. Ferguson, B. Lacy, & R. Derrah (Eds.), *Learning *from students, educating teachers: Research and practice* (pp. 270–279). JALT. https://doi.org/10.37546/JALTPCP2022-31

Vinall, K., & Hellmich, E. A. (2022). Down the rabbit hole: Machine translation, metaphor, and instructor identity and agency. *Second Language Research & Practice, 2*(1), 99–118. http://hdl.handle.net/10125/69860

Xu, J. (2022). Proficiency and the use of machine translation: A case study of four Japanese learners. *L2 Journal, 14*(1), 77–104. https://doi.org/10.5070/L214151328

23

L2 Translation in US/Japan Classrooms: AI and Peer Feedback in Task-Based Language Teaching

Larry Walker, Masako Inamoto, and John Rylander

23.1 Introduction

The rapid expansion of the English language in North America in the nineteenth and twentieth centuries contributed to the growth of first language (L1) print cultures on the continent. This was accompanied elsewhere in the world by an increasing non-native second language (L2) population of English users, including in Asia, Africa and, especially in the post-war era, Europe. Participation in growing global trade, travel

L. Walker (✉)
Kyoto Prefectural University, Kyoto, Japan
e-mail: walker@kpu.ac.jp

M. Inamoto
Skidmore College, Saratoga Springs, NY, USA
e-mail: minamoto@skidmore.edu

J. Rylander
Kyoto University, Kyoto, Japan
e-mail: rylander.johnwilliam.3c@kyoto-u.ac.jp

© The Author(s), under exclusive license to Springer Nature Switzerland AG 2025
D. Coulson and C. Denman (eds.), *Translation, Translanguaging and Machine Translation in Foreign Language Education*,
https://doi.org/10.1007/978-3-031-82174-5_23

479

and education booms largely relied on English usage. With Japan as one example, in countries with less-translated languages (Branchadell & West, 2005), national borders often demark the limit of their languages' usage.

Japanese is the main language of elementary, secondary and tertiary education in Japan and is also rigidly bound to national identity. However, English continues to be important for the country's participation in the world economy, while interactions between L1 Japanese and English speakers are becoming more frequent across domains. Within this context, the contrasting language identities of Japanese and English speakers highlight a need to contextualize translation in the foreign language classroom where AI technology is now taking root.

This chapter examines learners' attitudes and perceptions regarding two key constructs: the role of translation in second or foreign language (S/FL) learning and the use of generative AI in S/FL learning. Participants in this study included students in Japan who were studying English, and students in the USA studying Japanese. The project incorporates translation activities, intercultural peer feedback exchanges with speakers of the target language and learners' opinions about DeepL translation outputs. Additionally, participants' thoughts on the project, as elicited post-project, are presented.

23.2 Literature Review

23.2.1 Translation and L2 Translation

Translation is very much about languages and borders. The unraveling of Latin as the primary means of discourse on the European continent in the seventeenth century inversely mirrors English as an L2 on the rise in the twentieth century. In Japan, students learn about English in an environment where largely the language is not actively in use. A contrastive and Japanese-centric grammar-translation method, still in place today, has long been employed for the study of English (see, for instance, Fukuda (1908) more than a century ago). A millennium prior, when written Chinese became a model of scholarship, an intricate method was devised to invert Chinese texts to a Japanese SOV pattern with added reading-order marks for Japanese readers to decipher a text. This resulted in Kanbun Kundoku (Japanese reading of Chinese texts), and this source-adapted approach remains intact (Sato-Rossberg & Wakabayashi, 2012). The ingrained tradition of translation in Japan and the spread of English and the use of communication technologies are the variables under study here.

Much of the debate about translation and its usage in S/FL courses hinges on terminology that defines its usage. Koskinen and Kinnunen (2022) argue for the term *translatoriality* in foreign language learning (FLL) and explain their rationale to consider "translatoriality as a clarifying term for identifying, analyzing, teaching, learning and assessing particular practices within a wider spectrum of operating across and within several linguistic codes" (pp. 11–12). This moves beyond the traditional reductive concepts of translation and allows for full consideration of the terms under the umbrella of translanguaging, code-meshing and plurilingual modes. It surpasses a solitary act of translation, by making room for and raising consciousness of, such language phenomena within the scope of the classroom. It is this dialogue about language that requires attention.

The challenge posed is one of navigating a transformation of in-class language usage in the midst of the changes being brought about in classrooms by AI. The use of L1-L2 in Japanese and American settings is typical of language classrooms in transition, but their educational cultures vary. As such, translatoriality offers a suitable framework to embark on an exploratory practice of FLL, translation and neural machine translation (NMT) in these divergent settings.

23.2.2 Task-Based Language Instruction

In recent decades, task-based activities have remained relevant to S/FL learning (Jackson, 2022), with importance placed on a chain of activities that build to an overarching outcome. As in translation, such activities are both a process and have an end product. The process aspect is clearly provided for in pedagogic activities. With a translation brief acting as a roadmap for students (Nord, 1997), it can, through instructor guidance, be utilized as an authentic student-centered task that directs learning practices toward professional behaviors as a means of co-creating a finished product (González Davies, 2004).

A number of translation scholars recommend the use of a realistic translation assignment to help students situate a text and conceptualize it within language use (Kiraly, 2000). This aligns tasks designed to enhance language skills practice, while the decision-making requires teamwork. As the translation takes form and is edited and revised, students are guided in this ongoing dialog.

23.2.3 Corrective Feedback, Japanese and US Foreign Language Courses

The FL setting has additional constraints to consider when handling feedback. In Japan, with established hierarchical social norms, a prescriptive approach to education is the default. Translation from Japanese to English is taught throughout the six years of secondary school and is referred to as *eisakubun*, or "English composition". The written output of a student is expected to conform to the example answer. In a country that values educational ranking, students' agency in the process of composition is secondary to the prescribed answer in a textbook when grammatical structures are the learning targeted. This presents a dilemma for communicative classroom activities, where agency and creativity are in the students' domain.

The FL classroom in the USA, at the beginning to lower-intermediate levels, has a similar reliance on L1 text materials as learners have not yet developed active lexical knowledge. In this context, students are aware that Japanese as a foreign language (JFL) has less global reach than English. Yet, learner motivation to develop JFL interests may tend toward specific aspects of the target culture such as cuisine, music or a passion for popular products like anime or manga. Translation tasks allow students to step into the world of the source culture and engage in a communicative challenge beyond textbook grammatical structures and lexical items. The feedback employed is important to the success of the task and learners' self-esteem.

For this reason, instructors in this study relied on scaffolding throughout the group project and clues provided by peers in a nurturing learning environment. The students are informed that the concept of a correct or perfect translation is logically inconsistent. If it were so, a retranslation would not occur.

Kiraly (2000) suggests the goal of such projects is "to construct multiple and viable (rather than 'correct') solutions to problems that emerge naturally from authentic projects" (p. 67). Similarly, Lee (2023) notes the following with regard to writing English as a global language:

> As we forgo the 'corrective' emphasis in favor of a broader concept that focuses on language use—namely 'feedback on language use', we emancipate teachers and learners from an obsession with an error-focused approach to writing and error-free writing, respectively, to embrace a more open, critical attitude toward language use (p. 795).

This is not to suggest that misuse of language is ignored, but rather that students are allowed to use language creatively, to reflect on it and to rework it.

The idea of translation reflecting the writing process is a staple of Translation Studies as discussed in the seminal edited volume by Hermans (1985). In the current Japan/US relationship, we are less concerned about the ideological implications of soft power, but remain conscious that any exchange between cultures retains such a dynamic. In a pedagogical setting, we focus on tasks for learners that lead to an improvement of their skills. Translation, as in writing, requires reading and editing skills. This is in line with translatoriality, as noted above, and is not limited to any language pair. An essential part of a group translation experience is to work through inconsistencies that arise, make revisions where necessary and employ creative solutions, such as slang or neologisms, where appropriate.

23.2.4   Generative AI in the FL Classroom

Since online machine translation (MT) programs, like Google Translate, have become readily available to language learners, researchers have examined the role MT plays in language learning and teaching. In their study, Clifford et al. (2013) focused on perceptions of instructors and undergraduate students at Duke University regarding the use of MT. Among students, 85% indicated that MT aids in vocabulary enhancement, with many highlighting its utility for double-checking work. Among faculty surveyed, 42% considered students' use of MT a form of cheating. When asked about MT usage, 77% of faculty disapproved of MT use among students. The research emphasized a need to be proactive and forward-thinking to foster learning. A decade later, the go-to policy at many tertiary institutions is a ban on MT over concerns of plagiarism.

Now in the 2020s, generative AI is rapidly becoming a feature of all data sets. It is a fixture of online applications, shopping and social networking service (SNS) platforms and, unlike previous iterations, it processes new data independently and exponentially. It is widely agreed that NMT offers substantial improvement in rule-based MT software, but retains misappropriations inherent in the data it accumulates, such as gender bias, faulty register, inconsistent text type, an absence of cultural conventions and inaccuracies resurfacing in deceptively fluent prose (Klimtova et al., 2023). Previous studies in FL have been based on student writing or translation performance or a comparison of both.

Klimtova et al. (2023) reviewed the findings from diverse FLL settings of thirteen journal articles indexed in the Scopus and Web of Science databases from 2016 to 2022. The researchers surmise that, with guidance on software usage, the featured studies suggest NMT tools are beneficial for FLL, and note that less proficient students can use NMT in their FLL to develop vocabulary and writing skills. Without training, the mere use of NMT itself within the FLL context does not necessarily result in vocabulary retention or post-editing skills.

In the pairing of Japanese-English translation, Aikawa (2023) reported that different NMT engines produce different outputs, as each is trained on different sets of data. Further, in terms of directionality, the author continues that Japanese-to-English translation is more complex due to the specificity of English morphology, stating, "English is linguistically or morphologically more specified" (Slide 14). Notwithstanding, Aikawa notes DeepL can produce impressive levels of quality translation in either direction. She also reports on use of ChatGPT in scenarios that led to improved learner awareness of vocabulary and syntax.

This study builds upon the current literature by engaging with students of both target languages (i.e., Japanese and English). It seeks to gain a deeper understanding of their views on technology in FLL and the role translation and peer exchange plays in the secondary education experience.

23.3   Method

23.3.1   Design

This study focuses on students translating from their L1 to L2. Japanese-English language learners translated a 514-character text from a Japanese newspaper into English. The newspaper article covers promotional activities related to the release of the 2023 movie-length animation directed by Miyazaki Hayao, a founder of Studio Ghibli. Learners of Japanese in the United States translated a portion of a Studio Ghibli movie script (295 words) from English into Japanese. Bilingual dictionaries were allowed, but the use of online dictionaries or translation software was not. All work throughout the project was done on paper by the students.

The translation exchange employs a three-phase process that covers two classroom sessions per phase. The first phase is the introduction of the activity, which involves explaining the project stages and obtaining written permissions from students to participate in the study. The use of a "translation brief" is integral to the lesson plan design. The brief brings a sense of realia to the classroom, provides knowledge of translation workflow and includes authentic task content. Students work in groups to produce a draft translation.

The second phase is the exchange of the draft translations with the cohort group in the participating university. The participating group reviews the text translated into their L1. The instructors introduce a copy of the translation brief that participants' overseas peers were to work from, along with copies of the original text. Students at both universities discuss the concept of constructive criticism in groups as a way to create and focus on feedback and revisions. The translation briefs use a color-coded scheme or numbers to indicate where grammatical, vocabulary, punctuation or other improvements could improve the translation. Teachers encourage students to suggest actionable feedback to their respective peer group as a guide. The feedback phase does not include revisions.

The third phase involves returning the materials with written feedback to the original authors for final revisions, along with NMT output of the source text. Students are allowed to ask about the peer feedback and, along with reference to the NMT, negotiate the creation of a final translated version of the text.

In this study, Japanese students are upper-intermediate level, while US students are lower-intermediate. Both groups are novice translators and, as such, were matched to learning conditions that suited their present abilities. Micro- and macro-integration of textual meaning through the use of metalanguage is integrated throughout the task, and coherence is addressed to the whole text. The students experienced the entire translation process, a review stage and the opportunity for reflection based on feedback from their classmates, exchange cohorts, NMT and their instructors.

23.3.2 Participants

Participants included 11 Japanese university students majoring in English at Kyoto Prefectural University and 14 students studying Japanese at Skidmore College in the United States. Students' participation in the exchange was voluntary and the data collection process ensured their anonymity by using codes when answering survey questions.

Students in Japan were at least in the second semester of their third year. Their English level ranged from B1 to B2 on the CEFR scale.

They had taken six years of compulsory English courses in secondary school and at least two years at university. Students in the USA were in a third-semester Japanese language class. Except for one student, none had studied Japanese before college. Their proficiency levels ranged from novice-high to intermediate-low on the ACTFL Proficiency Scale. Their Japanese language program in the university's Department of World Languages and Literatures spans three years (i.e., six semesters) and leads to a bachelor's degree with a minor in Japanese. Out of 14 students in the study, 13 planned to undertake this minor.

For the project, participants, hereafter referred to as the Instructional Group (IG), at both universities were divided into four groups: A, B, C and D. Each group collaborated with its counterpart in the exchange country (i.e., group A at the Japanese university collaborated with group A at the American college). Non-instructional groups studying the same L2 at both institutions, hereafter referred to as the Reference Group (RF), participated in the pre- and post-surveys and provided a reference point for analysis.

23.3.3   Data Collection and Analysis

A survey, administered to students pre- and post-project, was developed to clarify learner opinions on components of the exchange experience. During survey development, we designed statements to measure two underlying constructs. The first construct was created to tap into respondent attitudes toward translation in the S/FL learning environment. The first construct contains 23 statements (see Appendix for survey access link). The second construct, which contained 15 statements, was designed to measure personal or institutional use of generative AI (e.g., DeepL, Google Translate) in S/FL learning.

Achieving construct equivalence in cross-cultural research that utilizes translated survey statements can prove challenging (Dörnyei & Taguchi, 2010), as respondents can engage with constructs in culturally-bound ways. In topics relevant to the present research—translation and AI—institutional frames of reference, such as educational, professional or media coverage, can influence how individuals perceive topic-relevant content. In the tables presented below, due to differences in how the learner populations responded to statements during data collection, contexts are presented separately.

Respondent attitudes represented in survey statements are assumed to have a link with behavior (Csizér & Dörnyei, 2005). Instrument validity, similar to survey data, rests on providing empirical evidence that the attributes espoused through statements measure the intended constructs. Establishing a survey's reliable and valid psychometric properties ensures greater generalizability of claims made based on its results.

Analysis for the present research relied on data composed of participant response strings from a Likert-scale survey instrument, with respondents selecting from a six-point response scale—1 representing Strongly Disagree and 6 Strongly Agree. Data collection occurred at two time points, prior to and following the period of intervention and participants included two distinct sets of learners at each participating institution (i.e., the Instructional and Reference Groups).

Data analysis involved the Rasch rating scale model (RSM) using the computer program *Winsteps* (Linacre, 2016). RSM describes the log odds of a person (n) choosing a specific category (k) of an item (i) (Bond & Fox, 2007) and is presented as the equation: $logit = Bn–Di–Fk$, where Bn denotes the person level, Di denotes the endorsability of an item, and Fk denotes the threshold between categories. Measures of item performance are indicated through fit statistics. The reported infit mean square (IN.MSQ) estimate is sensitive to unexpected responses nearest to the item estimate and is used as a reference for item fit. Linacre and Wright (1994) suggest that infit mean square values between 0.6 and 1.4 are considered good for RSM data. Item and person reliability estimates extend from 0.0 to 0.9, with higher values for items and individuals (e.g., >0.8) suggesting a greater degree of range between statement endorsability, and lower values (e.g., <0.5), potentially revealing evidence of homogeneity in the item pool or sampled participants.

In addition, lower sample sizes can result in muted person and item reliability estimates, as variance increases in smaller n-sizes. Unidimensionality is indicated through a coefficient measuring the size of dimensionality beyond the Rasch measure, with estimates below 2.0 viewed as desirable, and below 3.0 as acceptable. Measures reported beyond 3.0

suggest the need for a larger sample size or instrument redesign to include a greater number of items for the associated dimension.

Post-project discussion sessions were held at both institutions where students reflected on the exchange and offered their opinions, with excerpts from these offered below.

23.4   Results and Discussion

Table 23.1 (US) and Table 23.2 (Japan) are presented here with the commentary for the respective context. The endorsability of a statement is listed from top to bottom in the order selected by participants. The numbering of a statement represents the order it appeared in the surveys. The abbreviations *C* and *P* stand for Construct and Partition, respectively, in the table titles. The commentary for Tables 23.3–23.10 appears below. Tables 23.1–23.10 can all be accessed via the link in the Appendix.

Table 23.1 shows that the IG and RG find that sentence translation activities in L2 classes lack authenticity and perceive such exercises as overly intricate. This may relate to the manner in which published FL instructional materials provide learning content. At times, this content provides a mismatch with real-world language use. In class, the Japanese L2 textbook begins with the polite speech form, which is the predominant speech style used during instruction. Language encountered by students outside class predominantly appears in casual form. The disconnect between formal instruction and informal exposure might explain why the students perceive sentences as "unconnected to how (they) think people naturally speak" in Japan. Another mismatch may be due to the role language plays. Translation exercises done in class are typically L1 to L2, with the aim to enhance grammar proficiency for assessments. Tests are strictly graded, contributing to the perception of translation exercises as overcomplicated. Learners may perceive that grammar practices and assessments of this type lack an authenticity found in language for communicative purposes.

Table 23.2 shows that the IG and RG agreed that the exercises they had experienced in courses were too complicated, reporting little change

Table 23.1 US context: C1 translation in the S/FL classroom; P1 translation in LL experiences

	Instructional Group (IG)					Reference Group (RG)				
	Post	IN.MSQ	Pre	IN.MSQ	Change	Post	IN.MSQ	Pre	IN.MSQ	Change
N =	10					38				
Person Reliability	0.6					0.7				
Person Separation	1.3					1.6				
Item Reliability	0.8					1.0				
Item Separation	1.8					5.6				
Dimensionality in Contrast One	3.1					2.6				
Statement										
13. The sentences I normally have to translate for L2 classes seem unconnected to how I think people naturally speak in the L2	**59**	1.0	63	0.9	-4.6	**61**	0.07	62	0.8	-1.7
17. Translation exercises in the L2 class often seem overly tricky or complicated	**53**	0.4	56	1.3	-3.4	**63**	1.1	66	1.1	-2.3
16. In language classes, I often need to translate sentences from the L2 into my L1	**51**	1.7	49	1.1	2.1	**45**	0.9	47	1.1	-1.9
6. For much of my language learning, teachers have taught me how to communicate in the L2	**44**	0.5	44	0.7	0.0	**37**	0.8	39	1.1	-1.6
1. For much of my language learning experiences, teachers have taught me how to translate	**40**	1.1	42	1.0	-2.3	**37**	0.7	43	1.2	-5.9

from the pre- and post-surveys. As discussed above, much of the instruction is directly linked to grammar assessment, which can be the source of frustration. This could indicate a need to offer more authentic tasks to increase the meaningfulness of learning activities. Only Statement 16 regarding being assigned translation from the L2 into the L1 rose, moving from the bottom to the second position of the IG's statements. It is possible the L1-to-L2 project brought this to the fore, as this approach was not the typical exam-based exercise. In contrast, the RG non-participants remained virtually unchanged.

Table 23.3 (as above, see Appendix for the link to all subsequent tables) shows students in both groups hope to use L2 in their careers and that standardized language tests (e.g., Japanese-Language Proficiency Test), offer little incentive. Notably, some Japanese universities now offer programs with English as the medium of instruction. Consequently, students contemplating study in Japan may perceive little need to take formal language proficiency exams.

Table 23.4 reveals that students in Japan reacted similarly to their counterparts in the USA, showing interest in using English in a future career but not for standardized language tests. Table 23.5 shows that students in both groups tend to disagree with statements that translation exercises contribute to improving L2 skills, including L2 vocabulary, understanding the meaning of L2 words better, and understanding L2 grammar better. There is reluctance toward translation, according to the students in the IG. For instance, during the post-project discussion session, one student commented that translation could make learners reliant on their L1. Another acknowledged the helpfulness of translation exercises, yet emphasized that thinking in the L2 proves more beneficial. Additionally, a student noted the potential confusion from differences in syntax, stating that translation from English to Japanese often confused them. This result suggests that students apparently perceive their L1 as an impediment to constructing sentences in L2. Their concept of translation is as a learning tool rather than an active process. This perspective is understandable, given their Japanese language level (novice-high to intermediate).

Table 23.6 features little movement between surveys beyond an uptick in the idea that translation helps learners gain a better understanding

Table 23.2 Japan context: C1 translation in the S/FL classroom; P1 translation in LL experiences

	Instructional Group (IG)					Reference Group (RG)				
	Post	IN.MSQ	Pre	IN.MSQ	Change	Post	IN.MSQ	Pre	IN.MSQ	Change
N =	5					59				
Person Reliability	0.8					0.5				
Person Separation	2.2					1.1				
Item Reliability	0.8					0.9				
Item Separation	2.1					2.4				
Dimensionality in Contrast One	5.0					2.3				
Statement	**Post**	IN.MSQ	*Pre*	IN.MSQ	*Change*	**Post**	IN.MSQ	*Pre*	IN.MSQ	*Change*
17. (as above)	**83**	0.8	88	1.9	-4.9	**56**	0.6	56	0.9	-0.5
16. (as above)	**49**	0.8	39	0.8	10.2	**49**	0.9	48	1.1	1.1
6. (as above)	**42**	0.8	46	0.8	-3.4	**52**	0.9	51	1.1	1.2
12. In language classes, I often need to translate sentences from my L1 to the L2	**42**	0.7	42	0.5	0.0	**49**	1.3	53	1.2	-3.3
13. (as above)	**42**	0.5	49	3.3	-7.1	**43**	1.0	46	1.4	-2.5
1. (as above)	**39**	0.4	39	0.8	0.0	**49**	0.9	50	0.9	-1.0

of L2 word meanings in the IG. The person and item reliability were in acceptable ranges. Both groups in Japan saw Statement 10, finding themselves "better at translating from my L1 to the L2 than from the L2 to my L1", persisting as the most endorsable of this set of statements. The IN.MSQ here is slightly beyond parameters in the IG, but the RG numbers indicate stable responses. This is unexpected in that convention dictates translating into one's L1 is preferred. A divide between the perfection long expected of students, and a less prescribed framework to use during the task, with peer support, is likely behind this. L1 baggage, acting as a hindrance and interfering with the goal of thinking in the L2, was a point raised by cohorts in both contexts.

In Table 23.7, the pre-project survey results contrast with the post-project results. The change is minimal in the RG. In both the pre- and post-responses, this group endorsed the statement, "I use AI when I work on L2 homework". On the contrary, statements related to student confidence in learning new computer software programs or adopting new technology resulted in the lowest approval for both sets of results. Differences emerge in the IG between the pre- and post-survey outcomes. The most endorsed statement before the project—"I am a capable user of AI"—showed a decline. Likewise, the statement "I feel confident learning new technology to help me study the L2" saw the least endorsability in the post-project survey. These shifts highlight distinct patterns of change in perceptions and attitudes in the IG compared to the more stable trends observed in the RG.

The IG exhibited greater confidence in AI for language learning before the project. However, usage during the project indicated current limitations of the tool and the participants' own proficiency with it. While technology can be a valuable tool for L2 acquisition, there are exceptions. This is evident for lower-proficiency L2 learners, unable to assess the authenticity of the output generated by AI.

Table 23.8 shows that survey item reliability was consistent between the groups. The confidence reported in "learning new software" declined in the most endorsed statement, as did that of "learning new technology to help me study the L2" as the least endorsed. Applications tend to be user-friendly, while at the same time, the hype surrounding AI may have introduced some confusion. In this study, questions over AI, in the form of DeepL, seem to induce doubt over whether its output can be trusted for students' learning. The L2 user is at a disadvantage in discerning the quality of output versus what is learnable, and no group reported an increase in the confidence of its usage. The opposite result was interest in more peer feedback opportunities reported by members of both IG groups after the exchange.

Table 23.9 shows the perceived utility of AI, attitudes toward its application and values associated with AI use. Similar to the results in Table 7, a disparity in changes between the pre- and post-survey exists between the groups. Within the RG, minimal differences appear in the pre- and post-results. Statements regarding AI's role in aiding the comprehension of vocabulary and grammar mistakes receive the highest agreement, while the statement "AI will make it easier for people to become fluent speakers of foreign languages" has lower agreement.

In contrast, IG exhibits differences from the pre- to post-survey. The most endorsed statement in the pre-project survey, "I can use AI to help me understand grammar mistakes I make when writing in the L2", declines post-project. The most substantial change occurs with one of the least agreed-upon statements in the pre-project survey, "I find using AI helps me understand vocabulary mistakes I have made in the L2", which becomes the most agreed-upon post-project. Additionally, the second most endorsed post-project statement for the IG, "AI is helpful when I am translating from my L2 into my L1", becomes one of the least endorsed statements in the RG's post-project survey. These results suggest increased awareness in the IG about the benefits of using AI in their L2 learning after participating in the project.

Post-project, the students in the IG became aware of the limitations of using AI based on their L2 language proficiency. They found AI less helpful when translating from L1 to L2 due to their inability to evaluate the authenticity/appropriacy of AI-generated L2 output. This is corroborated by the feedback provided by students during the post-project discussion. Students said that referencing the AI output in the L2 was not helpful because unknown grammar appeared, making it difficult for learners to judge its accuracy. Students agreed that AI would be useful for translating L1 to L2 when they become more proficient. They perceived AI as helpful when translating from L2 to L1 (Statement 7), because the grammatical correctness could be easily judged. Discerning lexical differences (Statement 6) is easier than grammar. One student mentioned they would go to AI rather than the textbook to find an unknown L2 vocabulary item. Thus, students find AI helpful when its usage aligns with their proficiency and their interests, especially when their textbooks lack ease of use or topics of interest.

Table 23.10 shows responses that are evident most clearly in the Japanese context in Statement 6 regarding AI being helpful to understand vocabulary, with a boost in the post-survey, and remaining first in endorsability. A drop in the endorsability of Statement 15, on AI being of help to "understand grammar mistakes" when translating, was seen in both groups in Japan. Compared to the RG, the IG showed the opposite trend in Statement 4 about AI being helpful to "study the L2", moving downward. Statement 9, about AI being helpful when translating "from L1 to L2", rose compared to the decline observed in the RG. This may be attributed to focused instruction on how NMT output can be judged against feedback from overseas peers, and thus a more realistic and limited set of expectations.

For Statement 7, on AI as helpful when translating from L2 to L1, the IG remained unchanged, while it jumped from fifth to second in terms of its endorsability in the RG. The reliability figures here are stronger, indicating that the larger sample size was more representative of the groups. Both groups responded that AI should be used "when working on L2 activities" (Statement 8), but the RG, which had no treatment, more strongly endorsed this idea. This likely represents limited experience using AI in classroom learning activities.

23.5 Conclusion

The purpose of the study was to examine language learners' attitudes and perceptions toward translation in FLL learning environments, as well as the use of generative AI in FLL learning in a translation project that incorporated intercultural exchanges of peer feedback. The survey findings reveal that, as part of their educational experience, standard translation exercises are met with limited enthusiasm among both US and Japanese students in FL coursework. This perception may stem from the close association of such exercises with assessment, textbook chapter tests or entrance exams and the prescriptive approach of a traditional classroom routine.

Conversely, discussions shed light on a more positive outlook when students engaged in translation projects, or participated in peer feedback. Participants described these activities as valuable opportunities to integrate learning and apply acquired knowledge. They showed an appreciation of the collaborative aspect, emphasizing that it felt like a shared journey with their peers rather than mere feedback on errors. This matches the practice of translatoriality, which encourages student engagement, not student separation.

Furthermore, students noted significant learning experiences during these collaborative endeavors, gaining actionable insights into sentence construction in the L2. They found the process instrumental in understanding grammar nuances and refining their choices. As indicated in the discussion of Table 23.2 results, these findings underscore the importance of incorporating activities that highlight the real-world application of L2 sentences. Aligning translation tasks with student interests, allowing opportunities to work with and mentor classmates in cooperative, cross-border learning projects, and to reach the world beyond, offers a productive way to shut out the isolation of recent years and further adapt coursework in the digital age.

Acknowledgements Data collection for the initial trial survey runs and the pre- and post-surveys was conducted with the written consent of each student and done under the auspices of the relevant conditions of the institutional review board. This work was supported by JSPS KAKENHI Grant Number 23K00734.

Appendix: Surveys and Result Tables 23.1–23.10

Survey for American Students: https://doi.org/10.7910/DVN/9SDQ3Z.
Survey for Japanese Students: https://doi.org/10.7910/DVN/DDIPDP.
Tables 23.1–23.10: https://doi.org/10.7910/DVN/SWCUAF.

References

Aikawa, T. (2023, August 18). *A use case scenario of machine translation for language instruction* [Paper presentation]. The 17th International Conference of the European Association for Japanese Studies, Ghent University, Ghent, Belgium.

Bond, T. G., & Fox, C. M. (2007). *Applying the Rasch model: Fundamental measurement in the human sciences.* Lawrence Erlbaum.

Branchadell, A., & West, M. (2005). *Less translated languages.* John Benjamins.

Clifford, J., Merschel, L., & Munné, J. (2013). Surveying the landscape: What is the role of machine translation in language learning? *The Acquisition of Second Language and Innovative Pedagogies, 10*, 108–121. https://doi.org/10.7203/attic.10.2228

Csizér, K., & Dörnyei, Z. (2005). Language learners' motivational profiles and their motivated learning behavior. *Language Learning, 55*(4), 613–659. https://doi.org/10.1111/j.0023-8333.2005.00319.x

Dörnyei, Z., & Taguchi, T. (2010). *Questionnaires in second language research: Construction, administration, and processing* (2nd ed.). Routledge.

Fukuda, H. (1908). *How to translate current Japanese into current English.* Kembunkwan.

González Davies, M. (2004). *Multiple voices in the translation classroom: Activities, tasks and projects.* John Benjamins.

Hermans, T. (Ed.). (1985/2014). *The manipulation of literature: Studies in literary translation.* Routledge.

Jackson, D. O. (2022). *Task-based language teaching.* Cambridge University Press. https://doi.org/10.1017/9781009067973

Kiraly, D. (2000). *A social constructivist approach to translator education.* Jerome Publishing.

Klimtova, B., Pikhart, M., Delorme Benites, A., Lehr, C., & Sanchez-Stockhammer, C. (2023). Neural machine translation in foreign language teaching and learning: A systematic review. *Education and Information Technologies, 28*, 663–682. https://doi.org/10.1007/s10639-022-11194-2

Koskinen, K., & Kinnunen, T. (2022). Mediation in FL learning: From translation to translatoriality. *STRIDON: Journal of Studies in Translation and Interpreting, 2*(1), 5–29. https://doi.org/10.4312/stridon.2.1.5-29

Lee, I. (2023). Problematising written corrective feedback: A global Englishes perspective. *Applied Linguistics, 44*(4), 791–796. https://doi.org/10.1093/applin/amad038

Linacre, J. M. (2016). *Winsteps® Rasch measurement computer program user's guide*. Winsteps.com.

Linacre, J. M., & Wright, B. D. (1994). Dichotomous infit and outfit mean-square fit statistics. *Rasch Measurement Transactions, 8*(2), 360. https://www.rasch.org/rmt/rmt82a.htm

Nord, C. (1997). Defining translation functions. The translation brief as a guideline for the trainee translator. *Ilha do Desterro. A Journal of English Language, Literature in English and Cultural Studies, 33*, 41–55.

Sato-Rossberg, N., & Wakabayashi, J. (2012). *Translation and translation studies in the Japanese context*. Continuum International Publishing.

Index